With best wishes

MARK STEYN

D0003412

The Face Of
The Tiger

AND OTHER TALES FROM
THE NEW WAR

Columns and essays
from September 11th 2001 to September 11th 2002

STOCKADE
BOOKS

Published in 2002 by
Stockade Books
CP 843, Succursale H
rue Ste-Catherine ouest
Montréal, Québec
H3G 2M8

Printed and bound in the Province of Québec (Canada)

ISBN 0-9731570-0-3

First Edition

The only change that occurred on September 11th was a simple one. When Osama bin Laden blew up the World Trade Center, he also blew up the polite fictions of the pre-war world...

MARK STEYN on the fictions and facts of a new world...

..."the brutal Afghan winter":
Whatever happened to the "brutal Afghan winter"? It was "fast approaching" back in late September, and apparently it's still "fast approaching" four months later.

...the "whereabouts" of Osama:
He's stiff, he's six feet under, he's pushing up daisycutter bits in the Hindu Kush, he's bin Laiden to rest.

..."homeland security":
Under the new high-alert procedures, security personnel demonstrate their sensitivity by looking for people who don't look anything like the people they're looking for. Never in the field of human conflict have so many been so inconvenienced to avoid offending so few.

...a "bombing pause for Ramadan":
As Bill Clinton remarked, "Military action during Ramadan would be profoundly offensive." I'm no Islamic scholar, but given that during the holy month of Ramadan Muslims are expected to live in simple fashion, it's hard to see in what way taking out the water lines, the electric supply, etc is disrespectful. Quite the contrary, one would have thought. Happy Holidays from the Great Satan!

...Palestinian "martyrs":
Saudi TV has just had a hugely successful charity telethon raising $56 million for the families of Palestinian "martyrs". One Saudi Princess donated both her Rolls and her ox, a double jackpot sure to inspire any West Bank suicide bomber hoping to transform his relicts into a two-car family. Maybe they'll make it a weekly show: "Who Wants To Be A Million Air Particles?"

...the heroes of Flight 93:
Flight 93 is the key event of September 11th. Faced with a novel and unprecedented form of terror, American technology (cellphones) combined with the oldest American virtue (self-reliance) and stopped it in its tracks in just 90 minutes. The foiling of the hijackers of 93 began the transformation of Osama from a jihadi to a jihas-been.

MARK
STEYN

can be read regularly in Britain's *Daily Telegraph* and *Sunday Telegraph*; *The Spectator*; *The National Post* of Canada; *The New Criterion*; *The Chicago Sun-Times*; *The New York Sun*; many other publications around the world; and at SteynOnline.com.

ALSO BY MARK STEYN

Broadway Babies Say Goodnight (1997)

CONTENTS

ACKNOWLEDGMENTS

"God Bless America" (1938) by Irving Berlin © Trustees of the God Bless America Fund
"Imagine" (1971) by John Lennon © Lenono Music
"Last Christmas" (1984) by George Michael © Dick Leahy Music/Warner Chappell Music
"Let's Roll" (2001) by Neil Young © Silver Fiddle Music
"Some Enchanted Evening" (1949) by Richard Rodgers and Oscar Hammerstein II © Williamson Music
"Wake Me Up Before You Go-Go" (1984) by George Michael © Dick Leahy Music/ Warner Chappell Music

<u>NOTE</u>

These columns appeared in the year after September 11th 2001 in the following publications: The Chicago Sun-Times, *Britain's* Daily Telegraph *and* Sunday Telegraph, *Canada's* National Post, *America's* National Review *and* New Criterion, The Spectator *and* The Wall Street Journal. *They are reprinted here more or less as they were first published. As a rule, this collection retains the spellings of the originating publication, whether British, American or Canadian. So, if you dislike finding a "u" in the middle of "honor" or a "z" in the middle of "organisation", have patience: the word will likely recur with an entirely different spelling two or three pages further on. Or farther on.*

PRELUDE

Smelling blood

December 26th 2001
The Spectator

THE LAST THING I wrote before September 11th was a column for the preceding weekend's *Sunday Telegraph*. It was about shark attacks, which had exercised the Eastern Seaboard's fevered imagination all summer, ever since eight-year old Jessie Arbogast had his arm torn off just off the Florida coast. The boy's uncle wrestled the shark back to the beach, killed him, and retrieved Jessie's severed limb from his mouth.

In an eerie pre-echo of the world to come, progressive opinion came down on the side of the shark. *The New York Times* said that we should bear in mind all the sharks we humans kill, and fretted that the uncle's retaliation might have been disproportionate. The experts agreed we needed to look at the "root causes", to understand "why they hate us": just blundering into their territory in ever larger numbers was only going to provoke them into even bolder assaults on our shores; above all, we should resist any hysterical over-reaction to the many non-violent members of the shark community. Substitute "Islamists" for "sharks" and you'd have a dandy post-September 11th editorial thumbsucker. Go on, try it. Here's the *Times* back in July:

> *Knowing something about the biology, behavior and world status of sharks* [Islamism] *does not mitigate the terror... Even knowledge cannot alter some emotions. But many people now understand that an incident like the Arbogast attack* [World Trade Center attack] *is not the result of malevolence or a taste for human blood on the shark's part* [Islam's part]*... Inevitably, an incident like this one reinforces a nearly pleasurable cultural hysteria about sharks* [Islam]*... when what it should really do is remind us yet again how much we have to learn about them and their waters* [them and their extraordinarily rich culture]*...*

3

It was that kind of summer. We weren't playing croquet on sun-dappled country-house lawns in August 1914, we were splashing in the shallows, fleeing screaming for the shore at the first sight of a black snorkel. But we were enjoying the same complacent holiday from history. The week before September 11th, the US, Canada, Britain and Europe gathered at Durban under the auspices of the UN to apologise for western civilisation to the massed ranks of gangsters and dictators (supported as always by various NGOS – "non-governmental organisations" – led by the Rev Jesse Jackson, President-for-Life of the Republic of Himself). There was complete unanimity between all parties - from Robert Mugabe to the EU - that the west had a lot to apologise for. The only arguments were over how abject the apology should be and whether there should be a large cheque attached. Durban marked the zenith of the western world's 30-year campaign of self-denigration. Watching CNN in his cave, Osama bin Laden could reasonably have concluded that he was up against a soft culture ashamed of itself and its history.

For Americans, September 11th brought to a close the post-Cold War era, the period that began with the fall of the Berlin Wall. For a significant proportion of Muslims, September 11th was the culmination of a quite different timeline - an era that was inaugurated on October 23rd 1983, when Hezbollah suicide bombers killed 300 American and French soldiers in Beirut and prompted their governments to pull out of Lebanon. From a Muslim point of view, the suicide bomber is as reliable as the Maxim gun was: sometimes he brings victory, as in Beirut; sometimes he attracts a barely minimal response, as in Bill Clinton's desultory retaliations to bin Laden's ever more brazen provocations during the Nineties; and sometimes he is rewarded by public admonitions to his victims, as when the EU et al urge "restraint" on the part of Israel after Hamas or Islamic Jihad have blown up a few more pregnant women in a shopping mall.

Before September 11th, we saw the events, but not the pattern. America has been galvanised in the last three months: the Islamofascists loathe the rest of the west almost as much as they hate the US, but the difference is that, for the most part, those countries are content to be, as the Canadian columnist David Warren put it, "mere spectators in our fates". They're still in Durban mode, more inclined to apologise than act. Robert Fisk of *The Independent* nicely captured the likely fate of the apologists, not in anything he wrote (he's been pretty much wrong on everything since September) but in the simple act of getting beaten up by the people he's championed so long. His column on the lessons to be drawn from his savage assault by disaffected Afghans was a gem of self-parody:

> *Then young men broke my glasses, began smashing stones into my face and head … And even then, I understood. I couldn't blame them for what they were doing… If I was an Afghan refugee in Kila Abdullah, I would have done just what they did. I would have attacked Robert Fisk. Or any other Westerner I could find.*

It's not their fault, their "brutality is entirely the product of others" – i.e., us. Mr Fisk is the quintessential New Racist - he believes that, while he and Bush are sophisticated human beings who should be held accountable for their actions, the noble savage (and no one's done more to ennoble him than Fisk) should be offered moral absolution for assaulting a civilian on no other basis than his ethnic identity. As Salman Rushdie has said, this denies "the basic idea of all morality: that individuals are responsible for their actions." Mr Fisk's exquisite condescension to the people he claims a unique insight into is indestructible. The difference between him and the President is that Bush treats them as he'd treat Texans, who are at least members of the human race (however primitive and barbaric). Fisk regards Muslims as exotic wildlife.

Which is where we came in, in the turbulent waters of last summer. Read that column again, substitute "Jessie Arbogast" for Fisk and "the shark" for the Afghans, and you're back in the world before September 11th:

> *Then the sharks began chewing off Jessie's arm… And even then, I understood. I couldn't blame them for what they were doing… If I was a shark off the Florida coast, I would have done just what they did. I would have attacked Jessie Arbogast. Or any other human I could find.*

September 11th was a call to moral seriousness. You cannot compromise with a shark, you cannot negotiate with a suicide bomber. And, if you can't see that, you must have rocks in your head, and it wasn't the Afghans who put 'em there. The next shark to chew up a Florida moppet will get a tougher press, even from *The New York Times*.

SEPTEMBER 11th

A war for civilization

September 12th 2001
The National Post

YOU CAN UNDERSTAND why they're jumping up and down in the streets of Ramallah, jubilant in their victory. They have struck a mighty blow against the Great Satan, mightier than even the producers of far-fetched action thrillers could conceive. They have driven a gaping wound into the heart of his military headquarters. They have ruptured the most famous skyline in the world, the glittering monument to his decadence. They have killed and maimed thousands of his subjects, live on TV. For one day they reduced the hated Bush to a pitiful Presidential vagrant, bounced further and further from his White House to ever more remote military airports, from Florida to Louisiana to Nebraska, by a security staff which obviously understands less about the power of symbolism than America's enemies do.

And, for those on the receiving end, that "money shot", as they call it in Hollywood - the smoking towers of the World Trade Center collapsing as easily as condemned chimneys at an abandoned sawmill – represents not just an awesome loss of life but a ghastly intelligence failure by the US and a worse moral failure by the west generally.

There was a grim symmetry in the way this act of war interrupted the President at a grade-school photo-op. The Federal Government has no constitutional responsibility for education: it is a state affair, delegated mostly to tiny municipal school boards. But one of Bill Clinton's forlorn legacies is that the head of state and the Commander-in-Chief of the most powerful nation on earth must now fill his day with inconsequential initiatives designed to soothe the piffling discontents of soccer moms and other preferred demographics of the most pampered generation in history: programs to connect elementary schools to the Internet, prescription drug benefits for seniors, government "lock-boxes" for any big-ticket entitlement the focus groups decide they can't live without, and a thousand and one other woeful trivialities.

And so the President was reminded of his most awesome responsibility at a time when he was discharging his most footling. If you drive around Vermont and Massachusetts and California, you spend a lot of time behind cars with smug bumper stickers calling for more funds to be diverted from defence to education, because this would prove what a caring society we are. Tuesday was a rebuke to those fatuities: the first charge of any government is the defence of its borders – and, without that, it makes no difference how much you spend on prescription drug plans for seniors. From the moment Colin Powell advised against marching on Baghdad and ended the Gulf War, the world's only superpower has been on a ten-year long weekend off. It loaded up the SUV, went to the mall, enjoyed the good times and deluded itself that in the new world politics could be confined to feelgood initiatives – big government disguised as lots and lots of teensy-weensy bits of small government. Yesterday's atrocities were a rude awakening from the indulgences of the last decade, with some awful stories to remind us of our illusions – disabled employees in wheelchairs, whom the Americans with Disabilities Act and the various lobby groups insist can do anything able-bodied people can, found themselves trapped on the 80th floor, unable to get downstairs, unable even to do as others did and hurl themselves from the windows rather than be burned alive.

On Tuesday, the post-Cold War era ended and a new one began.

The first named victim I was aware of was the wife of the Solicitor-General, Barbara Olson, whom I sat next to at dinner a few weeks ago. She was one of the "blonde former prosecutors", which sounds like a rock band but was the standard shorthand for the good-looking female commentators who turned up on CNN every night during impeachment – she was smart, witty, a fearless scourge of the Clinton Administration. She'd postponed her trip to California by a day so she could wish her husband Ted a happy birthday on Tuesday morning and so found herself on American Airlines flight 11. She had time to call to tell him her plane was being hijacked and that she had been hustled to the back of the cabin with the other passengers and flight crew. By then, the Solicitor-General knew that two planes had deliberately crashed into the World Trade Center. He told Barbara what was happening –that she wasn't in the hands of some jerk who wants his pals sprung from jail and a jet to Cuba but cooler customers with bigger plans. A few seconds later her flight ripped through one side of the Pentagon.

I'm sure Ted Olson, in the course of the day, saw some of those TV pictures of taxi drivers, merchants and schoolchildren in Egypt, Lebanon and Palestine passing out candy to celebrate the death of his wife and thousands of others. This is not terrorism - five guys in ski masks plotting in a basement. This is war, waged in the shadows but openly cheered by millions and millions of people and more covertly supported by their governments, including some who are, officially, our "allies". America lost 2,403 people at Pearl Harbor, 2,260 in the War of 1812, 4,435 in the entire Revolutionary War, and 4,710 on the worst day of the Civil War. It is entirely possible that the final loss on Tuesday will exceed those totals combined. That's war.

What matters now is how the US reacts. President Bush, echoing a long line of British Prime Ministers responding to IRA attacks, called the perpetrators "a faceless coward". "Cowardly," agreed Rudy Giuliani, and Jim Baker. Those Prime Ministers were wrong and so are the President, the former Secretary of State, and the Mayor of New York. The men or women who do such things are certainly faceless but not, I think, cowards. A coward would not agree to hijack a plane. Many others might do it for, oh, $20 million, a change of identity and retirement in the Bahamas: those would be the stakes if life was run by Warner Brothers or Paramount and the terrorist was played by John Travolta or Bruce Willis. But very few of us would agree to hijack a plane for the certainty of instant, violent death. We should acknowledge that at the very least it requires a kind of mad courage, a courage 99% of those of us in the west can never understand and, because of that, should accord a certain respect. Assuming (as Barbara Olson's phone call seems to confirm) that no United or American Airlines flight crew would plough into a crowded building even with a gun at their heads, the men who took over the controls were sophisticated, educated people, perhaps even trained jet pilots who could be pulling down six-figure salaries in most countries but preferred instead to drive a plane through crowded offices in one all-or-nothing crazed gesture. If these men were cowards, this would be an easier war. Instead, they are not just willing to die for their cause, but anxious to do so.

And what causes are we willing to die for? By "we", I mean "the west", though in truth these days that umbrella doesn't cover a lot – the United Kingdom, most of the time; France, when it suits them; Canada, hardly at all, not in any useful sense. Even America's sense of purpose has shrivelled away since the Gulf War: Why was there such a comprehensive intelligence failure? Is it because the US has come to rely too much on electronic surveillance – satellites, telephone interceptions - and virtually eliminated human intelligence – the old-fashioned spies who go into deep cover at great risk to themselves? And is the delusion that you can fight terrorism with computers from outer space just another wretched example of the nouveau warfare pioneered by Mr Clinton in Kosovo? Or, to be more accurate, not *in* Kosovo but far above it and then only after dark on clear nights, dropping Tomahawks at a million bucks a pop on empty buildings. One quasi-governmental network of killers can find four fellows who can fly a jet willing to commit suicide on the same day, but the Clinton Doctrine tells the world that the greatest military power on the face of the earth no longer has the stomach for a single body-bag. The doughboys of the Great War went off singing, "We won't come back till it's over/Over There!" But not Mr Clinton's army: We won't go over till it's over/Over There! Such a craven warmonger cannot plausibly call anybody else a "faceless coward". In Kosovo, America declared it was prepared to kill, but not to die. Their enemies drew the correct lesson.

There are cowards elsewhere, too. The funniest moment in the early coverage came when some portentous anchor solemnly reported that "the United Nations building has not been hit". Well, there's a surprise! Why would the guys who took out the World Trade Center and the Pentagon want to target the UN? The UN is dominated by their apologists, and in some cases the friends of the friends of the fellows who did this (to put it at its most discreet). All last week the plenipotentiaries of the west were in Durban holed up with the smooth, bespoke emissaries of thug states and treating with them as equals, negotiating over how many anti-Zionist insults they could live with and over how grovelling the west's apology for past sins should be. Yesterday's sobering coda to Durban let us know that those folks on the other side are really admirably straightforward: they mean what they say, and we should take them at their word. We should also cease dignifying them by pretending that the foreign ministers of, say, Spain and Syria are somehow cut from the same cloth.

There is also a long-term lesson. The US is an historical anomaly: the first non-imperial superpower. Britain, France and the other old powers believed in projecting themselves, both territorially and culturally. As we saw in Durban, they get few thanks for that these days. But the American position – that the pre-eminent nation on earth can collectively leap in its Chevy Suburban and drive to the lake while the world goes its own way – is untenable. The consequence, as we now know, is that the world comes to you. Niall Ferguson, in his book *The Cash Nexus*, argues that imperial engagement is in fact the humanitarian position: the two most successful military occupations in recent history were the Allies' transformation of West Germany and Japan into functioning democracies. Ferguson thinks the US, if it had the will, could do that in Sierra Leone. But why stop there? Why let ramshackle economic basket-cases like the Sudan or Afghanistan be used as launch pads to kill New Yorkers?

Instead of an empire, the US belongs to Nato, a defence pact of prosperous western nations in which only one guy picks up the tab, a military alliance for countries that no longer in any recognizable sense have militaries. The US taxpayer's willingness to pay for the defence of Canada and Europe has contributed to the decay of America's so-called "allies", freeing them to disband their armed forces, flirt with dictators and gangster states, and essentially convert themselves to semi-non-aligned.

The British no doubt will respond by pointing out how lax American security is, compared to Heathrow or even Waterloo Station. And they're right. Granted, every democratic government knows that sometime somewhere some killer will wiggle through the system. But yesterday all the killers got through. Had the conspirators attempted to seize four planes but succeeded in taking only three, we could have consoled ourselves with the knowledge that we had merely a 75% failure rate. But they successfully commandeered every plane they aimed for: a 100% systemic failure.

The killers picked their point of embarkation well: Boston's Logan Airport is a joke. It is, first of all, not an airport but a building site, and has been for years, a maze of extremely permanent temporary signs, construction sheeting and makeshift walkways, all adding to the chaos. I wasn't catching a flight a couple of weeks back, just meeting one, but it was delayed and I wanted a coffee and newspaper and discovered I had to go through to the "secured" area to get them.

Overwhelmed by unnecessarily increased traffic, the security guards could give only a cursory glance to most bags, and a few sailed through the scanner while their eyes were elsewhere. At Logan, "airport security" is an oxymoron.

So let the British gloat: they've got great security systems. But on the other hand what was the point, given that they've decided to surrender slowly, piece by piece, to the IRA? When a great power is faced with a terrorist enemy, it has to win – fast and decisively. It has to identify the leaders, remove them silently and ruthlessly, shred their infrastructure and thus deny them the kind of victories that encourage civilian supporters to think their cause is a going concern. In the Fifties, the British did that in Malaya and saved that country from Communism. A decade later, when the IRA re-emerged, they no longer had the stomach for it.

Let us hope that America doesn't show the same lack of will. This is, as the German government put it, an attack on "the civilized world", and it's time to speak up in its defence. Those western nations who spent last week in Durban finessing and nuancing evil should understand now that what is at stake is whether the world's future will belong to liberal democracy and the rule of law, or to darker forces. And after Tuesday America is entitled to ask its allies not for finely crafted UN resolutions but a more basic question: whose side are you on?

⌐

The above column is virtually as it appeared in print, including a few things I was wrong about. The death toll: more than Pearl Harbor and the War of 1812 but less than the Revolutionary and Civil Wars. I was wrong, too, about the "courage" of the suicide bombers: I was not yet sufficiently immersed in the psychosis of Islamism and its perverted death-cultism, in which before committing mass murder one carefully prepares one's genitals because paradise is a brothel. Many readers objected to the passage about the Americans with Disabilities Act, and I apologize for giving offence – I'd probably just skip the point if I were writing it today. But the images and stories of the disabled were among the most heart-wrenching of the day, including that of the able-bodied man who stayed – and perished - with his wheelchair-bound friend because he could not bear to leave him and let him die alone. I don't understand why we sue small mom'n'pop businesses because their general store in a remote rural town has no wheelchair ramp, but we cheerfully encourage the disabled to work on the 80th floor of skyscrapers whose first move in an emergency is to shut down the elevators.

Everything else – the ugliness of the Arab street, the uselessness of Nato, the self-loathing of the west, the incompetence of Logan Airport – is sadly just as true today as it was then.

THE FIRST DAYS

Primal

September 22nd 2002
The Daily Telegraph

IT WAS THE accumulation of events that set the tone. One plane hit, then another, then the Pentagon was smoking, the White House was evacuated, the towers crumbled, a plane crashed in Pennsylvania, there were other flights missing, there were bomb scares... For a few hours that Tuesday it felt like the Third World War, and so commentators fell into war mode. And by the time the networks had shuttled Diane Sawyer, Barbara Walters and the other empathetic glamour gals to the scene it was too late to revert to the banality of "healing" and "closure" and all the other guff of a soft-focus grief wallow.

Even on that first day they were saying "everything's changed". But what exactly? The main difference seemed to be tonal. These days, an army of grief counsellors can arrive at a high school shooting quicker than a SWAT team. But, when they showed up last week to ply their grisly trade, they found few takers. In my general store, on the TV up above the ammunition and tampons, the local station, temporarily lacking any other local angle, fished a pain-feeler out of the Rolodex. "But a lot of people are saying they feel very angry," the interviewer gamely pointed out.

"That's okay," said the grief counsellor. "Often, in the early stages, when we're processing pain and hurt and sorrow, it can emerge as anger. So it's okay to feel anger."

Clustered round the TV, sipping coffee, the guys were vaguely irritated by this, raising the interesting question of whether it's okay to feel anger toward the grief counsellor. "Processed pain" is as bland and unsatisfying as processed cheese, and its self-evident irrelevance to the occasion seemed the most pitiful bad taste. It reeked of victimhood, the cult of the age but the last thing most Americans wanted to project at a time when there were so many real, actual victims under the rubble in

New York and Washington. The New York Fire Department lost more members in one day than the US armed forces have lost in the last 20 years. And they had no time to have their grief professionally counselled, just a few moments to blow the soot and dust off their helmets and get back in there.

If you want a word for the mood of this immediate aftermath, try "primal". In a feminised culture, guys were back – big burly firemen evoking Iwo Jima and raising the flag atop the ruins of the World Trade Center. Watching tanks rumble down the street, Manhattanites were amazed to discover that the Seventh Regiment Armory on Park Avenue really is an armoury, and not just, as it is to most New Yorkers these days, a heritage site you can rent for art and antique shows. On the steps of the Capitol, members of Congress broke into a spontaneous performance of "God Bless America". "The Star-Spangled Banner" is about an historic event, "America The Beautiful" is about the topography, but, when it comes to the nation, Irving Berlin said it simplest and said it best:

God Bless America
Land that I love.

Berlin wrote those lines sincerely and without embarrassment. He was a Jew and he endured slights: When he married a society girl, Ellin Mackay, she was dropped from the Social Register. When Ellin's sister took up with a Nazi diplomat in New York and went around sporting a diamond swastika, she suffered no such social disapproval. Throughout his life, fate seemed determined to test to the limit Berlin's faith in both America and the simple certainties of popular song. But he never forgot being a child in Temun, Siberia, when the Cossacks rode in and razed his village, sending his parents scuttling west. About his adopted land, he had no doubts, and his were the words Americans turned to. Sung on Federal property in normal circumstances, they'd be considered religious enough to attract a lawsuit from the American Civil Liberties Union:

Stand beside her
And guide her
Through the night
With a light from above…

But even the ACLU isn't dumb enough to launch church-and-state lawsuits when half of Lower Manhattan is filled with prayer vigils. Prayer, not grief counselling: the real thing, not its ersatz lo-cal substitute.

In my state, New Hampshire, the "Live Free Or Die" state, there were thousands of flags. Dawn Dupont of Pembroke stood out on the road holding her "Beep To Bomb Bin Laden" sign, and the overwhelming majority did. The students at Plymouth State College made a huge "Live Free Or Die Against Terrorism" banner and unfurled it in the state capital, Concord. A neighbour of mine put up the biggest flag in town and demanded a massive military response. "But she's a Democrat," I said to a friend. "And a lesbian." "Ah, yes," he replied, "but she belongs to the hawkish wing of the lesbian movement."

There are a lot of them around. *The New Statesman* would be foolish to assume the warmongers are all GOP cowboys.

In the midst of all this, the globetrotting celebrity Bill Clinton, making a rare appearance back in the United States, showed up on the streets of Lower Manhattan and, for the first time, looked oddly anachronistic. America's would-be Ex-President-For-Life, he suddenly seemed irretrievably stuck in the day before yesterday. If the Clinton era was characterised by anything, it was public passivity – sometimes because people were content (the economy), sometimes because they were ambivalent (abortion), sometimes because they just didn't want to know about it (his sex life), sometimes because they were scrupulously non-judgmental to the point of ennui (altogether now: "Everybody does it"). The GOP seemed to find the era tonally offensive as much as anything else. In 1996, Bob Dole howled, "Where's the outrage?" Three years later, William Bennett wrote a book called *The Death Of Outrage*.

Well, there's outrage now, as well there should be, though how it will be directed remains to be seen. If September 11th marked the close of the passive era, then it ended in a spectacular, awful but telling way. The perfect symbol of what Dave Kopel (in *National Review*) calls "the culture of passivity" is the airline cabin, the most advanced model of the modern social-democratic state, the sky-high version of trends that, on the ground, progress more slowly. Massachusetts and California can only aspire to cloud cuckoo land, but up there where the air is rarefied a Federal regulatory authority can bring Utopia into being at the stroke of a bureaucrat's pen. The commercial airliner is an Al Gore dream. There is no smoking. There is 100% gun control. You are by obliged by law to do everything the cabin crew tell you to do. If the stewardess is rude to you, tough. If you're rude to her, there'll be officers waiting to arrest you when you land. The justification for all this is a familiar one - that in return for surrendering individual liberties, we'll all be collectively better off. That was the deal: do as you're told, and the Federal Aviation Administration will look after you.

Last Tuesday morning, the FAA failed spectacularly to honour their end of the bargain – as I'm sure the terrorists knew they would. By all accounts, they travelled widely during the long preparations for their mission, and they must have seen that an airline cabin is the one place where, thanks to the FAA, you can virtually guarantee you'll meet no resistance. Indeed, in their FAA-mandated coerciveness the average coach-class cabin is the nearest the western world gets to the condition of those terrorists' home states. We've all experienced those bad weather delays where you're stuck on the runway behind 60 other planes waiting to take off and some guy says, "Hey, we've been in here a couple of hours now. Any chance of a Diet Coke?", and the stewardess says he'll have to wait, and the guy's cranky enough to start complaining. And one part of you thinks "Yeah, I'm pretty thirsty, too", but the rest of you, the experienced traveller, goes, c'mon, sit down, pal, quit whining, don't make a fuss, they'll only delay us even more.

And so, on those Boston flights that morning, everyone followed FAA guidelines: the cabin crew, the pilots, the passengers. There were four or five fellows with knives or box-cutters, outnumbered more than ten to one. If they'd tried to hold up that many people in a parking lot, they'd have been beaten to a pulp. But up in the air everyone swallowed the FAA's assurance: go along with them, be cooperative, the Feds know how to handle these things. I'm sure there were men and women in those seats thinking, well, there's not very many of them and they don't have any real weapons, maybe if some of us were to… But by the time they realised they were beyond the protection of the FAA it was too late.

The full story of what happened on three of those four terrible flights will never be known. But we do know something about the final moments of United Airlines Flight 93, the decisive event of the day.

Thomas Burnett, Jeremy Glick, Mark Bingham and others phoned their families to tell them they loved them and to say goodbye. Denied even that consolation, Todd Beamer couldn't get through to anyone except a telephone company operator, Lisa Jefferson. He explained three men were on board and one seemed to have a bomb tied around his waist. She told him about the planes that had smashed into the World Trade Center and the Pentagon. Mr Beamer said they had a plan to jump the guy with the bomb. He asked her if she would pray with him, so they recited the 23rd Psalm:

> *Yea, though I walk through the valley of the shadow of death, I will fear no evil: for thou art with me...*

Then they rushed the hijackers.

Miss Jefferson kept the line open. At 9.58am, the plane crashed, not at Camp David or the White House, but in a field in Pennsylvania. Jeremy Glick knew that he would never see his three-month old daughter again, Todd Beamer that he would never know the baby his wife is expecting in January. But both men understood that they could play their part in preserving a world for their children to grow up in. By being willing to sacrifice themselves, Mr Glick and his comrades saved thousands, perhaps including even the Vice-President and other senior officials. They were not passive.

One of the smartest observers of the American scene, Virginia Postrel, noticed something about these men: they were all technology-company executives. David Brooks, the author of *Bobos In Paradise* ("bobos" being "bourgeois bohemians", the new ruling class) has been mocking these tech execs for years. They put their companies in low-rise identikit buildings in boring office parks, a feature of the landscape I have no strong views on one way or the other but which Brooks feels symbolises the deficiencies of the age:

> *Nowadays when you walk amidst the office parks, you see a country that is great but insufficient too - great in its scientific accomplishments, in its tolerance and in its industriousness.... and yet insufficient because of its self-satisfaction and complacency.*

Warming to his theme, he comes close to indicting the office park as an un-American activity:

> *When you scan through the great figures who are supposed to represent the American spirit, almost all of them seem hopelessly out of place in office parks. We used to think America was a pioneer nation, but the people in the office parks haven't thrown off the comforts of civilisation to strike out on their own: This isn't the realm of the Puritan, the Cowboy, or the Immigrant.*
>
> *So too you can't fit George Washington in an office park. He may have embodied the American spirit when we were a nation fighting great wars for freedom and democracy, but it is hard to see Cincinnatus getting excited about an IPO.*
>
> *Nor is it easy to imagine Lincoln parking his Chevy Suburban in one of the oversized spaces and fiddling with his Palm Pilot on his way to the morning meeting. Lincoln was too grand and too political for an office-park nation.*

I don't suppose Lincoln would have given his office park any more thought than he gave his log cabin. But, insofar as there were any consolations on September 11th, it was because of the heroism of the "office-park nation". Why's that so surprising? Thomas Burnett headed a company that's making the devices that replace heart valves smaller. These men worked in the most dynamic sector of the economy, where people start their own businesses, develop new products, and maybe don't worry enough about how swank their office is. *Pace* Brooks, they're the new pioneers, the first settlers: they strike out for new territory – the undeveloped plot on the sub-division on the edge of town – throw up a rude dwelling and get on with the important stuff. According to a friend, Burnett was a "patriot", a hunter and military history buff whose office had busts of Lincoln, Churchill and Teddy Roosevelt. It's what's inside the office park that counts.

Miss Jefferson believes she heard what were Todd Beamer's last words: "Are you guys ready? Let's roll!" Then they jumped the hijackers.

"That's Todd," his wife Lisa said. "My boys even say that. When we're getting ready to go somewhere, we say, 'C'mon guys, let's roll.' My little one says, 'C'mon, Mom, let's roll.' That's something they picked up from Todd."

As it turned out, the men from the office park would have been instantly recognisable to Washington and Lincoln. They weren't self-satisfied or complacent at all.

Could you or I do what they did? This will be a long, messy, bloody war, in which civilians – salesmen, waitresses, accountants, tourists – are in the front line. America will need more Todd Beamers and Jeremy Glicks, and not just in the air. The culture of passivity is spread very wide throughout the west - the belief that government knows best and that citizens have sub-contracted out their responsibilities to protect and defend their liberty.

We know now that, for all its promises, the Federal Government wasn't up there over upstate New York when Flight 11 doglegged and began homing in on Washington. We know, too, that when you're facing terrorists willing to kill and die that the decisive moments are the first – the few minutes before they've established control or killed their first stewardess. So the next time it happens, Americans have a choice: they can follow FAA guidelines – or they can say screw 'em and their worthless assurances, and rush forward to overpower the fanatics, even if the FAA has seen to it they've nothing to charge them with except the rubber chicken. If you want a name for it, try the "Minutemen" – after the men of the Revolutionary War who were pledged to take the field at a minute's notice.

Across the placid, prosperous post-war decades, all the great words have been appropriated: if "courage" means facing up to your drinking problem, what's left for a fellow on a business flight who jumps the whacko with the bomb? In his Inauguration Address, George W Bush enjoined the American people to be "citizens, not subjects" and, although no one paid much attention at the time, last week gave us some fine examples. *Slate*'s Mickey Kaus thinks nothing's changed – that the sleeping giant will get bored, go back to sleep and this will all be off the front pages by Thanksgiving. But at least the horror and heroism of September 11th has usefully brought into focus the two alternatives the next time this happens (and it will, sooner than we think): you can be the kind of citizen who acts, or you can be the kind who just sits there and lets the Federal Government regulate his cutlery.

C'mon, guys. Let's roll.

LIKE A MOVIE

September 22nd 2001
The Spectator

"IT WAS LIKE something out of a movie."
Not everyone said that, but enough people did, watching on television or from the streets of Lower Manhattan. At times it was even shot like a movie, the low crouch of an enterprising videographer capturing the startled "What the fuh…?" of a street-level New Yorker as high above him in the slit of sky between the buildings the second plane sailed across the blue and through the south tower. The "money shots" were eerily reminiscent, the towers falling to earth with the same instant, awesome symbolism as the atomisation of the White House in *Independence Day*. In *Swordfish*, just a few weeks ago, a plane clipped a skyscraper; I thought at the time how bored John Travolta's innocent hostages looked, as he and the featured players spat inane dialogue at each other, and his supposedly terrified victims – Equity-minimum extras - sat blankly in the background, the director having neglected to direct them. It must have been different last Tuesday, but they couldn't show us that scene.

Still, the dialogue was the same: "Make no mistake – we will hunt down the enemy, we will find the enemy, and we will kill the enemy." George W Bush? No, Bruce Willis in *The Siege*, the 1998 film about Arab terrorists inflicting on New York "the worst bombing in America since Oklahoma City".

The headlines were the same, too: "Veteran Firefighter's Wife And Child Killed In Bomb Blast." *The New York Post*? No, the subway posters for Arnold Schwarzenegger's new movie about the bombing of a skyscraper, *Collateral Damage*, whose ad campaign uses mock newspaper headlines. That's what Manhattan commuters were looking at last Tuesday morning on their way to work in the financial district, if indeed they noticed them at all, so familiar a part of the cultural landscape are Hollywood's explosions and fireballs.

It even played like a movie, starting at 8.48am, when the first plane hit, and ending just under two hours later with both towers reduced to rubble. Then, instead of going to dinner and talking about it for ten minutes, America talked about it all day, and every day since.

Of course, there were things that weren't quite right: The after-effect of the towers' collapse, when the great balls of smoke and debris billowed out and pinballed down the canyon streets, sent pedestrians running in terror. But they couldn't outrun it, as in the movies people – or at any rate the above-the-title stars – do so easily. And the real heroism of the day was too primal for Hollywood – the guys on United flight 93 who called their families to say goodbye and wish them a good life, then rushed the hijackers and overpowered them only to crash in a Pennsylvania field. In the Hollywood version, they'd have skimmed the trees, skidded through some scrub, lost the tail and wings, burst into flames, but through the smoke and ambulance sirens at least some of the sooty heroes would have emerged to embrace their sobbing wives. September 11th was like a movie, but with none of the guaranteed consolations.

When I saw *Independence Day*, the big moment – the evaporation of the White House – brought the audience to wild whoops and cheers. They were reacting to it not as a dramatic moment, not as a plot point, but as an effect. This is not an especially American characteristic, or even a movie one. I remember years ago attending the first night of *Winnie*, a musical about Churchill, at the Victoria Palace. The big set-piece was the recreation of the bombing of the Café de Paris, a crowded dance floor suddenly blown to pieces. The contrast between the carnage and the gaiety of only an instant before should have been shocking. Instead, even as the bodies were hitting the stage, the audience burst into delirious applause. Their appreciation of the technology required to bring off the moment overrode any emotional engagement with it. And, say what you like, until last Tuesday the cinematic incineration of American urban landmarks was strictly hypothetical. In London, as in Europe's other great cities, these things really happened, within living memory.

If I had to identify the point at which the disaster overwhelmed the disaster movie, it would be when the networks realised the small, dark pinpricks on the ledges of the shattered towers were people. When aliens blow up the White House in *Independence Day*, it's a computer-generated model that gets demolished, and we give no thought to the secretaries, ushers, aides and sightseers who would have been interred within. In the non-movie, humanity asserted its primacy over technical spectacle: on those top floors, faced with a choice between burning alive or taking one last gulp of oxygen, people jumped. Traders, receptionists, clients, one couple choosing to die together and falling through the air hand in hand. Who were they? Men, women, we didn't know. For a moment, the cameras seemed to close in on the falling bodies. What a shot! The faces, the agony. But then they thought better of it, and stayed back.

Schwarzenegger's forthcoming film won't be coming forth any time soon: *Collateral Damage* is indefinitely postponed. Couldn't he lean on Warners just to drop it? Couldn't he do what Frank Sinatra did after the death of Kennedy, when he yanked his assassination thriller *The Manchurian Candidate* from cinema screens and kept it out of circulation for a quarter-century? We should expect no less of Arnie, who might like to ponder a move into costume drama or musicals or anything except formula video games that encourage us to admire destruction as choreography. Perhaps, at some level, those killers thought it would be an especially black jest to use the clichés of Hollywood's synthetic pain to inflict real pain. Even in America, life isn't a movie.

~

THE QUEEN'S TEARS

September 17th 2001
National Review

THE FOREIGN leader who said it best last week was the Queen, though she didn't really say a word. I have met Her Majesty from time to time (I am one of her Canadian subjects), and to put it at its mildest, for those with a taste for American vernacular politics, she can be a little stiff: the Queen stands on ceremony and she has a lot of ceremony to stand on. But on Thursday, for the Changing of the Guard at Buckingham Palace, she ordered the Coldstream Guards to play "The Star-Spangled Banner" – the first time a foreign anthem had been played at the ceremony.

The following day something even more unprecedented happened: at Britain's memorial service for the war dead of last Tuesday, the first chords of "The Star-Spangled Banner" rumbled up from the great organ at St Paul's Cathedral, and the Queen did something she's never done before – she sang a foreign national anthem, all the words. She doesn't sing her own obviously ("God Save Me"), but she's never sung "*La Marseillaise*" or anything else, either; her lips never move.

And at that same service she also sang "The Battle Hymn Of The Republic", for the second time in her life – the first was at the funeral of her first Prime Minister, Winston Churchill. On Friday, she fought back tears. When she ascended the throne, Harry Truman was in the White House. The first President she got to know was Eisenhower, back in the war, when he would come to the Palace to brief her father. She is the head of state of most of the rest of the English-speaking world – Queen of Britain, Canada, Australia, New Zealand, the Bahamas, Belize, Papua New Guinea, Tuvalu, etc. But she understands something that few other leaders of the west seem to - that today the ultimate guarantor of the peace and liberty of her realms is the United States. If America falls, or is diminished, or retreats in on itself, there is no "free world". That's the meaning of the Queen's "*Ich bin ein Amerikaaner*" moment.

Don't ask me who else you can count on. The Nato declaration was impressive, but, even as the press release was coming off the photocopier, a big chunk of America's 18 allies were backsliding. Norway, Germany and Italy said they had no intention of contributing planes, ships or men. Even as purely political support, the first ever invocation of Article Five was written in disappearing ink. The Italian Foreign Minister – speaking for Europe's most conservative government – said "the term 'war' is inappropriate". "We are not at war," said Belgian Foreign Minister Louis Michel, his nation's signature on that Nato document notwithstanding. Belgium holds the current Presidency of the EU and was last seen apologizing for slavery, colonialism, etc at Durban's recent UN Conference Against Whitey, Hymie And Capitalism.

The Royal Air Force will be alongside the USAF. The Aussies will send something. The Canadians will manage a token rustbucket like HMCS Toronto, the ship we dispatched the last time things started heating up in the Gulf. And New Zealand's recalcitrant Prime Minister may yet be forced by popular opinion into showing a bit more muscle. If these are the only active participants, so be it: in a war about "values", responsible government, the rule of law and individual liberty are essentially concepts of the English-speaking world that the rest of the west has only belatedly caught up to. Just a quarter-century ago, let's not forget, most of southern Europe – Portugal, Spain, Greece – was run by dictators. These people are used to making their accommodations with history.

Many consequences will flow from September 11th. The reactions of Continental governments confirm the worthlessness of Cold War alliances. Collective security, far from binding the western world, has corrupted it: the "free world" is mostly just a free ride. America's "moderate" Arab "allies" will find their relationship with Washington shift, too. The FBI list of those involved in the four hijackings makes instructive reading: no Afghans, no Iraqis, no Iranians, but many Saudis and Egyptians. What's the point of having "moderate" "allies" among the region's dictators if it only intensifies their subjects' hatred of America? And what's so "moderate" about these countries anyway? On the news networks, the standard incantation is that Pakistan is "one of only three countries that recognizes the Taliban regime". No one mentions that the other two are Saudi Arabia and the United Arab Emirates. With "friends" like these…

The worst time in the last half-century was the period when the west did everything *The Guardian* wanted - the years after the withdrawal from Vietnam, the years of "détente", the years when dolts like Pierre Trudeau allowed Cuban military planes to refuel in Canada en route to Moscow and military adventures in Africa, when Jimmy Carter dispatched a half-hearted rescue mission to Iran that resulted in the corpses of US soldiers being gleefully poked and prodded by the Ayatollahs on Teheran TV. The more "restrained" and "understanding" the west was, the more the Soviet Union increased its power, prestige and territory, from Ethiopia to Grenada. That period ended when the British, to everyone's surprise, retook the Falklands. They had behind-the-scenes intelligence support from the US, but otherwise they did it alone. That's as it should be. When America's attacked, it doesn't need to ask permission from Italy to strike back.

That's why I thank the Queen, a non-American but, unlike so many of America's moral relativists, not one who's uncomfortable with the emblems of the great Republic that overthrew her forebear. And so at St Paul's – symbol of British resistance during the Blitz – she sang the words written by Francis Scott Key on the last occasion the Eastern

Seaboard came under sustained bombardment – by the ships of the Royal Navy.

~

TAKING RESPONSIBILITY

September 17th 2001
The National Post

THERE ARE standard formulations even for atrocity. "The Provisional IRA," some BBC announcer would intone week after week for 30 years, "has claimed responsibility for the bomb which exploded at…" Enniskillen, Canary Wharf, Omagh, Hyde Park, wherever.

No one in the Middle East has yet "claimed responsibility" for the massacres of last Tuesday. So perhaps it would help if someone in the United States did. The obvious candidate is the Federal Aviation Administration, which is guilty on two counts.

First, it failed to prevent last week's hijackings: had the killers attempted to seize another 30 planes, who can doubt that they would have maintained their pristine 100% success rate? What happened on Tuesday was not the odd guy slipping through a few "cracks in the system", but a completely cracked system, whose failure was total. The scale of the disaster was constrained only by the murderers' ambition and manpower.

Secondly, and more importantly, the many and elaborate "security" measures the FAA did have in place contributed directly to the transformation of a small contained horror into a mass catastrophe. The FAA is perhaps the third most famous US governmental acronym on the planet, after the FBI and CIA. Any foreigner flying on foreign airlines into Chicago or Dallas or Atlanta gets used to the rote incantation that "FAA regulations prohibit" this or that humdrum manoeuvre. What an awesome agency: don't light up a furtive cigarette in the bathroom over Greenland; the FAA will know and they will get you! In the small municipal airport of Lebanon, New Hampshire, the only signs behind the ticket desk solemnly inform you the FAA has determined that, say, Lagos International Airport in Nigeria is unsafe. You can't fly to Lagos from Lebanon, New Hampshire. There are merely a couple flights per day to New York and Boston. But, whether because they were preoccupied with grading Lagos or for some other reason, no one at the FAA ever determined Logan Airport, Boston was unsafe – though, as we now know, it is, profoundly so. The FAA's non-security procedures would be laughable if they weren't doubly harmful: they delude the average citizen into believing the state is ensuring his safety, while letting the professional terrorist know he can get away with anything.

It's for that reason that it's important that the FAA Administrator, Jane Garvey, and her senior staff are asked to resign. It is time for them to acknowledge "responsibility". If this is, as President Bush says, "the first war of the 21st century", then here are a couple of relevant precedents:

After the fall of Norway, Neville Chamberlain resigned.

Two days after the Argentine invasion of the Falklands in 1981, Peter Carrington, Britain's Foreign Secretary, Humphrey Atkins, the Lord Privy Seal, and Richard Luce, the Minister for Latin-American Affairs, all resigned. Lord Carrington felt "it was a matter of honour" – they were the men charged with both guaranteeing the security of the Falklands and evaluating General Galtieri's regime in Buenos Aires. "I was wrong in the assessment of what they were doing," said Carrington, "and therefore I am responsible" – that word again. In interviews he reiterated the point: "There has been a British humiliation. I ought to take responsibility for it."

If those comparisons are too highfalutin, then let's keep it simple: if a municipal highway engineer had four bridges collapse on the same day, he'd be expected to quit. It's easy for bureaucrats to hide under the language of grief that the media instinctively deploy – "tragedy", "sorrow", "pain". What happened on Tuesday may well be a "tragedy", but it is also, for the responsible regulatory agency, all the things Fleet Street called the Falklands invasion: a "humiliation", "fiasco", "disgrace".

And yet it seems that no one is planning to resign. And, worse, they're carrying on exactly as before, with another ton of cumbersome regulations that won't improve the safety of a single American. No steak knives in first class! Gosh, how they must be quaking at Osama's training camps. This is a classic example of what brought us to this pass: a regulatory inconvenience that gives the illusion of security.

So, on the one hand, we have Norm Mineta, the unimpressive Transportation Secretary; on the other, the heroic passengers of Flight 93. The latter deserve not just America's highest (posthumous) honours, but an understanding of their sacrifice. Instead of indulging in gestures like confiscating eyebrow tweezers, the US government should summon up the will to match their courage.

~

THE NAMES OF THE DEAD

September 22nd 2001
The Spectator

THE BEST QUOTE of the war so far came from George W Bush's meeting with the four senators from New York and Virginia (the two states that came under attack). "When I take action," said the President, "I'm not gonna fire a $2 million missile at a $10 empty tent and hit a camel in the butt. It's going to be decisive."

I don't suppose Senator Rodham Clinton cared for this implicit rebuke of her husband and his intermittent Cruise-waggling over the Sudan and Afghanistan, but she kept quiet – as, by Monday, most of Bush's critics were doing. The jeers at his style had obscured the amazing substance: The President didn't shy away from the word "war", but rushed to embrace it. Unlike the last crowd, which announced beforehand that there would be no ground troops in Kosovo, Defence Secretary Don Rumsfeld refused to rule anything out, including nukes, which he seemed quite eager to rule in. His deputy, Paul Wolfowitz, pledged to "end" states that sponsor terrorism. By the time you read this, he may have begun the process, at least in respect to the Taleban. Meanwhile, even Mister Moderate, Colin Powell, under the guise of building a "broad-based coalition", is putting the screws to some of the more idiosyncratic regimes. General Musharraf told his senior commanders that he had no desire to help the Americans one jot but that he'd concluded Pakistan's "national survival" was at stake.

It would have been so easy to go the other way, the Clinton route – get the President drooling about building a better world "for all our children", make the Defence Department talk not of war and victory and vanquishing evil but only, as Clinton's Secretary Bill Cohen did, of "degrading" the enemy's capability. The new Administration did not exactly raise the stakes – they were all too clear from 9am last Tuesday - but by raising the rhetoric they acknowledged them in a way their predecessors would surely have ducked. It will not now be possible merely to whack a Cruise missile up some camel's butt.

To most of the rest of the world, this Rumsfeldian rhetoric is precisely the wrong tack. "Americans simply don't get it," wrote Seumas Milne in *The Guardian*: the Yanks should be trying to figure out what they did to get those terrorists all steamed up. It's the Louis Farrakhan line: the Jews just don't get it, they should give more thought to what they did to make Hitler so mad at them. Instead, tragically, all this war talk will only postpone the much-needed terrorist outreach, fulfilling the worst fears of left-wing commentators. Rana Kabbani, also in *The Guardian*, "hopes that the painful lesson that Americans have had to learn is not drowned out by cowboy ravings about 'getting the bastards'." The "painful lesson" she refers to is the murder of thousands of American civilians, as well as hundreds of Britons, Japanese, Australians, Koreans, Canadians, Mexicans, Zimbabweans and, at the time of writing, the nationals of some 35 other countries, including France, where Ms Kabbani resides. (And, incidentally, how come all these *Guardian* anti-racists and identity-politics obsessives reach instinctively for all this cheap cowboyphobia and rampant Texism?)

It's Ms Kabbani and Mr Milne who simply don't get it. Bill Clinton, no cowboy or Texan, asked Yasser Arafat to the White House more often than he invited any other world leader. In July last year, in the final stretch of his Presidency, he talked "Chairman" Arafat and Ehud Barak into holing up at Camp David and "going the extra mile" for peace. During these talks, by the way, last week's mass murderers were already well advanced in preparing their "painful lesson" for America: the British left may delude itself into thinking this is some sort of payback for Bush's hubris in rejecting Kyoto, but these fellows were busy taking their jet-flying courses even when Al Gore was ahead in the polls. Meanwhile, back at Camp David, Clinton schmoozed

Barak into offering up concessions that no previous Israeli Prime Minister had ever contemplated – including a Palestinian state with its capital in a shared Jerusalem. Okay, for Ms Kabbani and Mr Milne that might not be enough to justify calling off the "painful lesson", but you'd have thought it would be a basis for negotiation. Yet the great Chairman not only turned Barak down, he never even bothered making a counter-proposal.

If it were about Israel, it would be easy – to cut them loose, to abandon them to their fate, to singalong to the current big pop hit in Egypt and Syria, called with admirable clarity "I Hate Israel". But it's not about Israel, except insofar as eliminating Israel is the first stage. On Tuesday, I lost no close friends, only acquaintances, friends of friends, and distant neighbours over the far hills, the pilots and nurses and businessmen from southern New Hampshire who were on board those flights from Logan Airport. But the pool of blood crept close enough, and the "painful lesson" I learned was a simple one: that these guys can kill me and my family, and do it very easily, using a couple of cellphones, credit cards, online booking and commercial airlines – deploying western technology to bury western values. And, given that sometime soon they're likely to try again, I think it's worth doing something about it. Something "decisive", as the President said.

Now I know "western values" elicits titters from the Kabbani-Milne tendency. No doubt you've all had a hoot at the sappiness of American media coverage: Danny Lee died on American flight 11, rushing home for the birth of his child; she was born two days after his death, Allison, 8lb 12oz. Ha-ha, these Yanks are so sickeningly sentimental, aren't they? Christine Hanson, two years old, was sitting between her parents en route for Los Angeles. Lauren Grandcolas, two months pregnant, was on United flight 93 and called home, "There's a little problem with the plane, but I'm fine. I'm comfortable... Please tell my family that I love them."

Ms Kabbani would want to know why I'm not moved by the deaths of Palestinian mothers and fathers and children. Well, I am, and I realise that in this awful war we too will end up killing pregnant women, young sons, beloved grandmothers. But it's not me who accords less value to an Arab life than an American one. The Arab states do that when they deny their subjects the little bundle of rights and responsibilities loosely known as "liberty" that every American takes for granted. The western media diminish every Arab man, woman and child when they want to re-re-re-re-re-count every last dimpled chad in Palm Beach County while writing off the utter absence of democracy in the Arab world as just an example of quaint, charming, authentic Eastern "culture". In the Middle East, you can choose to live under a theocracy, an autocracy, a plutocracy, a kleptocracy or a nutocracy, but the only Arabs living in freedom are the two million who live in the United States and the others who live in Britain, Canada, Ms Kabbani's France, the rest of Europe and, come to that, Israel. If Washington treated Arabs the way Damascus does, you'd never hear the end of it at UN conferences.

As for Ms Kabbani's cowboy clichés, take a look at some of the faces under those ten-gallon hats. The names of the dead of September 11th tell their own story: Arestegui, Bolourchi, Carstanjen, Droz, Elseth, Foti, Gronlund, Hannafin, Iskyan, Kuge, Laychak, Mojica, Nguyen, Ong, Pappalardo, Quigley, Retic, Shuyin, Tarrou, Vamsikrishna, Warchola, Yuguang, Zarba. Black, white, Hispanic, Arab, Asian – in a word, American. There is a reason why people of every conceivable hue and ethnicity lie beneath the rubble, and it isn't because of what Ms Kabbani calls America's "unchecked arrogance". Western liberal democracy offers its citizens longer, better, healthier lives, freedom of speech, freedom of religion, freedom to travel, freedom to trade.

It even offers freedom to come here and become a wealthy, influential, famous cultural figure attacking the very notion of "the west" and "democracy" and their opposing bogeymen, "rogue states" and "terrorism", as "counterfeit" "confections" concocted by a dark "unseen power" to "create content and tacit approval". Thus, Edward Said's latest meditation for *The Nation*, which with exquisite timing appeared on their website round about the precise moment the first plane hit the World Trade Center. Could Said, a New York resident, get paid for writing that stuff in Lebanon or Syria, never mind Afghanistan? For a counterfeit confection, the west is providing Said with a pretty nice living.

But then that's the genius of the system. As readers will know, I'm no fan of Trudeaupian "multiculturalism", but let us acknowledge at least that it's a unicultural concept: it exists only in the west. As George Orwell wrote in 1945, "There is a minority of intellectual pacifists whose real though unadmitted motive appears to be hatred of western democracy and admiration of totalitarianism. Pacifist propaganda usually boils down to saying that one side is as bad as the other, but if one looks closely at the writings of younger intellectual pacifists, one finds that they do not by any means express impartial disapproval but are directed almost entirely against Britain and the United States." It is ever so. The 300 firemen who died on September 11th died in part for their fellow New Yorker Edward Said, though he is too stupid and graceless to understand.

As for those of us in the new front line, I don't want to end up in some weepy CNN montage of dead commuters because third-rate *Guardian* columnists think it's my fault that charlatan Arafat couldn't be bothered coming up with one lousy proposal at Camp David. Bush is right: this is the first war of the 21st century and we will win it – in spite of our "allies".

LATE SEPTEMBER

History's calling card

September 22nd 2001
The Daily Telegraph

ON WEDNESDAY I finally saw "Ground Zero". For those of us who've watched the endless TV replays of that second plane slamming into the tower again and again and again, what's most chilling about the scene in real life is how settled, how established it seems. I was in Oklahoma City six years ago, and in the days afterwards the Murrah Building looked like what it was: a big office block with a huge hole in it, something familiar that's been ruptured. But here you can no longer discern what the normality was before it got disrupted. It looks, in our terms, like a huge version of a New Jersey landfill that's gotten a little out of hand. Or, in a broader historical context, like the latter stages of the Germans' long siege of Stalingrad. Not the opening rounds of a first attack, but the vast accumulated detritus of a long, ongoing war – which, in a sense, is what it is. People are busy at the site, but the urgency has gone. The thousands of flyers posted by wives, husbands, parents and children are still up, but the word "MISSING" has slid from a long shot to a euphemism.

It impressed the celebrated German composer Karlheinz Stockhausen, who told a radio interviewer the other day that the destruction of the World Trade Center was "the greatest work of art ever". I'm reminded of the late Sir Thomas Beecham when asked if he'd ever played any Stockhausen: "No," he said. "But I once stepped in some." Last week, Stockhausen stepped in his own.

At Oklahoma City I remember the smell of the bodies. At Ground Zero's burial mound the devastation is so total that there are no bodies to smell. Thousands of people lie under there, all but atomised by their killers and all but forgotten by the appeasing left. At San Francisco's service of remembrance for its dead this week, Amos Brown, representing the city's Board of Supervisors, used the occasion

33

to launch into an examination of the "root causes" of the regrettable incident. "America, what did you do," he wailed, "in Africa, where bombs are still blasting? America, what did you do in the global warming conference when you did not embrace the smaller nations? America, what did you do two weeks ago when I stood at the world conference on racism, when you wouldn't show up?" The Bay Area lefties roared their approval.

Paul Holm, the partner of Mark Bingham, a gay 6'5" rugby jock who died on Flight 93, felt differently. He walked up to Senator Dianne Feinstein and said sadly, "This was supposed to be a memorial service." Then he quit the stage. Mark Bingham died heroically, and all the City of San Francisco can do is denigrate the cause and the nation for which he gave his life.

The totalitarian left has finally found its perfect soulmate. With Communism, the excuse was always that, whatever the practical difficulties on the ground, it retained its theoretical idealism. But the Taleban and Osama bin Laden are perfectly upfront: they're openly racist; they'd strip Dianne Feinstein of her Senatorship and make her a mere chattel; they'd execute Paul Holm for being gay, by building a wall and then crushing him under it. True, I don't know their position on global warming, but it doesn't seem to be a priority.

A few blocks north of Ground Zero, I dined with some friends. "This is the biggest event in my life," said one. "Bigger than the death of Kennedy." Even the Pearl Harbor comparison doesn't seem quite right. I wonder if we aren't revisiting August 1914, when the Archduke Franz Ferdinand was assassinated in Sarajevo. It seemed a simple war: the British Tommies marching off were told it would all be over by Christmas, as today *Slate*'s Mickey Kaus is confident the World Trade Center will be off the front pages by Thanksgiving. By the time the Great War was really over, four of the world's great powers lay shattered – the German, Austrian, Russian and Turkish Empires, all gone and so easily, though who would have predicted it in that last Edwardian summer? We don't know what this latest thread of history will unravel. But we should at least understand the stakes.

⌐

THE COALITION

September 23rd 2001
The Sunday Telegraph

THE FIRST battle has already been won – the critical battle over what kind of war we're in. As President Bush said on Thursday, it won't be like Kosovo or the Gulf. You can take this any way you like, though the omissions in the Presidential address suggest at least a couple: there was no mention of grand coalitions, the United Nations, the French, the Italians or any other Continental military power, and he doesn't seem to expect much from the rest of the world except a bit of inter-jurisdictional police cooperation and the occasional glance at any big wire transfers out of Osama's building society account.

That's very wise. In the Gulf, the "moderate" Arab states acted as a brake on the US; in Somalia, the Italians were giving nods and winks to the local warlord, General Aideed; and in Kosovo, the allies' insistence on advance operational information – even though for the most part they weren't actually contributing to any of the operations they were informed about – was not particularly helpful. As General Wesley Clark, Nato's former Supreme Commander, notes in his recent memoir *Waging Modern War*, "One of the French officers working at Nato headquarters had given key portions of the operations plan to the Serbs."

The difference is that, in those conflicts, the US military was engaged in saving far distant Muslims – Kuwaiti Muslims, Bosnian Muslims, Somali Muslims, Albanian Muslims (as should be obvious but sadly isn't, the US armed forces are the world's pre-eminent defender of Muslims) – and it was felt politic to observe the pretence that the ideal expeditionary force should look like a global affirmative-action program. This time, however, Boston and St Louis, Miami and Denver are at stake, and the Bush Administration sees no reason to mortgage their future to any country which thinks de-mothballing a rusting frigate entitles it to a set of keys to the command module. Of the attenuated militaries still in a position to contribute anything useful, Washington will welcome the British, than whom "America has no truer friend", said Bush, which is correct, but, alas, isn't saying much. This was a speech almost wholly free of the polite fictions of the foreign policy establishment. His murdered compatriots deserve no less.

So the first American victory in the war on terrorism goes to the Pentagon – to Defence Secretary Don Rumsfeld and his deputy Paul Wolfowitz, whose views have prevailed over those of the more famous and glamorous Colin Powell, Secretary of State. Last week, Powell was asked about Wolfowitz's comment that the US would "end" states that sponsor terrorism and publicly slapped him down, saying Wolfowitz spoke only for himself. But the Wolfowitz agenda seems to have taken the President's fancy: Bush told Afghanistan to "hand over the terrorists or share their fate"; he said, "Our enemy is a radical network of terrorists, and every government that supports them"; and he promised that they'd wind up with Nazism, Fascism and totalitarianism in "history's unmarked grave". That was the only concession to the mandarins, the substitution of "totalitarianism" for "Communism", for fear of waving a red flag (so to speak) at the Chinese.

Powell wants a limited action against Osama bin Laden, for all the usual reasons: there's less chance of running into problems with America's reluctant allies and cool press. Wolfowitz would like to take out Saddam now. Rumsfeld is more of an opportunist, willing to get rid of Saddam if the moment presents itself, happy to concentrate on the Afghans for the moment, while recognising that there's no point going to this much trouble for piffling aims. The Defence Secretary is not a man for empty threats: "If you're going to cock it, you throw it," he said the other day. On Thursday, the President cocked.

Like all sinister types Rumsfeld sits off to the side during the group photo, so he's not terribly well known to the Talebanophiles of the British media. But give 'em a week or two and he'll be the designated Dr Strangelove of this new world war. Indeed, he's the Strangelove's Strangelove: Henry Kissinger called Rumsfeld "the most ruthless man I've ever met" – dictators and despots included. *The Mirror* has already picked up on the remark, though they neglected to mention that the good Doctor insists he meant it as a compliment: "He would have made an outstanding President," said Kissinger of Rumsfeld's short-lived campaign for the nomination in 1988.

But the feeling, after he returned to Washington in January, was that the master had lost his touch. The press mostly took their cue from the shrill caricature by *The New York Times'* elderly schoolgirl columnist Maureen Dowd, to whom the returning Defence Secretary was "Rip Van Rummy", an ancient, cruel but out-of-touch Cold Warrior who'd been outmanoeuvred by the Pentagon brass in his attempt to return the world to the ideological conflicts of the Seventies. *Au contraire*, after the inertia of the Clinton years, Rumsfeld was the first to argue that a Cold War military was no longer sufficient for America's needs and that we needed faster, lighter, more adaptable forces.

Then came September 11th. He was the only Cabinet member whose offices were attacked, the only one to lose members of his own staff, the only one to pull the injured from the rubble, and even more amazingly the only one whose old memos seemed to have any relevance in the remade world. By contrast, Powell's platitudinous evenhandedness in the Israeli/Palestinian dispute barely passes muster even as conventional wisdom. Bush, for his part, seems to have split the difference between Rumsfeld and Wolfowitz, suggesting to the Taleban that it's time to start packing but not directly mentioning Iraq, Syria and Iran, thereby giving them one last chance to "straighten up and fly right" (as President Reagan told Colonel Gaddafi) without it looking as if they're knuckling under to Washington.

The President found his voice last week, splitting "compassionate conservatism" into two separate operating units: on the non-military stuff, Bush visits mosques, raves about how much he loves Islam, does a lot of male bonding with firemen, gets teary with widows of the Flight 93 heroes; but, on the war itself, he's steelier than many on the right expected. He knows you can't fight a terrorist war defensively. You have to take the fight to them, hard. Bush made that promise on Thursday, and that in itself was a break with the recent past. Asked to commit to Bosnia, General Powell declined: "We do deserts, we don't do mountains," he said. This week, mountains are back.

～

MENTIONING CANADA

September 24th 2001
The National Post

L AST FRIDAY, while Canadians were demanding to know why they didn't rate a name-check in President Bush's speech, a unit of Britain's special forces, the SAS, came under enemy attack deep inside Afghanistan.

There's the answer.

If affronted Canucks would step back a moment, they'd see that the unusual feature of the Presidential address was that it was almost entirely lacking in State Department guff, Foggy Bottom fog. The word from both countries is that this "coalition", on the battlefield, will be an Anglo-American affair: the US is not interested in letting anybody else into the inner sanctums of joint command. The minimum entry qualifications are that a) you have a professional, modern military and b) you share America's war aims. The French meet the former but not the latter. The Mexicans the latter but not the former. The British meet both. The Canadians meet neither.

This is a simple truth, and we should be mature enough to acknowledge it. When M Chrétien says that Canada will stand "shoulder to shoulder" with the Americans, he is, in fact, describing exactly where we *won't* be standing. "Shoulder to shoulder" is a military expression, for comrades in arms marching forward on the field of battle. The Prime Minister is happy to deploy the term metaphorically, but that's it. Just over a week ago, when I mentioned the pitiful state of our forces, I received a lot of indignant e-mails from Canadians insisting that they were ready to enlist. I don't doubt you. But, if you did enlist, they'd have no uniforms to give you, no weapons except for Papa Jean's spare set of clubs from Royal Montreal, and no means of getting you to the battlefield except a commandeered school bus. Of the 13 Nato air forces flying missions over Kosovo, ours were the only planes without anti-jam radios, forcing all the others to downgrade their communications to the Canadian level and use a jammable single frequency. Up against a far more ruthless foe than Slobo, Don Rumsfeld is not going to increase the risk to his pilots for the privilege of having a couple of maple tailfins up there.

If Canada applied to participate in joint military operations, it would be turned down – which is why John Manley's belated promise of ground troops is less manly than it sounds. He knows full well they won't be required. His generous offer is as laughable as me offering to play in the Wimbledon men's final. The reality is that what's left of Canada's forces is too poorly equipped to share a battlefield with the Americans, the British, the Australians or any reasonably funded army.

Intelligence? CSIS is underfunded and politically irrelevant: when they report that 50 global terrorist groups are actively operating in Canada, the Prime Minister files it in the bottom drawer under his golf-club bill-of-sale napkins and, if anyone brings it up, flatly denies its conclusions. Canada is the only G7 country whose government is involved in covert sabotage of its own intelligence gathering.

Yet, confronted with an obvious truth, we persist in hunting for ludicrous alternatives. Is it that Bush personally dislikes Chrétien? You couldn't blame the guy. In his speeches, our Prime Minister has a half-dozen jokes about what a dummy Dubya is: "I explained to him that Alberta is in Canada", etc. In person, he's boorishly patronizing:

Chrétien welcoming Bush to the Summit of the Americas in Quebec: *"Bienvenue."*

Bush: "Thank you, sir."

Chrétien: "That means welcome."

But, believe it or not, when you've got a mound of 10,000 corpses, getting in a dig at some irrelevant old coot is not what's on your mind. There's a reason why Tony Blair was the foreign leader in town for the day of the big speech, and not Chirac (who dropped by the day before) or Chrétien. Had Chrétien been sitting next to the First Lady and Bush had singled him out for the same lavish praise as Blair, it would have communicated not strength but weakness, not resolve but fundamental unseriousness, as though this was just another Clintonian marshmallow campaign.

It's not. That's why Canada's war is already over. It ended when all those diverted planes took off from Gander and Halifax and Calgary and their stranded passengers bid farewell to the many kind and generous Canadians who'd helped make those involuntary layovers as comfortable as possible. In Washington today, President Bush, who is always polite, will thank M Chrétien for Canada's assistance that terrible morning, and may even venture something Colin Powellish about the non-service of remembrance on Parliament Hill. But what else can he say? As Francie Ducros, speaking for the Prime Minister, explained, America's friendship with Canada is so deep it "goes without saying". In that case, Bush is happy to go on not saying it for a long time. A friend who dozes in a hammock on the front porch and gives a sympathetic wave as his neighbour's being mugged is of limited value.

One can regret this, but really, why bother? The 55% of the population who support the Liberal Party evidently believes it's more important for the state to invest in the Auberge Grand-Mère than in the defence of the realm. Those of us who disagree must respect the democratic will. Canada, after all, believes that it can best project itself as (in Lloyd Axworthy's exquisite banality) a "soft power". That may be right - as long as Osama bin Laden's boys can tell the difference between Minneapolis and Edmonton.

But since September 11th it's hard power that's needed. This will be a long and difficult campaign, and, if Canada can't make a contribution, it could at least quit whining about why its non-contribution isn't getting enough respect. As of today, the British already have SAS units and MI6 agents inside Afghanistan, plus 20,000 troops in Oman, and a Royal Navy task force, including a nuclear sub, steaming through the Red Sea. On Thursday, the President, mourning the loss of thousands of his fellow citizens, gave a sober businesslike outline of his response to the massacre. If we can no longer fight, we could at least have the good taste not to go, "But enough about world war. Let's talk about me."

POWELL, AGAIN

September 27th 2001
The National Post

TONY BLAIR backs the President, General Musharraf backs the President, even Hillary Clinton backs the President. But Colin Powell persists in treating him like a junior colleague with a tendency to wander off-message. In his address to Congress, George W Bush devoted more time to the Afghans than any Bush speech has ever given to a foreign country. He dwelled at length on all manner of Talibanic arcana. "A man can be jailed in Afghanistan if his beard is not long enough," he pointed out. Hordes of insufficiently hirsute Afghans, surreptitiously listening to the Voice of America from short-wave radios barely concealed in their stunted beards, would have been forgiven for concluding that help was on its way, that the land of the free and the home of the shave had the Taliban in its cross-hairs.

Certainly the hairy mullahs thought so. There were reports of massive defections from the ranks, and huge waves of refugees at the border. The pillars of the regime seemed to be crumbling around them, like Samson after his haircut, if they'll forgive a filthy Jew anecdote. Without even having to de-beard the enemy in his den, Bush seemed to have him by the long and curlies.

But not so fast. Within three days, Colin Powell was all over the talk-shows insisting that, despite Bush's "non-negotiable" demands, the Administration had no strong views on these chaps one way or the other. All we're after is getting them to cough up bin Laden. "If they did that we wouldn't be worrying about whether they are the regime in power or not," the General told the Associated Press. And he certainly doesn't foresee any large-scale military operations there: "It's a tough place to fight conventional battles," he said.

Instead, he figures it's possible to find more moderate elements within the group to work with. It seems even the most Neanderthal political movements (if my Neanderthal friends will forgive the comparison) can reform themselves – New Labour, New Democrats, New Taliban. And, if the Taliban were to be cooperative, "there may be significant benefits for them – having a better relationship with the west, with the United States." You Taliban fainthearts, halfway out of town, heading for the hills, tripping over your beards, come on down. Not only does the General have no wish to punish you for your hospitality to the mass murderers of American civilians, but he's happy to reward you for it.

The benign explanation is that Powell and the Bush hardliners are doing a good cop/bad cop routine. But, even as soothing rhetoric, it's deeply damaging. It gets reported in the Muslim world and elsewhere as evidence that the Great Satan is just as soft and decadent as they thought he was.

It's tempting to say that Colin Powell sounds like a holdover from the Clinton Administration. But it's worse than that: Colin Powell sounds like Colin Powell.

Ten years ago, the General was the only guy in the inner circle who didn't want to fight the Gulf War and the only one to come out of it an unqualified winner. Saddam survived, of course, but it took him a while to figure out how to make a laughingstock of UN inspectors and to pluck up the courage to start firing on Anglo-American air patrols over northern Iraq.

Still, he did better than his opposite number. George Bush père, after supposedly winning the war, lost the election, badly. With Bush went the Desert Storm war cabinet - James Baker, Brent Scowcroft - their political careers over. General Norman Schwarzkopf, the gruff, pugnacious commander in the field, came home a war hero, only to be advised by Powell, "Now is the perfect time for you to retire... You'll be getting all kinds of offers." He's not been heard of since.

But Powell, Chairman of the Joint Chiefs, graduated from Desert Storm a celebrity. Though he'd spent the war sitting in Washington, he, not Stormin' Norm, was the conflict's designated "hero". Men are from Mars, women are from Venus, but here was a martial man for a Venusian age. Warning Bush Sr against trying to push on to Baghdad and topple Saddam, he embodied America's preferred image of itself: the strong man who never wants to use his strength. He was an African-American, yet wholly untouched by bitterness. He was a Republican, but so "moderate" about it you hardly noticed.

In 1995, he parlayed his fame into a smash autobiography and set off on a spectacular book tour. Bill Clinton had just been hammered by the Republicans in the Congressional elections and all the party needed to complete its sweep was a viable Presidential candidate. The General's numbers were phenomenal. Heavyweight Republican backers across the country signed on to a "Draft Powell" movement and the money all but dried up for anybody else. But then, as in Iraq, with the capital in sight and victory his for the asking, he announced that he wasn't going to go for the big prize. As before, those who suffered most were his supposed pals –those Republicans who did bother to run and were inevitably found wanting by comparison with the great prince who'd disdained the crown.

Amazingly, Powell's careless, self-indulgent unbalancing of the Presidential race did nothing to harm his reputation. The only people who seemed antipathetic toward him were the African-American grievance-mongers. When the General remarked that his favourite music was Andrew Lloyd Webber, Jesse Jackson wondered whether the guy was even black. But, if you think about it, it's an apt choice: like Lloyd Webber, Powell is bland but huge. He's the *Cats* of American politics: no-one can quite explain why, but he runs forever.

Powell is not to blame for the inconclusive end to the Gulf War. That responsibility rests with Bush Sr, who as commander-in-chief accepted his general's advice. But Powell has been the most vigorous in defence of the decision not to push on to Baghdad. In his 1995 memoir, he credits his restraint with keeping the Gulf War coalition intact, with bringing Yasser Arafat to the negotiating table with Israel, and with ensuring that Iraq "remains weak and isolated, kept in check by UN inspectors. Not a bad bottom line."

Maybe not in '95. But six years on, Arafat's waging a new intifada; the UN inspectors have been kicked out; the coalition Powell prized above all else has dribbled away to the US and Britain, the last enforcers of Iraq's no-fly zone; France and the other "allies" have figured that, if Washington hasn't the guts to take him out, they'd like to get back to business as usual with Saddam. And, worst of all, ten years of economic sanctions have given the old butcher a grand propaganda coup, as the west's peacenik boobs line up to denounce the Americans for systematically starving Iraqi children. It should be said, loudly, that they're not. Saddam's personal fortune is estimated at $7 billion. (Who knew a career in Iraqi public service could be so rewarding?) If there'd been no sanctions, the kids would still be starving and his personal fortune would now be up to $10 billion. But sanctions have enabled him to portray Washington as the source of his people's woes, and there'll always be a big audience for that in the west. The net result of Powell's "moderation" has been to tarnish the morality of our cause.

True, there are no Tony Blairs or Al Gores waiting in the wings in Baghdad. The only way you could make Iraq democratic would be through colonial occupation, and, as we know from UN conferences, colonialism is A Very Bad Thing. So realistically the best we could hope for in a post-Saddam Iraq is a thug who's marginally less bloody. But a new thug is still better than letting the old thug stick around to cock snooks at you. If Saddam had been toppled, the nutter du jour would have come to power in the shadow of the cautionary tale of his predecessor.

Powell's famous restraint has now come back to haunt if not him then his countrymen. There are strong circumstantial links between Saddam and Osama bin Laden, from the 1993 World Trade Center bombing through to Saddam's support for one of Osama's subsidiaries, Jund al Islam ("Soldiers of Islam"). But Powell sees no reason to change his tune. He called it wrong ten years ago, and he's doing the same now. And, to all those naysayers who are suddenly big experts on Afghanistan as the graveyard of empires, let me recommend the most pertinent critique on the subject: the low-budget Brit comedy, *Carry On Up The Khyber* (1968), its title alluding not just to geography but to Cockney rhyming slang (Khyber Pass – arse). In the film, the 3rd Foot and Mouth Regiment are under attack from the Khazi of Kalabar and his revolting tribesmen, but no matter how ferociously the rebels shell the legation Sir Sidney Ruff-Diamond and his fellow officers are in the middle of tea and refuse to respond. This only makes the Khazi more enraged.

There, in a nutshell, is the Powell Doctrine. A friend reminded me this week of that British expression, a "parade general". Under its parade general, the US military became a parade army, and among the consequences is one astonishing statistic from September 11th: more members of the New York Fire Department died that day than members of the US armed forces have died in battle in the last 15 years. To the General, this is a source of pride: he was "relieved", he wrote, that he didn't have to say, "I'm sorry your son or daughter died in the siege of Baghdad." But Saddam and Osama saw it another way: if your enemy won't go to war, the war must go to the enemy. To die, your son or daughter won't have to go to Baghdad, but only to work - in New York or Washington or wherever's next. Even Powell, who thought he could defy the rules of conventional warfare, must surely now recognize the alternative forms are bloodier.

Rereading the Powell Doctrine – essentially a long list of reasons not to go to war – you realize it's a document from a lost world: the General's paramount concern is "Exit Strategy", but how can you exit when your own land is the battlefield? The Powell Doctrine takes into account every possibility except one: your enemy launching a sudden, brutal, bloody assault on your own territory.

Given that oversight, you'd think the General would have the decency to recognize its obsolescence, rather than trying to force it on the White House one more time. Life isn't a Republican Presidential nominating season: if you start something, you have to see it through. You can't fight a desultory war against terrorism, and, if Colin Powell thinks you can, it's time for George W Bush to remind him who the President is.

EARLY OCTOBER

Peace

October 6th 2001
The Spectator

WHAT HAVE we learned since September 11th? We've learned that poverty breeds despair, despair breeds instability, instability breeds resentment, and resentment breeds extremism.

Yes, folks, these are what we in the trade call "root causes". Which cause do you root for?

"Poverty breeds instability" (*The Detroit News*)?

Or "poverty breeds fanaticism" (Carolyn Lochhead in *The San Francisco Chronicle*)?

Bear in mind that "instability breeds zealots" (John Ibbitson in the Toronto *Globe And Mail*), but that "fanaticism breeds hatred" (Mauve MacCormack of New South Wales) and "hatred breeds extremism" (Mircea Geoana, Romanian Foreign Minister).

Above all, let's not forget that "desperation breeds resentment" (Howard Zinn in *The Los Angeles Times*) and "resentment breeds terrorism" (Eugene G Wollaston of Naperville, Illinois) but sometimes "desperation breeds terrorism" (a poster in Lower Manhattan) as surely as "despair breeds terrorism" (Ian Lawson in the San Diego *Union-Tribune*), though occasionally "despair breeds pestilence" (James Robertson of Ashland, Oregon).

Moreover, "injustice breeds hopelessness" (Stephen Bachhuber of Portland, Oregon) and "hopelessness breeds fanaticism" (Mark McCulloch of Forest Hills, Pennsylvania) and "injustice breeds rage" (the National Council of Churches).

Also, "ignorance breeds hate" (Wasima Alikhan of the Islamic Academy of Las Vegas), just as "hostility breeds violence" (Alexa McDonough, leader of Canada's New Democratic Party), and "suffering breeds violence" (David Pricco of San Francisco) and "war breeds hate and hate breeds terrorism" (Julia Watts of Berkeley,

California) and "intolerance breeds hate, hate breeds violence and violence breeds death, destruction and heartache" (David Coleman of the University of Oklahoma).

"Injustice breeds injustice" (Dr L B Quesnel of Manchester) and "suffering breeds suffering" (Gabor Mate, author of *Scattered Minds: A New Look At The Origins And Healing Of Attention Deficit Disorder*) and "instability breeds instability" (Congressman Alcee Hastings) and "hate breeds hate" (a sign at the University of Maryland) and "hatred breeds hatred" (the Reverend Charles A Summers of the First Presbyterian Church of Richmond, Virginia) and "anger breeds anger. Hostility breeds hostility. And attacks are going to breed other attacks" (Dania Dandashly of the Governor Bent Elementary School in Albuquerque, New Mexico), all of which only further confirms that - all together now - "violence breeds violence". So say Bishop Thomas Gumbleton of Detroit, and Kathleen McQuillen of the American Friends Service Committee, and Chris Struble, President of Humanists of Idaho, and Riane Eisler, international activist for peace, human rights and the environment, macro-historian, systems and cultural-transformation theorist and President of the Center for Partnership Studies.

Breeders, breeders everywhere. A large swathe of the left has settled into an endless dopey roundelay, a vast Schnitzlerian carousel where every abstract noun is carrying on like Anthony Quinn on Viagra. Instability breeds resentment, resentment breeds inertia, inertia breeds generalities, generalities breed clichés, clichés breed lame metaphors, until we reach the pitiful state of the peacenik opinion columns where, to modify the old Eyewitness News formula, if it breeds it leads. If I were to say "Mr Scroggins breeds racing pigeons", it would be reasonable to assume that I'd been round to the Scroggins house or at least made a phone call. But the "injustice breeds anger" routine requires no such mooring to humdrum reality, though it's generally offered as a uniquely shrewd insight, reflecting a vastly superior understanding of the complexities of the situation than we nuke-crazy warmongers have. "What you have to look at is the underlying reasons," a Dartmouth College student said to me the other day. "Poverty breeds resentment and resentment breeds anger."

"Really?" I said. "And what's the capital of Saudi Arabia?"

It's certainly possible to mount a trenchant demolition of US policy toward Israel, Kuwait, Iraq, Iran, Afghanistan and Pakistan, but that would require specifics, facts, a curiosity about the subject, and this breed of rhetoric is designed to save you the trouble. It's certainly not worth rebutting: if poverty and despair breed terrorism, then how come Aids-infested sub-Saharan Africa isn't a hotbed of terrorism? This line of attack is implicitly racist, or more accurately culturalist: the non-western world is apparently just one big petri dish full of mutating globules, eternally passive, acted upon but never acting. As Salman Rushdie wrote of September 11th, "To excuse such an atrocity by blaming US government policies is to deny the basic idea of all morality: that individuals are responsible for their actions." And the fact that only one side is denied this essential dignity of humanity tells you a lot about what the peace crowd really thinks of them.

But the breed screed is revealing of the broader disposition of its speakers. In America, the right tend to be federalists, the left centralists. The right are happy to leave education to local school boards, the left want big Federal government programmes. The right say hire a new local police chief and let him fix the crime problem, the left demand Federal "hate crimes" legislation. The right favour individual liberties, the left are more concerned with group rights. In a nutshell, the right are particular, the left love generalities (if you'll forgive a generalisation).

And so faced with the enormity of September 11th the pacifist left has done what it always does – smother the issues in generalities and abstractions – though never on such an epic scale. On that sunny Tuesday morning, some 7,000 people died – real, living men and women and children with families and street addresses and telephone numbers. But the language of the pacifists – for all its ostensible compassion – dehumanises these individuals. They're no longer flight attendants and firemen and waitresses and bond dealers, but only an abstract blur in some global theorising – if not mere "collateral damage" (the phrase they loved to mock the militarists for), certainly collateral. Of course, real live folks die in the Middle East, too, and their stories are worth telling. But in between the bonehead refrains of this breeding that and that breeding the other you'll search in vain for a name or a face, a city or sometimes even a country. Just the confident assertion that one abstract noun breeds another.

The totalitarian grotesqueness of the "peace movement" was nicely caught in the photos of last weekend's demonstrations in Washington. The usual anti-globalisation crowd had pencilled in the end of

September for their protest against the IMF and World Bank. The IMF and World Bank decided to postpone their meeting, but the glob mob figured there was no reason to call off the demo. So instead they got their rewrite guys in and switched all the placards from anti-capitalist slogans to anti-war slogans. This prompted a counter-protest by locals who held up signs reading "SHAME FOR DISTURBING A CITY IN MOURNING".

Quite. These people are mourning family, neighbours, acquaintances. If you're going to intrude on that, you could at least come up with something more pertinent than boilerplate sloganeering. It's true that with so many corpses – I use the term loosely as most of the victims were atomised – it's hard to focus on the individuals, the faces in the crowd. But, as Anna Quindlen wrote in *Newsweek*, our common humanity requires us "to see ourselves in them all: the executives, the waiters, the lawyers, the police officers, the father, the mother, the two-year-old girl off on an adventure, sitting safe between them, taking wing." At one brokerage firm alone – Cantor Fitzgerald – there are 1,500 children who've lost one of their parents. Picture a four-year old girl on an otherwise perfectly normal day wondering why mommy's crying and why daddy isn't there to tuck her in bed, and the next day he's still not there, and the next, and then mommy tells you he won't be coming home any more and that he's gone to heaven which is nice for him, but you wish he would come back to read you one more story. And you get older and go to school and daddy fades into a blur, just a couple of indistinct memories of a face leaning over your pillow and you feel him only as an absence, a part of your childhood stolen from you. Multiply that by 1,500 for Cantor Fitzgerald and then throw in all the other orphans. From the unending roll-call of the dead, I caught the name of Carol Flyzik, a lesbian nurse who'd got up early and headed for Logan Airport in Boston from Plaistow, a town in southern New Hampshire I drive through from time to time. She lived with her partner and their children and, although I'm a notorious homophobe and no respecter of "alternative families", I can't see what on earth those kids did to deserve having a great bleeding wound slashed into their lives.

Why do some people look at a smoking ruin and see the lives lost – the secretary standing by the photocopier – and others see only confirmation of their thesis on Kyoto? This isn't being sentimental. Any real insight into the "root causes" has to begin with an acknowledgment of the human toll, if only because that speaks more eloquently than anything else to the vast cultural gulf between the victims and perpetrators. To deny them their humanity, to reduce them to an impersonal abstraction is Stalinist. Bill Clinton at least claimed to "feel your pain". The creepy, inhuman formulations of the peace movement can't even go through the motions.

Few of us would have bet on the professors, preachers and the rest of the educated, articulate left performing in quite such a feeble, slapdash fashion. But in bringing war to the East Coast for the first time in two centuries the terrorists have also brought the fellow travellers home. It was easy to slough off the dead in the gulags, far away and out of sight. But could they do the same if the dead were right here on this continent, and not in some obscure cornpone hicksville but in the heart of our biggest cities?

Yes, they could, and so easily. At one level, it's simply bad taste – a lack of breeding, so to speak. But the interesting thing, to those of us used to being reviled as right-wing haters, is how sterile the vocabulary of those who profess to "love" and "care" is. In some weird Orwellian boomerang, the degradation of language required to advance the left's agenda has rendered its proponents utterly desiccated. The President gets teary in the Oval Office, the Queen chokes up at St Paul's, David Letterman and Dan Rather sob on CBS, New Yorkers weep openly for their slain fireman, but the dead-eyed zombies of the peace movement who claim to love everyone parade through the streets unmoved, a breed apart.

ROOT CAUSE

October 6th 2001
The Daily Telegraph

SAY WHAT YOU like about those Talebanophiles in the leftie press but at least they've chosen one of the two available sides. For others,

September 11th appears to be little more than a high-octane Rorschach test. The dust settles on the spectacular heap of rubble and, lo and behold, your favourite bugbear comes crawling out from it unscathed.

"The blind side is always the blind side. By focusing on one source of devastation, we build more blind sides. As long as we believe that our biggest threat is terrorism, we will never be truly prepared," Carl Russell of Bethel, Vermont wrote to my local paper, *The Valley News*. "Humans are behaving like all living organisms whose habitat becomes depleted of necessary resources. Global warming, pollution, soil depletion, plant and animal extinction, etc are all signs of environmental degradation, too complex for most of us to agree on, let alone find solutions to. Our subconscious reflex to this lack of control is anxiety. Anger, intolerance and violence, however inappropriate, are common expressions of anxiety."

Osama may have thought he was ordering his boys into action because he hates America, but subconsciously he was merely acting out, however inappropriately, his anxieties about plant extinction.

"We are going through a maturing process for the human species, and for the Earth," Mr Russell concluded. "Human lives have been lost and devastated, but our connections go deeper than that. Think of our Earth."

So September 11th was about soil depletion? Talk about a root cause!

But, whoa, not so fast. "The recent attacks do not mark the start of a fearful life for many Americans. For many of us, living in a perpetual state of fear began long before we ever heard of Osama bin Laden or witnessed the obliteration of the World Trade Center. The fear we live with is the fear of sexual violence," wrote Sara Machi in the University of Wisconsin's *Badger Herald*. "Here at UW-Madison, 58 students reported being sexually assaulted during the year 2000. Unlike the surviving victims of the World Trade Center or Pentagon attacks, many of these survivors cannot share their pain with others. They must live in silence, unable to speak about the trauma they endured. Whereas the terrorists can be ferreted out of their caves and hiding places by the force of the US military, the perpetrators of sexual assault cannot be stopped or eliminated so easily. The offenders live among us as our friends and our relatives… Unlike our country's proposed war against terrorism, this war against fear cannot be fought with bombs or guns; it must be fought in more indirect ways: through education and empowerment."

So September 11th isn't about soil depletion at all, but merely a timely reminder of the need for increased funding for the Rape Crisis Center?

Not at all! It's really about Bill Clinton, just like everything else. The anguish of the Narcissist-in-Chief was reported in *The New York Times* by the eternally understanding Richard Berke. "Former President Bill Clinton," he wrote, "is described by friends as a frustrated spectator, unable to guide the nation through a crisis that is far bigger than anything he confronted in his eight-year tenure... A close friend of Mr Clinton put it this way: 'He has said there has to be a defining moment in a presidency that really makes a great presidency. He didn't have one.'" It's so unfair: why did 7,000 people have to die on Bush's watch? That birdbrain gets all the luck.

Good old Bill. Whatever the story – Paula Jones or thousands of dead civilians – he always gets the victim role. This time round, though, the missus is giving him a close run. *The New Yorker* asked Senator Rodham Clinton how she thought Americans would react to being "on the receiving end of a murderous anger".

This is how she replied: "Oh, I am well aware that it is out there. One of the most difficult experiences that I personally had in the White House was during the health-care debate, being the object of extraordinary rage." She recalled a speech in Seattle. "Radio talk-show hosts had urged their listeners to come out and yell and scream and carry on and prevent people from hearing me speak. There were threats that were coming in, and certain people didn't want me to speak, and they started taking weapons off people, and arresting people. I've had firsthand looks at this unreasoning anger and hatred that is focused on an individual you don't know, a cause that you despise."

You think these suicide bombers are a tough crowd? Wait'll you meet conservative radio listeners. You'll wish you were playing a rape crisis centre in a soil-depleted neighbourhood.

~

ON THE TOWN

November 2001
The New Criterion

A DECADE AGO, Louis Benjamin, then the head of Stoll Moss, London's dominant theatre owners, showed me the graphs for West End ticket sales and pointed out the clutched straws with which each dip in receipts was rationalized: "Libyan crisis", "Royal wedding", "Weather v. bad", "Weather v. good".

"We've got an awful lot of excuses," he said. "But it's all rubbish. It's like the old excuse when takings were down at the Finsbury Empire [a raucous music hall]: 'Polo at Hurlingham'. I took £300,000 at the Palladium last week. D'you think I care what the bloody weather was like?"

This was 1991, Gulf War time, when Saddam Hussein, despite being preoccupied with brutalizing Kuwait and fending off the Great Satan, had apparently found time to close two West End musicals, *Children Of Eden* and *Matador*. I'm all for blaming Saddam for as much as possible, but, in fairness to the old mass murderer, most of *Children Of Eden*'s and *Matador*'s wounds were self-inflicted. On balance, Saddam's invasion of Kuwait was probably marginally good for business, if only because the potential theatregoing population was significantly increased by the vast number of al-Sabah princes who fled to London for the duration.

But ten years on and Osama bin Laden seems to be doing a pretty thorough job on the Grim White Way (as it's now called). By some estimates, 75% of New York theatre business is from tourists, and tourists are in short supply right now. In the suicide bombers of al-Qaeda, even Andrew Lloyd Webber may have met his match: you can get two on the aisle for *Phantom* any night you want now. Five other shows closed immediately, most of the rest took big pay cuts, and the Roundabout Theatre Company cancelled its opening next month of Stephen Sondheim and John Weidman's 1991 collaboration *Assassins*. This is a "revue" about the various men and women who've tried to kill American Presidents, from Lincoln to Reagan. Sondheim and Weidman are nothing if not protective of their cult status, and ten years ago took the precaution of opening it during the Gulf War. You can sense the theatre's reluctance to give up on it this time round. "An experience like this makes me want to produce it more than ever," said Todd Haimes, Artistic Director of the Roundabout. And you can see why: the revue's evocation of President McKinley's assassination exactly a century ago certainly has topical resonances.

But Sondheim and Weidman have nothing to say about their Presidential assassins other than that they're not "misfits" but all too typical Americans claiming their right to pursue their own somewhat darker version of happiness: to that end, the authors take all the most "innocent" musical forms – the beloved 19th century American songbook of cakewalks and Stephen Foster ballads – and gleefully transform them into a soundtrack for psychopaths. To kill a President, says the show, is the quintessential American dream. This would have been just another of the theatre's faux provocations before September 11th, and no doubt soon enough its time will come again.

Right now, though, it provides an insight into why the theatre provides so few insights. Many of the most idiotic reflex reactions to September 11th came from show people, from John Lahr, Harold Pinter, Dario Fo, as predictably perverse, paranoid and troglodyte as ever. All the really stupid things are said by all the really clever people: you'll search long and hard to find a grease-monkey who's offered up anything as dumb as some of the apparently widely-held beliefs of Ivy League professors. On stage, in the weeks after September 11th, a similar rough'n'ready rule held: It was possible to return to *The Music Man*, a revival whose hokiness I'd originally found as slick and insincere as the principal character, and find that somehow the show's fundamental harmlessness had combined with the audience's goodwill to produce a weirdly moving testament to the transcendent optimism of America. On the other hand, the following night I went to the Pearl Theatre Company's revival of the 1962 play *Exit The King*, Ionesco's celebrated meditation on the inevitability of death, the loneliness of life, and the usefulness of death as a prism through which to understand life. The protagonist is, as usual, Ionesco's alter-ego Berenger, better known from the earlier work *Rhinoceros* but here elevated to King Berenger I, an aged buffoon of a monarch presiding over a crumbling realm. At the opening of the play, his first wife Queen Marguerite tells him, "You're going to die at the end of the show."

The King is reluctant to "deal with" this precise death sentence. He insists his remorseless paralysis is lumbago, he fudges, obfuscates, plays for time, weeps, rages, and demands to know, "Why was I born if it wasn't forever?"

And answer comes there none, which is the point. Ionesco is one of the colossi of the Theatre of the Absurd, whose basic thesis is that man lives in isolation, an isolation so profound that he cannot even acknowledge it because it renders meaningful communication impossible, and thus makes meaningless life itself. Futility is all. Pointlessness is the point. That the depressive dramatist sincerely believed this and could not have foreseen the bizarre context in which this first New York revival would be played doesn't compensate for the fact that the forced comic nihilism just seems terribly silly. Not offensive, just wrong. It's like *King Lear* without the insight into human nature and played as a vaudeville sketch. Joseph Hardy's production manages to make a dated fraudulent irrelevance even more tiresome by ignoring the Absurdism and playing it with a leaden earnestness. The company seems to have been selected principally for their tin ear for comedy, and Hardy's careless decision to render the Royal court in contemporary fashion – the servant girl wears jeans, the throne is an office chair – only adds to the gloom: remote, exotic figures talking twaddle about life and death is one thing, but folks who look like New York office workers doing so is quite another. As the evening grinds on, the lack of laughs becomes embarrassing, beaching the actors and exposing the play as morbid indulgence by someone whose obsession with his own anxieties was at the price of any sense of anybody else's.

It may be that almost all writers write because of a fear of mortality, but they don't all write *about* the fear of mortality. The fleetingness of life is one of those things most of us adjust to. Recalling walking with his mother among the winter crowds at Place de Vaugirard, Ionesco said, "Whenever the picture of this street lives again in my memory, and when I consider that today almost all of these people are dead, everything strikes me as indeed shadow and evanescence. I am seized with dizziness, with anguish. There, in effect, goes the world: a desert of dying shadows." But, when just a short walk from this theatre in St Mark's Place, you're confronted by a real desert of shadows, shadows of thousands of evaporated lives, Ionesco's weary nihilism seems absurd rather than Absurd, a revelation of his disconnection from humanity rather than his understanding of it.

I've written before about the role of the audience – the way, say, Caryl Churchill's West End hit *Serious Money* was a savage indictment of Eighties greed when played before season-ticket lefties at the Royal Court but a raucous night out when played before City bond dealers. That's what's happened across town since September 11th: the plays are the same, but the audience isn't. As a rule, the more amiably escapist the fare the more resilient it is. But even evenings with the lightest touch go oddly awry: *Rude Entertainment* (at the Greenwich House Theatre) is a gay cornucopia – a horn of plenty - by Paul Rudnick, a prolific author who occasionally hits the big time, as he did a couple of years back with the Kevin Kline film *In And Out*. Mr Rudnick is a youngish fellow but as a "gay writer" somewhat old school, happier with Barbra Streisand gags than with the dreary preoccupations of the politicized gay left. His *Rude Entertainment* is a trio of playlets whisked through in a brisk 90 minutes that's best seen as a response to recent shifts in the gay sensibility.

The first offering, *Mr Charles, Currently Of Palm Beach*, is a cheerful throwback to the days when homosexuality was one of those things that was, in Lorenz Hart's words, "Too Good For The Average Man". Mr Charles, an exquisitely plumed and gilded gay stereotype of a certain age, resplendent from his aubergine espadrilles to his blonde rug, sits on a throne far more impressive than anything in King Berenger's court. He is the host of a cable show called "Too Gay", which can be seen on Channel 47 every other Thursday at 4am, between "Adult Interludes" and "Stretching With Sylvia". Mr Charles has what he describes as "nelly breaks", bursts of flaming queenery when he starts babbling in the hysterical gay dialect he calls Shebonics. He is assisted by his tank-topped "ward" Shane ("*Danke*, Shane"). But what he mainly does on his show is read viewers' letters:

"What causes homosexuality?"

"I do."

It's undemanding fare, extravagantly shallow and intentionally constrained by its TV format but rendered very enjoyable by Peter Bartlett's absolutely fagulous turn as Mr Charles. At its best, it's an elegy for a disappearing world. Aware that he is a gay dinosaur, a tyrannosaurus regina, he lets rip in a late "nelly break" about contemporary gayness and its need to prove that "we can hold jobs, go to church, raise children, just like everyone else." What's the point of that? "Being gay," he sighs amid a blizzard of farewell kisses, "there's a romance!"

Very Special Needs brings us up to the minute with Timmy, a menswear designer, and his partner Trent desperate to have a child. "It's all I've been dreaming about!" says Timmy. "I mean, all our friends, almost every gay couple, they all have babies!" Rudnick seems to sense the ice is a little thinner here, and the jokes get more tangential, like a variety-show sketch trying to avoid confronting its subject.

And then comes Rudnick's finale: *On The Fence*. Yes, Matthew Shepard, again. Unlike previous, documentary reconstructions of the events leading to his murder in Wyoming, Matthew (Neal Huff) is this time caught in a limbo between life and death, where his only companions are a gay saint, Eleanor Roosevelt (Harriet Harris), and a gay devil, Paul Lynde (Bartlett), the flamboyant favorite of "Hollywood Squares" restored to life clad in a caftan and armed with a cocktail. Rudnick, hitherto happy to bounce from queeny quip to queeny quip, is suddenly in the mood for a thoughtful debate on gay iconography. But who, honestly, needs such a debate? The reason why there are so many plays and TV movies about Matthew Shepard is because what happened to him three years ago is so rare: he's a poster-child for an epidemic that doesn't exist. In a country of a quarter-billion people, one vile gay-bashing is enough to prompt a summer-long torrent of media anguish about the "climate of hate", just as in the wake of 9/11 a few dozen intemperate anti-Muslim incidents threatened to do the same. But thousands and thousands of people died on September 11th and none of them will ever be as famous as "Matthew". The endless pages of dead firemen alone are so numerous that it's all but impossible to stop and focus on the human interest. To offer yet another fetishistic wallow in Matthew Shepard in the shadow of a huge pile of anonymous corpses suggests a culture whose deranged self-absorption in the peripheral is irredeemable.

Rudnick, I suspect, knows this. The climax of *On The Fence* is a *coup de théâtre* so lurid and unjustified that most theatregoers on the night I went charitably assumed it had been written before the big event. But it seems to me more likely that it's a hasty, misguided but intentional response to September 11th.

What happens is that Matthew, Paul and Eleanor turn their guns on the audience and shoot us at random.

The moral of the story? "Maybe the world is divided into two groups," says Paul Lynde. "The people who can kill other people. And the people who only wish they could." Maybe. But I think it's more likely the world is divided into the people who've entirely forgotten Paul Lynde, if they were ever aware of him, and the people who are reluctant to accept pat little homilies on the world's woes from a sour showbiz loser.

But Lynde isn't done yet. "Perhaps," he says, "the most that anyone can hope for is to want to be good."

The antidote to such a shriveled moral is Ovid's *Metamorphoses*, adapted and directed by Mary Zimmerman as a shimmering storybook production at the Second Stage. The evening is a literal oasis from the outside world, its various tales played out on a simple set centered on a shallow 27-foot pool of water. There are times when Miss Zimmerman teeters on a bad case of the cutes and when her actors get as sappy as the script, but these are momentary lapses. The production is suffused in loss conjured in the simplest of images - like a picture book you remember from childhood but didn't fully understand at the time.

So, for example, we meet Alcyon, who stands at water's edge waiting for the ship of her long-dead husband Erysichthon to reappear on the horizon, as she waited till it disappeared into the blue on the day he set sail. One day she finds his body in the ocean, and she embraces him, and, as she does so, they rise from the water, reborn as seabirds. It is a memorable stage picture, but also more than that: a vision of love transcending death that seems truer than anything in Ionesco.

Perhaps the signature image of the production is Orpheus, who in variation after variation of the famous myth is forced to relive again and again his famous, fatal error, like a man trapped in memory, playing it over and over like a video, though the ending will always be the same — as he looks back at his beloved and she vanishes forever into the underworld. No one needs to labor any parallels: in Alcyon and Orpheus and the story of Baucis and Philemon, who pray only that they will not die apart, our own sorrows find eloquent expression. It's not that the characters articulate grief, so much as capture it — in a glance, a sigh, the sense of sudden eternal wonder. The metamorphosis is in our ability to find the consolations in pain. The final tale concludes in a candlelight vigil, whispers in the darkness in the face of death. Many of those around me had tears streaming down their faces. *Metamorphoses* speaks from the ancient world to ours even as *On The Fence* and *Exit The King* seem trapped in an age now dead and gone.

Venturing back to the theatre a few days after September 11th, I decided to treat myself to some happy musical revivals and found myself dreading only the moment at the curtain when the designated spokesperson would step forward from the company and offer a few words. I dreaded not so much moral equivalence or Pinteresque bloviating but the life-sapping pieties of some dimestore Oprah. Yet I underestimated Broadway's luvvies. In most cases they contented themselves with a few words in memory of the dead, before the orchestra struck up "God Bless America" - written as a theatre song but currently more popular than the national anthem:

> *God Bless America*
> *Land that I love,*

wrote Irving Berlin, untroubled by the self-loathing that afflicts so many theatrical luminaries. "God Bless America" has everything – uncomplicated patriotism, something about the landscape, a call for divine protection, an implied martial beat and the confidence to set the climactic high note of the tune to the word "God". As a national song, it's ingeniously, unobtrusively comprehensive – a testament to the American theatre's ability, every once in a while, to rise gloriously to the occasion.

~

SO SEPTEMBER 10th

October 11th 2001
The National Post

ON SEPTEMBER 11th, just an hour after those planes slammed into the World Trade Center, Jo Moore, a senior adviser to

Britain's Secretary of State for Transport, Local Government and the Regions, turned away from the TV and composed an e-mail for departmental circulation:

It's now a very good day to get out anything we want to bury.

Ah, politics. How often does fate provide such excellent all-purpose cover for embarrassing statistics and minor policy reversals? Ms Moore is a spin doctor, and spin doctors are paid to be cynical, so in a sense Ms Moore was only demonstrating a supreme mastery of her black art. No doubt across the chancelleries of the west less hardened spinners were wiping away tears and mumbling "Oh, my God, my ex-boyfriend's sister works in Lower Manhattan" and letting their spinning go to hell, but at the Department of Transport et al in Whitehall Ms Moore's steely resolve held firm.

It's become a commonplace to talk of war as dehumanizing – see Senator Bob Kerrey's defence of his atrocities in Vietnam – or of CIA covert operations as "too dirty" a job to ask civilized human beings to do. But Jo Moore's memo suggests contemporary politics may be even more dehumanizing and its routine operations so depraved that it's no wonder our citizens recoil from "public service" and despise those that prosper therein. When the memo came to light this week, Ms Moore apologized, sort of. But it's one of those political apologies, whereby one is obliged to distance oneself from an unintended self-revelation. September 11th was an unspun world: within 48 hours, we'd adjusted to the new reality and were expressing ourselves accordingly, but for a few hours that Tuesday what we said and did as we saw office workers jump to their deaths offered a glimpse of who we really are and how we really think. How callous do you have to be to watch the twin towers collapse and think Ms Moore's thought, never mind put it in writing, happily append your name to it and send it to hundreds of people? No apology can ever take it back: we know her now.

Almost as revealing as the heartlessness was the careless expression of it – "anything we want to bury", even as thousands of people were literally buried before her cold eyes. This is the language of political operatives: bury it, shoot 'em down, take him out. These days, your average Chief of the Defence Staff is a meek, mild-mannered, caring general who speaks softly and explains that the purpose of the highly limited bombing is to make it safe for our planes to go in and drop TV dinners. Meanwhile, for at least a decade, the Jo Moores of this world have sounded like Patton on testosterone.

Why, even the Prime Minister of Canada has an attack dog, Warren Kinsella, whose new book is called *Kicking Ass In Canadian Politics*, the macho swagger of the first half of the title somewhat undermined by the territorial qualifier. Warren proclaims himself the Dominion's all-time champ at "kicking the living shit out of the other guy". If a gung-ho colonel talked like that, he'd be court-martialed. But, in the interests of promoting socialized health care or increased education funding or free bicycling helmets for seniors, this language is not only acceptable, but to be encouraged. As the memory of real war recedes, the ersatz warriors of the political ops rooms have eagerly appropriated the martial imagery. For the gulf between past and present look no further than one testy exchange from Bob Dole's 1996 Presidential campaign. Apropos Pat Buchanan's experience as the host of "Crossfire", a CNN gabfest, Dole muttered, "I was in the real crossfire. It wasn't on television. It was over in Italy somewhere, a long time ago."

But in the world before September 11th the metaphoric crossfire of CNN was far more real than any real crossfire. The documentary of the 1992 Clinton campaign was called *The War Room*. In 1996, wherever the President went, the local Democratic warm-up act would introduce Mr Clinton by hailing his "undaunted courage" and "bravery". A candidate for the Michigan legislature in Battle Creek was even able to say with a straight face: "This President is tough. Battle-tested." Of course, this President was famously un-battle-tested. But, before September 11th, it was the very notion of "battle" that sounded creaky - the notion of men putting it all on hold to slog it out in some patch of mud five thousand miles away.

And so, flipping on the TV a month ago, Jo Moore, who works for a Minister of the Crown, instinctively calculated not Britain's interest but her party's opportunity. She was, in that sense, an exceptionally advanced practitioner of politics pre-9/11: what counted was not governing but campaigning - the "permanent campaign", as the Clintonites put it. That's not what matters now: we have a real war room, not a political one; real crossfire, not the talk-show kind.

It's no coincidence that George W Bush found his Presidential voice only when September 11th rendered obsolete permanent campaigning, politicking and spinning, all of which he's lousy at. For his part, our own dear leader has been much criticized in these pages by "the mullahs of the media right", as Parker Barss Donham amusingly calls us in *The Daily News* of Halifax. Mr Donham presents the familiar defence of the Prime Minister: "To judge from the public opinion polls, it was, as usual, Chrétien who correctly read the mood of the Canadian public," he writes. "Approval of the Prime Minister's cautious handling of the terrorist crisis runs in the high 60s."

If the gig is to "read the mood of the public" and then voice it, that's fine – though why any self-respecting fellow would want such a diminished job is another matter. I don't believe Churchill took a poll after Dunkirk or that, on the morning of December 8th 1941, FDR said, "Maybe we should run this past the focus groups." This is not the time for a leader who follows. You can focus group every soccer mom on the continent and the result will be of strictly limited value. It's M Chrétien who gets the classified foreign intelligence, not Mrs McGillicuddy of Etobicoke. He knows the CSIS evaluation of current security threats, not you. He knows how well our emergency services could cope with a bioterror assault, you can only guess. He knows how secure our borders are, you have mere suspicions. He knows what needs to be done, you don't. And his job is to get you to follow him, not the other way round. That's why he's Prime Minister and you're an accountant, short-order cook, disc-jockey, housewife, deranged right-wing columnist, whatever.

The great game changed after the Cold War but it never went away. The only difference was that we thought it had. Books like *Kicking Ass*, whatever its merits might have been in early September, now seem like artefacts of a lost age – the post-modern era of politics, when the backroom boys came out front and, as in the Pompidou Centre, the plumbing was all on the outside. Operatives discussed their political masters as empty shells, creatures of polls, dependent on spinmeisters. It won't wash now: it's not about campaigning now, but about governing, in the most basic sense - about protecting our people, securing our borders, eliminating our enemies. What got buried on September 11th was the shrivelled pygmy vision of cynics like Jo Moore.

IMAGINE

October 15th 2001
National Review

ON SEPTEMBER 11th, a colleague of mine rang Henry Kissinger to ask if he'd write something for the op-ed page of Sunday's paper. On the Thursday, he called him back just to check the piece was still on. "Ah," the good Doctor growled dryly, "so this story has not been superseded?"

Dr Kissinger makes a good point, though not just about the news media. The urge to (in the dread Clintonian phrase) "move on" is the natural condition of our culture. If anything, the news operations tend to be a little behind the curve. When so many people watching TV that morning said it was "like a movie" – like *Independence Day* or *Armageddon* – I began to get nervous. Not because it wasn't like *Independence Day*, but because the defining characteristic of those movies is not the "money shot" of the atomized White House or any of the other special effects but the fact that they're huge, boffo, smash, record-breaking, mega-blockbusters for three weeks and then they're utterly forgotten. Movie's over. What's next?

Is something similar happening here? On Saturday September 22nd, the Miss America pageant went ahead as scheduled. If ever there was an event ripe for a bit of star-spangled symbolism, Old Glory wrapped around the young flower of American maidenhood, this was it. Tony Danza began by justifying the decision: "We don't carry on to make less of what happened, we carry on to make more," he said. One of the producers had explained beforehand that they'd had to make a lot of changes – as a result, it would be "more of a USO show".

I wish. The desire to "move on" was almost palpable. When Danza asked Miss New York what she liked about Manhattan, she replied cheerily, "More than any other city I've ever visited, it's just so full of life!" I wouldn't have minded if this had been delivered as an infelicitous cry of defiance, but instead its blank-eyed perky ingenuousness all but advertised the fact that Miss New York had entirely forgotten the slaughter of ten days earlier. Instead of awkward, clunky, heartfelt patriotism, the whole event was suffused in an awkward, clunky, desperate embarrassment at even having to acknowledge what had happened.

What would a 2001 USO show look like? There was a report that Bob Hope is anxious to stage a special benefit. Bob is 98, just back from the hospital and recuperating from pneumonia, but he may be the only guy in Hollywood who's not uncomfortable with uncomplicated flag-waving. 60 years ago, the radio shows were full of lame gags about the Yanks putting ants in the Emperor's Japants. On the comic-book covers, Batman and Superman forgot about the Joker and the Penguin and took on Nazi spies. Can anyone imagine popular culture conscripting itself to battle the enemy in similar fashion today? Indeed, there's a reluctance to admit that there's any "enemy" at all. It was not a good sign when New York City decided to entrust its special prayer service at Yankee Stadium to Oprah, and it would have been too much to expect Oprah to forgo Oprafying: "May we leave this place," she concluded, "determined to now use every moment that we yet live to turn up the volume in our own lives, to create deeper meaning, to know what really matters. What really matters is who you love and how you love."

Not right now, Oprah. What really matters is who we get to Afghanistan and what they do once they're there. Oprah's line isn't pacifist. Pacifism in the honorable sense is Mahatma Gandhi, a determined non-violence that bent a mighty empire to his will. Pacifism even in the corrupted American sense is at least self-interested – the middle-class college boys of the Sixties who didn't want their lives inconvenienced by anything so quaintly déclassé as service to one's country: when the draft ended, so almost instantly did "the peace movement". But, whether you agree or disagree with Gandhi or the Ivy League poseurs, their pacifism had a point: they wanted something.

What's happening now is not pacifism but passivism – a terrible inertia filled with feel-good platitudes that absolve us from action, or even feeling. This stuff is far craftier than old-style pacifism or open anti-Americanism, and after a decade of self-indulgence it reaches deep into the national psyche. It was thus inevitable that the all-network, all-star telethon should have featured John Lennon's dopey anthem for fluffy nihilists:

> *Imagine there's no heaven*
> *It's easy if you try*

No hell below us
Above us only sky
Imagine all the people
Living for today...

You may say he's a dreamer, but he's not. A couple of years ago, it emerged that Lennon was a very generous contributor not just to organizations that support and fund the IRA, but to the IRA itself. He could imagine there's no countries and nothing to kill or die for, but until that blessed day he was quite happy to support an organization that blows up shopping centers and railway stations. It's heartening to know that, though he grew rich peddling illusory pap to the masses, he didn't fall for it himself.

Robert Hilburn in *The Los Angeles Times* summed it up better than he knew:

> *The rock'n'roll descendants of blues and folk artists, who would have been excluded from earlier prime-time showcases as voices of rebellion, have become the ones the country turns to as voices of unity.*
>
> *The defining moment during a national World War II radio benefit: Bing Crosby singing Irving Berlin. There was still a place for Berlin on Friday, as Céline Dion sang 'God Bless America.' But the telethon's central moments involved rock artists, including Bruce Springsteen, U2 and Neil Young, who drew upon the music and/or spirit of Bob Dylan and John Lennon.*

If John Lennon and U2 are now the "voices of unity", it's worth asking: unity for what? "God Bless America" is a song to go to war to. Is "Imagine"? We need something a little more robust than the soothing drone of Lennon and Oprah. We need people willing to speak truth to evil. The Oprahvian line is not even old-school Pierre Trudeaupian moral equivalence, but something worse: moral nullity, a reflexive cringe from the very idea of position-taking.

Osama bin Laden, being a member of an NGO (non-governmental organization), can easily "imagine there's no countries": he's been doing it for some time. By contrast, the distinguishing characteristic of people who stand around holding candles and singing John Lennon seems to be a colossal failure of imagination. You can't begin "healing" until the guys have stopped firing. And in this case they haven't. This isn't *Independence Day*. It's not a movie. It's an old-fashioned radio serial, with cliffhanger endings week after week after week. If we can't get outraged – not sad, not weepy, not candle-in-the-windy but *outraged* – over thousands of people killed for no other reason than that they went to work then we're really in trouble. If cultural passivity – love the world, be non-judgmental, everybody does it – co-opts even this awesome event, then the sleeping giant isn't sleeping so much as comatose.

The people responsible for September 11th already have well advanced plans for the next atrocity – probably nothing to do with planes; maybe a gas line, maybe just a shopping mall in some town you've never heard of. A terrorist is an opportunist warrior. If he can kill the President, he will. But, if he can't, he'll kill you.

Imagine that.

LATE OCTOBER

War

October 13th 2001
The Daily Telegraph

IT'S A SHAME the White House has asked the networks to hold off on airing Osama bin Laden's live-from-the-cave specials. They were worried he was broadcasting coded messages to his supporters, but, on the other hand, the subliminal messages he was broadcasting to the rest of us were oddly reassuring. Many of my neighbours were stunned by their initial glimpse of the new bogeyman, the first 11th century guy to get his own CNN gig: *This* is who we're at war with? He *really* lives in a cave?

Evidently, life in the batty cave is taking its toll. No Saddamite gimlet eye transfixing the faithful. Osama looked like hell. Maybe there's some stump of a stalagmite under his matting wrecking his sleep. Or maybe being cooped up with four wives in one small cave is getting to him. Or maybe, when he's in the mood late at night, he can never figure out which wife is under which burqa.

Since his last jihad-inciting special, the cave man seemed to have aged dramatically. That floor-length beard could have used a couple of vats of Grecian 2000. Ah, you say, he'd have no truck with such a filthy infidel product. But take away all the infidel products and you'd be left with a loser in yak-wool boxers standing in a cave shouting to himself. Osama had an infidel watch (Timex Ironman Triathlon), infidel fatigues (army-surplus US battle dress), infidel hand-mike, infidel camera.

This is presumably an example of what Professor Edward Said, the distinguished New York-based America-disparager, calls the "interconnectedness" of the west and Islam. The Prof deplores the tendency, in the wake of September 11th, to separate cultures into what he called "sealed-off entities", when in reality western civilisation and the Muslim world are so "intertwined" that it's impossible to "draw the line" between them.

This pitch isn't getting a lot of respect. "The line seems pretty clear," said Rich Lowry, editor of *National Review*. "Developing mass commercial aviation and soaring skyscrapers was the west's idea; slashing the throats of stewardesses and flying the planes into the skyscrapers was radical Islam's idea."

Let me be a little more charitable to Professor Said and say that, as a Canadian, I'm all too familiar with the desperate need of certain cultures to overcompensate, however pathetic and tortuous it might seem. Osama, for his part, seems a lot more relaxed about this "interconnectedness". This week, at an anti-American demo in Dhaka, the usual excitable types jumped up and down waving giant placards bearing a montage of bin Laden portraits. When photos of the crowd were published in the US, eagle-eyed observers noted that appearing side by side with Osama on the posters was Bert, a tufty-haired orange Muppet from "Sesame Street" who's usually paired not with Osama but with his fellow felt-head, Ernie.

How did Bert get on a gazillion pro-Osama posters? It seems the great terrorist's supporters carelessly downloaded images of their hero from the Internet and failed to notice that one was from a spoof "Bert Is Evil" site that puts up doctored images of the irascible Muppet with Adolf Hitler, OJ Simpson, etc. Just as there's something inherently ridiculous about a man standing in a cave and shaking his fist at the civilised world, so it's hard to take seriously a bunch of angry guys yelling "Death to the Great Satan!" when they're waving placards showing a character from "Sesame Street".

For their part, the show is furious. "We're outraged that our characters would be used in this unfortunate and distasteful manner," said spokesperson Beatrice Chow. "The people responsible for this should be ashamed of themselves. We are exploring all legal options to stop this abuse." In other words, if the bombs don't get him, Osama bert Laden is looking at the mother of all breach-of-copyright suits. And you don't get much more "interconnected" with western culture than getting your ass sued off.

Meanwhile, it emerged that not all Osama's attempts to "intertwine" with the west have proved successful. The three people (so far) to have been contaminated by anthrax all work for *The Globe*, a supermarket tabloid which recently suggested that Osama's problems arise from the fact that he has a small penis. Apparently, these Taleban broads don't make a big deal about it, but back in the Seventies Osama bin Laden picked up some American chick at a Beirut disco and the evening didn't go well. Had Osama bin laiden that night, history might have been very different. As "root causes" go, this strikes me as more plausible than any of *The Guardian*'s poverty-breeds-resentment shtick: humiliating one-night stand breeds intense hatred of Great Satan.

So at the end of the first week since battle was joined I'm pleased to report that, in the anxious dreams of many Americans, Osama bin Laden seems somewhat shrunken. Er, not that I'm saying I think there's anything in this small-penis business – at least not until I've got the bioterror sniffer dogs in place. [Note to *Telegraph* mailroom: Keep an eye out for small packages – and no, that's not another reference to his you-know-what.]

~

THE HEAD THAT WORE THE CROWN

October 7th 2001
The Sunday Telegraph

HE'S THE COMING man, the go-to guy, the Afghan they all want to hound. Every EU apparatchik and Washington bigshot is beating a path to his door and emerging enraptured half an hour later, lovingly dropping insider lingo like *"loya jirga"*. "There is an age-old tradition in Afghanistan in which the King calls a '*loya jirga*' or 'grand assembly' of leaders from all over the country to address issues of great concern," explained Congressman Joe Pitts of Pennsylvania. "Zahir Shah is able and ready to call a *loya jirga*, help set up a transitional government, and bring peace to his country."

The *loya jirga* of the international community is already agreed that Zahir is everything you're looking for in a dynamic leader. In an interesting variation of the traditional line on local strongmen – "He may be a sonofabitch but he's *our* sonofabitch" – Washington's take on Zahir is that he may be an 87-year old shy modest retiring loner in variable health, prone to depression, who enjoys photography, but he's *our* 87-year old shy modest retiring loner in variable health, prone to, etc. The photography may be a problem when he returns from exile as there's little to photograph except rubble, and by the time he gets there many of Kabul's most scenic mounds of rubble may have been reduced to smaller bits of rubble. But Zahir is the best we can come up with. If you object that he's been in retirement for nearly 30 years, don't forget that in Kabul that's a unique distinction. If you're looking for someone with experience of running Afghanistan, he's the only available candidate who isn't a corpse. Zahir was deposed in 1973 by his cousin and brother-in-law Daoud, who was killed by his successor Taraki, who was suffocated by his successor Hafizullah Amin, who was executed by the Soviets, who installed Babrak Karmal, who died in hospital in Moscow but in a rare break with tradition managed to outlive his replacement, Najibullah, whom the Taleban wound up hanging from a traffic post.

You can understand why the King is an appealing figure among such company. Still, there's an element of wishful thinking about the constant refrain that he could be "a unifying figure" for his troubled land. Robert Hardman turned in a classic of this genre the other day in *The Daily Mail* after visiting Zahir Shah in Rome and discovering that he still has vivid memories of his trip to London in 1971 when he was treated to a private "90-minute riding display" by Princess Anne, which is more than Babrak Karmal ever got from Andrei Gromyko.

Zahir's finest hour came in the moment of his father's assassination, when he was shot during a school prize-giving in the Palace grounds and the teenage Prince, already Acting Minister of Education, leapt into the fray to come to his father's aid, alas too late. It was September 1933, and the 19-year old King was just one more new leader on the world stage, along with Herr Hitler in Berlin and President Roosevelt in Washington. George V was on the throne in England, his son had caught the eye of Mrs Simpson, Ramsay MacDonald was in Downing Street and wondering whether this loincloth chappie Gandhi needed watching. The League of Nations was the world's power broker and saw Afghanistan as a buffer state between the Soviet and British Empires. Now both are gone, Zahir receives Kofi Annan's emissary, and Afghanistan is a buffer between very different kinds of competitors. Not only is the King's political currency remarkable by Afghan standards, but by everyone else's too. If he were still in Kabul, he would today be the world's longest-serving monarch.

In 1963, he transformed himself into a constitutional monarch and introduced responsible government, a free press, women's rights, etc. He was a moderniser, and not just by the standards of the current crowd, who evidently regard the Dark Ages as decadent sissy-boy stuff. But, by the middle of Zahir's reign, Afghanistan was one of the few nations on earth receiving aid from both the US and the USSR, and the palace compound at Kabul was a strange mix of traditional pursuits, like hunting, and newer activities, like the competing cells of political theorists among his various cousins. Today, older Afghans recall Zahir nostalgically as the last good time, which admittedly isn't saying much. They also respect him for his sheer antiquity: he has lived more than double the average lifespan of an Afghan male (40 years); they feel the same awe as we would meeting a 150-year old Englishman.

So they've warmed up to him retrospectively. However, Zahir also allowed the agencies of the state to become hopelessly penetrated by Moscow's local stooges. This in turn led to the birth of an Islamic fundamentalist movement, alarmed by His Majesty's indifference to Communist subversion. So the two malign forces which have laid waste his kingdom – godless Marxism and Islamofascism – were at least partly the creation of his moderation, diffidence, gentle nature, and all the other characteristics the west now loves about him. Given the various forces the King hopes to bring under his umbrella, it's not unreasonable to wonder why things would go any differently this time round. A far more ruthless operator, King Sihanouk, found himself feebly endorsing the hijacking of Cambodia's multilateral settlement a couple of years back and going along with the Khmer Rouge. But then the monarchical "unifying figure" usually winds up providing a polite cover for whatever the ambitious politician below thinks he can get away with – that's why Mussolini saw no need to get rid of Victor Emmanuel, nor Maurice Bishop and Grenada's New Jewel Movement any need to dispense with Her Majesty The Queen. Indeed, that even our own sovereign was willing to accept a revolutionary coup leader as "her" "Prime Minister" should be a sobering lesson in the limitations of constitutional monarchy as a democratic bulwark.

In Zahir's case, scepticism that he can bring stability to Afghanistan is compounded by the noticeable indifference of his sons. Crown Prince Ahmad Shah is happy writing poetry in suburban Virginia. The next in line, Mohammed Nadir, is "a successful sitar player in Canada". I'm as fond as the next fellow of Sitar Night at Bud's Grill in Yellowknife, but when a throne is no longer competitive with playing Ravi Shankar medleys on the frozen tundra you've got problems.

The King, of course, has been here before. 1983: Zahir, "as figurehead leader of the Afghan resistance, could play a significant role in unifying its divisive guerrilla movements." (*The Christian Science Monitor*) 1988: "Zahir Shah could be a force for unity in the country in the event of the withdrawal of Soviet troops." (*The Atlantic*) 1992: UPI reported "a growing movement to return the monarchy from exile" as more and more Afghans realised that "Islamic fundamentalism runs counter to the Afghan way of life". But each time some innovative horror leapt into the breach.

The difference now is that the distinctively virulent local strains of both Communism and fundamentalism seem exhausted. Both are, by Afghan standards, exceptionally intrusive. In 1978, when the country fell into the hands of Taraki, a Communist too hardline even for Moscow, it marked the first time in Afghan history that the national government had ever really impinged on village life. The best thing about Zahir's rule was that many folks were barely aware of him, and that's more than you can say about the Taleban, as they descend on remote villages to torch women and bury alive suspected sodomites. Afghanistan has always been happiest existing somewhere between massive decentralization and semi-anarchy, something Zahir's father certainly understood when he overthrew the Tajik folk hero Bacha-I-Saqao ("son of the water carrier") in 1929. After decades of secular and religious totalitarianism run from Kabul, what the country could really use is a benign non-unifying figure.

~

THE SNAKES OF ARABY

October 20th 2001
The Spectator

BEFORE THE White House decided to lean on the networks and get him off air, Osama bin Laden popped up on the TV in my general store in another rerun of his caveman special. Off he went with his usual shtick about "the tragedy of Andalusia".

"What's he on about?" asked my friend Judy.

"It's a reference to the end of Moorish rule in Spain in 1492," I said.

"That's our fault?" she said. I started to say something about how, as Osama saw it, the roots of Islam's downfall in Andalusia lay in its accommodation with the Christian world and the move towards a pluralistic society, etc, etc, but Judy wasn't in the mood. "You know why this is a great country?" she said. "Because none of us have a clue what he's on about."

This is a common theory. There's a wonderful screed floating around the Internet called "We're more nuts than you and it should scare you shitless", which works up to a grand assurance to al-Qa'eda that, even after we've killed them, our schoolchildren still won't have a clue who they are, where they're from or what was bugging them in the first place. The clichémongers of the global media like to talk about "America's Loss Of Innocence", but that innocence is more properly understood as "ignorance is bliss" – America is where you go to get away from guys hung up on whatever it was that happened in Andalusia in 1492. Pat Buchanan, in his book *A Republic Not An Empire*, argues that the US has drifted away from its original vision by getting mixed up in all kinds of imperial adventures that are more suited to old-school European powers than the aloof yeoman republic its Founders foresaw.

On the other hand, there are those who think the events of September 11th prove that you can't buck millennia of tradition: a non-imperial superpower is a contradiction in terms and it's time for America to embrace its fate and start colouring the map red-white-and-blue. My neighbour Tom, who's painting my house at the moment and who always carries a copy of the Constitution with him, thinks this

73

is a filthy unAmerican idea. "You Commonwealth guys," he says. "You can't let go of the whole colony thing." He's right, of course: the Founders would be horrified at the idea of the White House appointing chaps in solar topees with ostrich feathers. But, simmering under the talk of immediate war aims in Afghanistan, a Republic-versus-Empire debate is already under way.

Let's start with Osama bin Loser's main beef, about the US military presence near Islam's holiest sites in Saudi Arabia: he's right; it *is* a humiliation that one of the richest regimes on earth is too incompetent, greedy and decadent to provide its own defence. But it's not America's fault that those layabout Saudi princes, faced with Saddam's troops massing on the border, could think of nothing better to do than turn white as their robes and frantically dial Washington.

In fact, insofar as the Middle East's the victim of anything other than its own failures, it's not western imperialism but western post-imperialism. Unlike Africa, Asia, Australasia and the Americas, Araby has never come under direct European colonial rule. The Ottoman Empire was famously characterised by Tsar Nicholas I as "the sick man of Europe", which would seem to concede admission to the club, but also suggests that its sickness was at least partially due to its lack of Europeanness. These effects linger long: the difference in progress between parts of the former Yugoslavia seems to owe as much to whether the territory was previously Habsburg (Slovenia) or Ottoman (Macedonia) as anything else. The Turks backed the wrong man in the First World War more by bad luck than by anything else, and one can sympathise with the more sophisticated terror-apologists in the west who argue that the Ottoman Empire should never have been broken up. Turkey, for its part, was more European in the 1920s than it ever was under the Sultans: indeed, it remains the only Muslim territory to have successfully embarked upon a redefinition of the relationship between Islam and the state. Turkey gave women the vote before Britain did – the sort of supporting evidence the west's self-loathers might find useful, if they troubled themselves with supporting evidence.

But in the Arabian peninsula the Ottoman vacuum was filled not with dependencies but with "spheres of influence", a system that continues to this day. Rather than making Arabia a Crown colony within the Empire, dispatching Lord Whatnot as Governor, issuing banknotes bearing the likeness of George V, setting up courts presided over by judges in full-bottomed wigs and introducing a professional civil service and a free press, the British instead mulled over which sheikh was likely to prove more pliable, installed him in the capital and suggested he send his sons to Eton and Sandhurst. The French did the same, and so, later, did the Americans.

This was cheaper than colonialism and less politically prickly, but it did a great disservice to the populations of those countries. The alleged mountain of evidence of Yankee culpability is, in fact, evidence only of the Great Satan's deplorable faintheartedness: yes, Washington dealt with Saddam, and helped train the precursors of the Taleban, and fancied Colonel Gadaffi a better bet than King Idris, just as in the Fifties they bolstered the Shah and then in the Seventies took against him, when Jimmy Carter decided the Peacock Throne wasn't progressive enough and wound up with the Ayatollahs instead. As noted earlier, this system of cherrypicking from a barrel-load of unsavoury potential clients was summed up in the old geopolitical realist's line: "He may be a sonofabitch but he's *our* sonofabitch."

The inverse is more to the point: he may be our sonafabitch, but he's a sonafabitch. Some guys go nuts, some are merely devious and unreliable, some remain charming and pleasant but of little help, but all of them are a bunch of despots utterly sealed off from their peoples. As we now know, it was our so-called "moderate" Arab "friends" who provided all the suicide bombers of September 11th, just as it's in their government-run media – notably the vile Egyptian press – that some of the worst anti-American rhetoric is to be found. The contemptible regime of President Mubarak permits dissent against the US government but not against its own, licensing the former as a safety valve to reduce pressure on the latter. This is a classic example of why the sonofabitch system is ultimately useless to the west: the US spends billions subsidising regimes who have a vested interest in encouraging anti-Americanism as a substitute for more locally focused grievances. As a result, the west gets blamed for far more in a part of the world it never colonised than it does in those regions it directly administered for centuries.

The worst example of this is Saudi Arabia, the source of many – if not all – of our present woes. It's remarkable how, for all the surface flim-flam about Afghanistan, Israel, Iraq and Pakistan, everything specific about this crisis circles back to Saudi Arabia: most of the suicide bombers were Saudi, Osama's a Saudi, the Taleban were trained in Islamic terror schools in Pakistan funded by the Saudis. American defence of Saudi Arabia gave Osama bin Laden his cause, American investment in Saudi Arabia gave him the money to bankroll it. If we're looking for "root causes" to this current situation, American support for Israel is a mere distraction next to its creation and maintenance of modern Saudi Arabia.

The Beltway guys may talk about realpolitik, but they're pikers compared to the House of Saud. After all, as this last month has proved, you can be one of only three states with diplomatic relations with the Taleban, you can be militarily uncooperative, you can refuse to freeze Osama's assets, you can decline even to meet with Tony Blair, you can do whatever you like, and Washington will still insist you're a "staunch friend".

The joke in all this is that Saudi Arabia as a functioning state is an American invention: In 1933, just a year after founding his kingdom, Ibn Saud signed his first oil contract with the US and eventually gave them a monopoly on leases. Saudi Arabia was the prototype of latter-day hands-off post-imperialism and a shining example of why it's ultimately a waste of time. A century ago, Ibn Saud was a desert warrior of no fixed abode. Today the House of Saud has approximately 7,000 members and produces about 40 new princes a month. Chances are, while you're reading this, some hapless female member of the Royal House is having contractions. Because if there's one thing Saudi Arabia can always use, it's another prince. The family hogs all the cabinet posts, big ambassadorships and key government agencies and owns all the important corporations: that takes a lot of princes. Public service in Saudi Arabia is an expensive business because salary is commensurate with Royal status: cabinet ministers can earn over $6 million (base).

This isn't some quaint ancient culture that the US was forced to go along with, but rather one largely of its own creation. American know-how fuelled Saudi Arabia's rapid transformation from reactionary feudal backwater into the world's most technologically advanced and spectacularly wealthy reactionary feudal backwater. They've still got beheadings every Friday but the schedule is computerised. As Ibn Saud told Colonel William Eddy, the first US minister to Saudi Arabia in 1946, "We will use your iron, but you will leave our faith alone."

It's possible to foresee (admittedly some way down the road) Jordan evolving into a modern constitutional monarchy, but not the decadent, bloated, corrupt House of Saud. It's not a question of if the Royal Family will fall, but when. Even if they were really the "good friend" Washington insists they are, their treatment of women, the restrictiveness of the state religion and their ludicrous reliance on government by clan make it impossible for the Saudi monarchy to evolve into anything with a long-term chance of success. By backing and enriching Ibn Saud's swollen progeny, the US has put all its eggs into one basket-case. If Washington wasn't thinking about these things before September 11th, it ought to be now. America may be the engine of the global economy, but Saudi Arabia is the gas tank, producing more oil more easily than anywhere else on earth. No one could seriously argue that Washington's Frankensaud monster is the best way to guarantee long-term access to that oil.

By comparison with the sonofabitch system, colonialism is progressive and enlightened. If, as the bonehead peaceniks parrot, poverty breeds instability, then what's the best way to tackle poverty? The rule of law, a market economy, emancipation of women – all the things you're never going to get under most present Middle East regimes or any of the ones likely to overthrow them. Osama bin Laden may disagree on the third point, but he should appreciate the first two. His real grievance is with his fellow Muslims. In the Nineties, when he was living in the Sudan, the thug regime in Khartoum persuaded him to invest heavily in the country, in various enterprises of one kind or another. Doing business in such an environment involves an awful lot of palm-greasing. Osama's bookkeepers figured out his business interests in the Sudan had lost $150 million, at which point the great humanitarian cut his losses and moved on to the Hindu Kush. If he wasn't so consumed by his own psychopathology, he could have learned far more about the Arab world from this experience than from any number of books about who did what in 1492 or 1187. Even in Afghanistan, the savagery of whose menfolk has been much exaggerated by the left's nervous nellies, such progress as was made in the country came when it fell under the watchful eye of British India, as a kind of informal protectorate.

What will we do this time round? Will we stick Zahir Shah back on his throne to preside over a ramshackle coalition of mutually hostile Commies, theocrats and gangsters, and hope the poor old gentleman hangs in there till we've cleared Afghan airspace? Or will we understand that only the west can make his kingdom a functioning state once more? Afghanistan needs not just food parcels, but British courts and Canadian police and Indian civil servants and American town clerks and Australian newspapers. So does much of the rest of the region.

America has prided itself on being the first non-imperial superpower, but the viability of that strategy was demolished on September 11th. For its own security, it needs to do what it did to Japan and Germany after the war: civilise them. Kipling called it "the white man's burden" – the "white man" bit will have to be modified in the age of Colin Powell and Condi Rice, and it's no longer really a "burden", not in cost-benefit terms. Given the billions of dollars of damage done to the world economy by September 11th, massive engagement in the region will be cheaper than the alternative. If neo-colonialism makes you squeamish, give it some wussified Clinto-Blairite name like "global community outreach". Tony Blair, to his credit, has already outlined a ten-year British commitment to rebuilding Afghanistan under a kind of UN protectorate. But, given the appalling waste and corruption that attends any UN peacekeeping mission, it would be better to do it directly under a select group of western powers. We can do it for compassionate reasons (the starving hordes beggared by incompetent thug regimes) or for selfish ones (our long-term security) but either way the time has come to turn "American imperialism" from a cheap leftie slur to a formal ideology.

SUSPICIOUSLY CONVENIENT

October 20th 2001
The Daily Telegraph

I WOKE UP YESTERDAY and was halfway down the front steps before I noticed the white powdery substance on my hands. My initial reaction was: Aaaaaargh! Head for the hills! But then I noticed the hills were also covered with a white powdery substance and remembered that, the evening before, the sensible weather girl on Channel 3 Vermont, had predicted the first light snow of the winter.

And, to be honest, why would anyone mail any anthrax to a right-wing warmonger like me? For as George Monbiot shrewdly observed in *The Guardian*, "The anthrax scare looks suspiciously convenient. Just as the hawks in Washington were losing the public argument about extending the war to other countries, journalists start receiving envelopes full of bacteria, which might as well have been labelled 'a gift from Iraq'. This could indeed be the work of terrorists," George conceded, somewhat reluctantly, "but there are plenty of other ruthless operators who would benefit from a shift in public opinion."

In other words, what better way for those of us in the vast right-wing conspiracy to firm up support for our ridiculous war than by sending anthrax to left-leaning American journalists and powerful Democrats?

Well, I myself have personally mailed George a white powdery substance – Epsom salts, which I hope will help settle his nerves and tide him over until his next column on how the American right has been itching for years for an excuse to seize Afghanistan, a country rich in highly valuable natural resources such as rubble.

The Monbioterror crowd looks at things this way: who has "the most to gain"? As the Muslim website, themodernreligion.com, said of September 11th, "The FBI and Mossad, acting either together or separately, have the most to gain from the attacks: the abolition of civil liberties in the US, which make it possible for Americans to criticise US government support for Zionism."

There's a lot of conspiracies around. In the Middle East, it's perfectly correct to say that most Muslims do not support what happened on September 11th, but that's because most of them – or, at any rate, most with a public platform – figure Mossad hijacked and crashed those planes. Americans "knew very well that the Jews were behind these ugly acts," Imam Muhammad al-Gamei'a told an interviewer in Egypt the other day. "Only the Jews are capable of planning such an incident, because it was planned with great precision of which Osama bin Laden or any other Islamic organisation or intelligence apparatus is incapable." This sounds like what the Great Satan's grade-school teachers would call a self-esteem issue: we Muslims just aren't smart enough to pull off a Jew stunt like this.

But, if Mossad are behind September 11th, does that mean Osama bin Loser is a Mossad agent? Almost certainly. The more interesting question is: is he a woman? Mossad are notorious in the Arab world for preferring to use female agents, who then seduce Muslim men. There's an entire genre of Egyptian pulp novels about Zionist "honey traps", with titles like *The Hookers' War: Jewish Women And Arab Politicians*. Of course, Arab men wouldn't fall for these women if it weren't that, according to reports in Muslim papers, Israel laces Arab chewing gum with hormones to make the men hot for infidel babes.

So Osama bin Ladenberg seems to me a pretty obvious Mossad honey trap. For a start, if you put him in a burqa, he'd look just like a woman. Then there's the fact that this cave business seems, as Monbiot would say, "suspiciously convenient". What better way than living in a cave and restricting access to a few hand-picked lieutenants to keep people from spotting your false beard?

Even the *National Enquirer* story, noted here last week, that Osama had the smallest penis in Araby even before Bush froze his assets may be "suspiciously convenient". Who has "the most to gain" from all these Tiny bin Laden rumours if not Tiny herself? When she's power-lunching with the Taleban boys at the Kabul Ivy and finds herself standing next to Mullah Omar in the men's room, what better cover for her strange modesty than the small-penis rumour?

The other thing I couldn't help noticing about that Tiny bin Ladenstein live-from-the-cave video is how she holds the hand-mike while looking straight ahead with those big soulful eyes. It's exactly the same way Barbra Streisand holds the mike when she does "The Way We Were" at her semi-annual farewell concert. I'm not saying Tiny and Barbra are one and the same, but Tiny does bear an odd resemblance to a lounge act I caught in the Catskills in 1988. On the face of it, the idea that dozens of Islamic suicide bombers would be prepared to die for a singing Jewess seems far-fetched, but don't you think the alternative – that she's just a psychotic Islamofascist with a small penis – looks suspiciously convenient?

I did think of offering George Monbiot my theory for his next *Guardian* column. But, on reflection, the ease with which those right-wing nutters at the *Telegraph* have been able to discredit him looks more suspiciously convenient than anything else. It couldn't be that George's column is a classic CIA dirty-trick psy-ops plant, could it?

THE HOME FRONT

October 28th 2001
The Chicago Sun-Times

BUCKINGHAM Palace received nine direct hits during the London Blitz, including one occasion when a single German bomber flew low up the Mall and dropped its load directly above the living quarters. The King and Queen were in their drawing room and showered with shards of glass. The first bomb fell on the Palace 61 years almost to the day before the attacks of 9/11, on September 13th 1940. Afterwards, Queen Elizabeth (mother of the present Queen) said, "I'm almost glad we've been bombed. Now I can look the East End in the face."

One shouldn't exaggerate the privations of the Royal Family during wartime – I recall one sycophantic courtier explaining that, because of wartime economies, the footmen ceased serving marmalade in a dish, which was felt to be wasteful, and the King was forced to spoon it direct from the jar. War is hell. Nonetheless, the Queen's remark captures precisely the unspoken pact between the rulers and the ruled: they should be able to look us in the face; they should not require of us things that they are not willing to endure themselves.

You would think, in a democratic Republic of free-born citizens, such an observation would be a statement of the obvious. But a lot of Washington bigshots seem to be having a hard time grasping what the dear old Queen Mother, the last Empress of India, instinctively understood. It's bad enough that, at the first whiff of anthrax in the House of Representatives, Speaker Denny Hastert and the rest of the leadership rushed outside, announced they were shutting the place down for the week and scrammed out of town. The one-word headline on *The New York Post* was to the point: "WIMPS!" Worse was the House Republican Whip's attempt to reassure the little folk. "The American people need to know that these terrorists are going after specific people," said Tom DeLay. "People that are symbols. Somebody in Sugerland, Texas shouldn't worry about anthrax."

Got that, you losers? You're not important enough to be targeted. You're not a symbol, as Tom is, though a symbol of *what* he didn't say (suggestions welcome, but try not to spill confectioner's sugar on the postcard). Given that the comparative losses of the war since September 11th are Nobodies: 5,000 Symbols: zip, DeLay's remark is at the very least in extraordinarily bad taste. I can't speak for Sugerland, Texas but I know of, for example, a lady from Plaistow, New Hampshire who died on September 11th for no other reason than her choice of flight.

Even with anthrax, the grandees are so insulated that to get to the symbols you have to go through an awful lot of non-symbols. Yet, after its discovery in a letter to Tom Daschle, the initial response was to offer widespread testing to any Senate aide who wanted it but none to postal workers through whose facility the mail had to have passed en route to Congress. Two postal employees are now dead, and those deaths most likely could have been avoided. The impression that our leaders are looking out for number one and leaving the little people to fend for themselves is not exactly conducive of public trust. In that respect, the stories of medics having to plead with Senate staffers to stop trying to pull rank and cut in line but just wait their turn are also very instructive. They contrast sharply with the survivors of the twin towers waiting calmly and politely to be treated by emergency workers.

"Wait your turn": that's not something government bigwigs like to do. Speaking of New Hampshire, what's your preferred image of the state's famous primary? A candidate wandering into a diner or Legion hall and trying to get the attention of some cranky guy in plaid? Here's another view, from a couple of weeks before Primary Day last year: I'd just pulled up to the toll booth on the turnpike between Manchester and Concord and was about to toss my 75 cents in, when I was blinded by the flashing lights of the world's longest motorcade – I counted at least 12 cars plus an ambulance – coming in the opposite direction. They roared through the toll plaza without stopping, defying red lights and scattering meandering old biddies in beat-up sedans.

"What's going on?" I asked.

"Al Gore," replied the toll lady. "Does it every time. Never pays. He can't stop for 'security' reasons," she said with a chuckle. Even with a 13-vehicle motorcade, that's only $9.75 and she'd have been happy to take a single payment for the entire camel train. But a lofty fellow like Al Gore is too busy fighting for the little man to trouble himself with any of the things little men have to do, like paying tolls.

I think it's worth subjecting every new anti-terrorism measure to the Al Gore motorcade test: are the politicians burdening us with stuff they themselves don't have to bother slowing down for? A key Senate aide is on the fast track to nasal swabs and Cipro; a mail sorter has to take a number. We've already had one incident of Hillary Clinton's "security detail" attempting to crash through a barrier at the airport. Do you figure the junior Senator's having her tweezers and nail-file seized every time she hops a flight? Think she has to get there two hours beforehand so her undies can be emptied out on the conveyor belt?

I have to confess that my first reaction, on hearing that 34 staffers in Tom Daschle's office had tested positive for anthrax, was a gasp of amazement: Tom Daschle has 34 staffers? *Why?* These aren't the citizen legislators foreseen by the Founders so much as mini-sultanates, with all the inevitable consequences.

Journeying round the country, I find more and people wondering why politicians and the media seem so uniquely panicked. They get all this intelligence, folks say; they must know something. But maybe it's more basic. Politicians, like showbiz types, are now so unnaturally sealed off from the world by their vast entourages that the piercing of the perimeter has utterly confounded them: suddenly, they feel vulnerable, as many Americans do in a thousand situations – walking down an empty city street after dark, working the midnight shift at a convenience store in a crummy neighborhood. The gap between the people and the elites is easily measured by the way the spore bores at the networks have driven away their audiences: since they stalled their war coverage on Anthrax Avenue, CNN's ratings have apparently dropped 70%.

As it happens, Tom DeLay is precisely wrong: One reason why the world has terrorism is because in the last century it's become all but impossible for fanatics with political causes to kill politicians, so they have to slaughter grannies and toddlers to make their point. The safer you make politicians, the less safe you make the public. Given that grim equation, we are entitled to expect that our war leaders at least act like war leaders. If Tom DeLay is really a symbol, he should start behaving like one.

YELLOW STREAK

November 3rd 2001
The Spectator

IT'S NOT EASY being a compassionate warmonger. This week, it came to the notice of the Bush Administration that, due to poor communication at the design department, the TV dinners and cluster bombs they're dropping on the Hindu Kush are the same colour. That meant they had to rush out a new radio ad: "Attention, people of Afghanistan!" began the announcer in what the White House hopes is fluent Pashto. "As you may have heard, the Partnership of Nations is dropping yellow Humanitarian Daily Rations. The rations are square-shaped and are packaged in plastic. They are full of good nutritious, Halal food."

That's the good news. On the other hand, "in areas far from where we are dropping food, we are dropping cluster bombs. Although it is unlikely, it is possible that not every bomb will explode on impact. These bombs are a yellow colour and are can-shaped... Please, please exercise caution when approaching unidentified yellow objects in areas that have been recently bombed."

Please, please exercise caution: it could be a Big McHalal burger, fries and a vanilla sheik; it could be a cluster bomb; or - most worrying of all – that unidentified yellow object could be western resolve curdling under the klieg lights of Taleban media savvy. By the time you read this, the rumoured Halloween atrocities may have come to pass in America, and we will have been reminded once again of why we're fighting this war. Alternatively, among our allies, the clamour will have increased for a "bombing pause", to enable the aid agencies to go in and re-stock their bombed warehouses so that the Taleban can steal all the supplies before the USAF blows the buildings up again.

And then there's Ramadan. As Bill Clinton remarked during one of his own perfunctory bombing campaigns, "Military action during Ramadan would be profoundly offensive to the Muslim world." Jack Straw and Geoff Hoon, speaking for the rear end of our pantomime coalition, have similar reservations. Unlike every other white-boy pundit, I'm no Islamic scholar, but given that, as I understand it, during the holy month of Ramadan Muslims are expected to live in simple fashion, it's hard to see in what way taking out the water lines, the food warehouses, the electric supply, etc is disrespectful. Quite the contrary, one would have thought. Happy Holidays from the Great Satan!

But where's the American Civil Liberties Union lawsuits when you need them? If American flyboys taking Ramadan off isn't in breach of the separation of church and state, what is?

With hindsight, some of us were foolish to assume that, being Neanderthal racist misogynist homophobic fundamentalists, the Taleban would get at least as bad a press as the average GOP Congressman. We underestimated the contempt in which the US is held by global opinion. Why, *The Guardian* has mocked the very idea of America fighting for civilisation: "Which bits of the planet does Mr Bush term uncivilised?" sneered their leader writer. "Some would say Afghanistan; others might nominate west Texas." How true. Remember their stirring editorial from 46 years ago? "Which bits of the planet does Mr Truman term uncivilised? Some would say Dachau; others might nominate Missouri."

And so after three weeks the US has somehow contrived to get blamed by world opinion for the "humanitarian disaster" in Afghanistan. We need a "bombing pause" to enable the Taleban to come to their senses, even though they don't have any senses to come to and the quickest way to end the "humanitarian disaster" is to liquidate its direct cause: the weirdbeards. But, having framed the war in idealistic terms, Bush shouldn't be surprised that a lot of the world's most tedious self-proclaimed idealists want to muscle in on it. He made more sense when he was in cowboy mode, doing his "Wanted Dead Or Alive" shtick.

The President says that this is a "war against terrorism" and Don Rumsfeld claims we may never know when it's over. Neither statement is correct, though, if you believe the former, the latter goes with the territory. This is a war against the forces that attacked the United States: al-Qa'eda and the regimes that support and fund them. It will be over when Osama bin Laden and his closest colleagues are dead, al-Qa'eda is destroyed, the Taleban are removed, Saddam Hussein is overthrown, and the House of Saud has at the very least had its collective genitals squeezed and been persuaded to exile those princes who've been kissing up to terrorists. This is a fight for America, not for an abstract principle. America's immediate objective in

Afghanistan is destroying the Taleban. A benign, social democratic coalition government would be a nice bonus, but to fret about it now will only get in the way of bombing Mullah Omar's yak cart.

For a month now, the Administration has gone the Colin Powell route – restrained warfare, multinational mumbo-jumbo, would-you-like-the-chicken-or-beef? – and the result has been jeers all round from Mary Robinson, the aid agencies, the European press, Tony Blair's twitchy backbenchers and at least some of his cabinet. This is not an audience worth playing to. And the only audience that does matter – America's more equivocal "friends" in the Arab world – respects might far more than Halal McNuggets. It's time to stop trying to be liked and start trying to be feared.

~

HELLO, MULLAH

November 3rd 2001
The Daily Telegraph

In late October, the first British Muslims were captured in Afghanistan – young men, born and bred in Luton, Crawley and other quintessentially English towns, who had nevertheless decided to sign up with the Taleban and/or al-Qa'eda. Herewith, a dispatch from some of our plucky boys fighting the good fight out in the Hindu Kush (with acknowledgements to Alan Sherman and Ponchielli):

Hello, Fadduh, Hello, Mama
Here I am at Camp Osama
Camp is really very thrillin'
And they say we'll have some fun when we start killin'

There's no chip shops, there's no telly
And the cave is kinda smelly
And Osama can be crabby
But what else do you expect from a Wahhabi?

WAR

All the women are in burqas
And we're looking out for Gurkhas
Death to Bush and Blair and Putin!
Death to all the non-Islamic parts of Luton!

I've come home
Oh, Fadduh, Mama
I've come home
To Camp Osama
Don't make me
Come back and be a Brit
Until
I've seized some plane's cockpit

I've come home
I'm on my way to
Paradise
Like Bedfordshire but
Twice as nice
And not an avenue
That's got one single Jew

Hello, Mullah, Hello, Luton
Here I am without a suit on
Camp is very satisfyin'
And they say we'll have some fun when we start dyin'

Goodbye, Britain, stuff your passport
Goodbye, snooker, that's not our sport
Robin Cook and his Marsala
You can bet I won't be eating that with Allah

I've come home
Oh dearest granny
I've come home
I'm Talebanny
Don't make me
Forsake Osama bin
And head
Back much to my chagrin

I've come home
I'm on my way to
Paradise
It's really worth the
Sacrifice
It's not like Beds or Herts
But more
Like Kandahar in parts

Dearest Mullah, lotsa Fateh
On a theologic matter
I don't mean to raise your hackle
But you're sure up there I'll have my wedding tackle?

Wait a minute, bombs are falling
Buildings burning, Allah's calling
If I'm wounded, skip the surgeons
'Cause I'm first in line for all those pantin' virgins

And when I'm in Paradiseland
And they say, "You from some nice land?
Were you wafted from some fair port?"
I will tell them proudly, "Nah, mate. Luton Airport."

NOVEMBER 11th

Remembrance

November 11th 2001
The Chicago Sun-Times

O N CNN THE other day, Larry King asked Tony Blair what it was he had in his buttonhole. It was a poppy – not a real poppy, but a stylized, mass-produced thing of red paper and green plastic that, as the Prime Minister explained, is worn in Britain and other Commonwealth countries in the days before November 11th. They're sold in the street by aged members of the Royal British Legion to commemorate that moment 83 years ago today, when on the eleventh hour of the eleventh day of the eleventh month the guns fell silent on the battlefields of Europe.

The poppy is an indelible image of that "war to end all wars", summoned up by a Canadian, Lieutenant-Colonel John McCrae, in a poem written in the trenches in May 1915:

> *In Flanders fields the poppies blow*
> *Between the crosses, row on row,*
> > *That mark our place; and in the sky*
> > *The larks, still bravely singing, fly*
> *Scarce heard amid the guns below.*

Row on row on row. And, in between, thousands of poppies, for they bloom in uprooted soil. Sacrifice on the scale McCrae witnessed is all but unimaginable in the west today – in Canada, in Britain, even apparently in America, which instead of sending in the cavalry is now dropping horse feed for the Northern Alliance, in the hope they might rouse themselves to seize an abandoned village or two, weather permitting.

Nonetheless, though we can scarce grasp what they symbolize, this year the poppies are hard to find. Three Canadian provinces had sold out by last Monday, and by the time you read this the rest of the

Royal Canadian Legion's entire stock of 14.8 million will likely be gone. That's not bad for a population that barely touches 30 million and includes large numbers of terrorist cells plus the students at Montreal's Concordia University who openly celebrated the attacks on the World Trade Center. Evidently, the public has made a connection between September 11th and November 11th, though no one seems quite sure what is: A general expression of solidarity with the victims? Or a renewed respect for the men who gave their lives so we could get fat and complacent and read celebrity features about Britney?

> *We are the Dead. Short days ago*
> *We lived, felt dawn, saw sunset glow,*
> *Loved and were loved, and now we lie*
> *In Flanders fields.*

This year, President Bush has declared the week of Veterans' Day to be National Veterans Awareness Week, which is just a terrible name and makes America's armed forces sound like a disease ("National Breast Cancer Awareness Week"). He's also announced an initiative to get every school, in the week ahead, to invite a veteran to come and speak to students. A fine idea, but one likely to run into problems in a culture where not just tony bastions like Harvard but many less elevated outlets of academe decline to permit the ROTC on campus. When Oxbow High School in the small North Country town of Bradford, Vermont mooted a JROTC program, the proposal was quickly shot down by the usual activists protesting JROTC's policies on gays. (JROTC doesn't have any policy on gays – that's the problem.) "Being a teenager," said one middle-aged, graying hippy-dippy Vermonter, "is not about wearing a uniform and fitting in. It's about standing up and declaring who you are." There speaks the voice of the eternally adolescent Boomer in all its woeful self-absorption.

Actually, most Americans are already "aware" of their veterans, it's the elites who need reminding – like the chaps at *The New York Times* and other big papers who carry (by my estimation) less than a tenth of the military obituaries Britain's *Daily Telegraph* does. True, NBC's star anchor, Tom Brokaw, has found himself a lucrative franchise cranking out books about "The Greatest Generation" – the World War Two generation – but Brokaw's designation is absurd and essentially self-serving. The youthful Americans who went off to war

60 years ago would have thought it ridiculous to be hailed as "the greatest". They were unexceptional: they did no more or less than their own parents and grandparents had done. Like young men across the world, they accepted soldiering as an obligation of citizenship, as men have for centuries. In 1941, it would have astonished them to be told they would be the last generation to respect that basic social compact. They understood that there are moments in a nation's history when even being a teenager is about standing up and declaring who you are by wearing a uniform. When we – their children and grandchildren – ennoble them as "the greatest" and elevate them into something extraordinary, it's a reflection mainly of our own stunted perspective.

So for many of us "sacrifice" is all but incomprehensible. Responding to Robert Putnam's recollections of "civic community" in World War Two – "victory gardens in nearly everyone's backyard, the Boy Scouts at filling stations collecting floor mats for scrap rubber, the affordable war bonds, the practice of giving rides to hitchhiking soldiers and war workers" - Katha Pollitt in the current edition of *The Nation* sneers: "Those would be certified heterosexual, Supreme-Being-believing scouts, I suppose, and certified harmless and chivalrous hitchhiking GIs, too - not some weirdo in uniform who cuts you to bits on a dark road." Somehow I don't think poor paranoid Ms Pollitt has met that many fellows in uniform, weirdoes or otherwise.

To the broader constituency for which Katha speaks, those guys in uniform *are* weirdoes – not because they want to cut her to bits but because they're willing to go and slog it out on some foreign hillside, getting limbs blown off by grenades, blinded by shrapnel – and for no other reason than something so risible as "love of country"!

Today, across the western world, the generals dislike conscript armies. They want light, highly trained, professional regiments. But it's hard not to feel that the end of the draft – the end of routine military service – has somehow weakened the bonds of citizenship. Citizenship is about allegiance. We benefit from our rights as citizens of the state and in return we accept our duties as citizens of the state. And let's not be embarrassed about supposedly obsolescent concepts like the "nation-state". If we've learned anything since September 11th, it's that, if it were left to the multilateral acronyms – the UN, EU, even Nato – Osama bin Laden would have the run of the planet. The great evil of September 11th is being resisted by a small number of nation-states, by the United States, the United Kingdom and a handful of others. Ultimately, it is as Americans or Britons, Australians or Canadians that we resist the assault on our liberties.

But how do we play our part in this war? Hug your children, advised the President, and shop till you drop. Ask not what your country can do for you, ask what you can do for your outlet mall. But, for most Americans, that's not enough. They're ready to do more, and Mr Bush isn't giving a lead. We may not be asked to scramble up over a trench and across a muddy field in Flanders, but it's all too possible we may be called upon to demonstrate great heroism close to home, as the firemen of New York and the passengers of Flight 93 were. They are the Dead. They lived, felt dawn, saw sunset glow, loved and were loved. They did not deserve their premature deaths. But they join the untold legions who helped the Union win the Civil War, the Americans and the British Empire win the Great War, and the Allies the Second World War. And every single American alive today – including Katha Pollitt – enjoys the blessings of those victories.

> *Take up our quarrel with the foe:*
> *To you from failing hands we throw*
> *The torch; be yours to hold it high.*
> *If ye break with us who die*
> *We shall not sleep, though poppies grow*
> *In Flanders fields.*

In Thursday's otherwise unsatisfactory speech, the President finally used the words he should have spoken a month ago, the last words of Todd Beamer before he and his ad-hoc commando unit took out the hijackers of Flight 93 at the cost of their own lives. And so Mr Bush ended his address by informally deputizing the citizenry: "We have our marching orders. My fellow Americans, let's roll."

It's not as poetic as John McCrae, but then, in the dust of Ground Zero, no poppies blow nor ever will.

NOVEMBER

Quagmire

November 17th 2001
The Daily Telegraph

THIS WAR IS in trouble. We're bogged down, getting nowhere and staring at a Vietnam-style quagmire. The Taleban's grip on the country remains total. These famously tough warriors of iron resolve are unlikely to be…

Whoops, sorry, that was last week. Just let me punch up this week's Conventional Media Wisdom. Ah, here we go:

Things are moving too fast. There's a dangerous power vacuum in the country. The Taleban, being famously tough, etc, have pulled off a brilliant double bluff by abandoning every major city and lever of government. Their grip on selected southern and western caves remains total. The Northern Alliance are too vicious, unfairly targeting enemy soldiers instead of just killing unarmed women and homosexuals. The collapse of the burqa market will devastate the Afghan fashion industry. The removal of 90% of Afghan beards could leave vital supply routes choked with facial hair. The re-introduction of music has raised serious fears that many western aid workers will become disc-jockeys on KBUL ("No Beards, No Burqas, No Bee Gees"). The Pushtuns will be pushed out, the Tajiks will be tragic, the Uzbeks want their Uzis back, and in Punditstan and Rootkhazia many top western commentators remain cut off from reality, facing a bleak winter unless they can come up with a new title for *Afghanistan: The War We Can't Win* before Random House stops the cheque.

Here's Maureen Dowd in *The New York Times* on November 7th, moaning that the Northern Alliance are a bunch of pussies "who smoke and complain more than they fight" and look "sillier and sillier". "Let's cut the chitchat," she urges.

Here's Maureen on November 14th, aghast to discover that the Northern Alliance are a bunch of bloodthirsty thugs who'll stop at nothing: "Some Alliance soldiers looted dead bodies for valuables," she squeals. "We give the Northern Alliance an air force and they embarrass us with savage force." Alliance field commanders, having acted so impressively on Ms Dowd's earlier advice, must be wondering if she's going for the Pulitzer for columnar whiplash.

Instead of pining for the slap of firm government from Mullah Omar and his fellow members of the region's ferocious Loonitun minority, Maureen and co should be asking themselves why the media has got everything wrong so far. One reason is that most of the "experts" are frauds: The ones who've been to Afghanistan tend to be misty-eyed westerners for whom, reasonably enough, the Hindu Kush will always be more romantic than a strip mall in Newark. Jason Burke, billed in *The Observer* as "an expert on Afghanistan", reminisced fondly about "Mohammed Ghaffar, the white-bearded waiter at Kabul's battered Intercontinental hotel who grimly counted off the regimes that have successively run and ruined his country on his fingers", and confidently declared that "the Afghans are now falling in behind the Taleban. The strikes are swiftly radicalising what was an essentially moderate country." (Please, no tittering. He's an expert, remember.) "You cannot bomb these men into submission."

Back on the home front, American columnists rushed to agree: Afghanistan's the "graveyard of empire", everyone knows that. Actually, Afghanistan was an informal British protectorate for some 60 years (as I noted here a month ago) and the only reason they never officially colonised it was because they felt it was less trouble to keep it as a buffer state rather than a common border between the British and Russian Empires. The truth about Afghanistan is verifiable to anyone willing to spend ten minutes with a history book.

Likewise, in all their droning about it being impossible to colonise Afghanistan, the experts failed to notice that it was already a colony: the Taleban was propped up by Osama's money, Islamabad politicians and military recruits from Pakistan and the Arab world, plus a few western Muslim losers. The dead in the streets that Ms Dowd finds so "chilling" are mostly foreign Taleban soldiers killed by Kabul civilians. If they were, say, British soldiers, most western lefties would be delighting in a popular uprising against a colonial oppressor.

And then there's the grandees, fellows like Arthur Schlesinger Jr, who being an Ivy League history prof knows that Afghanistan is in the same general east-of-Martha's-Vineyard direction as Vietnam. "Our leaders gambled on the supposition that the unpopularity of the regime would mean the bombing would bring about the Taleban's rapid collapse," he wrote in *The Independent* earlier this month. "Vietnam should have reminded our generals that bombing has only a limited impact on decentralised, undeveloped, rural societies."

The history guy has missed the point. From the Second World War on, most local squabbles – from Vietnam to Grenada – were proxy wars for the great game between Communism and the Free World. The difference between Vietnam and Afghanistan is that, as the Taleban were heading for the hills, the President of the Russian Federation was kibitzing with his buddy Dubya at Crawford High School in some Russo-Texan Borscht Belt routine. In this war, all the major powers are on the same side – America, Russia, Britain, Germany, Japan, even China. The only countries who aren't with us are the basket-cases – Iraq, the Sudan, Cuba, North Korea – a handful of irrelevant loser states who contribute nothing, economically, culturally, technologically. We are at war with the world's losers. And losers tend to lose. If Osama really spoke for the entire Muslim world, we'd be in trouble. But, as we now know, Osama bin Loser doesn't even speak for the Muslims living ten miles from his cave. Some jihad.

True, Mullah Omar has told the BBC that the Taleban will refuse to take part in any new "broad-based government", presumably on the grounds that any government based on broads is repugnant to them. (All Taleban jokes must go, folks, in our never-to-be-repeated grand warehouse clearance sale, this weekend only.) The one-eyed Mullah insists that relocating from his executive office to a cave is all part of the Taleban's master plan to bring about "the destruction of America", which "will happen within a short period of time". Dream on, weirdbeard. That faint background noise outside the cave is approaching Delta Force commandoes playing Céline Dion's *Greatest Hits* really loud. Granted, he could have a dirty nuke. The unthinkable is thinkable – in the sense of the levelling of an American city. But long-term these guys are already history.

Let's make it easy for Professor Schlesinger and co, and spell it out: In liberated Kabul, people are VERY HAPPY. In Pakistan, anti-American protests are POORLY ATTENDED. In Iran, the Ayatollahs are more worried about PRO-AMERICAN DEMONSTRATIONS. In Bangladesh, the world's third most populous Muslim nation, in an election held at the height of the US bombing, Islamic fundamentalists got LESS THAN FIVE PER CENT. In repressive Saudi Arabia, the shifty, decadent House of Saud has instructed its vile press to SUPPORT AMERICA. Two months after the bloody attacks on American cities, the government that supported the men who did it has been OVERTHROWN and its troops are CORPSES IN THE DUST, picked at by birds and spat on by the civilian population they enslaved. It's early days, but that alone is cause for all Americans – and Britons - to rejoice. Even journalists.

Last week, President Bush said, "Let's roll." We're rolling.

KANDAHAR – THE MOVIE

November 17th 2001
The Spectator

K*ANDAHAR* – The Movie! Talk about a hit title, and just in time for liberation. A few months ago, this picture would have been *Kandahoo?* But now even President Bush has seen it, and he hasn't seen a film since *Austin Powers: The Spy Who Shagged Me.*

Whether he enjoyed it as much, I cannot say. Mohsen Makhmalbaf, the Iranian director, has produced an inside-the-burqa look at women's life under the Taleban. It's not a documentary, so much as a drama in which real people play fictionalised versions of themselves. The star is Niloufar Pazira, a 25-year old Afghan refugee who now lives in Canada. Three years ago, she received a letter from a friend back home who said life was so intolerable under the Taleban she was going to kill herself. Miss Pazira took the premise to Makhmalbaf, and the result is a film in which Niloufar plays Nafas, an Afghan-Canadian who's received a letter from her sister in Kandahar threatening to commit suicide on the last eclipse of the 20th century. Her sister was unable to flee the country because she made the mistake of picking up a pretty doll left in a minefield and lost both her legs. (There seems to be a general shortage of limbs in Afghanistan: *Kandahar* has more one-legged actors than you'd find this side of a Sarah Bernhardt impersonators' convention.) Aside from an Afghan-Canadian playing an Afghan-Canadian, the rest of the cast is made up of villagers playing villagers, aid workers playing aid workers, amputees playing amputees, etc. The villagers had never seen a film, never mind been in one, and it would be nice to report they took to it like naturals. But, to be honest, the acting here isn't really very good, especially the speaking parts, whether English or Farsi.

The film opens with Nafas on the Iranian border, hoping to find someone who can take her across into Afghanistan and on to Kandahar. She is in a Red Cross helicopter, and that gives Makhmalbaf his first great visual image. The chopper drops its cargo – a pair of prosthetic legs dangling from a parachute – and a gaggle of young Afghan men on crutches hobble across the sands in a race to be the first to get to them. If you're wondering what Makhmalbaf's second great image is, well, it's the prosthetic legs floating through the sky again, but this time a couple of days east with multiple pairs of legs and even more Afghan men hobbling frantically after them. This is a film where the same scenes and sights and lines are repeated over and over. As a director, Makhmalbaf is usually subtle, allusive, oblique, you name it, but in this instance the tone of the movie appears to have been hijacked by the crusading Miss Pazira.

As a Canadianised Afghan, she is unfamiliar with the burqa, but is aware that, in order to smuggle herself across the border as an old Afghan's third or fourth wife, she'll have to climb into one. Miss Pazira had never worn one before and says that she found it hard to breathe inside. Hence, her character's name: "Nafas" means "to breathe". As she disappears from view, she muses, "Does love pass through the covering of the burqa?" She's not a good enough actress to pull off lines like that, but she has a very expressive face and beautiful, sharp features, and she's never more eloquent than in those moments when she's forced to reveal herself, raising the covering so that we see her chin and mouth and nose while the eyes remain dappled and mysterious, shaded by the burqa's grille. Incidentally, now that the streets of Kabul are carpeted with discarded burqas, *Kandahar* may be the first and last great burqapic. I had no idea they came in such vibrant colours – the turquoise and orange were particularly striking, and the moment when an all-female wedding party comes scrambling up the hill is really rather beautiful. A yard off the hem, a foot off the neck and a droptop hood, and Mullah Omar would have had a great export.

The best actor in the picture is the old guy Nafas persuades to take her across the border. He's a leathery weatherbeaten thing who's got a wife from every Afghan ethnic group. But no sooner have they crossed the border than they're robbed and he decides to retreat back to Iran, leaving Nafas to make her way to Kandahar with a succession of increasingly unsuitable escorts, including a black American living in Afghanistan and wearing a false beard – "the male burqa" – because he can't grow one himself. Of necessity, all the film's characters, apart from Nafas, are male, because female identity has simply been abolished. You would think, after making a movie that's basically a public service message about Afghanistan's all-pervasive violence, disease and oppression, that Miss Pazira would welcome the liberation of her people from Mullah Omar and co. But no: she's "passionately" opposed to the US bombing, and thinks instead Washington should have leaned on Saudi Arabia and Pakistan merely to stop funding the Taleban. Would that have worked? Don't hold your breath, Nafas.

FLIGHT FROM REALITY

November 17th 2001
The Spectator

ON THE FACE of it, it seems statistically improbable. A waitress who escaped from the burning World Trade Center moments before the tower collapsed books a seat on American Airlines Flight 587 to San Domingo, and this time her luck doesn't hold. Two months after American Airlines lost two planes to a group of Islamakazi terrorists bent on turning them into flying bombs, they lose a third, which drops out of the sky onto a neighbourhood that lost 75 residents in the first disaster.

And yet there is, apparently, no connection - any more than there is between those two events and the dominant intervening story: the anthrax attacks on selected Washington and New York mailrooms, which, according to the official FBI profile, are most likely the work of "an adult male", "something of a loner", who "chooses to confront his problems long-distance". Hmm. That could be Saddam. Or it could be me, or any number of other crazy guys holed up in the hills. But, as things stand, it seems that in the last two months New York has suffered an unprecedented terrorist attack, an unprecedented biological attack and an unprecedented airline crash, all entirely unrelated but all contributing to what the media call the "climate of fear".

If there is a "climate of fear" it's largely confined to the TV networks and those who appear on them – politicians and celebrities, two groups hitherto unnaturally sealed off from the world by their vast entourages and thus unusually panic-prone. I once recounted in these pages the occasion when I had to accompany Whitney Houston across Sixth Avenue because she didn't feel "comfortable" crossing the street unescorted. It's unlikely that toppling buildings, lethal spores and planes dropping out of the sky will have made Whitney feel any more comfortable about the perils of midtown boulevards. In this respect, I was saddened to see another old friend, Liza Minnelli, pull out of a Los Angeles charity gala because her "contacts" in Washington had advised her not to fly. "I should risk my life for one fucking song?" she asked, rhetorically. Liza, Liza: in Kabul, where until Tuesday music was banned, there were brave dissidents willing to risk their lives for one fucking song from the *Liza At Carnegie Hall* two-CD set.

Contrast this behaviour with the folks at Rockaway Beach, just a few miles from Liza's midtown pad but another world. As soon as they saw the plane come down, the residents grabbed fire extinguishers and hoses and rushed toward the blazing buildings. We are all firemen now, we all want to be not Whitney or Liza but Michael Moran, a Rockaway member of the FDNY who lost his brother, a battalion chief, on September 11th but stood on stage at the New York benefit concert and declared, "Osama, you can kiss my royal Irish ass!" When Gray Davis, the Governor of California, announced that the terrorists had plans to blow up major bridges in the state, the camera crews descended on the Golden Gate Bridge to see if they could detect any downturn in traffic. "Come and get me, Osama!" roared one motorist. Another said she had no plans to change her route but was planning to improve her odds by speeding even more than usual.

By contrast, the only real significance of Monday's air crash was that, even if it wasn't a bomb, it could have been. It reminds the already shrunken pool of airline passengers that, while the fellows at the metal detectors are now ostentatiously confiscating every pair of tweezers, most of the checked baggage goes into the hold subject only to random and cursory examination. It thereby provides yet another reason not to get back on a plane, as if we needed one. Even before this week's "mechanical failure", the industry was predicting a 27% drop-off in next week's Thanksgiving traffic, usually the busiest travel period of the year. The 73% who haven't cancelled are enjoying hastily introduced bargain fares that ensure just about every flight is flying at a loss. By the end of October, American, Continental, Delta, Northwest, United and US Airways were each losing between $5 million and $15 million per day. So if you can't make money on the busiest travel period in the year, when can you? Anxious to prevent any further slippage, the experts patiently explain that flying is still the safest form of travel: if you fly every single day of your life, you would have to live 26,000 years to face the statistical likelihood of dying in a plane crash.

But that's missing the point. If you fly every single day of your life, by the end of the first week it already feels like 26,000 years. What the airlines and the Federal Aviation Administration and Underperformin' Norman Mineta, the Transportation Secretary, don't seem to realise is that, as far as Mr and Mrs America are concerned, the issue isn't the "fear of flying" but the crappiness of flying. This was true well before Mohammad Atta booked his first pilot's lesson. Domestic air travel has long been the exception that proves the rule about American service: in a British restaurant or store, I pine for American waitresses and sales clerks, but on United or US Air or Delta or Continental I dream fondly of the smart, solicitous cabin crews of Virgin or British Airways. Or even Lufthansa.

Still, even with the world's surliest trolley dollies in their worn, shiny, shapeless navy stretch pants – okay, let's not be sexist here: if you want to see America's worst-dressed gay men, take a plane – and even with their minimal standards of "cabin service" (a bag of mini-pretzels) and the delays on landing and take-off, at least pre-9/11 you could turn up ten minutes before the flight and, thanks to the perfunctory security, know you'd get on the plane.

September 11th was a catastrophe for the industry, but also an opportunity. They seized it, and got a $15 billion emergency bail-out from the Feds. They needed the money even before that Tuesday morning; the only difference is they wouldn't have got it. And what did they do with it? They laid off thousands of employees, so that, even without the new security procedures, the check-in lines have got longer. If you go to a supermarket at certain times of the day, you'll find that the deli counter can be quite busy, so you pull a little ticket from the dispenser and mooch around in the general area, loading up the yoghurt and Pop-Tarts until your number's called. For 15 billion bucks, maybe the airlines could buy a couple dozen dispensers apiece. But apparently not. They *want* you backed up in lines shuffling your bags forward a couple of inches at a time because your misery is their convenience.

And now the FAA has vastly increased the opportunities for commercial aviation to chastise its customers. Norm Mineta's strategy for the world post-9/11 is to replace the pre-9/11 useless joke security with useless joke harassment: if you buy a plastic fireman's axe at Toys R Us for your favourite nephew, it will be confiscated as a dangerous weapon; if you're sitting at the gate reading a thriller with a cover showing an explosion, you will be prevented from boarding as a security risk, as happened to one young man recently; if you stand up on a flight within 30 minutes of Reagan National, your plane will be diverted to Dulles, as happened a couple of hours before Monday's big crash because a guy needed to use the bathroom. On the other hand, a fellow at New Orleans forgot he had a handgun in his briefcase and it sailed through the scanner undetected. On the plane, he suddenly remembered and gave it to the stewardess, who promptly ensured the poor law-abiding citizen was detained on arrival and harassed by law enforcement for what was, in fact, the airline's incompetence.

At the moment, the Senate and the House of Representatives are split over whom to entrust with airport security: the House favours private firms (as at Heathrow and Tel Aviv), the Senate wants them federalised, so that instead of being bored minimum-wage illegal-alien incompetents who quit after four months they'll be bored highly-paid government incompetents you can never fire. If you seriously think these new fellows will now be "accountable" for any slip-ups, try counting the number of FAA, INS or other Federal officials who've been dismissed for what happened on September 11th. Answer: not one.

Are these pols on the same planet? Senators will never have to endure any of these insane measures themselves but the rest of the citizenry are assumed to be willing to get to the airport four hours early for a one-hour domestic flight in the interests of "security". It's true that air travel is now safer than it was before September 11th, but that's not due to Secretary Mineta so much as the splendid example of the passengers on Flight 93. These days, if you're sitting next to a burly guy or a woman with severe PMS or even an 87-year old arthritic granny, you can feel they're itching for someone to start something just so they can rush the punk and beat him to a pulp. A roused citizenry is more use than all Mineta's bans on plastic knives and long fingernails.

But, in the end, even the prospect of kneeing Osama's boys in their meticulously depilated goolies isn't enough. Long before 9/11, regulations on smoking and seatbelts had remorselessly expanded into a culture of trivial but total coerciveness that Americans would rightly reject in any other environment. Airlines assume passengers will put up with anything because they've got no choice. But, while's it true this is a big country, an awful lot of travel is discretionary. Even business travel. Psychologically, we're stuck in the mid-19th century when the original travelling men spent eleven months of the year on the road because there was no alternative. The railroads have gone, the telephone's arrived, and so's video conferencing, and electronic networking, but guys are still on the road, flying off to lunch in Houston and a presentation in Denver and all kinds of other engagements they don't really need to be physically present at. The FAA and the airlines have blithely assumed that they can triple the amount of time you have to allow for a flight to New York for a business lunch without companies calling into question the necessity of that lunch.

If next week's numbers are off by more than 20%, that's the death knell for the airlines: if Americans won't fly for Thanksgiving, they won't fly at all. And that's good news for oil prices, which have already fallen in part due to the airlines' reduced need for jet fuel, and even better news for customers. The sooner the current lousy carriers go out of business, the sooner the FAA will be forced to change its ways, the sooner we'll get some new companies that give serious thought to winning patrons back with decent food, perky stewardesses and efficient service. The American people aren't afraid of flying, but, if airlines aren't yet afraid of the American people, they ought to be.

~

BIG SHIFT

November 19th 2001
National Review

W E'RE ALL INTO government now. Not just Senator Rodham Clinton – on September 11th, "we saw government in action" - but also Vice-President Cheney – "One of the things that's changed so much since September 11th is the extent to which people do trust the government – big shift – and value it, and have high expectations for what we can do."

If that's true, it's hard to see why. But the Rodham-Cheney line is now received wisdom. There was even a hint of gloating in the way Albert Hunt, in *The Wall Street Journal*, noted that the heroes of September 11th – firemen, cops, rescue workers – were all government employees. That's correct, as far as it goes. But by which government were they employed? What worked on September 11th was municipal and state government. What failed – big time, as the Vice-President might say – was federal government, all the hotshot money-no-object sweeping-powers fancypants acronyms – FBI, CIA, INS, FAA.

Indeed, if Hill and Al are determined to goad us small-government nuts into beastly partisanship, one could argue that September 11th vindicates perfectly the decentralized, federalist, conservative view of the world. We all love firemen. On Fourth of July, in small towns across America, the fire department leads off the parade, as it should. Proponents of small government don't want to sell off the fire trucks, they want to get rid of all the stuff that distracts from the fire department. The debate over government is between folks who want a fire chief and those who want a fire chief plus a transgendered cultural outreach officer. Fellows like Edgar Rosenblum of Connecticut's Long Wharf Theatre: "The fire department is not more important than art," he said at some arts gabfest a few years back. "If you will save people, what will you save them for?" Big government wants it all: a fireman to bring you out of the blazing skyscraper and then deposit you in front of the homoerotic performance artist waiting in the piazza.

Incidentally, in many parts of the country, even the emergency services exemplify the American ideal of an engaged citizenry - the Fire

Departments and FAST Squads are volunteer, and the police officers are part-timers recruited from willing residents. I'm not suggesting this would work in New York, only that both the big town and nowheresville exemplify the same principle – that remote government is bad government. And the remoter it gets the worse it gets. It was somehow inevitable that, even as the left were demanding that any response to September 11th should be done through Kofi Annan and international law and the other putative organs of "world government", it emerged that the UN had given money to one of Osama bin Laden's front organizations. Not because they meant to give millions to terrorists, but because the likelihood of that happening increases the further away government gets from the volunteer fire department level.

Big government failed all over the world in the run-up to September 11th: the suicide bombers and their support networks lived openly in the US, Canada, Britain and Western Europe, crossing and re-crossing borders, flying back and forth, waved through each and every time despite invalid visas, outstanding warrants and behavior so suspicious they might as well have had "TERRORIST" blaring in neon from their heads. But let's be as generous as the Bush Administration apparently is, let's wipe the slate, and judge these agencies strictly by what they've done since 9/11: The FBI is in some snotty turf war with the NYPD. At the FAA, Jane Garvey is refusing to support the pilots' demand to be allowed to carry guns but does support driving what's left of commercial air travel further into the ground by forcing passengers to arrive two hours beforehand so their jewelry and "Bob The Builders" toys can be confiscated. And at the INS their first reaction to September 11th was to write to Deena Gilbey.

Who's Deena Gilbey? She's one of several hundred foreigners widowed by the events of 9/11. Her husband Paul was a trader with Euro Bank who worked on the 84th floor at the World Trade Center. Mr Gilbey was British and had been admitted to the US on a long-term work visa that allowed his family to live here but not to work. The Gilbeys bought a house in Chatham Township and had two children, born in New Jersey and thus US citizens. All perfectly legal and valid. A few days after September 11th, Mrs Gilbey received a form letter from the INS informing her that, upon her husband's death, his visa had expired and with it her right to remain in the country. She was now, they informed her, an illegal alien.

Well, as on September 11th, the local guys came through. The Chatham Police Chief was outraged and took up her case, and eventually it came to the attention of the President and in late October he signed special legislation for the hundreds in Mrs Gilbey's position. But what the big government boosters need to address is the peculiar mentality of a swollen bureaucracy whose first priority on the morning of September 12th is to traumatize further the law-abiding widows and children: that's an "intelligence failure" even more profound than the CIA's. The INS blithely admitted to the country Mohammed Atta with an invalid visa for the purpose of his stay. Given that he went on to murder Mrs Gilbey's husband, the INS harassment is at the very least in the most appalling taste.

But big government will do that to you. I'm Canadian and I have a romantic fondness for the famous motto of the Royal Canadian Mounted Police, the one about the Mounties always getting their man. But the bigger you make the government, the more you entrust to it, the more powers you give it to nose around the citizenry's bank accounts, and phone calls, and e-mails, and favorite Internet porn sites, the more you'll enfeeble it with the siren song of the soft target. The Mounties will no longer get their man, they'll get you instead. Frankly, it's a lot easier. And so the INS failed to get Mohammed Atta, but they did get Deena Gilbey. Congratulations, guys.

That's why Dick Cheney's "big shift" is in precisely the wrong direction. What should have died on September 11th is the liberal myth that you can regulate the world to your will. The reduction of a free-born citizenry to neutered sheep upon arrival at the airport was the most advanced expression of this delusion. So how's the FAA reacting to September 11th? With more of the same kind of obtrusive, bullying, useless regulations that give you the comforting illusion that if they're regulating you they must be regulating all the bad guys as well. We don't need big government, we need lean government – government that's stripped of its distractions and forced to concentrate on the essentials. If Hillary and Co want to argue for big government, conservatives could at least make the case for what's really needed - grown-up government.

THANKSGIVING

November 24th 2001
The Daily Telegraph

THANKSGIVING in America, and this year my neighbours have much to be thankful for.

We can be thankful that this month, for the first time, the UN has met its monthly target for getting sufficient supplies into Afghanistan to feed its starving people. It turns out the quickest way to end the humanitarian crisis in Afghanistan is to remove its idiot government. Conversely, the best way to keep people starving is to cook up new wheezes to maintain the thugs in power, as Christian Aid tried to do when it demanded a humanitarian "bombing pause" for Ramadan.

I am thankful that Mohamed Atef, a key al-Qa'eda lieutenant blown up in a devastating US raid, has gone off to Paradise to claim his 72 virgins. Paradise must be running quite low on virgins these days. I hope Mr Atef pulled rank on all the other martyrs. It would be a pity if virgin-wise he wound up having to make do with some of the chunkier American models. Perhaps *The Guardian*, Christian Aid et al could denounce US aggression for causing a massive humanitarian crisis in virgin shortages. Incidentally, while Muslims and Europeans mock the US for being soft, decadent, crass, materialist, etc, you notice it's not the Americans who frame the unseen world in terms of earthly pleasures. If my local Baptist Church told us that Christian martyrs would be welcomed into Heaven with premium cable service and get their fries supersized for free, I think I'd be a bit suspicious.

I am also thankful I don't live in a cave. That the son of a successful Saudi building contractor, made spectacularly rich by western investment, should have wound up digging himself his own personal hole is in its way a poignant emblem of the Middle East's perverse misunderstanding of modernity. Since the Taleban's collapse, the gloomy gussies at CNN and elsewhere have been touting Osama as a kind of troglodyte Trump with a canny eye for underdeveloped mountains. They point out he moved in a lot of his dad's heavy equipment (Osama himself is famously light in the equipment department) back in the Eighties and extensively renovated the caves.

CNN has had a lot of fancy computer-generated models made up so that the camera can swoop in and take you on a cyber-tour through the various levels and labyrinths until finally you wind up down in the luxurious mastercave with en suite latrine. It's like the penthouse in Trump Tower, but without any of those pesky views. It's Rockefeller Center, but upside down. There is a strange symmetry about the man who demolished the World Trade Center meeting his own end at Sub-Basement Level 14 of his personal inverted skyscraper. As Cagney almost said, "Made it, Ma! Bottom of the world!"

And how about Osama's nuclear plans? The ones downloaded from a How-to-build-your-own-bomb spoof. I am thankful for the Internet, which is suckering al-Qa'eda on a regular basis. Ask those Pakistani shopkeepers how many unsold posters of Osama and Bert the Muppet they've got clogging up the back room.

I am thankful I'm not anti-American, which is utterly self-corroding. As evidence of the growing alienation of Muslims, *The New York Times* reported this touching vignette: "Eight years ago, the al-Munaif family slaughtered sheep in tribute to one President Bush, as that leader was hailed as the liberator of Kuwait." But last year the al-Munaifs chose to give their newborn son "a name meant to send a very different signal to the west. The little boy is Osama." On NBC, there was a spirited discussion about how to address this "ingratitude", with much talk from the expert Arabists of the problems of the Kuwaiti media, the need for democratic reform… But no-one made the observation Joe Sixpack would have – that there's no point worrying which way a guy who sacrifices sheep will jump. I'm sure the Duke of Edinburgh is pleasantly flattered by those Cargo Culters in the Pacific who worship him as a god. But, if they suddenly switched to Princess Michael of Kent, he wouldn't start holding strategy sessions on how to win them back. The point about Muslim "hatred" of America is that it's a problem for Muslims, not Americans.

Finally, I am thankful for Turkey – not the plump gobblers roaming wild across my land but the Muslim nation, which for all its imperfections and unlike almost all its former provinces, has made the transition to a modern, secular state. Turkey has dispatched special forces to Afghanistan and sees itself as a bulwark against Islamic fundamentalism in Turkic-speaking Central Asia. Hey, Euro-whiners, if you're so keen on Islamic outreach, when are you letting Turkey into the EU?

OMAR'S GIRLS

November 29th 2001
The National Post

ALL OF THE west's flabby intellectual elites have had problems with September 11th, but it's the professional feminists who are really feeling the squeeze (if they'll pardon the expression). They started confidently enough. In the stirring clarion call of Professor Sunera Thobani of the University of British Columbia (your tax dollars at work!), speaking at a feminist conference two weeks after the attack, "There will be no emancipation for women anywhere on this planet until the western domination of this planet is ended."

Meanwhile, the Worldwide Sisterhood Against Terrorism And War, which includes Susan Sarandon, Gloria Steinem, Alice Walker and about 75 other sisters and is "Worldwide" mainly in the sense the World Series is, organized a petition called "Not In Our Name". "We will not support the bombing," they declared, and who can blame them? I dropped out of women's studies in Grade Two, but, as I recall, a bombing campaign is a quintessential act of patriarchal oppression and sexual domination. The male pilot, looming over the curvy undulating form of the Third World hillside, unzips his bomb carriage and unleashes his phallic ordinance to penetrate his target. Needless to say, he explodes on contact, typical bloody men.

Unfortunately, this thesis, while it may get you a Federal grant from Hedy Fry, took a bit of a knock after the fall of Kabul, when to the surprise of the Worldwide Sisterhood the Afghan sisters began emerging from their hoods. Momentarily stunned, the feminists nimbly discovered a whole new set of grievances. Oh, sure, Bush is making a big deal about women's rights in Afghanistan now, but where was he five years ago when the Taliban first showed up? Well, five years ago, he was in Austin, Texas, and the guy with his feet under the desk in the White House never did a thing - though, if ever there was a fellow with a vested interest in ensuring that impenetrable facial hoods for ladies never caught on, it was surely Mr Clinton.

But now the Taliban's gone and, of all the various factions negotiating a broad-based government, only the original patriarch – the old king – has plans to include any broads. Washington, said

Gloria Steinem, was colluding in "gender apartheid". Well, yes, it's regrettable that there appear to be no Pashtun Janet Renos on the horizon in Kabul, and the Jalalabad Playhouse has yet to book *The Vagina Monologues*, and that Take Your Daughter To Work Day has not been written into the Constitution. But, on the other hand, Don't Take Your Daughter To School Year is now off the calendar; Afghan females will be able to be educated, get jobs, receive proper medical treatment, walk unaccompanied in public, show their faces and dress as they wish.

It was this last point that the more inventive feminists seized on. As *The Boston Globe* put it, "The war on terrorism has certainly raised our awareness of the ways in which women's bodies are controlled by a repressive regime in a far away land, but what about the constraints on women's bodies here at home?" This was in a column entitled "The Burka And The Bikini" by Jacquelyn Jackson, a "women's health advocate", and Joan Jacobs Brumberg, a historian at Cornell University and author of *The Body Project: An Intimate History Of American Girls*. "Taliban rule has dictated that women be fully covered whenever they enter the public realm, while a recent US television commercial for 'Temptation Island 2' features near naked women," they pointed out. "American girls and women have been stripped bare by a sexually expressive culture whose beauty dictates have exerted a major toll on their physical and emotional health."

Got that? Afghan men make their women cover up, western men make their women strip off.

But, according to the Montreal *Gazette*, quite the opposite is true: Afghan men make their women cover up – *and so do we!* "The burqa has many forms," writes Linda Gilman Novak. "North American females are urged to wear burqas of a different sort. Their appearance is subtle and sophisticated and not as easy to identify." I'll say.

Still, Ms Gilman Novak does her best. She has noticed that various advertisements for Say What? Sweaters, Cover Girl mascara, Bonnebell makeup and Esprit clothing show models with turtlenecks pulled up to cover their mouths and copy lines like, "I let my eyes do the talking."

"This is the sporty, outerwear version of the burqa," writes Ms Gilman Novak. "Young girls learn from these images what society expects of them when they mature, and the message that rings loud and clear is that to speak out is not 'ladylike'. Girls grow up conditioned to be silent. Advertising tyrannizes women in our culture. It is the Taliban of North American society."

To be honest, the only reason I stumbled across the column was because of the come-hither eyes of the Esprit model, which the *Gazette*'s editors placed slap in the centre of the comment page. Ms Gilman Novak wouldn't be impressed to learn that, long before *Say What?* Sweaters came along, people were letting their eyes do the talking. The gateway to the soul, and so forth:

> *Some enchanted evening*
> *You may see a stranger*
> *You may see a stranger across a crowded room*
> *And somehow you know...*

True, you may make your way across the crowded room and find yourself trapped in a corner listening to a stranger hector you on the iniquities of Madison Avenue for the rest of the evening while you wonder if it would be bad form to playfully roll up her turtleneck and whirl her out on the dancefloor. But that's the way it goes. The first glance, the eye contact, symbolizing a world of possibilities. I looked at that Esprit ad and saw in those eyes not oppression but the supreme confidence of the modern western woman.

Who's right? The *Boston Globe* gals or the Montreal *Gazette*'s? Are we western Taliban making women strip off or cover up? Well, the answer is: Both. Neither. Who cares?

The point the Misses have missed is that the burqa was not a "cultural confine", but the law: if you went for a stroll in Kabul wearing a turtleneck, you'd be arrested. And even "cultural confines" are mostly confined to non-western cultures – for example, to those Muslim societies where it's the "cultural tradition" for men whose sisters get raped to kill them. In 2001, North American women face no "cultural confines". If relentless messages about "body image" are tyrannizing American women into bulimia, how come it's the fattest society in human history? Go to a suburban Multiplex any night of the week and you can watch Julia Roberts or Gwyneth Paltrow surrounded by an audience whose distaff side weighs an average 250 lbs and is happily chowing down on supersized extra-buttery popcorn. Whatever oppressive messages about "body image" are being transmitted, these gals are cheerfully ignoring; they long ago burst any "cultural

110

confines". Men, on the whole, don't go for the Kate Moss type but would prefer something a little under 300 lbs, but it's perfectly obvious that their views on the matter are utterly irrelevant. If you stroll around downtown Washington, you can't help noticing that, in contrast to the heels and cleavage of Paris and Rome and almost every other western capital, there's nothing but a vast tide of women in sneakers and comfortable, shapeless clothing.

This is their right as free citizens. But, when feminists yak on about "cultural confines", they're denying the very essence of liberty – that each of us is free to choose and therefore responsible for his or her actions. To equate the turtleneck with the Taliban requires a failure of the imagination bordering on the psychotic: imagine never being allowed to feel sunlight on your face – by *law*.

Most women understand this. The traditional "gender gap" in wars - women are usually between 10 and 15% behind men in their approval of military action – has statistically all but vanished: 86% of American men back the Afghan campaign, 79% of women. So the more interesting question is why there's such a huge gap between the overwhelming majority of women and the feminists who claim to represent them. *Pace* Professor Thobani, the west does not dominate the world because it "exploits" people, but because it emancipates them – it untaps its greatest resource, its citizens, and invites them to exploit their own potential. Some will rise to high office (Condi Rice), some will make a nice living cranking out ridiculous theses for a lucrative niche market (Joan Jacobs Brumberg). But, if you want one phrase that encapsulates the difference between the society we live in and the ones our enemies wish to impose, it's this: the treatment of women. The gal in the street gets it. A pity the stars of the sisterhood don't.

DECEMBER

Don't mention the jihad

December 1st 2001
The Spectator

ARE YOU A WESTERN leader of the Judaeo-Christian or Agnostic-Atheist persuasion? Want to issue a public statement on how much you respect and value Islam as a peaceful religion of moderation and tolerance? Take a number, pal. The line's longer than the waiting list at a Birmingham hospital. The Queen's spoken of her respect for "the Islamic community", so's the Pope, and Tony Blair. President Bush does it at least a couple of times a day. A week ago, he hosted the White House's first ever Ramadan dinner – not a banquet, that would have been insensitive, and the whole point of the Administration's "Ramadan public relations offensive" is, according to *The Washington Post*, to "highlight its sensitivity to Islamic tradition". At this difficult time, politicians are sensitive about being thought insensitive, so there's not point being too sensitive about how you advertise your sensitivity. In Canada, it can't be said that the Prime Minister, Jean Chrétien, has made anything in the way of a coherent statement on the subject, but he has visited a mosque, as he never ceases to remind folks. Ask him about border security or troop deployments or post-9/11 economic issues and he says, "I was proud to visit da mosques because dat to me is da Canadian value."

This is the most sensitive war in history. The President has urged Americans to be especially solicitous and protective of what he calls "women of cover". He has recommended that each American schoolchild get a Middle Eastern pen pal, though, with the current anthrax scare, I don't suppose the US Postal Service is especially eager for a lot of envelopes with childlike handwriting from Mullah al-Mahrah's Fourth Grade in Jeddah.

Should the US Government be in the business of Ramadan PR? The Republic is founded on the principle of separation of church and state, but, judging by the unnerving silence from the usually litigious American Civil Liberties Union, the separation of mosque and state is quite another matter. Last time round, FDR interned Japanese-Americans. Not only has Bush no plans to intern Muslim Americans, it wouldn't surprise me if he interned himself, just to "send the right message".

Do you find our language too insensitive? Fine. Let's make "Koran" "Quran", or better yet, "Qu'ran", or, if you prefer, "Qu'~*ran", whatever you want, the more the merrier, toss a couple of wingdings in there. In the Thirties, when Churchill was attacking the Munich Agreement, the sensitivity-check didn't automatically amend it to "München". But the other day, in the 24 hours between appearing in Britain's *Daily Telegraph* and Canada's *National Post*, Janet Daley's column had every single "Afghan" surgically removed somewhere over the Atlantic and replaced with "Afghani", including the pull-out quote. Janet is a ferocious American of robust views and anyone less likely to say "Afghani" is hard to imagine. Hitherto, Anglicisation of foreign place names has been an accepted custom, just as we accept that in Iraq America is spelt G-R-E-A-T-S-A-T-A-N. But, if appellatory sensitivity requires us to use the foreign version, let's do it right and rename Princess Patricia's Canadian Light Infantry the Infidel Dog's Lackeys of Zionism.

Our enemy, of course, has no name, or at least, as with Harry Potter's arch-enemy Voldemort, no name one can safely mention. Bush gets much mocked by progressive opinion for persistently referring to our opponents as "the evildoers", but if he used anything more precise they'd be the first to complain. We're at war with …Afghanistan? Heaven forfend! Militant Islam? Whoa, there's that word again. The Taleban? Well, hold on, Colin Powell wants "moderate Taleban elements" to be part of a "broad-based government". If Powell calls on "moderate evildoers" to be included in any new government, Bush's Enemy Nomenclature Team will really have its work cut out.

Meanwhile, our airports have been told to look out for …evildoers. How will we know who they are? When they do something evil, like running up an escalator to retrieve a forgotten Palm, as one poor boob did in Atlanta last week, causing a four-hour evacuation of the airport and the grounding of half the planes on the continent. The guy didn't fit the profile of the suicide bombers, but neither does your 88-year old granny and that's why we're emptying out her underwear on the conveyor belt. Under our new high-alert procedures, security personnel demonstrate their sensitivity by looking for people who don't look anything like the people they're looking for. Never in the field of human conflict have so many been so inconvenienced to avoid offending so few.

And, as always, the Tolerance Police are very intolerant of insufficient tolerance. As *The Toronto Star*'s wearily damning headline put it, "Harris Finally Listens To Muslims". Mr Harris is the Premier of Ontario, but unfortunately for him a Conservative one. "Forty-three days after the events of Sept. 11," began Ian Urquhart, "Premier Mike Harris finally sat down last week with leaders of the Muslim community to provide them with reassurance that the provincial government does not see them as the enemy." Ah, that's lovely, and such a useful formulation: "President Bush finally sat down with leaders of the feminist movement to provide them with reassurance that the Federal Government has no plans to rape and torture them."

Did some errant provincial government clerk at Queen's Park accidentally issue a declaration of war on Muslims? Apparently not. But the 20 community leaders present were concerned that the Premier had yet to visit a mosque to "show solidarity", as Bush, Blair, the Prince of Wales and a gazillion others have done. Ontario's Citizenship Minister, Cam Jackson, had gone to one, but this was felt to be a bit of an insult, like the Queen sending Princess Michael to open the Commonwealth Games. Maybe Harris didn't go because he didn't want to be sitting on the Queen Elizabeth Way backed up in mosque photo-op drivetime. Or maybe he was just busy with other stuff – meeting with Governor Pataki in New York, dealing with trade and security issues, governing, etc. Either way, the Muslim spokespersons didn't care for it. Concerned about public ignorance of Islam, they called for a world religions course to be made part of the core curriculum in Ontario schools. That's not a bad idea. An even better idea would be a world religions course in Saudi schools. I'll pay the airfare of any Ontario Muslim leader who manages to get an appointment with whichever layabout prince heads up the Saudi education department.

For its part, the American Muslim Council, which has yet to find time to condemn al-Qa'eda, has launched an attack on the insensitive US Postal Service. On September 1st, the Post Office released its "Eid stamp", commemorating the Islamic festivals of Eid al-

Fitr and Eid al-Adha. Sadly, after September 11th, it seems that an exotic blue stamp covered in gold Arabic calligraphy wasn't what most postal customers were looking for. Sales were unimpressive, at least in comparison to stamps of Old Glory, the American eagle, etc. But the AMC claims the Postal Service has been deliberately failing to promote the stamp, an accusation that prompted the Postmaster General to recall 75,000 advertising posters and replace them with ones displaying the Eid commemorative. The Post Office is "proud to feature the Eid stamp," he said, "in recognition of the many outstanding contributions of the Muslim community here in the United States and throughout the world." But Aly Abuzaakouk, director of the AMC, remains pessimistic. September 11th, he told *The Kansas City Star*, "has become a catastrophe for the stamps, too."

British Muslim bigwigs went the North Americans one better, and came up with an ingenious wheeze. The Islamic Society of Britain drafted a "Pledge To British Muslims" and then demanded that prominent political, religious and media figures sign it. Tony Blair did, thereby giving everyone else the choice between opting for an easy life and signing, or refusing and getting pilloried as a racist. After all, it's only a pledge to be "tolerant", and what could be more unobjectionable than that? One simple signature and all the accusations of insensitivity and racism will go away. The impeccably tolerant Islamic Society of Britain, just for the record, has denounced the Israeli Government as "inhuman savages and murderers".

But a "Pledge Of Tolerance" would sound pretty lame to the President, who seems to have signed his own personal "Pledge Of Tolerance Of Intolerance". No matter how wacky a Muslim "community leader" is, he'll be entitled to a meet-and-greet with Dubya. "Islam is peace," declared Mr Bush at the Islamic Center of Washington, surrounded by representatives of the Council on American-Islamic Relations and the American Muslim Alliance. CAIR has objected, on the grounds of "ethnic and religious stereotyping", to the prosecution of two men in Chicago for the "honour killing" of their female cousin, and sponsored a rally in Brooklyn at which an Egyptian cleric led the crowd in a rousing singalong of a number whose chorus goes, "No to the Jews, descendants of the apes." The AMA, on the other hand, distributes Holocaust-denying literature. When this was brought to the attention of White House press secretary Ari Fleischer, he said, "You should never assume that when the President meets with a group for important reasons of meeting with a group that he would ever agree with anything anybody in that group has said." And he has a point, sort of: Mr Bush meets with these groups for important reasons of meeting with groups.

True to the Bush spirit, London's *Sunday Times* managed to come up with an even better headline than *The Toronto Star*'s: "Muslims In Britain Come Under Attack". If you read on, you discovered that oddly enough the only verifiable attacks mentioned were the attempted burning of an Anglican church by a masked Muslim gang in Bradford and a rampage through Leeds by Muslim youths. At the former, though the discreet reporters forbore to mention it, the Reverend Tony Tooby was pelted with stones by men who shouted, "Get the white bastard!"; a Brownie troop of small girls was threatened; and its leader, Lucy-Jane Marshall, was stoned and jeered at as a "Christian bitch". At the latter incident, a mob vandalised cars, yelling "Get out of Afghanistan!" and forcing drivers to repeat, "Osama bin Laden rules!"

Nonetheless, we sensitive media types understand that the main significance of these events is that they could provoke a "backlash", no matter how theoretical. Hence, "Muslims In Britain Come Under Attack". To be fair, although no Muslims have been physically attacked as the Christian bitches and white bastards were, there was one reference right at the end of the *Sunday Times* piece to ten pigs' heads being left in the car park of an Islamic centre.

Not all battle conditions are as favourable as Brownie night in an English churchyard. After September 11th, several British Muslims decided to sign up, with the Taleban. Some, alas, happened to be standing under the B52 at the wrong time and will not be returning. But those who've survived and escaped the especial wrath the liberated Afghans reserve for foreign Taleban have announced that they're coming back and don't want any "hassle" from the authorities. By "hassle", they mean prosecutions for terrorism, treason and so forth. London's Mayor Ken Livingstone agrees. "These people went off because of a deep sense of injustice," he says. So we should understand their need to join a foreign army and wage war against their own (nominal) compatriots.

We madmen on the right dislike this identity-politics business. So I accept there are all kinds of Muslims. In Luton, whence came many of the Taleban's British volunteers, the mainstream moderate

Muslims, angry that a few extremists were getting the community as a whole a bum rap, beat up the principal local jihad-inciter. As *The Wall Street Journal*'s James Taranto commented, "Extremism in the pursuit of moderation is no vice." Doubtless the same differences of opinion exist among Muslims in Chicago, Boston and Saskatoon.

But the fact – the *fact* – is that, since September 11th, the remarks by the Queen, the Pope, the President and almost every other pasty face have earned no similarly warm, unqualified response from Muslim "community leaders". In *The Ottawa Citizen*'s coast-to-coast survey of imams, all but two refused to accept that Osama bin Laden was responsible for September 11th, even though he himself has said he did it. Imam Yahia Fadlalla of the Hamilton mosque is convinced neither bin Laden nor any other Muslims were involved. Every single imam was opposed to the US bombing campaign against the Taleban. (In that, they differ sharply from their happily liberated coreligionists in Afghanistan.) In Washington, the best the Administration could turn up for the multi-faith service at the National Cathedral was Dr Muzammil Siddiqi, of the Islamic Society of North America, who told the President and the nation that "those that lay the plots of evil, for them is a terrible penalty". Does that mean Osama's gonna get it? Or that the Yanks were asking for it? Hey, let's not get hung up on specifics. In Bush's Islamic home guard, it's strictly don't ask, don't tell.

In his splendid address to the United Nations, Bush told the world that expressions of sympathy weren't enough; it was time for other countries to get on side. Yet, back home, he's happy to hold photo-ops with fellow Americans you can't squeeze anything but the vaguest expression of sympathy out of. He schedules visits with groups that are either covertly hostile, deeply ambivalent, or deafeningly silent. This unreciprocated abasement is unworthy, and merely a fluffier variant of the west's cult of self-denigration that reached its peak in Durban a week before September 11th. Islam wouldn't be the fastest-growing religion in the US, Britain, France and Canada if Muslims were thought to be "the enemy". Conversely, Christianity is the fastest-shrinking religion in the Sudan, where they really are thought to be the enemy. In Pakistan the other week, six children and nine adults were gunned down as they worshipped in a Christian church.

Had some "Christian fundamentalists" slaughtered thousands of civilians in the name of their faith, I doubt whether Bush and Blair would be worrying whether they'd swung by enough Methodist chapels and Baptist vestries. And the airwaves would be clogged with Cardinals and Archbishops denouncing the perpetrators by name and deed. If the west's Muslim "community leaders", for whatever reason, are reluctant to speak truth to evil, that is a matter between them and God. Their opposition to the war is their right as free citizens. So is their belief that the Holocaust never happened and that honour killings are a valuable cultural tradition. I don't even care particularly about prosecuting the Taleban's Anglo-American volunteers: to hell with them. All I ask is an end to the deeply unedifying spectacle of western politicians jumping through increasingly obnoxious tolerance hoops. Bush, after all, doesn't waste time fawning on any other anti-war constituency. What was remarkable after September 11th was that 99.99% of the American population displayed no animus whatsoever toward Muslims. What's even more remarkable is that they've put up with weeks of being lectured not to surrender to their natural racist urge to pogroms, and two months of preposterous fetishisation of a sub-group of American citizens that's chosen for the most part to sit this war out. One-sided outreach is demeaning. It suggests we have something to feel guilty about. We don't.

THE NEXT QUAGMIRE

December 1st 2002
The Daily Telegraph

I KNOW EVERYONE'S moaning about Microsoft's new Windows XP, but apparently it has one absolutely marvellous new programme for us pundits. With Quagmire '75 (the year the software was written), you simply press a button and your redundant doom-mongering column on the Taleban – bombing never works, merely unites the civilian population against us, etc - is instantly updated to the next unassailable fortress.

Take Chris Matthews, who appears in the New York *Daily News* and also hosts TV's "Hardball". A month ago, Chris was full of dire warnings about Afghanistan. This week, he had, as Bill Clinton likes to say, moved on:

"To attack Iraq now would forfeit all that the American President has won since Sept. 11: the backing of the United Nations... the support of the Arab League... and a 90% job-approval rating from the American people.

"It would be nothing like the recent successes in Afghanistan.

"To topple Saddam would take a half-million to a million U.S. troops. It would require an occupying force capable of policing a civilian population that would be embittered by a brutal bombing campaign..."

Fantastic stuff, eh? I'll bet Chris is already in the Virgin Islands sipping his margarita, secure in the knowledge that Quagmire '75 will simply insert new quagmires as necessary: "To attack [Iran/North Korea/Wales] now would forfeit the support of the [Arab League/EU/Milton-under-Wychwood Women's Institute]... To topple [Assad/Voldemort/the Queen Mother] would take two to four million [US troops/broomsticks/souvenir mugs]..."

A war with Iraq, says Chris, will put an end to America's national unity. Hmm. This week a *Washington Post*/ABC poll asked, "Would you favour or oppose having U.S. forces take military action against Iraq to force Saddam Hussein from power?" 78% said they were in favour. That's not because they're rallying round the President. The President has barely said a word about Iraq, for fear of distressing Colin Powell. But it doesn't look as if daisycutters over Basra are going to be denting his numbers.

As for "the support of the Arab League", that's one of those exotic shimmering mirages that fades to nothing when you try to drink from its limpid pool and wind up with a mouthful of camel dung.

Besides, it's an open question how many actual Arabs the Arab League speaks for. On the supposedly seething "Muslim street", bin Laden T-shirts are gathering dust on the discount racks. When Baghdad's day of liberation comes, the civilian population will be too busy dancing in the street to be "embittered".

I see that back in the summer I mentioned Saddam's musical, *Zabibah And The King*, currently playing at the Iraqi National Theatre. It was supposed to be Baghdad's answer to *Cats*. My advice is see it before New Year, even if you have to make do with a couple of restricted-view seats in the upper balcony. If they haven't hung up the "Limited Season Only" sign yet, they ought to.

MEANWHILE, BACK ON THE WEST BANK...

December 6th 2001
The National Post

O N NBC'S "Meet The Press" last Sunday, Donald Rumsfeld was asked if he thought Yasser Arafat was a terrorist. "It's not for me to characterize him," said the Defence Secretary circumspectly, "but if one looks historically, he has been involved in terrorist activities."

That "Chairman" Arafat *was* a terrorist is not in doubt. The more important question is whether he's capable of being anything else. And the answer to that, too, is not in doubt.

Under the terms of the Oslo "peace process", he has been a head of government – not of a sovereign state, but of an embryo state. The "Palestinian Authority" is not a viable entity in and of itself, being merely selective areas of Israel's "occupied territories", but within it "the Palestinians" had, give or take, the same degree of autonomy that the Province of Quebec does today or the Irish Free State did in 1922. Arafat had an opportunity to demonstrate he was capable of governing – in matters of law and order, health, education, the economy. Had he done so, the movement toward a fully-fledged Palestinian state would have been unstoppable. He didn't have to be perfect. The expectations in the reformed-terrorist category are not high – Jomo Kenyatta, Robert Mugabe – but Arafat has failed to make even this minimal grade. His Palestinian Authority is a swamp of corruption and organized crime presided over by trigger-happy goon squads from the Chairman's dozen competing state security agencies. If you gave this guy Switzerland to run, he'd turn it into a sewer.

At one level, this is a crisis for Israel: as George Will noted in yesterday's *National Post*, more of their citizens have died from terrorism in the eight years of the "peace process" than in the 45 years before. But, in a more profound sense, Arafatism is a crisis for the Palestinians: if their cause remains mortgaged to the Chairman, their prospects of any kind of viable future are precisely zero. The Palestinians' problem is not Israel: last year at Camp David, Ehud Barak offered Arafat over 90% of the West Bank and the Gaza Strip and part of Jerusalem. Nor is the Palestinians' problem Washington: President Bush has come out in favour of a Palestinian state. Rather, the Palestinians' problem is Yasser Arafat, his stunted lieutenants, their dark subsidiaries and the impulses of a substantial percentage of the population. Invited to choose between building a country or killing Jews, they choose Jew-killing. Every time.

That's why last weekend's carnage usefully clarified the situation. Once upon a time, professional Arab armies were prepared to fight for Palestine. Unfortunately, they kept losing. (Not to be mean-spirited but Arab armies are among the lousiest in the world, at least since King Hussein sacked General Sir John Glubb in the Fifties.) So they contracted the job out to the PLO who in the Seventies waged a campaign of vicious but targeted terrorism. Then came the Eighties and the intifada, in which the new front-line warriors were rock-throwing nine-year olds. And now it's down to suicide bombers detonating themselves in shopping malls for the glory of killing kids and pregnant women – the final stage of Palestinian nationalism's descent into nihilism. What other once credible liberation movement has so willingly embraced such awesome, total self-degradation?

Arafat has been successful only in one particular: landing Israel with the blame for the situation and persuading the Arabist romantics in the west to frame the debate entirely in his terms. I see even Anton La Guardia in Monday's *National Post* wrote that "the Palestinians are a stateless people". In fact, there is a Palestinian state: it's called Jordan, whose population has always been majority Palestinian. It's not as big a state as it used to be, but that's because King Hussein, in the worst miscalculation of his long bravura highwire act, made the mistake of joining Nasser's 1967 war to destroy Israel. Hence, the "occupied territories": they're occupied because the Arabs attacked Israel and lost. And, unlike, say, Alsace-Lorraine or Hong Kong, Israel uniquely is prevented from returning the occupied territories to the guys they occupied 'em from. The West Bank cannot be given back to Jordan, because in 1974 the Arab League declared Arafat's PLO to be the "sole legitimate representative of the Palestinian people", an impressive claim for an organization only five years old.

The Arabs did this to punish King Hussein because they were steamed at him for sitting out their 1973 war against Israel. That's a perfectly good reason from their point of view, but what's amazing is that they've talked the entire world to accept their little exercise in political muscle as the only valid position on the issue. There are no equivalent situations anywhere where the global community has instructed a country to hand over conquered territory not to the state from which it was won but to a third-party terrorist, and even trying to invent an analogy will drive you nuts: Imagine if Quebec attacked English Canada but lost and, as a result, English Canada occupied Montreal and was then instructed by the world that Montreal had to be handed over not to Quebec but to a second francophone state headed up by a, er, Haitian-born terrorist based in, um, Guadeloupe...

The Arab League didn't take its bizarre position because it cares a fig for the Palestinian people, or indeed for Arafat: until he landed in the Palestinian Authority, he'd spent his career being booted out of one Arab state and on to the next. The League chose to endow the PLO because the "Palestinian problem" is more useful to them than its resolution would ever be. Since the collapse of the Ottoman Empire, Arab leaders have tried and failed to promote a viable, sustained pan-Arabism. Today, the only tattered remnant of the pan-Arab cause is Palestinian nationalism, and very helpful it is, too. Why, only the other day a wealthy Saudi assisted by Egyptian lieutenants and Iraqi intelligence blew a hole in the middle of New York and the world rushed forward to insist that this proved the need for a Palestinian state. For the squalid thug regimes of the region, giving the impression to their hapless peoples that they're engaged in an epic struggle with the Jews helps excuse their own failures as nation states. It costs the Arab dictators very little in blood or treasure. They have no desire to lose any more wars against Israel, and most of their financial contribution has been in the longstanding arrangement by which "taxes" are deducted from the paycheques of Palestinian workers in the Gulf and wired direct to the PLO.

The League's 1974 coronation made Arafat, a pipsqueak militarily, into a political powerhouse. The UN began treating him as the leader of a sovereign nation, as if to underline his inevitability: he's already a head of state; all he needs is a state to be head of. And so in 1993 Israel consented to the creation of the Palestinian Authority. For Hamas and Islamic Jihad, this offered the prospect – since taken up with gusto – of being able to kill Jews *from within Israeli territory!* But for their protector Arafat it also offered an opportunity for a little bit of what the IRA calls "internal housekeeping": since moving into the PA from their most recent lodgings in Tunis, Arafat's boys have successfully cowed into silence or interrogated to death many of the less radical, more accommodating West Bank Palestinians who might have made the Authority a going concern. If there seem fewer alternatives to Arafat than there used to be, it's because a lot of them are six feet under.

Much of this activity has been funded by the west, which has given billions to something called PECDAR, the Palestinian Economic Council for Development And Reconstruction. Set up under the Oslo accords, PECDAR was supposed to be entirely independent of the Palestinian Authority. Instead, Arafat's gang have creamed off most of the dough either for their personal benefit or to shore up their police state. One of the biggest changes in the West Bank post-Oslo is that, even as ordinary Palestinians' economic prospects have withered, you see a lot more local officials riding around in Mercs. Meanwhile, the schools teach children about the heroics of the suicide-bombers and in geography class Israel has been literally wiped off the maps. Whether or not a second Palestinian state is desirable, it's perfectly obvious that this particular second Palestinian state is not in the least bit so, and after last weekend there's no reason for Israel to pretend otherwise.

Nor for America: in an interesting development, the US yesterday proposed Jordanian troops act as "international observers" in the West Bank. Symbolically, that would be the most serious challenge to Arafat's monopoly on the Palestinian cause in 27 years.

So the question that whatever's left of the respectable nationalist movement needs to ask itself is: do you want the rule of law, economic liberty, representative government, hospitals, schools and roads? Or do you want an abyss, in which the only consolation is that a few Jews will get sucked down to oblivion along with Palestinian aspirations? As we now know, that's all the Chairman can deliver.

I see *The New York Times* is warning the Israelis not to try getting rid of Arafat. They have a point. It's time the Palestinians got rid of him.

~

LET'S ROLL!

December 13th 2001
The National Post

WITHOUT doubt, the best Canadian response to the events of September 11th has been from Transport Minister David Collenette. Whoops, sorry, that's a typing error. I mean Neil Young – assuming, for the purposes of argument, the "Canadian rock legend" is still Canadian. It's hard to know these days. Jim Carrey's response to September 11th has been to apply for US citizenship. America, he says, "defined me". (It's not just Conrad, folks.)

Anyway, Neil's new song, "Let's Roll", takes its inspiration from the events on Flight 93, the one supposedly headed for the White House that Tuesday morning but whose passengers rose up and overpowered the Islamakazi hijackers. Flight 93 crashed in a Pennsylvania field, but its fallen heroes saved hundreds of lives, including perhaps the Vice-President's. Todd Beamer's last words, heard by a GTE operator to whom he'd been speaking, were, "Are you ready, guys? Let's roll!" Neil Young's dark, driving anthem begins with the sound of cellphones ringing. Then:

I know I said I love you
I know you know it's true
I got to put the phone down
And do what we gotta do

One's standing in the aisle way
Two more at the door
We got to get inside there
Before they kill some more

Time is runnin' out
Let's roll
Time is runnin' out
Let's roll...

Let's roll for freedom

Let's roll for love
Goin' after Satan
On the wings of a dove...

I'm not a big Neil Young fan. If I never heard the fey, dopey "Harvest Moon" or "Heart Of Gold" ever again, it wouldn't be too soon. But "Let's Roll" may well be my favourite CanCon number since …oh, let me see now …gosh, since Ruth Lowe of Toronto wrote "I'll Never Smile Again", a Number One hit for Sinatra and the Tommy Dorsey band in 1940. "I'll Never Smile Again" is really the other end of those "Let's Roll" cellphone calls: Miss Lowe had just been widowed and her ballad of love and loss caught the mood of Americans in that interlude between the start of World War Two and their own entry into it. Lisa Beamer would understand Ruth Lowe's song: for all her pride in Todd's heroism, honoured by Neil Young, President Bush and millions of his fellow citizens, it must be poor consolation for a lost husband and father.

With the benefit of hindsight, Flight 93 is the key event of September 11th. By all accounts, the hijackers of that plane weren't exactly the cream of Osama's diseased crop. The flight was halfway across the continent before the boobs made their move and started meandering back east to their target. By the time the passengers began calling home, their families were aware of what had happened at the World Trade Center. Unlike those on the earlier flights, the hostages on 93 knew they were a human missile intended to kill thousands of their fellow citizens. So they acted. As UPI's James Robbins wrote, "The Era of Osama lasted about an hour and half or so, from the time the first plane hit the tower to the moment the General Militia of Flight 93 reported for duty."

Exactly. No one will ever again hijack an American airliner with boxcutters, or, I'd wager, with anything else – not because of new but predictably idiotic FAA regulations, but because of the example of Todd Beamer and his ad hoc platoon. Faced with a novel and unprecedented form of terror, the latest American technology (cellphones) combined with the oldest American virtue (self-reliance) and stopped it in its tracks in just 90 minutes. The foiling of the hijackers of 93 began the transformation of Osama from a jihadi to a jihas-been. Sure, he might yet come up with something new, but invention and improvisation are the hallmarks of a dynamic culture not a fetid, stagnant one, like Islamofascism.

As for America being "soft" and "decadent", let Neil Young nail that one:

> *No one has the answers*
> *But one thing is true*
> *You got to turn on evil*
> *When it's comin' after you*
>
> *You got to face it down*
> *And when it tries to hide*
> *You got to go in after it*
> *And never be denied*
>
> *Time is runnin' out*
> *Let's roll...*

My goodness, sounds positively unCanadian, doesn't it? But here's a suggestion for the Prime Minister: Next time you're in the mood to give the Princess Pats a pep talk, instead of sending Mme Clarkson (Delete Queen and country, you're fighting for the diverse tolerance of our tolerant diversity), or Art Eggleton ("We're not going to send our people into a condition in which they're unwelcome"), instead of dusting off the old Shawinigan battle cry ("Once more not unto da breach, dear friends, dat be da Canadian value"), instead of all that stuff, why not read out the above lyric and listen to the roar of approval our troops would give you?

Ah, but September 11th demanded moral clarity, and, the odd grizzled rocker aside, that's not the Canadian way. As the great Christie Blatchford put it the other week, "Canadians consistently mistake the sidelines for more honourable ground."

Three months after the war began, the contours of the new world are emerging: an American "hyperpower" (as David Warren noted yesterday) able to project itself anywhere it wants, militarily, economically, culturally; below it, a second tier, entirely vacant; a little further below, a cluster of medium powers – Britain, France, Germany, etc – united in an ersatz federation defined mainly by its somewhat snooty attitude to the rawer liberty of the American Republic; and way, way, way down at the bottom of the list the Arab dictatorships, utterly irrelevant.

The Americans who died on Flight 93 are a big part of the reason why the US is outpacing the rest of the west: Thomas Burnett, Jeremy Glick, Todd Beamer and others were tech execs, working in the most innovative, vital sector of the economy. We shouldn't be surprised to find that their entrepreneurial spirit extends to the battlefield as well.

Where Canada fits in is somewhat problematic: it's a natural EU member beached on the wrong continent. Perhaps they'd take us anyway; who knows? We can get away with sitting out the war, and avoiding the moral clarity of Neil Young. But as a nation adrift we can't avoid the same choice that confronted the brave passengers of 93: can we act, or are we content to be, in David Warren's words, "spectators in our own fate"?

> *No time for indecision*
> *We got to make a move...*
>
> *Time is runnin' out...*

Let's find a role.

~

VIDEOSAMA

December 15th 2001
The Daily Telegraph

The Daily Telegraph *is pleased to present a worldwide panel of experts with the latest in-depth analysis of the new Osama bin Laden tape:*

MUHAMMAD AL-GAMEI'A, *A-list imam, live from Cairo:*

We know very well that Mossad are behind this video. Only the Jews are capable of pulling off a stunt like this. The brilliant audio quality. The lighting. The professional camera work. Our Muslim camcorders won't have that kind of technological capability for another 200 years.

JOHN PILGER, *veteran war correspondent, live in studio:*

Thanks, Mark. Great to be here. To help me identify the guys behind this tape, please welcome the guys behind me! My good friends, the Guardian Tabernacle Choir, accompanied by the New Statesman Sympathy Orchestra, with George Monbiot on snare drum. We'd like to do a medley of the only song in our act. So take it away, professor (that's Noam Chomsky):

> *You got to ac-cen-tchu-ate the negative*
> *E-lim-i-nate the positive*
> *Latch on to all the paranoid*
> *Don't mess with Mister In Between*

> *You got to ask yourself who has the most to gain*
> *Ask yourself who's the least to gain*
> *Figure out just who benefits*
> *It's always the US war machine*

> > *To illustrate*
> > *The stuff we check*
> > *Mention Vietnam*
> > *Bring up Mossadeq*
> > *That's what we do*
> > *Just when ev'rything looks a wreck*
> *Man, we say you gotta*

> *Ac-cen-tchu-ate the negative*
> *E-lim-i-nate the positive*
> *Latch on to all the paranoid*
> *Don't mess with Mister In Between!*

One hundred mo' times!

ROBERT FISK, *foreign correspondent,* The Independent, *hanging upside down in Madam Fatima's Discipline Parlour, Beirut:*

I was struck, quite literally – *ow!* – by the very unIslamic tone of the purported confession. That cowboy imagery about "a strong horse and a weak horse" hit me immediately – *aaaaieeeee! Thanks* – as less Saudi sounding and more Texan. Also that obsession with death, dying, killing – it all seems entirely foreign to the life-affirming culture of militant Islamism I know so well and smacks more – *yarrooooo! a little lower, please* – of the Texas penal system. Furthermore, though they appear to say "Allah be praised" continually, if you rewind – *aaaaaaaaaaargh! that's too tight* – and turn it up, it's clear that they're really saying, "Al'll be Prez". It's obvious this is a year-old video of Dick Cheney, Jim Baker and George Bush Sr sitting around in false beards kicking around – *uuuuuurgh!* – ideas on how to steal the Presidency from Gore by simply shredding his dangling chads – *aaargheurgheooo!! No, no, please…*

YVONNE RIDLEY, *author of* Yvonne Ridley's Diary, *live from the Ivy:*

This is conclusive proof of the humanitarian crisis in Afghanistan caused by the bloody Yanks' useless bombing campaign. I mean, flamin' Nora, would you go to a bash at Osama's? No booze, no fags, no music, everyone sitting around on old beanbags boring on about their dreams. And no chance of a UN relief convoy getting through with the chilled Chardonnay and hors d'oeuvres before winter sets in. The dull bloke on the right? Oh, I got stuck next to him the first night in Kandahar, just my luck. I pull up on the donkey figuring I'll crash the party, no problem. So I say to him, "Where do I park my ass?" And he says, "In the extra-large burqa, infidel harlot." Bloody hilarious, I don't think.

MULLAH OMAR, *interior decorator, live from Tora Bora:*

This video is obviously faked by the CIA. As I learned from your filthy Jew tabloids, Osama has a very small penis. That's why he always undresses down the dark end of the cave.

That's why his ex-wife says in your *Daily Mirror* that he wants to blow up Big Ben and the Eiffel Tower. That's why he feels the need to keep penetrating deeper and deeper into the mountain. I know this stuff. We get Dr Ruth on Radio Peshawar. Yet the man on the video has a pronounced bulge in his robes. My best guess would be Tom Jones. Whoops, he's coming back. And it's my turn to sauté the scorpions.

SIMON WILSON, *Communications Director, the Tate Gallery, live from London:*

Well, it was a late entry but the Turner judges were particularly taken by Osama's almost playful approach to contemporary notions of slaughter and horror. Although he's previously worked with rubble, in his first home video the gleeful attitude to mass murder poses a profound challenge to fundamental societal attitudes about what's funny. Okay, I know you *Telegraph* types will say it's just ugly and destructive, but he's actually immensely spiritual when you talk to him about it. He's worked in construction, he's worked in deconstruction, he's edgy, dangerous, explosive, but rarely so in your face. I did ask him to come to London but he says he's holed up in a cave dodging daisycutters with a one-eyed mullah and a lame goatherd who gets a faraway look in his eyes every time the radio mentions the $25 million reward. I said, "Do I hear next year's installation, or what!" Then there was a big noise and the line went dead.

THE HOLIDAY SEASON

If it's Tuesday it must be Yemen

December 9th 2001
The Sunday Telegraph

A FORTNIGHT ago, two Americans met in the northern Afghan desert, at the Qala-I-Jangi prison. One was a CIA special-ops man, Mike Spann. The other was a prisoner he was interrogating, a Taleban soldier called "Abdul Hamid", the *nom de guerre* of John Walker, formerly of northern California. Mr Spann will be buried tomorrow by his wife and three young children in Arlington National Cemetery. He was kicked, beaten and apparently bitten to death in an uprising of captured Taleban, who then booby-trapped his body with grenades. Mr Walker, by contrast, is one of 86 people to survive the four-day prison battle, and the question now is what to do with him.

If nothing else, he's usefully nailed one of the self-serving myths peddled after the awesome intelligence failure of September 11th: awfully sorry we failed to see it coming, said the high-ranking suits, but it's impossible to do any covert deep-cover stuff out in Afghanistan; these fellows are all cousins and brothers-in-law - a guy from Jersey would stick out like a lap-dancer in a burqa.

As we now know, instead of being full of fearsome Pashtun warriors renowned down the centuries, the Omar/Osama ranks were like a novelty Gap ad, "Losers of Many Nations" – misfit Saudis and Pakis, Brits and Californians. Anyone can walk in off the street and be assistant supervisor of the third-floor latrine in Tora Bora by nightfall. The only distinguishing feature about John Walker is that he's such an obvious compendium of clapped-out clichés from America's Left Coast the wonder is the mullahs didn't automatically take him for a CIA plant.

But no, Mr Walker is for real - born John Lindh in 1981, and from that bastion of well-heeled pothead progressivism, California's affluent Marin County. Just north of San Francisco, Marin is the kind of place where Taleban are rare and Republicans are rarer, and your

131

average hippy-turned-lawyer can stay true to his Sixties values while living on property that stays true to its late Nineties values (average house price: just shy of a million bucks). This is the aging of the dawn of Aquarius: a lotta latte, a little dope, environmentalism, multiculturalism, and everyone likes feeling religious, or at least "spiritual" - old *New York Times* headline: "Religion Makes A Comeback (Belief To Follow)". Following the traditional Marin pattern, his parents divorced, his father moved in with another man, his mother converted to Buddhism, and the children were taught Native American spirituality. John was sent to an "alternative" high school. (In the Bay Area, all the high schools are "alternative". The problem for parents is trying to find any alternative to the alternative.) The set texts included *The Autobiography Of Malcom X*, and John liked it so much that like the late Mr X he too decided to embrace Islam and change his name, to Sulayman. His parents, putting their foot down for what seems to be the first and last time, demanded the right to continue calling him John. They had, after all, gone to the trouble of naming him after one of the colossi of the age, John Lennon. To this, he consented. In return, they let him study at the Mill Valley Islamic Center.

In 1998, after an awkward trip to their ancestral Ireland in which John trudged dutifully round the auld sod wearing his turban and white robes, Frank Lindh agreed to let his 17-year old son spend a year in Yemen, on the next stage of his "spiritual odyssey". He was just another middle-class kid who'd gone off to find himself, but, like most of the others, he always knew how to find daddy when he needed to. Last year, John e-mailed home to say al-Qa'eda's attack on the USS Cole was justified – oh, and by the way he was off to enrol in a Pakistani madrassah. So Dad wired him a couple thousand bucks, which goes a long way in Bannu. Aside from a glowing school report from his imam, that was the last Mr Lindh heard from Junior until he turned up brandishing an AK47 while battling US armed forces and declaring his approval of the events of September 11th.

John Walker's CV bears eloquent testament to his parents' scrupulous observance of the Bay Area's First Commandment: Thou shalt be non-judgmental. Yeah, man, Yemen. Cool. Whatever's your bag. As one headline put it: "A Product Of Bay Area Culture". Exactly, I thought. But, this being *The San Francisco Chronicle*, they were applying the label with pride. Rhapsodising about the area's "religious tolerance" and the way children are taught "to accept other cultures" and value "critical thinking about the US role in the world", senior writer Louis Freedberg concluded that Walker's only misfortune was that "his search for identity intersected precisely with the World Trade Center attacks". If not for this unfortunate "intersection" Walker might have become an "idealistic doctor". The President, he said, should allow the boy home "and let him get his life back on track. We'd want nothing less for our own children, who could easily have found themselves in a similar mess."

In fairness to the youth of northern California, that last part is an unjust slur. The marvel is that, after labouring under the twin burdens of the education system's multicultural orthodoxies and the preening moral superiority of their boomer parents, no more Bay Area teens have signed on with Mullah Omar. Nonetheless, there is a difference between "tolerance" of other cultures and the moral void inhabited by the Lindhs. We can, in any case, guess the limits of Marin County's much-vaunted "tolerance". Imagine that the Marinated Muslim had instead announced that he was going to do what the late Mike Spann did at his age: enlist in the Marines. Would Marilyn Walker have seen that as a valid part of her son's "self-discovery"? Or would she have got out her joss sticks and wailed, "Oh, my God, where did we go wrong?"

Mom says she's "proud" of John, but is taking the line he must have been "brainwashed". From the look of him, his brain's the only thing that's been washed. John Walker resembles one of those hairy, smelly, cadaverous, vaguely deranged guys who stumble up to you late at night at remote Greyhound stations and demand money for medication. But right now that's shrewd image-positioning. President Bush seems to have bought the "misguided" line, describing Walker as a "poor fellow" who thought he was fighting for a "great cause". "I can't see him as being unpatriotic," says a neighbour. "This is where his journey led him." And, anyway, as everyone says, he's just a "boy".

John Walker is a 20-year old *man* – though one can sympathise if protracted exposure to the Bay Area's "critical thinking" (if only) has left him in a state of arrested development. For four decades, supposedly "non-judgmental" flower-children like Marilyn Walker have reflexively characterised CIA men like Mike Spann as the dark agents of right-wing militarism. We are entitled to judge Marilyn's son, the comrade of Spann's killers, as the dark agent of left-wing Marinism. Raised by peaceniks and Marinated in "tolerance", he took up an AK47 in defence of misogynists and gay-bashers: not an internal contradiction, but the logical reductio of the new left's moral nullity. Cocooned in one of the most prosperous enclaves on the planet, he was taught everything – from Buddhism to Indian spirituality to Malcolm X – everything except what it means to be an American citizen.

When a 13-year old girl wants an abortion, the Marin County crowd insists that "a woman's right to choose" is sacred. Twenty-year old men make choices, too. John Walker chose to go to war against his own country. Americans should respect his "right to choose" and let him live with the consequences.

I'm not in favour of trying him for treason: Alan Dershowitz and the other high-rent lawyers are already salivating over the possibility of a two-year circus with attendant book deals and TV movies. But there is another way, suggested the other day by *The Toronto Sun*'s Peter Worthington. In 1944, lacking the benefits of an immersion in Bay Area "critical thinking", the teenage Worthington volunteered for the Royal Canadian Navy. Unlike Walker's apologists, he at least treats him as an adult exercising free will. As Mr Worthington notes, on page four of John Walker's US passport, it states that any American who enlists in a foreign army can be stripped of his citizenship. Mr Walker wants to be Abdul Hamid: Mr Bush should honour his wishes. Let us leave him to the Northern Alliance and let his fancypants 'Frisco lawyers petition to appear before the Kabul bar, if there is one. It would, surely, be grossly discriminatory to subject Mr Hamid to non-Islamic justice.

~

HATE-ME CRIMES

December 14th 2001
The Wall Street Journal

HAVING SUCCESSFULLY introduced the novel legal concept of the "hate crime", progressive opinion has now taken it to dizzying new heights: the hate-me crime. In a traditional hate crime, you beat someone up not just for his fake Rolex but because you hate him on the basis of his race, creed or color. With the new hate-me crime, you beat someone up because you hate him on the basis of his race, creed or color – and hey, that's cool, he's okay with that, feel free to take another swing.

So the other day Robert Fisk, of the British newspaper *The Independent*, was set upon by a gang of Afghans. Mr Fisk has had decades of experience in the Muslim world and is a widely-acknowledged expert on the subject – that's to say, since September 11th, he's got pretty much everything wrong. (Sample Fisk headlines: "Bush Is Walking Into A Trap", "It Could Become More Costly Than Vietnam", "How Can The US Bomb This Tragic People?", "There Is No Easy Way For The West To Sort This Out", "We Are The War Criminals Now".) You can understand why Mr Fisk has been in low spirits of late: the much-feared "Arab street" is as seething and turbulent as a leafy cul-de-sac in Westchester County on a weekday afternoon; and poor old Afghanistan's reputation as the humbler of empires has gone south since Mullah Omar contracted out homeland defense to a bunch of Saudi, Brit and Californian losers. What's with these wussies?

But last weekend the people finally roused themselves – and beat up Fisky! His car broke down just a stone's throw (as it turned out) from the Pakistani border and a crowd gathered. To the evident surprise of the man known to his readers as "the champion of the oppressed", the oppressed decided to take on the champ. They lunged for his wallet and his credit cards, and then began lobbing rocks. And, even as the rubble was bouncing off his skull, Mr Fisk was shrewd enough to look for the "root causes":

> *Young men broke my glasses, began smashing stones into my face and head. I couldn't see for the blood pouring down my forehead and swamping my eyes. And even then, I understood. I couldn't blame them for what they were doing. In fact, if I were the Afghan refugees of Kila Abdullah, close to the Afghan-Pakistan border, I would have done just the same to Robert Fisk. Or any other Westerner I could find.*

It's not their fault, he insisted, their "brutality is entirely the product of others" – i.e., Bush, Blair, Rumsfeld, you. I would have beaten me up if they hadn't got to me first! In a flash, the gloom of recent weeks lifted and Mr Fisk turned in the heady, exhilarating columnar equivalent of a Sally Field acceptance speech: you hate me, you really hate me!

You'd have to have a heart of stone not to weep with laughter. Even as a mob is trying to kill him, he absolves them of all responsibility: it's "entirely" America's fault. Noam Chomsky, eat your heart out. Any old Ivy League professor can give droning speeches about America's "silent genocide", any third-rate EU foreign minister can swan off to UN gabfests in Durban to apologize to Robert Mugabe for western civilization. But, at a stroke, Mr Fisk has dramatically raised the bar for standards of western self-loathing.

By way of contrast, consider another Afghan story his paper carried – a call by Amnesty International, Human Rights Watch and others for "a full inquiry" into whether or not US forces in Afghanistan are guilty of torture. Torture? My God, what are our boys up to? Well, it seems that "very disturbing" "threats" were made to a member of the Taliban and captured on videotape. The offending party was the CIA team of Mike Spann and his comrade, known only as "Dave". They were at the Qala-i-Jangai prison, interrogating the celebrated Marin County Taliban, born John Yoko Ashram Fonda Country Joe And The Fish Walker Lindh but now going under the name Mustapha Jihad.

Mike and Dave seem to have been doing a good cop/bad cop routine on the "poor fellow" with Mike quietly pointing out that "there were several hundred other Muslims killed" at the World Trade Center and Dave stomping around in the background using the f-word a lot and muttering things like, "The problem is, he's got to decide if he wants to live or die. If he wants to die, he's going to die here. Or he's going to fuckin' spend the rest of his short fuckin' life in prison. It's his decision, man. We can only help the guys who want to talk to us."

Had the Marinated Muslim spent less time in the madrassah mastering the ways of his adopted people (how to brandish your AK-47 without getting it snagged in your floor-length beard) and more time watching traditional American pop-culture junk, he would have recognized the Mike/Dave scene from its equivalent in *There's Something About Mary*. But Kenneth Ross of Human Rights Watch thinks that Dave's "threat" would, under international law, be considered torture. Sticks and stones may break my bones, but words are illegal and constitute cruel and unusual punishment.

We can't bring Mike Spann before a war crimes tribunal and prosecute him for torture because unfortunately Tali-Boy's fellow prisoners rose up in what proved to be a bloody four-day battle and beat, kicked and bit the CIA man to death before booby-trapping his body with grenades. But Dave managed to fight his way to freedom and he could certainly be prosecuted by an international court. If the US refused to extradite, Dave could be tried in absentia. Perhaps he could even be bitten to death in absentia. I'm no expert in international law, so I'll leave that for others.

But these two stories usefully clarify the peculiar pathology of the anti-war left. On the one hand, we need international investigations if Americans are insufficiently decorous in their questioning. On the other, it's perfectly justifiable for disaffected Muslims to target western civilians purely on the basis of their ethnic identity. On the one hand, we can't do anything right. On the other, they can't do anything wrong. The Fisk Doctrine, taken to its logical conclusion, absolves of any responsibility not just the perpetrators of September 11th but also the Taliban supporters who've attacked several of his fellow journalists in Afghanistan, all of whom, alas, died before being able to file a final column explaining why their murderers are blameless.

In recent weeks, some of us have found it hard to suppress the occasional titter at President Bush's ongoing attempts at Islamic outreach, not least his suggestion that American schoolchildren should seek out pen pals in the Muslim world. But it testifies, if nothing else, to Mr Bush's humanity: he believes that the Third Graders at the Sword Of The Infidel-Slayer Elementary School in Kandahar are at heart no different from those in Crawford, Texas – that they have the same impulses and enthusiasms as any other children. He may be naïve about this: it could be that, even if he sat down and read *The Hungry Caterpillar* or *'Twas The Night Before Ramadan* to a bunch of six-year olds in Yasser's noxious classrooms in Ramallah, the little tykes would think it sucked compared to Suicide Bombing 101. But at least, whenever he talks about anyone, Texans or Tajiks, Afghans or Australians, the old right-wing Big Oil stooge accords them their fundamental dignity as human individuals.

By comparison, every argument the enlightened progressives over on the anti-war side make has at its core the basic proposition that these people are primitives, animals: they are no more culpable for tearing you apart than a pack of hyenas would be. As Mr Fisk sees it, the mob who mugged him and robbed him were "truly innocent of any crime except being the victim of the world". Not true. They had a choice, and to deny that they had a choice is to dehumanize them far more than Pentagon euphemisms about "collateral damage" do. For what could be more dehumanizing than to say that these people have no responsibility for their actions? But that's the anti-war crowd's view: they believe in Fiskal responsibility – it's always the Great Satan's fault.

Before the scenes of shaven Afghans cheering their liberation disheartened the peaceniks, you could go to most any college town and see signs saying "Stop your racist war!" As they no longer seem to need the placards, I was wondering if we warmongers could borrow them – because the fact is the intellectual assault being waged by the extreme left is explicitly racist. To old-school imperialists, these excitable Pashtun types were the "lesser breeds without the law". To self-loathing multiculturalists, they still are. Or, rather, they're still "without the law" but now they're the "superior breeds" – their moral integrity confirmed by their resistance to such concepts as individual responsibility. Rousseau's "noble savage" was savage because of his isolation from the west; the Chomsky-Fisk-Said "noble savage" is savage precisely because of the west, which you've got to admit is a dandy improvement, if only in terms of heightening the delicious masochistic frisson.

But if I were, say, Dr Abdullah Abdullah, the new Afghan Foreign Minister, I'd be getting a bit sick of the exquisite condescension of western liberals. From 1886 to 1973, Afghanistan was one of the more peaceful corners of the planet – at least when compared with, oh, Germany, Italy, France, Poland, Russia, Japan, China, etc. There's no reason why it can't be again. The Bonn talks went well. The new cabinet includes a woman. The interim government starts next week. And the only Yankee war crime to get steamed up about is the robust vocabulary of one agent: Hey, hey, CIA/How many naughty words did you use today?

It must all be very disheartening for the massed ranks of western doom-mongers. But, c'mon, don't beat yourself up over it. As Robert Fisk well knows, there's plenty of Afghans who'll do it for you.

MINETA

December 27th 2001
The National Post

PRESIDENT Bush's Transportation Secretary, Norm Mineta, told an interviewer the other day that, if "a 70-year old white woman from Vero Beach, Florida" and "a Muslim young man" were in line to board a flight, he hoped there would be no difference in the scrutiny to which they were subjected.

I'd love to see Norm get his own cop show:

"Captain Mineta, the witness says the serial rapist's about 5' 10 with a thin moustache and a scar down his right cheek."

"Okay, Sergeant, I want you to pull everyone in."

"Pardon me?"

"Everyone. Men, women, children. We'll start in the Bronx and work our way through to Staten Island. What matters here is that we not appear to be looking for people who appear to look like the appearance of the people we're looking for. There are eight million stories in the Naked City, and I want to hear all of them."

Last week, one of the widows of September 11th launched the inevitable lawsuit against United Airlines. If I was United, my defence would be that we were in full compliance with everything the Federal Government required of us: 9/11 was not a failure of security, but of policy. The official in charge of that policy, Mr Mineta, appears to have learned nothing – which, given that the put-upon passengers of his over-regulated airlines are now the last and only effective line of defence against terrorists, seems extraordinarily ungrateful. But he can't be sacked because, in Mr Bush's otherwise Republican team, he's the token Democrat, and he's also the first Asian-American Cabinet Secretary. He is, in that sense, the most prominent beneficiary of political profiling, which, unfortunately for the rest of us, is the only acceptable kind.

~

EUROPEANS, AMERICANS, ARABS, JEWS

December 29th 2001
The Spectator

MY COLLEAGUE Petronella Wyatt reported the other week that "since September 11 anti-Semitism and its open expression has become respectable at London dinner tables." Barbara Amiel then chipped in with the news that it's spread to lunch and afternoon tea, too.

Apparently, at a recent gathering chez Barbara, the Ambassador of "a major EU country" told guests that the current troubles were all because of "that shitty little country Israel... Why," he asked, "should the world be in danger of World War Three because of those people?" Next came a private lunch at which "the hostess - doyenne of London's political salon scene - made a remark to the effect that she couldn't stand Jews and everything happening to them was their own fault."

A few days after September 11th, Richard Ingrams wrote a column in *The Observer* headlined "Who Will Dare Damn Israel?" Answer: Take a number and join the queue.

This is the mood music of the new war, and more mellifluous in Britain than in the Arab world, with its amusing anti-Jew pop songs and droll sitcoms ("Plots Of Terror", featuring an Ariel Sharon who drinks the blood of Arab babies and then tosses them on the bonfire). It would be frightfully tedious if Jews were thin-skinned enough to make a fuss about this sort of thing when there are so many more important things to worry about – such as, for example, the potential backlash against Muslims that western leaders are always fretting about in between photo-ops at the mosque. President Bush and co have been so busy enjoining us not to beat up our Islamic neighbours that they've failed to notice an actual as opposed to hypothetical spate of "hate crimes": according to Rabbi Abraham Cooper of the Simon Wiesenthal Center, more European synagogues have been attacked and burned in the last year than in any year since 1938, the year of Kristallnacht. This doesn't seem to be getting a lot of press coverage.

Americans are resigned to Britain and Europe's need to "damn" Israel, if only because they're used to being on the receiving end themselves. Among British Conservatives, anti-Zionism tends to go hand in hand with anti-Americanism – or, to put it in a more positive light, Europhiles tend also to be Arabists (Iain Gilmour, etc). This is perfectly understandable: a certain type of Englishman looks at an Arab and sees a desert version of his most cherished self-delusions. Where Jews are modern, urban and scientific, Arabs are feudal, rural and romantic. Jews wear homburgs; Arabs wear flowing robes and headdresses. Jews are famously "in trade", Arabs are just as famously hopeless at economic creativity: they have oil, but require foreigners to extract it and refine it. A backward culture that loves dressing up and places no value on professional activity will always appeal to a segment of the English elite. Look at the Prince of Wales in that wannabee Bedouin get-up he wore to meet Brother bin Laden the other week. Scarcely had he tossed the Highgrove hejab in the washer then he went out and gave a speech denouncing the "arrogance" of skyscrapers. In America, blacks talk of the "white Negro"; the Prince is our white Arab.

Over on the other side, meanwhile, whether or not Jews are still regarded in Europe as grasping, taloned, sallow, hook-nosed usurers with eyes like rattlesnakes, the traditional defects pale in comparison to a more recently acquired trait: their Americanism. Americans and Jews are not entirely synonymous, but, to elderly European Jews of a certain age, criticism of the Yanks has a familiar ring to it. In 1937, Sacheverell Sitwell visited the Bukovina, formerly the easternmost province of the Habsburg Empire, then part of Romania and now in the Ukraine. Its capital city Czernowitz was a multicultural mélange of Romanians, Ruthenians, Poles, Germans, Armenians and Swabians, but, as Sitwell observed, you'd never know that from a stroll down Main Street:

> *There is not a shop that has not a Jewish name painted above its windows. The entire commerce of the place is in the hands of the Jews. Yiddish is spoken here more than German.*

Not any more - the Jews of Czernowitz are dead or fled - but the Hebrew hegemony in the Bukovina has a contemporary echo in the High Streets of modern Britain: There is scarce a shop that has not an

American name painted above its windows – McDonald's, The Gap, Dunkin' Donuts, Toys R Us, Starbucks. American is spoken more than British – "Have a nice day." "Would you like fries with that?" Resentment of US cultural imperialism is merely a supersized version of the charges levelled at 'tween-wars European Jewry: the anti-globalisation crowd, droning on about interlopers interested only in profits and swamping local cultures, are singing a very old song. Indeed, the savvier Aryans can claim to have seen it coming. As Werner Sombat wrote in *The Jews And Economic Life* (1911):

One can rightly say that the United States owes what it is entirely to the Jews: that is, its American nature. What we call Americanism to a large degree is nothing other than the influence of the Jewish spirit.

I don't entirely agree with that, but it seems to me Sombat is right to this extent: American sympathy for Israel and European support for the Arabs are essentially cultural statements, unrelated to the finer points of the "Palestinian question". America supports Israel not because it's Jewish but because it's democratic. In fact, Republicans support Israel despite the Jews. American Jews are urban liberals and one of the Democratic Party's most reliable core demographics. There is no political benefit whatsoever to Bush in taking a "hard pro-Israel line". *Au contaire*, Arab-Americans are just about the only immigrant group other than the Cubans that votes Republican. Yet that will never translate into GOP support for Arab states as presently constituted. My northern, rural, conservative neighbours are, when you prod 'em a little, mildly xenophobic and share a reflexive distaste for overt Jewishness. But they'll always back Israel over Syria or Egypt because to them liberty trumps everything else. They are also under no illusions as to the kind of state an Arafat-led Palestine would be. So Republicans look at Israel and see not Jews but a liberal democracy.

Funnily enough, that's also what the Arabs see. They don't hate America because it backs Israel; they hate Israel because it looks like America – it's a functioning state. If you get out a map of the world and look at the vastness of the Arab lands from North Africa to the Gulf with a tiny Israeli sliver in the middle (if you accept the 1967 borders, it's only 11 miles wide at one point) it's simply not possible for any rational human being to blame the tiny sliver for all the woes of the surrounding vastness. At least in the old days, Muslim victim culture sought out more plausible oppressors. Writing after the Great War, in which the Ottoman Empire picked the wrong side through bad luck as much as anything else, Albert Kinross recounted his discussions with an educated Turk:

> *The bey's politics amounted to this: why did British diplomacy allow German diplomacy to lead poor Turkey by the nose? He presupposed, firstly, that the Turk could do no wrong, and, secondly, that the Turk was an irresponsible and charming child whom it was the duty of the Great Powers to pet and spoil. To my unregenerate mind, a good hiding would have been more salutary.*

The Turk has grown up, rather impressively. But we're still trying to pet and spoil his former Arabian provinces – i.e., "win their hearts and minds" – when in truth the good hiding administered to Osama and Mullah Omar is far more salutary.

But, even if you accept that Jews are slavering money-lenders no London hostess can stand and that Israel is a shitty little country, so what? In the objective sense, the Arab states are failures. If Israel was "imposed" on the region in the Forties, the other nations date only from the Twenties. The only difference is the Jews have made a go of it. Both Israel and Egypt get massive subventions from Washington: Egypt, an economic basket-case, pisses it away; Israel is now a net technology exporter.

If America recognises a kindred spirit in Israel, then so does Europe in the Arab autocracies. After all, when King Fahd, President Mubarak et al sell themselves to the west as anti-democratic brakes on the baser urges of their people, they sound a lot like the European Union. As we've seen yet again, the principle underpinning the new Europe is not "We, the people" but "We know better than the people" – not just on capital punishment and the Treaty of Nice and the single currency, but on pretty much anything that comes up, including national elections. When 29% of Austrian voters were impertinent enough to plump for Joerg Haider's Freedom Party, the EU punished them with sanctions and boycotts. As the Swedish Prime Minister Goran Persson put it, "The programme that is developing in Austria is not in line with EU values." In the new Europe, the will of the people is subordinate to the will of the Perssons. Understandably, to such an elite, the Oslo "peace process" ought to be as remorseless and undeviating as the path to European unity: how preposterous to let something as footling as the wishes of the Israeli electorate disrupt it.

So each half of the west looks in the Middle East for what it values most in itself - for the Americans, liberty; for Europe, paternalism, benign or otherwise. The result is a mirror image: just as Israel is the odd man out in the Middle East, so increasingly America is in the west, wedded as it is to such bizarre concepts as capital punishment, gun rights, free speech, etc.

As for Barbara Amiel's EU Ambassador, fretting that shitty little Israel – "those people" – are plunging the world into war, let me propose an alternative theory: it's all his fault. The other day, Mickey Kaus, an iconoclastic neoliberal, noticed that Zacarias Moussaoui, the French national now charged with conspiracy in connection with September 11th, became an Islamic radical while living in London "drawing welfare benefits"; also, Ahmed Ressam, arrested on the eve of Y2K while en route to blow up Los Angeles International Airport, had been living in Montreal where he "survived on welfare payments"; likewise, Metin Kaplan, who heads a radical Islamist sect, "claimed social benefits in Cologne for many years until two million Deutschmarks in cash was found in his flat".

In other words, life in the Middle East may have fired their Islamic fundamentalism, but benefit cheques from the soft-west Euro-Canadian welfare states enabled them to pursue their obsession at the taxpayer's expense. If you're looking for "root causes" for terrorism, European-sized welfare programmes are a good place to start. Maybe if they had to go out to work, they'd join *The Daily Mirror* and become the next John Pilger. Or maybe they'd open a drive-thru Halal Burger chain and make a fortune. Instead, Tony Blair pays Islamic fundamentalists in London to stay at home, fester and plot. Having grown up in Arab countries that place no value on work and provide little incentive to economic activity, your would-be suicide bomber fits easily into the welfare culture of the European Union or Canada. He wouldn't last long in New Hampshire.

Say what you like about the Jews, but they don't sit around on welfare. In *St Urbain's Horseman*, Mordecai Richler recalled some of the routine slurs of the Quebec Government during World War Two, including an official pamphlet showing "a coarse old Jew, nose long and misshapen as a carrot, retreating into the night with bags of gold." A junior minister was dispatched to do damage control. "Anti-Semitism," he told the press, "is grossly exaggerated. Speaking for myself, my accountant is a Jew and I always buy cars from Sonny Fish."

Just so. In the Middle East, two cultures jostle side by side: one channels its citizens' energy into economic fulfilment, the other into pathetic victim fantasies. The sides the United States and the European Union have chosen to align themselves with say as much about themselves and their own psychological health as they do about Palestine.

NEW YEAR

Taking stock

December 15th/16th 2001
The Spectator/The Chicago Sun-Times

THE WORLD changed on September 11th. Nearly everyone said that, and nearly everyone meant it, even the French: "*Nous sommes tous Americains!*" declared *Le Monde*, and for a while they were. "This is no time to be an 80% ally," said Australia's Prime Minister John Howard, and he wasn't. But the moment of unity was just that, and, in the months since, our paths have been remorselessly diverging. Britain seems to me right now to be about a 60% ally and falling a little more each week. The initial assessment was right but there's a palpable urge in much of the rest of the west to pretend nothing's changed, to be back to the way we were.

The most obvious beneficiary of the "change" was President Bush. The guy had been in office since January, but in September he was still a hazy presence to most Americans. The columnists, the gag-writers, the zeitgeist set wrote him off as a boob and, worse, a dullard: no star power. They wished Clinton was still there, and Clinton did his best to pretend that he was, embarking like his chum Barbra Streisand on an unending round of farewell appearances and filling the front pages with a flurry of last-minute scandals. The same geniuses now assure us that Bush has "grown in office". *Au contraire*, he's the same fellow he was six months ago: what's changed is the terrain. It's propitious to him, in a way the Clintonian landscape pre-9/11 wasn't.

Back in March, I made what was if I do say so myself (and, let's face it, nobody else is going to) a brilliant observation. Defending their man in the storm over his last-minute pardons of various international fugitives, coke dealers, relatives and folks who wrote large checks to Hillary's brother, the last surviving Friends Of Bill conceded that, okay, the whole pardons business may have got out of hand but that's because the President was so busy personally immersing himself in the nuances of very complicated cases that it just overwhelmed him. "In its way this was the Clinton apologia pared to its essence: the President, say his defenders, is a 'complex' man, and he tends to make everything else complex," I wrote. "Bush's problem, of course, is that he's not 'complex'. Indeed, he is, as the press has assured us, a simpleton. And so his governance has an admirable simplicity to it." This wasn't entirely successful in the world before September 11th, but, as Michael Barone wrote recently in *US News & World Report*, "The war has weakened the liberal notion that all issues are complex and require the ministration of credentialed experts, but it has strengthened the conservative idea that big issues require moral clarity and decisive action."

This is Bush territory, and he has claimed it. With Clinton, everything got complicated, including the meaning of the word "is" and whether oral sex counts as adultery. What he would have done after September 11th, we do not know. But we do know that in his only significant speech on the subject he thought it all went back to Christian excesses during the First Crusade in 1095. 1095! That's 906 years. Even Paula Jones would have settled. If ever there was an occasion for the great Clintonian invocation that "we need to move on", a grudge over the First Crusade is surely it. But, as the speech went on, Mr Clinton managed to come up with several other examples of "terrorism". Here they are in full: southern plantation owners killing slaves, white settlers killing Native Americans, General Sherman burning farms in the Civil War ("a relatively mild form of terrorism"), and "even today," he concluded, "we still have the occasional hate crime rooted in race, religion, or sexual orientation. So terror has a long history." Osama is on a par with the drunken bozo who yells "Beat it, faggot!" at the guy in the parking lot. Terrorism is like oral sex with interns: Everybody does it.

By comparison, being a renowned simpleton, Bush is not the kind of fellow who feels the need to show off how much he knows about what was happening in 1095. He's a big-picture guy. He grasped the enormity of what had happened and spoke to it directly. It was a time for black and white, not the murky gray in which Bill Clinton swims. To be sure, the Bush strategy has its gray areas - General Musharraf, the love-in with Russia - but the object even then is to pull them out of the gray, towards you, not to get sucked in yourself.

As a result, a mere two months later Afghanistan has an interim government with a token woman in it. Whether it includes any gays, I cannot say, and you'll forgive me if I'm reluctant to ask the question of any Tajik warlord, no matter how Village People-like his moustache might be. But at least the weekly Crush-A-Fag-And-Win-A-Yak-Cart competitions have been suspended.

The Democrats and their media chums haven't quite adjusted yet. Three months in, the conventional wisdom is that, domestically, there's a new faith in "big government" that naturally favors the Dems, and that, internationally, the previously isolationist Bush has had to take on the entire Clinton/Gore agenda.

Chuck Schumer, New York's Other Senator, was touting the first half of this equation the other day: "Our society will have to examine the vulnerable pressure points in our country," he wrote in *The Washington Post*. "Only one entity has the breadth, strength and resources to lead this recalibration and pay for its costs—the Federal Government."

I'd quote more, but I'm too convulsed with laughter to type. Leaving aside that the only "resources" the Federal Government has is your paycheck, on September 11th the Cult of Regulation – the notion that some Federal hijack procedures from the Seventies transformed by antiquity into Holy Writ would guarantee our safety – contributed to the deaths of thousands. Meanwhile, the great American virtues of self-reliance and innovation, as practiced by the brave heroes of Flight 93, saved the lives of thousands. Anyone who thinks this has no implications for domestic policy is welcome to try running in a competitive election on an anti-gun platform. In some parts of the US, firearm sales are up by as much as 22%, especially sales to women. Want to make Americans safer? "Let's roll!" trumps gun control, any day. Politicians can't tell the citizenry they have to be on full alert and then turn around and announce new restrictions on the ability to defend yourself.

As for international affairs, let Congressman Barney Frank speak for the conventional wiseacres: "Bush has bought into the Clinton/Gore policy," he says with a straight face. According to *The Wall Street Journal*'s Al Hunt, the unilateral Bush has been forced to submit to all the big Gore themes from Campaign 2000: "state-building, a strong reliance on the United Nations, and multilateralism".

I'd quote more, but tears of laughter have made my copy of Al's column all wet. "State-building"? Nation-building is one thing, nation-building by the UN is quite another, and generally to be avoided. The distinguishing feature of Afghanistan so far is that it's not going to be another UN protectorate, which are swell for black marketeers and hookers but for little else. It looks as if the Afghans might dodge the fate of the Balkans and other territories (you can't call them "nations") which the UN maintains as the international equivalent of slum housing projects.

A "strong reliance" on the UN? Kofi Annan can't get a look-in. Most Americans would be forgiven for assuming that, after its Conference on Racism in Durban in early September, the UN had entered the witness protection program.

"Multilateralism"? All the multilateral stuff Bush was getting hassled over six months ago is deader than it's ever been. Kyoto anyone? The ABM Treaty? The International Criminal Court? Include us out, permanently. This new war isn't Kosovo, where 19 different Nato governments had to sign off on every target. Even the Brits are being kept at arm's length.

Introducing Tony Blair in Congress, the President was characteristically generous. But he's been very steely with London since. The Bush/Blair visions of this war veer off in separate directions very quickly, as the White House understands. The Defense Secretary, Geoff Hoon, has said that Britain would not extradite bin Laden to the US without assurances that he would not face the death penalty. Here's the response I'd give Her Majesty's Government if I were the US Attorney General: Fine, you keep him. Put Osama on trial, he'll have the jurors killed. Put him in Brixton or Pentonville, and it's your citizens who'll be seized in Palestine, Saudi, Kuwait, Egypt or Belgium and held hostage until he's released. So, if you and your EU pals want to preen that badly, you can explain it to the loved ones of your own kidnapped nationals.

In London, these and other differences provoked the Chief of the Defense Staff into launching the first assault on Washington by a British Admiral since they burned the White House in 1814: Sir Michael Boyce let loose with snide cracks about the "apparent" success of the air campaign and cheap cowboy imagery about "a high-tech 21st century posse in the new Wild West".

And guess what? Bush couldn't care less. If a multilateralism that barely stretches to 10 Downing Street is really what Al Gore campaigned on, then I grievously misunderstood the guy. The fact is you couldn't ask for a more unilateral war.

What's going on here? Well, let's take those few British men seeing action in Afghanistan. The SAS are one of the world's most renowned elite forces. For the last two months, *The Daily Mail* in London has been running snippy little comments about how Washington should let our chaps handle this bin Laden blighter because frankly the ghastly Yank special forces are an absolute shower and should just stay out of the way. There may have been some truth to this ten or twenty years ago, but not now. Today, the best you can say about the SAS is that they're about the last foreign force on the planet that can keep up with the US military. The rest just get in the way and clog things up.

This shouldn't surprise us: of the world's top ten military spenders, the US is not just Number One but outspends the other nine combined. As a result, the gap in capability and technological innovation widens every year. This is the logical consequence of the massive budget cuts by countries that a generation ago were still serious military powers. Last week, for example, New Zealand scrapped its air force. The whole thing. Wanna buy a fighter jet? Wellington's selling off the lot. Of course, New Zealand, like Canada and Europe, figures the US will ultimately guarantee its freedom. Bush is generous enough not to care about the free lunch, but he doesn't see why those guys should have a veto on what the chef's allowed to serve. If that's unilateralism, bring it on.

The French say the Americans have advanced beyond superpower to "hyperpower" status, economically, militarily and culturally. If US preeminence continues growing at the present rate, even "hyperpower" won't suffice. The Afghan campaign has been the first war of this new reality: Whatever the fantasies of Barney Frank, no nation in history has ever been less in need of "multilateralism".

~

LAND THAT I LOVE

December 23rd 2001
The Chicago Sun-Times

IN THE WEEKS after September 11th, several of my fellow columnists wanted to know why everyone was singing "God Bless America" rather than the national anthem. The song was everywhere in those early days, and various musicologists were called upon to speculate learnedly on why this song had caught the public mood: perhaps "The Star-Spangled Banner" requires too great a range, perhaps its complex use of melismas demands a professional vocalist, etc, etc.

All irrelevant. The reason the nation sang "God Bless America" is its first seven words:

> *God Bless America*
> *Land that I love.*

Berlin was a contemporary of Cole Porter, Ira Gershwin and Lorenz Hart, but, unlike those sophisticated rhymesters, only he could have written those words without embarrassment. As Jule Styne, the composer of "Let It Snow! Let It Snow! Let It Snow!", once said to me about Berlin, "It's easy to be clever. The really clever thing is to be simple" – to say it directly, unaffectedly, unashamedly:

> *God Bless America*
> *Land that I love.*

Now President Bush has quietly designated September 11th as Patriot Day. "God Bless America" is a good song for that day, just as Berlin anthems mark other high days and holy days on the American calendar – "Easter Parade" and "White Christmas". It was Philip Roth who said Berlin took the two most important dates in the Christian calendar and turned them into a song about a hat and a song about snow. But, in the latter case, there's a bit more to it than that. They had white Christmases in Temun, Siberia, where Berlin was born, but a white Russian Christmas wouldn't be the same: It's not about the

151

weather, it's about home. In 1942, those GIs out in the Pacific, who made the song a hit, understood that. Whatever his doubts about God, Berlin kept faith with his adopted land - and that faith is what you hear in "White Christmas". Irving Berlin embodies all the possibilities of this land: he came here as poor and foreign and disadvantaged as you can be, and yet he wove himself into the very fabric of the nation. His life and his art are part of the definition of America.

This year, as in 1942, our troops are on foreign soil and foreign seas dreaming of a white Christmas just like the ones they used to know. Spare a thought for them, and for the empty places at the American table this year – for CIA man Mike Spann, for the brave citizen-soldiers of Flight 93, and for all those who set off to work on a beautiful Tuesday morning in mid-September. They died in a great cause.

God Bless America
Land that I love.

~

MOST INTRIGUING

January 5th 2002
The Daily Telegraph

RING OUT THE old, ring in the old. According to *People* magazine, "The 25 Most Intriguing People Of 2001" include Julia Roberts and Jennifer Aniston. Jennifer was also one of "The 25 Most Intriguing People Of 2000" while Julia was one of *Ladies' Home Journal's* "Most Fascinating Women Of 2000". Am I the only one who feels Julia was actually far more fascinating in 2001 and a lot more intriguing back in 2000, when she appeared in London with unshaven armpits? As for Jennifer, I don't think she's really been intriguing since 1996, when she changed her hairdo.

But no matter how many New Years are rung in, there are some auld acquaintances we're never allowed to forget. What's really intriguing is: what has to happen in the world for Jennifer not to make the "Most Intriguing People" list? The Twin Towers crumble, the Taleban tumble, they both got blown away, but this list is here to stay.

Oh, sure, there's a nod to topicality – Bush makes the hit parade and, unlike last year, when she made the cut because "she got the husband everyone wanted", this year Jennifer's here because she "helped us muddle through these troubling times by providing reassurance, reliability and comic relief". But in these troubling times the reliability of the "25 People Most Likely To Turn Up On Lists" list is what's really reassuring. I was worried it might be a lot of gloomy world leaders, generals, Afghan warlords. But not a bit. Julia's there because she "won her first Oscar, starred in three movies and weathered a turbulent year on the romantic front". There's always a woman who "proudly showed fortysomething women how to stay sexy." This year it's Kim Cattrall of "Sex And The City". Next year, it'll be Sharon Stone, Michelle Pfeiffer, maybe Pam Shriver. Prince Harry, on the other hand, "emerged from his brother's shadow to become his own young man". Life would be a lot simpler if we could all be our own young man. Just ask Michael Barrymore.

But why Prince Harry and not Richard Reid? A shoe-in for most intriguing Briton of the year. Just what makes him tick? Could it be the timing device in his sock? But *People* couldn't care less. Instead they plump for Reese Witherspoon, because she "broke out from the pack".

What about Goran Persson? Hot from his stint as Euro President and with Gothenberg's first EU riot under his belt, the Swedish Prime Minister is unquestionably the most intriguing Persson of the year. But instead *People* gives us Nicole Kidman, who "rebounded gracefully from a shattered marriage".

Who could forget Mullah Omar? Please don't talk about him, one eye's gone! The intriguing mullah, who routinely turns down interview requests, proudly showed fortysomething women how to stay sexy – just step into this large shapeless tent and you too can look as foxy as Kandahar's teen chicks. But *People* went for Madonna, who offered "proof that middle age hasn't dimmed her star".

True, but you could say the same about General Musharraf. On September 10th, he was the Taleban's biggest backer. By September 15th, he was Bush's biggest backer. In a land of intrigue, no-one is more intriguing.

And even Osama himself loses out, though last year saw the intriguing evildoer break out from the pack and sheikh his booty big-time. He's the biggest thing on magazine covers since Princess Di – and hey, he's also got kohl-ringed eyes, just like her. We bet he'd look great in Versace, too, and he might even like hanging out with George Michael. Alas, he loses out to Mariah Carey, who makes the Top 25 because she "suffered a public breakdown after poor record sales and boyfriend problems". Worse, Osama's only mention is in a joke about him hiding out somewhere barren and deserted – theatres showing Mariah's floppo movie *Glitter*.

The salient point about *People's* Intriguing People list is that no-one intriguing ever gets on it. I'm not saying celebrities can't be intriguing. Pam Shriver, for example: she's marrying George Lazenby, the James Bond no-one remembers, the one between Sean Connery and Roger Moore. How did an Eighties B-list tennis player hook up with a Sixties B-list actor? Is there a magazine? Intriguing.

Finally, my tip for next year's Most Intriguing list: Janawar Afghanistan. This small town in the northwest corner of the war-ravaged nation could be generating a lot of buzz just because it sounds like Jennifer Aniston. You read it here first.

~

CRITIC OF THE YEAR

December 29th 2001
The Spectator

WHAT PRICE now the blockbusters of summer? They gross a hundred million in the first week, and are dead by the sixth. Even *Harry Potter*, barely a month old, is fading fast, and likely, I fear, to be frosted out come Oscar time. It was the 60th anniversary of Pearl Harbor a couple of weeks back and, amid all the commemorations, no one wanted to mention the motion picture of the same name, though it got more press than the original six months ago.

Like Japan in the war, it opened big. But, also like Japan, it soon stalled. No doubt there are still various elderly studio execs holed up in the jungles of Beverly Hills refusing to admit that it's all over and that *Pearl Harbor* The Movie wasn't the mega-smash it was supposed to be. If nothing else, the film nicely illustrates the problems Hollywood has handling even generally approved wars of long ago. Indeed, much of the exposition in *Pearl Harbor* eerily foreshadowed *The Guardian*'s leader page in late-September "root cause" mode: according to the film, Imperial Japan attacked the US fleet to protest Washington's oil embargo. Hmm.

In fact, with the benefit of hindsight, many of this year's pictures feel oddly like pre-echoes. When I saw Ground Zero, a few days after September 11th, my first thought, mainly because of the vastness and the carpet of ash, was of the early scenes of *Enemy At The Gates*, set in the siege of Stalingrad.

I'm also struck by the off-hand cunning in *Blow*, the latest in a line of coke movies, in which the hero (Johnny Depp) becomes a big-time drugs kingpin by using his stewardess girlfriend (the lovely Franka Potente) and her uninspected cabin-crew luggage to smuggle premium-quality marijuana from California to the lucrative East Coast college market. None of us watching that scene just a few months ago gave a thought to its wider implications.

Dumb Hollywood Comment Of The Year? It's gotta be Oliver Stone, back in September, noting the concentration of power in the movie industry. "Six men are deciding what you're seeing in film, and they own all the small companies... We have too much order," he said. "And I think the revolt on September 11th was about order. It was about 'Fuck you, fuck your order.'"

So Osama got sick of his movie being stuck in turnaround at Universal? Poor old Ollie, unable to make sense of the world except through the prism of his own narcissism.

Critic Of The Year? I'd like to nominate Egypt's leading archaeologist Zahi Hawass. Mr Hawass was one of 600 experts invited by the government film censor, Madkour Thabet, to take part in a conference on whether Egypt should permit *The Mummy Returns* to be screened. (The original *Mummy* was banned on grounds of historical inaccuracy.) The most controversial scene - whose significance we western critics once again failed to spot - was the moment when Brendan Fraser flees in terror from an Egyptian bathroom because it's so filthy. Affronted by this, the experts were on the verge of banning the picture, until Mr Hawass rose to speak. "First," he said, "our bathrooms are dirty, and we should clean them."

Good point.

"Second," he continued, "if the world thinks Egyptian bathrooms are dirty, we should know this."

Another good point. (An Arab equivalent to the west's "Why do they hate us?" agonising.)

Finally, he said, "If we don't like it, we should make a better film ourselves."

The best point of all. I'm not saying we necessarily need a film about great Egyptian bathrooms, but I'm sure many top-rank movie stars could be tempted to Cairo by the promise of a decent Egyptian toilet role. And, anyway, how hard can it be to make a better film than *The Mummy Returns*?

KNOW NOTHING

December 29th/31st 2002
The Daily Telegraph/The National Post

ABOUT 15 months ago, I went a little bit nuts. The sheer torpor of the Bush Presidential campaign paradoxically intoxicated me and in a fit of giddiness I predicted in these pages a Dubya landslide. Alan Rutkowski of Edmonton, Alberta wrote in to scoff. "All academics who specialise in such matters predict (on the basis of computer models) that Al Gore will win," he declared. "When he does, will Mr Steyn turn in his political pundit's badge?"

Hah! Any old sissy boy can resign from his job. I decided to go Mr Rutkowski one better. "If Bush loses," I wrote, "I hereby pledge that I will kill myself live on the Internet." Of course, I had no idea back then that my life would be hanging by a chad in Palm Beach County. I don't suppose I'd have actually killed myself, but at the very least I'd have had to fake my death, get a sex-change operation in North Africa, and re-emerge as a ferocious left-wing lesbian harridan at *The Guardian*. It would have been a frightful inconvenience, but I accepted Mr Rutkowski's premise: "It would be ridiculous," I agreed, "to continue posturing as an incisive analyst of US affairs once I have been exposed as a complete buffoon."

Well, I dodged that bullet, which is just as well as, twelve months on, the buffoon section at the Journalist of the Year Awards gala dinner is as packed as a passenger train in Madras on round-trip supersaver day. *The Wall Street Journal* had an hilarious piece the other day in which they called up the wise old birds of the "mainstream" media and read their words back to them. "We are mapless, we are lost," wrote *The New York Observer*'s Nicholas von Hoffman in a column that had the bad luck to appear the day Kabul was liberated and the cheers of the populace were drowned only by the mass whirr of rusty Remingtons consigning a thousand beards to the trashcan of history.

"Nobody knew anything about Afghanistan, myself included," says a chastened von Hoffman now. "We probably still are clueless."

Then there was Daniel Schorr, the gram'pa of gravitas at National Public Radio. "This is a war in trouble," he began one commentary. Reminded of this, he now says, "I have never been in Afghanistan and know nothing about Pashtuns and the rest of it."

But these belated confessions were as nothing compared to Jeffrey Simpson's column in the Toronto *Globe And Mail* apologising for all the things he got wrong this year. Well, not *all* the things – they'd have had to publish a collector's-item special section – but a representative sample, ruefully acknowledged with grace and humility, the bastard. That's gotta be the most cunning wheeze of the year! I'll bet even now the *Globe* mailroom is groaning under a ton of letters hailing him for his honesty and maturity. He's a dead cert for every newspaper award going. The minute I read the piece, headlined "Why No-One Should Pay Any Attention To Anything I Say" (I quote from memory), I cursed myself for not thinking of it first.

Yet, even if I'd come up with the idea for a massive apology column, I don't think I could have pulled it off as convincingly as Jeffrey. For, at the risk of being more insufferable than usual, I have to say my track record on this war has been pretty good. I won't bore you by pointing out all the things I've got right since September 11th, though a list is available on request and, attractively framed and mounted, makes an ideal post-Ramadan gift for *Observer* and

Independent columnists (framing and mounting not included, all sales final).

Oh, okay, if you insist, I'll point out a couple of things: The close of my column on September 17th predicted with uncanny accuracy the passengers' splendid behaviour on that Paris-Miami flight a week ago. On October 9th I declined to subscribe to the conventional wisdom about the invincibility of Afghanistan, "the savagery of whose menfolk has been much exaggerated by the left's nervous nellies." As for Her Majesty's frosty northern Dominion, on September 24th I wrote a column called "Canada's War Is Already Over".

Robert Turner of Toronto responded, "He is obviously one of Conrad Black's handpicked right-wing stooges, and I find his vindictive anti-Canadian diatribes ill-timed and in bad taste. His style of journalism offends me." "If *The National Post* alleges to be Canada's national newspaper, it should act like one, and not publish outrages and unpatriotic columns like those by Steyn," snorted Mr A J Lesyk. "It is a shame this five and dime reporter gets to publish this crap," said Jonathan Sellar. And from Lesia Dickson of Winnipeg: "I am e-mailing you to beg you to renounce your Canadian citizenship."

Dream on, Lesia. Here's the thing, guys: it's not about being a stooge of right or left, patriotic or unpatriotic, anti-Canadian or anti-American, conservative or liberal, in good taste or bad, fecal matter or the most exquisite truffles. At a certain basic level, a columnist has to be right every so often, otherwise you chaps are just wasting your time. You can sit through all that interminable will-they-won't-they guff on the CBC with Chrétien standing down the troops he stood up when he stood them down after putting them on stand-by to stand shoulder to shoulder, etc, but everything you need to know about our contribution to the war effort these last three months is in that September 24th headline.

My longer-term predictions – the removal of the House of Saud and the winding-up of Nato – have not yet come to pass but I'm happy to stick by them.

Before hailing myself any further, let me pause to salute some of *The National Post*'s elite commandoes, including especially the dashing Captain Coyne, Colonel Fulford and Sergeant-Major Blatchford. Credit where it's due also to Margaret Wente and Rex Murphy at the *Globe*, both of whom were on top of this thing from the beginning. Generally speaking, any columnist's strike rate this year depends on his answer to the most basic question of September 11th: "Is this wrong?" There were those who said "Yes" and a depressing number who said "Yes, but...", and generally the yes-butters sank further into their swamp from that point on. You could open the *Globe* at random and find the but-boys preening themselves: "While the President has reminded me of nothing so much as an old-time Texas gunslinger," wrote Peter Gzowski in September, "the Prime Minister has seemed ...well, wiser."

Yes, indeed. And, if the Prime Minister had been sitting in Washington on September 11th, presiding over a Trudeau-Chrétienised military, they'd be selling burqas at Neiman-Marcus now and wise old Papa Jean would be in a re-education camp growing his beard.

As for the secret of my success, it's as simple as George W Bush himself: know nothing. In this war, expertise is vastly overrated. Nothing is so certain as that, when a man appears on TV with the words "Professor of Middle Eastern Studies" under his name, everything he says will prove to be utter rubbish. Likewise, all the fellows with decades of experience in the Muslim world, like Robert Fisk of *The Independent*. Even if one cannot rise to the Rutkowski challenge, surely one should be expected occasionally to get *something* right, especially if one works for publications which have jeered endlessly at what a moron Bush is.

I made my prediction of a Dubya 2000 election victory for one reason. I was bored of reading lame-o columns repeating the stale old line that whichever candidate is ahead on Labour Day always wins the election. On Labour Day, Gore was ahead. So I plumped for Bush. If you learn only one lesson of history, make it this one: history repeats itself until it doesn't. The argument that simply because the US lost in Vietnam it would therefore lose in Afghanistan is tenable only if you believe that for the last three decades the US military has been as institutionally resistant to innovation as the John Pilger column. Fortunately, it hasn't.

In fact, if there's a broader lesson in Jeffrey Simpson's mea culpa, it's this: the criticisms our columnar and academic elites make of the military apply more accurately to themselves. Don Rumsfeld and the boys fought a brilliant, innovative, fast-thinking campaign, while the lamebrains of the press and the academy were a lock-step, unthinking, blank-eyed, flat-footed regiment marching their ancient clichés up and down the parade ground. If anyone's stuck in a "Vietnam quagmire", it isn't the US armed forces.

When I started dwelling on the potential Achilles' heel of Osama's rumoured small penis, friends told me, "I wish you'd stop doing those Tiny bin Laden jokes. Suppose he finds out where you live." But I rather hoped he would. I'd quite like to kill him and so would almost everyone I know. The evidence – not least of last weekend's Miami flight – suggests that when you go *mano a mano* with these dudes they're a pretty pathetic bunch. I'm armed to the hilt, and my recurring nightmare about the last moments of a woman I knew on one of those planes has gradually been replaced with a very pleasant dream in which I'm making a speech about giving away the $25 million reward money.

You may say I'm as big a crazy bearded psycho as he is, and you may be on to something: America is a much more primal federation than the EU. Before September 11th, we heard a lot from the Europoseurs about how the US was "out of step" with the rest of the civilised world: Chris Patten and co swung by Washington to lecture the Administration about capital punishment. But if the US wasn't out of step – if it was just another Belgium or Canada – Islamic fundamentalism would be unstoppable. It's because Americans are crazy enough to like owning guns and frying murderers and driving the world's biggest cars at the world's lowest gas prices that they're also prepared to maintain the only serious military in the western alliance. Don Rumsfeld can win this war, Geoff Hoon can't.

So that's my tip to the Quagmire Crowd on how to improve analytical accuracy: know nothing, do penis gags, buy a gun. And, for your New Year resolution, stop underestimating American resoluteness.

JANUARY

The brutal Afghan winter

January 7th 2002
The National Post

WHATEVER happened to the "brutal Afghan winter"? It was "fast approaching" back in late September, and apparently it's still "fast approaching" today. "Winter is fast, fast approaching," reported ABC's "Nightline" on September 26th.

Two weeks on, New York's *Daily News* announced that, "realistically, US forces have a window of two or three weeks before the brutal Afghan winter begins to foreclose options."

Two or three weeks passed and the brutal Afghan winter's relentless approach showed no sign of letting up. "A clock is ticking," declared *The Oregonian* on October 24th. "The harsh Afghan winter is approaching."

The clock ticked on. On November 8th NBC's Tom Brokaw alerted viewers to the perils posed by "a rapidly approaching winter". "They expect the conditions to deteriorate rapidly as the brutal winter soon sets in," wrote *Newsday*'s Deborah Barfield on November 11th updating her earlier sighting of "the typically brutal winter approaching" a month earlier on October 9th.

Another month ticked on, and the brutal winter carried on brutally approaching. "Winter is approaching fast," said Thomas McDermott, UNICEF's Regional Director, on December 9th. "With winter fast approaching, women wait in line for blankets," *The Los Angeles Times* confirmed, after the clock had ticked leisurely on a couple more days.

And not just any old approaching winter, but the "brutal Afghan winter", according to ABC, NBC, National Public Radio, *The Boston Globe*, Associated Press, Agence France-Presse, etc. "Former Canadian Foreign Minister Lloyd Axworthy is in Pakistan" - in case you were wondering - "to find out how to speed up aid deliveries before the brutal Afghan winter sets in," reported the BBC in November. "The temperature can drop to 50 below, so cold that eyelids crust and saliva turns to sludge in the mouth," said Tom Ifield of Knight-Ridder Newspapers.

Yesterday, it was 55 and clear in Kandahar and Herat. Ghurian checked in at 55, with 62 predicted for tomorrow. 57 and sunny in Bost and Laskar, with 64 expected on Thursday. In Kabul, it was 55, though with the windchill factored in it was only – let me see now – 54.

Meanwhile, in Toronto it's 28, New York 38. Overseas? Belfast and Glasgow report 46, London 44, Birmingham and Manchester 42. If those Afghan refugees clogging up the French end of the Channel Tunnel ever make it through to Dover, they face a gruelling battle for survival against the horrors of the brutal British winter.

Just under four months ago, when the doom-mongers first started alerting us to the "fast approaching" "brutal Afghan winter", it was 70 degrees and I was sitting here in shorts and T-shirt. Today, in my corner of Quebec, the daytime high is 21, the predicted overnight low is 5 degrees, and tomorrow we'll be lucky to hit 14. For Saturday, they're predicting 3 degrees. 3 Fahrenheit is, as the metrically inclined would say, minus 16 Celsius. So you'll understand my amusement at the *Sunday Telegraph* headline of October 21st: "British Unit Prepares To Defy Extremes Of The Afghan Winter. Crack Troops Will Have To Work In Temperatures As Low As -20C." Big deal. Crack columnist has to work in temperatures as low as –16C. And, for my neck of the woods, this is a very mild winter.

Now, pedants will point out that there are one or two brisk parts of the Hindu Kush. On top of Mount Sikaram, at 15,620 feet the highest elevation in Afghanistan's White Mountains, it would no doubt freeze the proverbial knackers off a brass monkey. Similarly, on top of Mount Washington, highest elevation in New Hampshire's White Mountains, it's –15 with the windchill, while down in the state capital of Concord it's a balmy 36. That's why no one except a couple of meteorologist types lives on top of Mount Washington, but thousands do down in Concord. Amazingly, despite the vast cultural differences, the same patterns of population dispersal prevail in Afghanistan. Up on Mount Sikaram, a convenient eight-day donkey-ride to the nearest 7-Eleven, the only guys interested in buying a ski condo are Osama and Mullah Omar. Al-Qaeda operatives aside, the overwhelming majority of the Afghan population live in towns currently enjoying temperatures most Canadians won't see for another three or four months.

So where did this "brutal Afghan winter" business come from? It came, pre-eminently, from spokespersons for the relief agencies. There are some special-interest groups – the National Rifle Association, Right To Life – whose press releases get dismissed by the media as propaganda, and others – environmental groups, for example – whose every claim is taken at face value. Into this last happy category fall the "humanitarian lobby". Throughout the rhetorically brutal autumn, they bombarded us: "Predicting even more desperate times for millions of Afghans, international relief groups and federal humanitarian aid officials are scrambling to get food and medical supplies into a country they say is on the verge of famine... They expect the conditions to deteriorate rapidly as the brutal winter sets in."

Gosh.

"The UN Children's Fund estimated that as many as 100,000 Afghan children could die of cold, disease and hunger within weeks if vital aid did not reach them."

Oh, my.

"The situation in Afghanistan is deteriorating rapidly, international aid agencies say, and they are predicting the worst humanitarian crisis ever."

The aid agencies, you'll recall, campaigned aggressively for a "bombing pause" during Ramadan. This would have enabled them to truck some food convoys through the mountains from Pakistan. These routes get snowbound and become impassable, and that's really the only salient fact about the "brutal Afghan winter".

Why are the roads to Pakistan more important than the roads to Iran, Turkmenistan, Uzbekistan and Tajikistan? Because Pakistan, being Afghanistan's most westernized neighbour, is where the western aid agencies are based. These are the fellows like my old chum Alex Renton – or, as the Canadian papers call him, "Toronto-born Alex Renton". Alex, the son of Lord Renton, is an Oxfam bigshot in the region. A lot of the other humanitarian coves running around out there are also English boarding-school boys, chaps with names like Rupert and Sebastian on a benign version of the journey of self-discovery that Taleban guy from Marin County went on. I'm sure they're all very well-intentioned, but when they start shrieking about the fast approaching brutal Afghan winter and the imminent deaths of millions what they're mainly doing is protesting that the American military action is disrupting their act.

Here's how you feed Afghanistan: You can get Rupert and Sebastian to load up the trucks in Peshawar and drive through to Kabul, where what isn't stolen by the Taleban can be distributed to the people. Or you can bomb the Taleban, drive them from office, put a non-deranged administration in place, re-open the year-round road-and-rail bridge to Uzbekistan, speed up construction on a second Uzbek bridge, and get air convoys to cover the places roads can't reach. In the seven weeks since the fall of Kabul, all this has happened. The millions who are supposed to be dying aren't. The hundred thousand child corpses are alive and kicking. The UN says all the supplies it needs to feed Afghanistan are now getting through.

Here's what would have happened had the aid agencies got their way and pressured the US into a bombing pause: many more Afghans would have starved to death, the Taleban would have been secured in power at least for another few months and perhaps indefinitely, but Rupert and Sebastian would have enjoyed the stage-heroic frisson of bouncing along in the truck to Jalalabad. That seems a high price for the Afghan people to pay. One expects a certain amount of reflexive anti-Americanism from these "humanitarian" types, but in the brutal Afghan fall they went too far: they ought at least to be big enough to admit they were wrong and be grateful the Pentagon ignored their bleatings.

Instead, they seem a little touchy about the fact that among the first food supplies to get through was a fresh supply of egg on their faces. When Axworthy and other self-proclaimed "humanitarians" start droning on next month about starving children in Iraq, always remember the lesson of Afghanistan: a bombing pause is not as "humanitarian" as a bomb. I would urge readers to be highly selective about supporting aid agencies who operate under tyrannies. Better yet, go see for yourself: after all, for Canadians, there's no better time than now to spend a sultry two weeks in Kabul enjoying the charms of the brutal Afghan winter.

~

WHAT NEXT?

January 6th 2002
The Sunday Telegraph

EVERY TIME I switch on the TV these days, there's a panel discussion on whom we should bomb next. On the need to bomb someone there's general agreement – not just from the ex-commando types in leather jackets who now run mysterious "consultancies" but also the pantywaist Democratic Party strategists and liberal California Congresswomen. It's like casting Scarlett in *Gone With The Wind*: Osama and Mullah Omar are being written out, and it's just a question of deciding which lucky evildoer lands the plum role of standing underneath the daisycutter. What a bewildering array of menu options the pundits offer: Yemen, Somalia, Iraq, Iran, Sudan, Canada, France …on and on the horizons roll. Some want to take out what they call "the low-hanging fruit", which I assumed was the Administration's new term for Saddam, what with that Village People moustache and frankly camp turtleneck. But it turns out "the low-hanging fruit" are the little fellers you nail before storming Baghdad: some useful mopping-up operations in the backcountry of Somalia and the Yemen. *Then* you hit Anthrax Boy.

Three out of four Americans support sending in ground troops to topple Saddam, and that's before the President's said a word on the subject. 93% are happy with Mr Bush's conduct of the war. He can invade anywhere he wants right now, and no, I wasn't joking about France. On the Internet sites and call-in shows, the "bomb France" option always scores well, the more so since they pompously "warned" Washington – apropos the so-called "20th hijacker" currently awaiting trial in the US – that "no person benefiting from French consular protection could be executed." Please - don't make us laugh when we're trying to find a vein.

When you're way up in the 90s, demographics are irrelevant, but it should be noted that, according to Democratic pollster Celinda Lake, this is the first war ever in which support for military action is as strong among women as men. Professor Glenn Reynolds, who runs the Instapundit website, calls them the Bellicose Women's Brigade, and these days you meet them everywhere, not least in the gun shop.

It's a different story in Britain, sorry to say. When this war began, the BBC quickly set up camp in an alternative universe of indestructible clichés: civilian casualties (actually very light), humanitarian disasters (the food's getting through) and always, always, the certainty of getting bogged down in the brutal Afghan winter. But it's not just the BBC/*Guardian* crowd that haven't warmed up to the war. Nobody really has. The British are more pro-war than the rest of the EU, but so what? That's like being less anti-semitic than the EU. In Greece, support for the war is at 5.2%.

Even in the first polls in mid-September, British backing for military action was about 70%, about 5% less than in Australia, over 10% less than in Canada. It's fallen significantly since then. When Tony Blair came out metaphorical guns a-blazing, I assumed it was because he didn't want to be wrongfooted by the tabloids as they reverted enthusiastically to "Kill an Argie, win a Metro" mode. But the truth is that the Prime Minister could probably have got away with doing nothing. Instead, General Blair took the rhetorical lead, and his people's reaction has been at best indifferent. Like General Musharraf, he speaks for himself and his security apparatus, but seems essentially disconnected from the broader populace.

I spent Christmas reading Lawrence James' riveting *Warrior Race: A History Of The British At War*, to which the present Blairite play-war is a forlorn coda. Though the Pentagon was very appreciative of those few brave SAS men, the UK alone could never have dreamt of waging such a war. It couldn't fight the Falklands War now. Every year, it falls further behind the US technologically. And, to coin a phrase, impotence breeds decadence. You see it most clearly in what to Americans seems the curious lack of outrage over the numbers of British Muslims who turn up on Osama's side every other day. Over here, they argue whether Tali-Boy John Walker should be executed for treason, jailed for life or tossed to the Afghans. By comparison, British public opinion is cheerily relaxed about Richard Reid, Her Majesty's nominal subject but Osama's loyal foot-soldier.

It turns out Mr Blair's re-election, the first break in a half-century of Anglo-American political synchronicity, symbolises a widening divergence, between an American people resolved to do what's necessary and a British public that, in all the most disturbing ways, is beginning to act more and more – gulp – European. Even if Mr Blair's on board for Iraq, how about the rest of you?

THE BRUTAL CUBAN WINTER

January 26th 2002
The Spectator

NOT FAR FROM me, in the small Coos County town of Stark, is an old German POW camp. Camp Stark was basically a logging camp with barbed wire. With so many of its men in uniform overseas, the Brown Paper Company agreed to take German prisoners in order to keep its forestry operations going. The detainees arrived in the depths of a White Mountains winter and were not impressed by the huts. There were wire mesh screens on the insides of the windows, so that even when you opened them up you couldn't stick your hand out. The Germans pointed out that this was in contravention of the internationally agreed rules on prisoner accommodation, and insisted that the screens be removed immediately.

The camp guards looked at each other, shrugged and said, "Sure, if that's what you want." The deep winter snows melted, and eventually it was safe to open the windows. A week later, Black Fly Season arrived – the black fly isn't New Hampshire's state animal but it ought to be – and thousands of the little fellers swarmed in through those big inviting apertures to chow down on all that good Aryan blood. There was a reason for the screens.

I mention this to make two points: one) there are things that are unforeseen by international conventions; two) let's talk about the weather. The British, if you'll forgive a gratuitous racist generalisation, seem to be remarkably obtuse about matters meteorological. Perhaps this is a natural consequence of living in a country where it's 54 and overcast all summer and 53 and overcast all winter, and the only divergence from that temperate constancy was missed entirely by your famous Mr Fish. But at least in the old days Britons were ignorant but fearless: you were the mad dogs and Englishmen out in the midday sun. Now, after four months of cowering in fear at the impending arrival of the entirely mythical "brutal Afghan winter" – currently 55 and sunny in Kandahar – Fleet Street's media doom-mongers have moved seamlessly on to the horrors of the brutal Cuban winter: oh, my God, how will these poor al-Qa'eda boys – you know, the ones who could supposedly hole up in the Khyber Pass eating scorpions all winter making a fool of those Yank ignoramuses – how will these fearsome warriors survive the Caribbean nights and the hordes of malaria-infested mosquitoes?

And this time it's not just the usual America haters at *The Guardian* and the BBC but the likes of Alice Thomson, Stephen Glover, Alasdair Palmer, Matthew Parris, my most esteemed *Telegraph* and *Speccie* colleagues: "They are kept in cramped outdoor cages, open to the elements and the attentions of possibly malarial mosquitoes," notes Mr Glover. "I mind the shark cages, with their concrete floors open to the elements and the 24-hour halogen flood lights, left near mosquito-infested swamps, so the prisoners can catch malaria when some already have tuberculosis," frets Miss Thomson.

I don't know whether Alice or Stephen has ever been to DisneyWorld. Doesn't sound like quite their bag, but you never know. DisneyWorld is in the middle of a swamp, and, if you use the employees' exit and turn right rather than left and then on to the dirt track and into the swampy groves you'll find within minutes the windscreen's full of squished, bloody bugs. Yet when you're on the other side of the fence waiting in the hot sun for two hours to go on a 60-second ride, there are, amazingly, no bugs. Find me a mosquito in DisneyWorld and I'll guarantee you it's an animatronic attraction. A local girl up here ran off to Florida and hooked up with some guy who worked for the Mouse. At their Disney wedding, he told me that, among his responsibilities, he was part of the crew who bombed the perimeter at the crack of dawn each day with industrial-strength bug spray. The same procedure is being carried out at Guantanamo: the camp is sprayed with mosquito repellent.

As for malaria, that seems to have been conjured entirely out of Miss Thomson's head. There is no malaria in Cuba. None. Risk of contracting malaria: Zero per cent. And before you Fidel groupies start putting that down to the wonders of the Cuban health system, do you know who eliminated malaria from the island? The United States Army, after the Spanish-American War and by draining swamps and introducing bed netting and (here they come again) window screens.

So there's no malaria, and a tiny risk of mosquitoes. As for the "cramped outdoor cages", they are, in fact, the factory version of Bloody Mary's exotic hut on the tropic isle of Bali Hai in the current West End production of *South Pacific*. They've got roofs, with eight-foot ceilings – not exactly a Kensington drawing room, but hardly "cramped". As for those concrete floors Alice disdains, all I can say is that a few years back I jacked up my old barn and poured a concrete foundation, and there are truly few more pleasurable sensations on a hot summer's day than putting one's bare feet on cold, shaded concrete. So these "shark cages" have sloped roofs and cool floors. Granted, they have no walls. If they did, they'd be sweatboxes that would likely kill you - unless, of course, you installed air-conditioning, which, as we know, you British types find frightfully vulgar.

Nonetheless, according to an ITN report carried on PBS over here, these poor prisoners will have to "endure the searing heat". Actually, these beach huts are perfectly designed for one of the most agreeable climates on earth - a daytime high in the mid-eighties and an overnight low in the low seventies, with a wafting breeze caressing one's cheek. My advice to Fleet Street is to steer clear of weather for the rest of the war. The merest nudge of the thermostat is enough to send excitable reporters rocketing from one extreme to the other, like the old cartoon of the shower faucet with only the tiniest calibration between "Scalding" and "Freezing": Kabul in the sixties is the "brutal winter", Cuba in the low seventies is the "searing heat".

So take it from me, Don Rumsfeld's Club Fed huts are cool in the day and balmy at night. They're a lot more comfortable than the windowless "concrete coffins" of Belmarsh in which your terrorist suspects are banged up 22 hours a day. True, it's a shame they have to have wraparound wire mesh to spoil the view and there's no banana daiquiris from room service, but the idea is (in case you've forgotten) that they're meant to be *prisoners*. And, unlike the three-to-a-cell arrangements in, say, Barlinnie, the Talebannies have a room of their own, so they won't be taking it up the keister from Butch every night. They get three square meals a day, thrice-daily opportunities for showers, calls to prayer, copies of the Koran, a prayer mat – all part of a regime *The Mirror* calls "a sick attempt to appeal to the worst redneck prejudices".

It's correct that, for hygiene purposes, they were shaved, which was "culturally inappropriate". But then, if the US wanted to be culturally appropriate, they'd herd 'em on to a soccer pitch and stone 'em to death as half-time entertainment. As to whether or not they are prisoners of war, there is a legitimate difference of opinion on their status: you can't ask them for name, rank and serial number, because the last two they lack and, if Richard Reid is anything to go by, they keep a handy stack of spare monikers. This is new territory. But surely the Fleet Street whingers must know, if only from the testimony of their fellow Britons among the inmates, that there is no "torture" (*The Mail On Sunday*), not even by the weather.

Still, my colleagues may be heartened to know that Britain's getting far more attention for its anti-Americanism than it did when it was backing Bush 100%. I drove from New Hampshire to Montreal the other day and, on both Vermont and Quebec radio, I heard references to the "British-led international protests" against Guantanamo. "British-led international protests" is a much more convincing formulation than the "American-led international coalition". Your side really has got a coalition: Britain, Mary Robinson, the EU, UN, Red Cross. And it's making quite an impression: many people over here had no idea quite how ridiculous you are. You're shocked by us, we're laughing at you.

In fairness, instead of coasting on non-existent diseases and wild guesses at the weather, the always elegant Matthew Parris at least attempted to expand Guantanamo into a general thesis. "We seek to project the message that there are rules to which all nations are subject," he wrote in *The Times*. "America has a simpler message: kill Americans, and you're dead meat."

This caused endless amusement over here. As the Internet wag Steven den Beste commented, "By George, I think he's got it!"

Mr Parris is right to the extent that there are varying approaches to terrorism. You can take the dead-meat approach, or you can do the British thing: hunker down, fight a defensive war, inconvenience your citizens by shrinking the slots on pillar boxes and eliminating the rubbish bins at railway stations, insulate your political leadership so that the terrorists have nothing to do but blow the legs off grannies and schoolkids, and then after three decades pack it in, give the blood-drenched thugs the red carpet treatment at the Palace of Westminster and make them Ministers of a Crown they don't even deign to recognise. That playbook wouldn't sell here. If Omagh had happened in, say, Wisconsin, the government would not allow Martin McGuinness to keep his secrets about the perpetrators merely because they had such a high regard for his talents as Education Minister.

"My difficulty is not with America as America, but with Washington as a hoped-for coalition partner," Parris continues. "Partnership in foreign policy is not in their nature." There's a very good reason for that. Partnership implies the burden is shared more or less equally. If I bought twenty quid's worth of shares in *The Spectator* and started swanning about bitching that Conrad Black didn't treat me as a partner, he'd rightly think I'd gone nuts. The British in their time were at least as ruthless about such realities as the Americans are today. For example, in September 1944, in one of the lesser-known conferences to prepare for the post-war world, Churchill and Roosevelt met in Quebec City. They had no compunction about excluding from their deliberations the Canadian Prime Minister, Mackenzie King, even though he was the nominal host. There's a cartoon of the time showing King peering through a keyhole as the top dogs settled the fate of the world without him.

And guess what? Militarily speaking, Canada was a far big player back then than Britain is today: the Royal Canadian Navy was the world's third-biggest surface fleet, the Canucks got the worst beach at Normandy - but hey, why bore you with details? In those days that still wasn't enough to get you a seat at the table.

So what exactly is it that Britain brings to the table today? The RAF did nothing in Afghanistan. The Gurkhas sat out the war in Oman. In the end, the only non-American contribution was a few brave British and Australian SAS men fighting alongside US Special Forces. We honour them for their service and their courage. But they weren't strictly necessary and in return the Pentagon had to put up with not just that idiot speech from Admiral Boyce but a lot of anonymous MoD pillocks sneering to the press about how Washington should let our chaps handle the show because frankly these Yank special forces have always been an absolute shower. Do you realise how pitiful this sounds? The way things are going in the prisoner round-ups, it looks like the major British participation in the war has been on the al-Qa'eda side.

"America has simple gods and likes to keep her satan simple, too," declared Matthew Parris. "In Salem it was once witches. In Senator Joe McCarthy's heyday it was Commies. Now it is al-Qa'eda."

Just for the record, the Salem witch trials were conducted not by citizens of the United States but by British subjects. As for Senator McCarthy's heyday, well, there were a lot of Commies around: in short order, they'd seized half of Europe, neutered much of what was left and had become the dominant influence on the Third World's political class. Suppose America had followed the rest of the west and elected a détente sophisticate like Helmut Schmidt or Pierre Trudeau, whose first act upon retirement from office was to take his young sons to see Siberia because "that was where the future was being made" – in 1984! The world would be very different today, and not to my liking. The west won't work if every country's Canada and every leader's Trudeau. The only thing that enables Belgium to be Belgium and Norway to be Norway and Britain to be Britain is the fact that America's America – for all the reasons my *Spectator* colleagues deplore.

~

BRUTAL AFGHAN WINTER UPDATE

January 24th 2002
The National Post

IT'S OVER. "The winter is over," Zbolon Semantov, one of the last two Jews in Kabul, told *The New York Times*. "Why shouldn't I stay for a while to enjoy the fruits of summer?"

The "fruits of summer", incidentally, is not a reference to the fetching young catamites now re-appearing on the streets of Kandahar, according to a story in *The Times* of London filed from the city known as the "gay capital of South-East Asia". "Such is the Pashtun obsession with sodomy," writes Tim Reid, "locals tell you that birds fly over the city using only one wing, the other covering their posterior." Apparently, it's common among swarthy Pashtuns to take an "*ashna*" – a "beloved" boy – and stroll the streets arm in arm of a balmy Kandahar evening in January. If the humanitarian lobby – Big Consciences – had made like the birds and worried a bit more about covering its posterior instead of playing Rent-A-Scare for lazy journalists, it wouldn't look quite so ridiculous now.

~

GENEVA CONVENTIONAL WISDOM

January 24th 2002
The National Post

A S YOU PROBABLY know, Article 26 of the Geneva Convention provides that prisoners shall be given access to tobacco. I'm sure I'm not the only humanitarian Canadian who's noticed the suspiciously small number of smoke rings wafting over Guantanamo. Furthermore, I was shocked by those pictures of arriving prisoners forced to wear shackles and surgical masks. This is in complete contravention of Article 26: How can you smoke your pipe when you're wearing a surgical mask? How can you bend down to reach your sock, where you keep the matches and plastic explosives, when you're in shackles? After all, in their own country, many of these young Talibs like nothing better than to light up a fag. As humanitarian Canadians, we should be organizing an emergency airlift of cigars to Cuba.

Oh, wait a minute. We're the guys who, as reported here in June 1999, deliberately withheld cigarettes from the Kosovar refugees at CFB Trenton and other Canadian bases, despite the fact that 98% of them were smokers and were twitchily prowling the perimeter fence in search of a kindly passer-by willing to nip down to Loblaw's for a pouch of Balkan Sobranie. The Red Cross, happy to subject its Kosovar charges to cruel and unusual punishment at Trenton, is now handing out smokes to the al-Qaeda terrorists. Isn't it about time there was an international human rights investigation into the outrageous torture inflicted on these Kosovo Muslims while in Canada? Where's Mary Robinson when you need her?

On second thoughts, you never do.

⌐

CAPTIVE COUNTRY

January 26th 2002
The Daily Telegraph

Live from the living hell of Guantanamo Bay, the brutally tortured British members of al-Qa'eda talk exclusively to the Telegraph *about the horrors they've experienced:*

"It's humiliating," says one. "They put you in these shapeless overalls, with a mask over your face – for your own protection, they tell you – but you're gasping for air as you try to breathe through your nose and there's bright lights blazing down on you and you're suffering sleep deprivation because you've been awake for 48 hours and any sharp instruments have been taken away from you. And eventually you think, 'I've had 30 years with the NHS and it's not getting any better.'"

That's when Mustapha hip Replacement (formerly Dr Nigel Tomlinson) decided to rethink his life. "So, when Osama called and suggested a mid-life career change, I was ready for it. It was the lack of sharp instruments that finally made me jack it in. It was a Tuesday morning hernia. I said 'Scalpel' and the nurse said, 'It's in Manchester.'"

"The journey was a nightmare," says another prisoner. "We just sat there hour after hour. In the dark. Freezing. No idea of where we were headed, and deprived of even the simple human dignity of being able to use the toilet. Then eventually we pulled out of the tunnel and the customer service representative said we were being diverted to Hastings St Leonards where customers should await a courtesy bus to Bushey."

That's when Aziz al-Daysupersaver (formerly Roger Threepwood) decided he'd had enough of commuting and maybe it was time to try international terrorism. "The final straw was during the two-hour wait in the Croissant de Paris burger bar when I read in the paper that they'd put Lord Birt in charge. And I thought, 'Well, I've always wanted to be a shoe bomber…' Strictly long-haul flights, Business Class all the way, executive check-in. Mohammed Atta said, 'Allah be praised, you spend eternity with virgin.' I said, 'Well, it beats spending eternity with Connex.'"

"You feel like you've been totally stripped of any individual identity," argues his fellow terrorist. "They make you wear a shapeless boiler suit and have your head shaved. And eventually you think, 'Do I really want to be in a lesbian theatre collective that hasn't had a good review since *Time Out* in 1983?'"

That's when Mufti al-Diva (formerly Fran Bogg) began to look into becoming a suicide bomber. "So when New Labour cut our grant it was really a blessing in disguise. A month off the Immac, and I was accepted by a madrassah in Yemen. I've never looked back."

"People can't imagine what it's like," says a fellow al-Qa'eda fanatic. "For your daily outdoor exercise, you're confined to this cramped, tiny space, shuffling up and down behind an 11-foot fence topped with razor wire. And eventually you think, 'Sod it, I'm sick of living in Fulham.'"

That's when Amin Riyahl Ustayt (formerly Rupert Scott-Thwaites) began to hear the call of the Hindu Kush. "I spotted the remodelled donkey stables in Kandahar while flicking through Country Life *and we moved in four weeks later. To be honest, until he came to the housewarming, I had no idea who Mullah Omar was."*

"The conditions are bloody awful," confirms another. "They give you toothpaste, toothbrush, and a towel, and then lock you up in this tiny space where you're visible to everyone. There's no privacy at all, even when you want to go to the bathroom. And the hot lights are bearing down on you 24 hours a day. And eventually you think, 'Flamin' Nora, why did I ever agree to do 'Big Brother 3'?'"

That's when Sayed bin Starkuz (formerly Del Sprong) began to consider a career in international terrorism. "To be honest, I'd have joined sooner if they hadn't kept going on about the 72 virgins. I said, 'Wot, you mean the dull mousey types in the beige cardigans who got rejected at the first audition? You're stuck in Paradise with these birds you can never get your leg over?' That's when Osama said I was asking too many questions and told me to get back to mopping out the cave."

"It's like you're totally disorientated," adds his fellow captive. "I thought I'd go mad. You're covered from head to toe in this suffocating suit with big ear muffs and huge mittens. It's hot as hell

in there, you're drenched in sweat, you're suffering complete sensory deprivation, and forced to crouch in all kinds of degrading positions. I've never felt so dehumanised. And eventually you think, 'Well, maybe 20 years in Cats *is enough, love.'"*

That's when e-Qu'ity Minnamum (formerly Ronnie Twinkle) began to wonder about breaking into infidel-slaying. "I was really chuffed when my agent said she could get me six months in an Islamic jihad. She said, 'They're looking for embittered losers with a death wish. Then I remembered you'd auditioned for Edward And Mrs Simpson The Musical.'"*

Meanwhile, in London, Robin Cook angrily dismissed accusations from human rights groups that Britain should be doing more to improve living conditions for its alleged terrorists. "I utterly reject that charge," he said. "We've moved Lady Thatcher to a cubbyhole under the stairs and given her office to Gerry Adams."

WHO'S MUSHARRAF?

January 12th 2002
The Spectator

THE TRICKIEST bit of the year-in-review wrap-ups over here was trying to explain why the famously moronic Bush seems to be doing such a good job of running the war. The conventional wisdom is that he's "grown in office". It may just seem that way to the pundits because so many of them have shrunk in office. A year ago, *The New York Times'* Pulitzer Prize-winning jingle-writer Maureen Dowd came up with funny names for the idiot frat-boy's Cold War keepers (Dick Cheney = "Big Time", Don Rumsfeld = "Rummy") and figured that would be enough to get her through the first term. Syndicated professional Texan Molly Ivins only came up with one funny name (Bush Junior = "Shrub") but managed to stretch it out to a full-length book.

Now both gals seem utterly lost, Maureen gibbering away in loopy introspection like a call-in host who's not getting any calls:

"Since Sept. 11, our long voyage of personal awareness has only intensified. Every day, we check our image, looking for ways, big or small, that we might have changed. We ponder if the changes are good or bad. We puzzle over whether the president has metamorphosed. We palaver about how the country has been transformed... We've absorbed 9/11 into our shallow fixation on self-image, turning the crisis into a makeover saga..." Speak for yourself, dearie.

Jacob Weisberg, whose latest volume of amusing *Bushisms* is rocketing up the amazon.com bestsellers list at Number 54,797, came up with a subtler explanation for Bush's apparent success. Having been an early convert to the boy-what-a-dummy school of Dubyology, he's sticking with his line that the guy's an idiot. But, fortunately for Dubya, war plays to an idiot's strengths: "Bush continues to exhibit the same lack of curiosity, thoughtfulness, and engagement with ideas that made him a C student. Nuance, complexity, subtlety, and contradiction are not part of the mental universe he inhabits. And curiously enough, it is these very qualities of mind—or lack thereof—that seem to be making him such a good war President," wrote Weisberg in *Slate*, arguing that his earlier thesis – that boneheads make bad Presidents – still held. "But there's a wartime codicil. In wartime, certain qualities sometimes associated with high intelligence—fascination with detail, a tendency to self-reliance, an awareness of ambiguity—become greater obstacles to effective leadership."

In war, the idiot President comes into his own, since war is a simpleton's game and does not require the grasp of nuance, subtlety, etc of more complex issues such as mandatory Federal regulations for bicycling helmets, or whatever it was Bill Clinton was busy with for eight years.

It's worth going back to the "root causes" of such exquisite condescension. Two years ago, a TV guy in Boston called Andy Hiller sprang a sudden "pop quiz" on the then Texas Governor and asked him to identify various world leaders – the President of Wackistan, the Prime Minister of Albiseenya, and so on. Bill Bradley, hailed as one of the greatest brains ever to bless the Senate, had refused to participate in a similar quiz, but genial ol' Dubya said sure, why not? He scored an impressive zero rating, and seemed entirely amiable about it, save for a counter-challenge halfway through, when he asked Hiller if he could name the Foreign Minister of Mexico. "No, sir," TV Boy replied. "But I would say I'm not running for President."

The Weekly Standard's Andrew Ferguson suggested that Bush should have switched to Hiller's own area of expertise. "Okay, you're in television. Who played the Professor on 'Gilligan's Island'?" But that's not Dubya's style and so, two years on, in September 2001, legions of journalists couldn't resist noting the "irony" that one of the world leaders he failed to recognise was General Musharraf, the Pakistani strongman on whose support Bush's fragile Afghan strategy depended so heavily.

Gosh! Fancy not knowing who General Musharraf was! But it turns out General Musharraf didn't know who he was, either. In the course of about 15 minutes in mid-September, he performed a 180-degree U-turn, cast off his old persona as principal Taleban patron and decided he was happy to be whoever the Administration wanted him to be: just fax him the script and he'll read it. Why waste your time knowing who the old General Musharraf was, when that person has effectively ceased to exist? The new General Musharraf is something of a work-in-progress, but, as additional demands are put on him, he responds swiftly and graciously: after complaints from Washington that his previous condemnations were too qualified, this week he declared that Pakistan rejects all terrorism, with no exceptions even for Muslim "liberation" groups in Indian-held Kashmir (which gives Islamabad a rather more robust line on terrorists than London or Dublin).

After September 11th, everyone was into the General – you couldn't open the papers without reading Musharraf this, Musharraf that. But, as the old song says, I dug Musharraf when Musharraf wasn't cool. In *The National Post* on October 21st 1999, I hailed the General's ascent to power. This was the time when Britain and Canada were agitating about sanctions, suspension from the Commonwealth, and all the usual hooey. In defiance of the Robin Cook line, I saluted Musharraf as a great improvement on his allegedly "democratic" predecessor, Prime Minister …well, come on, you clever-clogs types who sneer at Bush, what was the guy's name then? I'll give you a clue: he'd given his various unsavoury relatives not just all the plum jobs but also their own colour-coded Mercs, and he'd installed them in one purpose-built complex on the edge of Lahore, a kind of Pakistani Southfork. Anyone remember the fellow? Andy Hiller of Boston, like to take a shot?

Nawaz Sharif. He'd subverted the Constitution, Parliament, the Opposition, the courts and the media and was indulging in highly dangerous nuclear braggadocio with India. "General Musharraf," I wrote, "is supported at home because he's promised to end corruption; he should be supported abroad because, by removing Sharif, he's made the region safer." Had Robin Cook and Lloyd Axworthy, the Canadian Foreign Minister, had their way and restored the Sharifs, the nuclear stand-off these last couple of weeks could have gone very differently.

Musharraf was, on balance, the best man available. Left to his own devices, he might eventually have weaned the ISI, Pakistan's intelligence service, off its links with the Taleban and defused Islamist elements in the army. But it was only because in the days after September 11th Washington clamped the metaphorical electrodes to his genitals that he did it so swiftly. He went on TV and told Pakistanis that the survival of the nation was at stake.

Maybe that's what Washington told him, or maybe he was just covering himself. But it's not a bad way of putting it. Why, after all, does Pakistan exist? It exists because of a terrible failure of will on the part of the British. Indeed, all the problems Tony Blair has been swanking about Asia anxious to mediate are the fault of his compatriots and, come to that, his party. There wouldn't be two nuclear powers if there weren't two powers in the first place. If Lord Mountbatten had held out against partition for another year, Jinnah would have been dead and who knows how much steam the Muslim League could have mustered?

Conversely, the only reason India and Pakistan are squabbling over Kashmir is because Britain, having decided on partition, then, typically, screwed over the Maharajahs and Nawabs of the Princely states, which comprised a third of the sub-continent, and told them the jig was up and they had to choose which of the two nations they wanted to belong to. In Kashmir, the ruler was Hindu and the vast majority of his subjects were Muslim, but the British let him opt to join India. However you look at it, the creation of Pakistan was a mess: even the ISI was a British invention. More importantly, in stringing along with Jinnah's rejection of modern, pluralist, secular, democratic India, Mountbatten and co implicitly sanctioned Pakistan's development as the precise negative of its neighbour: backward, narrow, fundamentalist, dictatorial. If that's what centuries of expertise in the region produces, then I'll take a know-nothing like Bush any day.

Obviously, the President can't solve all the messes created by the Attlee Government: he's wise to leave that to SuperTone. Instead, he decided what he needed from Pakistan and invited them to agree with him. And it was all the more effective for being uncomplicated by warm personal relationships. Bill Clinton had Yasser Arafat over to the White House more often than any other foreign leader, and what did he have to show for his investment? Intifada, suicide bombs, arms shipments from Iran via Dubai to the Palestinian Authority. The problem with that Boston pop quiz is the assumption – very common among the Clinton-Gore tendency – that because you know the Deputy Fisheries Minister you somehow know the country. As we should surely know by now, to think of Araby as President Mubarak and King Fahd only obscures the real dynamics of the region. That's why, in this war, it's the fellows with the bulging Rolodexes – former US Ambassadors to Saudi Arabia, etc - who talk the most drivel.

A little after flunking the Musharraf quiz, Bush made a campaign stop where he was set up by a CBC comedian and appeared to give the impression he thought the Prime Minister of Canada was called "Jean Poutine" instead of …well, whatever his real name is. Poutine is the national dish of Quebec – a bowl of fries covered in gravy and cheese curds – and Bush was yet again much mocked for his ignorance. He was certainly at odds with the prevailing trend – in the eight years since Monsieur Non-Poutine has been Prime Minister, his name recognition in the US has doubled, from 1% to 2%. Sadly, Governor Bush was not among them.

But, look, I'm Canadian, and to be honest, given Prime Minister Wossname's performance since September 11th, it's hard to see why any American should know his name. Lacking both the resolve and the capability to make any contribution to the new war, Monsieur Whoozis proved unable to offer even rhetorical support, as his counterparts in Britain, Italy, Australia and elsewhere did. He assumed carelessly that, as in Kosovo and the Gulf, Bush would put together the usual multinational coalition – 99% American, 1% everybody else. But Bush didn't want anything and, even worse, when the international stabilisation force was being put together in London, the British didn't want Canada, either – even though Canadians are supposed to be the world's most sought-after peacekeepers. Ottawa went into panic mode and begged Washington to be allowed to do *something*. There's now an understanding that at some point 700 members of the Princess Patricia's Canadian Light Infantry will be allowed to join the Americans in stabilising Kandahar. As Rick Gibbons of *The Toronto Sun* drolly observed, "History is replete with examples of countries having to negotiate their way out of wars. Rarely does a country actually have to negotiate its way into one."

That's the problem with those impromptu pop quizzes on world leaders: you can't see the lack of wood behind the celebrity trees. A more important question than "Who's the Prime Minister of Canada?" is "What's the rest of the world for?" Americans know what they contribute: they're the engine of the global economy and the pre-eminent military power. But Canada and Europe expect the US to pick up the tab for their defence costs and yet still treat them as serious players. The big lesson of the war so far, as the American hyperpower gallops further and further ahead, is that, *pace* Tony Blair's ambitions, there are now no second-tier powers: that's not a healthy situation for the world. Let's take it as a given that George W Bush lacks the intelligence to hold down a really demanding job like columnist at *The New York Times* or *Slate*. Let's take it as read that he's a stupid man leading the stupid party of a stupid country. Granted all that, his blissful indifference to the hotshots of the *International Who's Who* is as brilliant a distillation of global reality as any. Bush couldn't name the Prime Minister of Hoogivsadamistan, but in the weeks before September 11th, having already spotted his predecessor's neglect of the matter, his Administration was working on new strategies to combat international terrorism. What a chump, eh? Too dumb to be Prime Minister of Canada.

~

EVERYBODY'S SHOT

January 19th 2002

The Spectator

THERE'S NO fat in *Black Hawk Down*. Everything's lean: lean actors, lean plot, lean script. Here's Tom Sizemore, a colonel in charge of a small convoy under heavy fire in Mogadishu, pulling a dead soldier out of the driver's seat of a Humvee and ordering a bleeding sergeant to take his place:

"Get into that truck and drive."

"But I'm shot, Colonel."

"Everybody's shot. Get in and drive."

Terrific. The best kind of screenwriting – raw, muscular, the American spirit in six words (by Ken Nolan). Peggy Noonan, the Reagan/Bush wordsmith, picked up on that line and devoted her *Wall Street Journal* column to its metaphoric power post-September 11th. *Black Hawk Down* is a movie for the times, and almost an act of redemption for its producer Jerry Bruckheimer and director Ridley Scott after such historical travesties, PC idiocies and flyboy fluffiness as *Pearl Harbor* (Bruckheimer), *GI Jane* (Scott) and *Top Gun* (Bruckheimer with Scott's brother Tony).

It's October 3rd 1993, Somalia. Remember that? Most of us can't quite recall what America was doing there, but we know some number of Special Forces died, their bodies dragged through the streets by the gleeful conscripts of General Aideed, the hotshot warlord du jour. Bill Clinton ordered a withdrawal of American forces, and the whole episode went down as a "failure" – according to taste, either a disastrous intervention in a territory in which the US had no interest, or proof that America was soft and weak and had no stomach for body bags. We know what conclusion Osama bin Laden drew. A journalist, Mark Bowden, started mooching around in the subject and discovered that the public's perception of the mission – a horrible fiasco – was completely wrong. There was, not for the first time, a failure of political will, but the military were heroic. If Somalia was an example of political weakness, this operation was also a demonstration of military strength.

The Rangers and Delta Force were there to help prevent famine by securing supply routes against General Aideed's thugs. Their mission that day was to kidnap a bunch of the General's lieutenants who were holding a meeting downtown. This they did, but two helicopters were shot down. The Rangers pride themselves on never leaving a comrade to fall into the hands of the enemy, and so they stayed in the city to search for and rescue survivors. It was a story of bravery and loyalty that Bowden felt deserved to be told. His book was a bestseller but not an obvious candidate for Hollywood, given that it's at odds with people's preconception of the event.

At first, you're not sure Scott can pull it off. Helicopters sail over glistening sand and for a moment we hover on the brink of the prettification – the cinematic flower-arranging – that so disfigured *Hannibal*. It's an external shot, too composed, too aware to get inside the subject – in the way that all the poets and novelists hired by glossy mags to write something arty about September 11th have been colossal flops – embarrassingly fussy and self-regarding - next to the straightforward account of a fireman or secretary. (Think John Updike in *The New Yorker* preening his subordinate clauses, "smoke speckled with bits of paper curled into the cloudless sky, and strange inky rivulets ran down the giant structure's vertically corrugated surface... it fell straight down like an elevator, with a tinkling shiver and a groan of concussion distinct across the mile of air... an empty spot had appeared, as if by electronic command," etc. Oh, for a monosyllabic tab hack! The ghastly false tinkle of all those shivers and groans and curling rivulets is a reminder that for the most part our great artists don't illuminate the human condition so much as offer an insulated retreat from it.)

But Scott pulls himself together, and henceforth it's all business. It's almost as if he feels duty bound to match the men's dogged, defiant, improvisational professionalism. No birds, no bonking, no backstory: Bowden's book tells us about these men's early lives and loves, Scott relies on the shorthand of casting – laconic Sam Shepard, idealistic Josh Hartnett, eager Ewan McGregor. The actors establish their identities in the early scenes and then submerge themselves in the unit. Once the battle starts there's little dialogue that isn't armyspeak barked into receivers (just as well, in the case of McGregor, whose accent is a little unreliable).

In one of the film's few departures from reality, Scott put name tags on the Ranger helmets because otherwise they'd be hard to tell apart in the battle scenes. But that's okay: the cast understands that the film's real star is the operation and that confusion about who's who is part of the story. A 16-hour all-night battle compressed into two and a half hours, *Black Hawk Down* does a brilliant job of placing you inside the heart of the event and plugging you into the rhythm of combat. Scott pulls off an extraordinary technical achievement: as the operation starts to unravel, the film becomes more vivid, unrelenting, intense, adversity heightening the reality. There's none of those *Private Ryan* interludes with the ennobling sentiment and uplifting rhetoric. The nobility and inspiration are in the action. It is in that sense a film very much in tune with America's mood: practical, resolute, fierce.

FEBRUARY

The face of the tiger

February 25th 2002
The National Post

There was a young lady of Niger
Who smiled as she rode on a tiger
They returned from the ride
With the lady inside
And the smile on the face of the tiger.

THE SMILE on the face of the tiger is the video recording of the death of Daniel Pearl. What an accomplished production it sounds. According to Pakistani authorities, somewhere between five and eight persons were present to choreograph and record the murder of the *Wall Street Journal* reporter. They wanted to get it right, and, from their point of view, they did. *The Arab News* describes the video thus:

> *As he finishes the statement, a hand appears from behind and grabs his head, while another hand appears and with a sharp-edged weapon cuts his throat.*

In an artistic touch, the camera zooms in for a close-up of Pearl's severed head. See? He is an American *and* a Jew. We hit the jackpot! And then we cut his head off. A pity the filthy Hollywood infidels have closed their Oscar nominations, or we'd be a sure thing for Best Foreign Short.

Three weeks ago, Robert Fisk, the Middle East Correspondent of Britain's *Independent*, offered a familiar argument to Pearl's kidnappers: killing the American would be "a major blunder, an own goal of the worst kind", "the best way of ensuring that the suffering" – of Kashmiris, Afghans, Palestinians, whatever – "goes unrecorded".

185

Others peddled a similar line: if you release Daniel, he'll be able to tell your story, get your message out.

Somehow we keep missing the point: the story did get out; the severed head is the message. By now, the tape has been duplicated, and re-duplicated, and copies are circulating through the bazaars and madrassahs. Apparently, it's even for sale on the Internet. It's a recruitment video – join the jihad, meet interesting people, and behead them – and a training video, too: this is how you do it – the statement, the knife, the defilement of the corpse. But in a more profound sense it's a boast, an act of self-congratulation, a pat on the back for a job well done: the smile on the face of the tiger.

Daniel Pearl reckoned he could ride the tiger: he was promised a meeting with an Islamofascist bigwig, so he got in a car with intermediaries he thought he knew. George Jonas wrote a brilliant column the other day on the delusions of those who think they can "establish a 'dialogue' with fanatics" or, as some of Pearl's friends put it, "bridge the misconceptions". The "misconception", presumably, is that these men are ruthless, violent, depraved. As surely we know by now, the only misconception is that that's a misconception.

Pearl thought he had won their trust, that they had accepted him as a honest broker, recognized his genuine sympathy for Muslim suffering, were willing to treat with him as one human being to another. But in the end they saw none of that: to them, he was an American, a Jew, a trophy. So they set a trap. According to one witness in a Karachi court, Omar Sheikh boasted two days beforehand that they were about to seize someone who was "anti-Islam and a Jew". By the time Robert Fisk issued his plea for mercy on February 4th, Pearl was already dead.

In Saturday's *Independent*, Fisk reflected on the death of the man described as his friend: "But why was he killed? Because he was a Westerner, a 'Kaffir'? Because he was an American? Or because he was a journalist?" Anyone spot the missing category? It's the one Omar Sheikh used, and the one acknowledged by Daniel Pearl in his last words: "Yes, I am a Jew..." Fisk can't bring himself to use the word in the entire column. Full disclosure: after noodling incoherently around possible reasons for the murder, Fisk settles on a "shameful, unethical headline" over an "article by Mark Steyn" in Pearl's own *Wall Street Journal*. It was about Fisk's bloody beating by an Afghan mob in Pakistan last December, after which he said that, in their shoes, "I would have done just the same to Robert Fisk. Or any other Westerner I could find." It's not their fault, he insisted, their "brutality is entirely the product of others". As Fisk sees it, the mob who attacked him were "truly innocent of any crime except being the victim of the world". In *The Wall Street Journal*, I called this "Fiskal responsibility – it's always the Great Satan's fault."

Insofar as there's any connection between the mugging of this vain buffoon and the murder of Daniel Pearl, it's this: History repeats itself, but, in this instance, the usual order – tragedy's recapitulation as farce – has been reversed. Is it too much to hope that militant Islam's apologists might finally put an end to their own "misconceptions"? Islam is not "the victim of the world", but the victim of itself. Omar Sheikh is a British public schoolboy, a graduate of the London School of Economics, and, like Osama and Mohammed Atta, a monument to the peculiar burdens of a non-deprived childhood in the Muslim world. Give 'em an e-mail address and they use it for kidnap notes. Give 'em a camcorder and they make a snuff video.

Let's assume that all the chips fell the jihadis' way, that they recruited enough volunteers to be able to kidnap and decapitate every single Jew in Palestine. Then what? Muslims would still be, as Pakistan's General Musharraf told a conference the other day, "the poorest, the most illiterate, the most backward, the most unhealthy, the most unenlightened, the most deprived, and the weakest of all the human race." Who would "the victim of the world" blame next? The evidence of the Sudan, Nigeria, and other parts of Africa suggests that, when there are no Jews to hand, the Islamofascists happily make do with killing Christians. In Kashmir, it's the Hindus' fault. There's always someone.

Musharraf is by far the most interesting character to emerge in that part of the world in some time. As I wrote recently, the British should never have created Pakistan (it was a typical botched job by that silly old queen Mountbatten). Nor should the British have created the ISI, the Pakistani intelligence service whose "rogue elements" (a term covering about 97% of employees) have their fingerprints on at least some of the outlying parts of the Pearl crime scene. Nor should Pakistan's charming, urbane, westernized elite – a ruling class whose only deficiency is that they're incapable of ruling – ever have acceded to the Islamicization of Pakistan's British-derived legal system, under which, for example, Muslims who behead Muslims face the death penalty but Muslims who behead non-Muslims don't. No matter how zealously the Pakistani police pursue Daniel Pearl's murderers, in law his life is of less value than theirs.

This then is Musharraf's moment. Will he allow his country's darkest forces to maintain his people in their squalor? Or will he do as Ataturk did after the collapse of the Ottoman Empire? If Pakistan did not exist, it would not be necessary to invent it. But it does exist, so it's necessary to reinvent it, to reverse the vast catalogue of errors made by every wretched administrator from Lord Mountbatten to Nawaz Sharif, Musharraf's corrupt predecessor. At the very least, the General needs to dismantle the ISI and announce immediately that the Islamic biases of the justice system are being abolished and that all individuals are equal before the law.

The Americans will provide certain incentives for him to do this. If Musharraf demurs, Washington will make other arrangements. It's his choice: he can try to ride the tiger, or resolve to kill it and hang it in his trophy room.

OLYMPIC ICE STORM

February 17th 2002
The Sunday Telegraph

ON MONDAY night, I had the TV on in the background while I was pottering about, when suddenly my ear caught the familiar strains of the theme from *Love Story*, one of those tunes you never hear any more except at skating competitions.

To be honest, I prefer Francis Lai's gloopy theme with its "Where do I begin?" lyric by my late friend Carl Sigman, and the magnificently deranged Shirley Bassey recording has more drama going on in it than Jamie Salé and David Pelletier's icy re-enactment of the entire plot will ever have. To anyone with even a nodding acquaintance with ballet and show dance, the most exacting part of a serious discussion of ice routines is trying to keep a straight face. I couldn't give a hoot for your double axels, triple lutzes or even the triple triple, whatever that is, but like most guys I always enjoy the bit where the fellow propels the gal toward the camera backwards on one leg while the wind blows her cute little skirt up her back.

Anyway, Jamie did a perfect triple gusset, to use the technical term, and happily, since Monday's outrage, NBC, south of the border, and the CBC, to the north, have been replaying the moment round the clock. The rest of the stuff – the giddy swirls, representing the scene in the movie where Oliver and Jenny caper in the snow; the sudden slipping apart, representing the moment when Jenny discovers she has a terminal illness – is fine as far as it goes: if you only see one "*Love Story* On Ice" this year, make it this one.

Before Salé and Pelletier, the Russian couple, Berezhnaya and Sikharulidze, had come out and crashed around for a couple of minutes to the Meditation from *Thaïs*, the perfect musical accompaniment for a sport that, as noted above, is often a meditation of thighs. Unfortunately, the guy stumbled on a double axel at the front end of a combination and, as experts agree, the one place you don't want to stumble on a double axel is at the front end of your combinations. Nevertheless, despite this error and to the astonishment of the crowd, the judges decided that these clumsy Russkies were the winners. Well, not all the judges: just the eastern bloc plus France. Despite the IOC's public deploring of politics, in figure skating the Cold War hasn't ended and the French are still non-participating members of Nato.

Something strange happened as the week wore on. The more the networks rebroadcast Jamie and David's entire routine, the more choreographically dramatic and passionate it seemed to become, heightened as it was by fresh revelations of the great injustice, and brief talk-show glimpses of the team's off-ice love for each other. By Valentine's Day, I was beginning to choke up at the bit where Jamie and David recreate the scene where Oliver and Jenny caper in the snow; my shirt front was sodden with tears as Jamie slipped apart from David, representing the moment when Jenny first discovers she's ill. For me, of course, it represented the moment when Jamie first discovers that lousy French broad has stiffed 'em.

This apparently is why pairs skating is big business: the audience projects its own romantic fancies on to the couples, no matter how fantastical it might be, especially in the case of some of those ice-dancing chaps. It's hard to imbue any other Olympic sport with affairs

189

of the heart. Few of us watch the two-man luge and coo, "Oh, it's so romantic! Look at how the top guy arches his back to avoid crushing the bottom guy's nuts! It's obvious they're in love!"

Romantic projection seems as sound a judging method as anything else. After Monday's fiasco, there were half-hearted attempts by the experts to attribute it to "cultural" differences: the Russians, Chinese et al would have preferred something classical rather than a sappy Seventies movie score. It was mooted that Jamie and David had made a big mistake by wearing sober, stylish, non-risible grey without any sequins or tassels. In other words, the judges are looking for high-toned symphonic music interpreted by guys in spangly pink bolero jackets. By interpreting cheesy music in serious clothes, Jamie and David had given the fatal impression they'd been reading the instruction manual upside down.

There may be something in this theory. I thought in the men's competition Tim Goebel's *American In Paris* routine was tops, but the judges hammered him in the "presentation" marks. By "presentation", it seems they resented the way he didn't flounce around twirling his arms and waggling his hips. The experts argue that the public doesn't understand the "technical" considerations, but in this instance the technical considerations boil down to mandatory screaming campness: you don't stand a chance unless you queen about like some bitch waiter at Miami Beach enraged at being told to hold the curly endive.

When it was pointed out that even these technical considerations didn't quite cover the outrageous farrago of the pairs results, the officials, privately and publicly, offered various explanations, all of which were notable for the almost insouciant lack of pretence that there was any integrity to the judging process. There were those who tried to pass it off as some sort of typing error on the memo: the mandatory ice-dancing fix had somehow erroneously got extended to the freestyle pairs. Asked to respond to rumours that the French judge, Marie Reine Le Gougne, had been pressured into voting for the Russians, the French Skating Federation said Mme Le Gougne was "emotionally fragile". They should know. By the end of the week, when she was ejected from the judges' panel, it emerged that they were the ones pressuring her to switch votes. Who, in turn, was pressuring the Federation was less clear, at least officially.

Five months to the day after September 11th, another sinister foreign conspiracy had struck on American soil, and once again underestimated American resolve. Had Skategate taken place in a foreign city before a foreign audience and been broadcast over here in the middle of the night, they might have pulled it off. Instead, despite IOC President Jacques Rogge's insistence that this is a new Olympic era, the usual corrupt officials blithely assumed they could get away with "victimising a North American pair on North American soil", as Cam Cole put it in *The National Post* – and live in US primetime, to boot.

For all that pious guff about not tainting the "Olympic ideals", the best Games have always been those infected by politics: a racially inferior Negro driving Hitler nuts by taking four medals in '36; the mad-as-hell Magyars who, a month after the Hungarian uprising, whupped the Soviets in a brutal water-polo match in Melbourne in 1956. Alas, the USSR went belly up and those genetically modified east bloc lady shot-putters with facial hair even Mullah Omar might find a tad excessive faded from the scene. And, to be honest, in the last decade the Olympics hasn't been what it was. But what happened this week was, like the 1980 US-Soviet hockey match, not just a clash of sportsmen, but a clash of the dominant political philosophies of the day: on the one hand, the moral clarity of post-September 11th America; on the other, the principal challenger to that vision - the multilateralists who insist that any international deal is worth going along with: Kyoto, Durban, the quickstep round of the ice-dancing competition. In the week before Jamie and David hit the ice, you couldn't pick up a paper without seeing something from Chris Patten or Lionel Jospin deploring the Americans' lack of "sophistication". Hubert Védrine, the French Foreign Minister, disdained what he called the "simplistic" approach of the Bush Administration.

Well, we got a good look last week at what French "sophistication" amounts to in practice. It doesn't matter whether it's because they're "emotionally fragile" (like Mme Le Gougne) or just duplicitous bastards (like her Skating Federation), those two options accounting for pretty much every significant event in modern French history. It's one thing for the "sophisticates" to insist in their own deranged media that the Americans didn't really win in Afghanistan, it's quite another thing to insist in the great state of Utah that two plucky Canadians didn't win in the figure skating. The ISU conceded on Friday that "public opinion" – i.e., Americans - had persuaded them to award a belated gold to Salé and Pelletier, implying that once they're on the plane back to Europe the skating establishment can resume business as usual. Maybe they can. But for now they've learned that, at least on US soil, the new Bush Doctrine applies not just to rogue states but to Rogge states, too.

~

THE AXELS OF EVIL

February 14th 2002
The National Post

WHERE DO I begin to tell the story of how great a wrong can be?

I was in the Canadian VIP pavilion at Salt Lake when Jamie and David were cruelly cut down last Monday – or, as I like to think of it, 2/11. "This is outrageous!" I cried, leaping to my feet, falling backwards and landing on top of Brian Tobin, Allan Rock and Bill Graham (a perfect triple putz). "Canada must reverse this injustice!"

"Well, now, hold on," said Naomi Klein, emerging from the no-hospitality suite. "Did Canada deserve to lose? Of course not. But there's a different question that must be asked: Did Canadian foreign policy create the conditions in which such apparently twisted logic could flourish? In other words..."

As if on cue, the massed ranks of the *Toronto Star* comment team, face down in the beer nuts, jerked instantly to life and droned in unison: "Why do they hate us?"

"Exactly," said Alexa McDonough. "Poverty breeds hopelessness, Hopelessness breeds resentment. Resentment breeds 5.0, 5.2, 4.9, 4.7 and in extreme cases 3.4. We need to address the root causes of what happened."

"Come off it," I said. "Look at that." Yet again the cameras showed that shocking moment in the warm-ups when the Russian pair collided with Jamie and sent her crashing to the ice.

"Hmm," mused *Globe And Mail* film critic Rick Groen, toying with a cocktail olive. "*Grey Skirt Down* is simultaneously an accomplished piece of kinetic brilliance yet highly suspect in its political resonance. Devoid of context, it presents us with an artificial choice between 'good' Canadians and a crude Slavic enemy straight from the Cold War era that reduces the narrative to feeble jingoistic propaganda."

John Ralston Saul strolled in from the balcony. As always in his appearances in this column, the Vice-Regal consort was completely naked, though, in deference to the sub-zero temperatures, His Excellency was wearing a Canada Council toque and a hand-knitted woollen condom. "It's too easy to deal in simplistic concepts such as 'winning' and 'losing'," he said, warming his frostbitten buttocks over the hot punch. "Clinging to outmoded certainties, reducing complex issues to black and white, is not particularly useful or helpful. It's a very American fault, frankly."

"Cowboy justice!" agreed Michele Landsberg. "'We wuz robbed.' 'I won, you lost.' 'Stick 'em up and hand over your medals.' 'Let's head 'em off at the pass.'"

"Just so," said John, presenting Michele with the Order of Canada and a signed copy of *Equilibrium: Towards A New Inertia*. "I sometimes feel that the almost psychotic Canadian aggressivity towards Russia has less to do with figure-skating scoring and more to do with a desperate attempt to avenge western Christianity's many failed attempts to conquer and subjugate Russian Orthodoxy. Hitler, Napoleon, the Crimea, etc, etc. (Memo to Rideau Hall stenographer: fill out with historical detail for a couple of paragraphs.)"

To be honest, I was glad to see my old friend Federal Ethics Counsellor Howard Wilson wander over from the bar. "In the four minutes since this alleged occurrence occurred, I have been able to conduct a full and thorough investigation," he announced. "I did not find any incidence of involvement on the part of the judges which could have given rise to any real or apparent impropriety on their parts. On the contrary, the high standards of the judging process have been completely respected. Move along, folks. There's nothing to see here."

"That's ridiculous!" I scoffed. "What about meeting up a month before the games to decide the results?"

"Under the new tightened-up ISU ethics guidelines," replied Howard, "that's no longer illegal. Ask Jean. He knows all about figure skating."

"Dat right," said the Prime Minister. "I skate over da figures all da time. I say, sure, I call da bank guy to loan da Grand-Mère a couple hunnerd thousan', but I already sold da golf course for half da millions, even though I have to loan da guy da money to buy da place, but I write da contract on da paper napkin so all da zeroes faded and blurry. So I know about skatin' on da thin ice. I'm not sayin' I'd have slam into Jamie in da rehearsal like da Russian skater did. I leave dat to Warren Kinsella. Dat da Canadian value."

Mr Chrétien glanced at the TV screen. "Beside, we winning lot o' da udder medal. Look at dis woman in da luge. Sure, she glance off da wall, which knock da twentieth of a second off da time, but she's really picking up da speed now."

"Er, Prime Minister," Allan Rock pointed out, "that's an 87-year old granny on a trolley rolling down a corridor at the Royal Victoria while the orderly gives an interview about health cuts to Lloyd Robertson."

"Yeah, well it still da phenomenals performance, and da personal best."

Before I could comment, Professor Sunera Thobani of the University of British Columbia had burst in on us. "There will be no emancipation for women anywhere on this planet until the western domination of figure skating is ended!" she roared to an inscrutable Hedy Fry. "Look at that!" She pointed at the TV, where the CBC were replaying in slow motion the bit where David is propelling Jamie backwards toward the camera on one leg as the wind blows her skirt up. "What message is that sending to Canadian lesbians?"

"Well," I said, "it's sending the message that Jamie has one hell of a cute…"

"It's saying that in our society women are expected go backwards at the behest of the white patriarchal oppressor," snapped Sunera. "It's a very old message that every aboriginal woman, every woman of colour, every woman of orientation will recognize."

"I dunno bout dat," said Jean, "but we don wan da racisms or da backlash against da ethnic types in da goofy clothes. Dat why I schedule da big fundraiser wit da Russian Mafia. Maybe I put anudder Ukrainian in Rideau Hall. Dat's da Canadian way, eh?"

"That's right," agreed Lloyd Axworthy, popping in en route to the Belarus Men's Curling Team disco. "The easy thing would have been to quit, to walk away from the table. But this defeat shows what can happen when Canadian soft power is projected at the international level. Sure, you have to compromise, you don't get everything you want, but we hung in there and we ended up, I think, with a very good result that reflects a broad-based global consensus – the Russians, the Chinese, our colleagues in the

Francophonie, emergent east bloc democracies. I'm only sorry we couldn't bring the Iraqis on board."

My head was beginning to reel, so I was glad to see long-time Finance Minister Paul Martin coming through the door. "What do you make of this, Paul?" I asked, handing him David and Jamie's scores.

"5.8, 5.8, 5.9, 5.8, 5.8, 5.9," he read. "Well, I've always said that the Canadian dollar would eventually stabilize, and this is a rate that's good for Canada, good for the economy, and leaves us very competitive internationally. On the other hand, if you're planning on staying down here through the weekend, I'm happy to give a speech and talk it up over six cents."

~

THE GREAT MORON

February 23rd 2002
The Spectator

SAY WHAT YOU like about those wacky Islamofascists but at least they revile America as the Great Satan. By contrast, to Europe, America is now and forever the Great Moron. Thus it was inevitable that, when George W Bush started going on about his "axis of evil", this would be just another excuse for cartoonists in the Rest Of The West to depict him as a bozo in a triangular (Iraq-Iran-North Korea) dunce's cap. To Joschka Fischer (Germany's Foreign Minister), Bush's rhetoric "gets us nowhere"; to Chris Patten (the EU's External Affairs Commissioner), it's unhelpfully "absolutist" and in "unilateralist overdrive"; to Hubert Védrine (the French Foreign Minister), it's "absurd".

Faced with this axis of snottiness, how should the Great Moron react? The formal State Department handbook says that, on being insulted by European grandees, Administration officials should endeavour not to titter, but even Colin Powell, Mister Moderate himself, is having a hard job keeping a straight face. Invited to respond to Mr Patten, the General said, "I shall have a word with him, as they say in Britain." Invited to respond to M Védrine, he suggested the poor fellow was "getting the vapours". In neither case did he think it was worth taking on their arguments, such as they are.

The "axis of evil" is actually a pretty sophisticated construct. When the Rest Of The West protests that it's not an "axis", they're missing the point. It's like the new *Ocean's Eleven*: they're not really buddies, but they've been cast together in a remake of an old-time buddy caper (the original Rat Pack: Adolf, Benito, Tojo). It's true that Iraq doesn't seem to have been as intimately involved in al-Qa'eda operations as, say, the Metropolitan County of the West Midlands, or whatever Heatho-Walkerian administrative unit Tipton is presently consigned to. But hey, that's the breaks, Saddam: toppling you for the World Trade Center is like nailing Al Capone for tax evasion; it'll do. The Administration intends to have a new Iraqi President visiting Washington and sitting up in the gallery by the time of Bush's next State of the Union address in January (the Hamid Karzai role's already been cast), and, if they have to snub Chris Patten to achieve their goal, then by jingo they're prepared to do so.

Sixty years ago, another simple-minded absolutist was in unilateralist overdrive. George W Churchill was in Downing Street filling the air with inflammatory cowboy rhetoric about "a monstrous tyranny never surpassed in the dark lamentable catalogue of human crime". Meanwhile on the Continent EU Marshal Chris Pétain was deploring this crude talk of "the abyss of a new Dark Age" as frankly unhelpful and certainly not as effective as "constructive engagement" with "moderate elements" in the Third Reich. At decisive moments in human history, someone has to be simple, someone has to be primal. For two crucial years in the mid-20th century, the British Empire played that role alone and in so doing saved the world.

This is one of those moments. If Osama had had a nuke on September 11th, he'd have used it. Maybe Saddam wouldn't, maybe he'd be more rational. But, honestly, I'd rather not wait to find out. Every option poses risks: The risk of doing nothing is that Baghdad will slip a little something al-Qa'eda's way and *hasta la vista*, the Empire State Building. The risk of doing something is that Lionel Jospin and Jean Chrétien and all your other "allies" will start making even snider cracks about you. Hmm. Tough choice.

As for Iran, consider a recent speech by Hashemi Rafsanjani, the former President and now head of the Expediency Council, which sounds like an EU foreign policy agency but is, in fact, Iran's highest religious body. Rafsanjani said that on that fast approaching day when the Muslim world gets nuclear weapons the Israeli question will be settled forever "since a single atomic bomb has the power to completely destroy Israel, while an Israeli counter-strike can only cause partial damage to the Islamic world."

Unlike Chris Pétain, I take these guys at their word. The EU supposedly fears massive "destabilisation" of the Muslim world. I say, bring it on, baby. If we don't destabilise them now, they're going to be destabilising us the day after tomorrow. The population of the Middle East is growing at a rate six times faster than that of western Europe, whose populations are either stagnant or declining. Islam is turning out ever greater legions of poorly educated young men with little or no economic opportunity at home and every incentive to head to Frankfurt or Marseilles or Luton and drift into Islamic terrorism while living off Euro-welfare. The refusal of the Continent's political class to adjust its support for Arafat no matter how many Israeli bat mitzvahs get blown up by suicide bombers may strike many Americans as repugnant, but it has a compelling demographic logic about it if you look at even the official figures for Muslim immigration in Europe. If the Great Moron isn't getting much support for its plans to take out Saddam now, France and Germany and co are going to be a lot less keen in five or ten years. If it were done, then 'twere well it were done quickly.

That's why I find it slightly perplexing to have my colleague Matthew Parris characterising my support for America's war as in some way unBritish. In the choice he posits between "America" and the "Rest of the World", I bet on form. Of the 20th century's three global conflicts – the First, Second and Cold Wars – who was on the right side each time? Germany: one out of three. Italy: two out of three. For a perfect triple, there's only Britain, America, Canada, Australia, New Zealand. Even now, with their military capabilities shrivelled to almost nothing, the only guys actually on the ground in any combat role with the Americans are the British, Aussie and Kiwi SAS boys and Canada's Princess Patricias. I think there's something to be said for being on the right side of history. In that sense, in my argument with the swelling ranks of *Speccie* and *Telegraph* doubters, I'm not the loud-mouthed Yank, I'm the British traditionalist.

Alas, Britain is no longer as British as I am. "Night after night," wrote Salman Rushdie in *The New York Times* recently, "I have found myself listening to Londoners' diatribes against the sheer weirdness of the American citizenry. The attacks on America are routinely discounted. ('Americans only care about their own dead.') American patriotism, obesity, emotionality, self-centredness: these are the crucial issues."

Quite. Not Our Kind Of People. Lardbutts. U! S! A! U! S! A! Healing. Closure. Would you like fries with that? Vulgar, vulgar, vulgar. In September, Maulana Inyadullah, one of the more quotable jihadi holed up in the Greater Kandahar area, nailed it perfectly in this pithy soundbite for *The Daily Telegraph*:

"The Americans love Pepsi-Cola, we love death."

The sodaphobe knew his audience well. You can almost hear Chris Patten, Hubert Védrine, Lionel Jospin, and a thousand others stampeding to agree: "*Exactly!* We hate Pepsi-Cola, too!" For the likes of Mr Patten, Ian Gilmour and Ted Heath, conservatism is as much about restraining the people's right to "pursue happiness" as liberating it.

For over five months now, a continuous stream of preposterous criticism of the Americans has had at its core the assumption that such a demotic culture must necessarily be a profoundly stupid one. Yet funnily enough it's the sophisticates who keep getting everything wrong: The Arab street will rise up! Musharraf will be overthrown! The Taleban will never surrender! Millions will starve! Thousands of Afghan civilians are dead! (Not true: see below.) There's evidently a powerful psychological need among the non-American western elites to believe that, if America is big, it must also be blundering; if it's powerful, it must also be clumsy; if it's technologically superior, it must also be morally inferior. Hence the frenzied rush to accuse America of "torture" in Guantanamo, a camp where the medical staff outnumber the prisoners. Atrocious, eh? I bet Rose Addis is glad she didn't get shipped there rather than the Whittington.

In September, I wrote here that one of the consequences of that awful day would be the end of Nato. Under Nato, America has over-guaranteed European security, reducing the Rest Of The West to the status of a neurotic girlfriend you can never quite shake off, the sort who insists on moving into your pad and then keeps yakking about how she needs her space. Officially, the ROTW is side by side with America in the "War on Terrorism". In practice, its principal contribution to the team effort seems to be sitting on the sidelines watching the Americans skate all over the rink and then handing them a succession of cranky 4.3s. That's where Mr Inyadullah's Pepsi line isn't quite right. America is Coca-Cola, the market leader. It would benefit from a Pepsi, a credible number two – emphasis on the "credible". Paavo Lipponen, the Finnish Prime Minister, was in London last week and gave a speech arguing that "the EU must not develop into a military superpower but must become a great power that will not take up arms at any occasion in order to defend its own interests."

Perhaps it lost something in translation.

As for Mr Inyadullah's choice between Pepsi and death, the Internet commentator Old Man Murray remarked the other week, "Well, it's January and I'm drinking a Pepsi and Mr Inyadullah is probably dead." So things worked out swell for both parties. It's only the Europeans who find themselves agonisingly caught between Iraq and a soft drink.

A NOTE ON CIVILIAN DEATHS

February 23rd 2002
The Spectator

MY COLLEAGUE Stephen Glover stands by his assertion that Bush and Rumsfeld have killed more Afghans than Osama killed Americans. This statistic derives from the work of Marc Herold, a Women's Studies professor at the University of New Hampshire (my tax dollars at work, I regret to say), whose study of civilian casualties in Afghanistan put the death toll at a little over 4,000. John Pilger insouciantly rounded this up to 5,000, and I fully expected it to rise over the weeks as spectacularly as Enron stock in the late Nineties.

Professor Herold's general methodology seems to be that if, on Wednesday morning, *The Peshawar Bugle*, *The Baghdad Courier* and *The Des Moines Register* each report that 20 people were killed overnight that adds up to a total death toll of 60. I'd mentioned that even Human Rights Watch put civilian fatalities at around 1,000, and Stephen Glover promptly called up a spokesperson at HRW's London office to chastise me for conjuring this figure up out of thin air. "We're very cross with Mark Steyn," she told Stephen. "We've never released figures for civilian fatalities in Afghanistan, nor have we speculated. It's all utterly made-up."

Actually, I got that figure of 1,000 from the HRW New York office, which offered it as a "rough estimate" to Murray Campbell in a Canadian Press story of January 3rd. His report appeared in several North American papers from Toronto to Seattle, and no one from Human Rights Watch went around huffing that they were "very cross" with Mr Campbell. The Associated Press, after studying fatalities reported by Afghan hospitals and tracking down families named in casualty reports, has come up with a civilian death toll of 600 or more. They also quote Afghan spokesmen who say the Taleban required them to exaggerate numbers. Reuters estimates 1,000. The Project for Defense Alternatives (a leftie group) reckons somewhere between 1,000 and 1,300. Even Professor Herold has revised his figures, abandoning his total of 4,050 and now placing the total between 3,000 and 3,600. So here's the current Hit Parade at a glance:

Associated Press	600
Reuters	1,000
Human Rights Watch (New York)	1,000
Project for Defense Alternatives	1,000-1,300
Professor Marc Herold (UNH)	3,000-3,600
The Spectator (Stephen Glover)	4,000
The Mirror (John Pilger)	5,000
Professor Noam Chomsky	7,000,000*

(*cautious estimate ventured in a speech in New Delhi in the middle of the campaign; it may be higher by now)

Right now, I'd say the balance of probability favours the AP-Reuters-HRW-PDA end of the scale rather than the Glovero-Pilgerian-Chomskyite end.

MARCH 11th

Six months on

March 10th 2002
The Chicago Sun-Times

SIX MONTHS on, they're still out there – in Frankfurt and Lyons and Rome, living on Euro-welfare and with the whole day free to liaise and plot. They're in Montreal, where the Province of Quebec operates an immigration policy independent of the rest of Canada and where young men from former French colonies in North Africa and the Middle East can blend in easily, knowing they're less than an hour's drive from New York and Vermont's low-security border posts.

And, of course, they're in Boston, and Dallas, and Chicago, on long-expired student or tourist visas, beneficiaries of an era when the INS had neither the resources nor the inclination to keep track of them. They have access to significant sums of money back in Saudi, but they don't need a lot, or at least not in the large one-off amounts that attract attention. You could finance another September 11th through ATM withdrawals in Newark, Boca Raton, Vancouver - a couple of hundred dollars here, a couple of hundred there – taken from accounts in the London and Paris branches of respectable Gulf banks. Unless the government's going to monitor every $40 withdrawal from the First National Bank of Dead Skunk, Idaho, no system can track such insignificant transactions.

They're almost always young men. Mostly they're called "Mohammed" or "Ahmed" and they have Saudi or Egyptian passports. But sometimes they're called "Richard Reid" and are bona fide British subjects with entirely legal documents issued in the name of Her Britannic Majesty. The so-called "20th hijacker" is a French citizen. Ahmed Ressam, arrested en route to blow up LAX two years ago, had a Canadian passport in a less obviously Arab name which he'd acquired by faking a Quebec baptismal certificate – an easy trick until the loophole was closed post-9/11, by which point who knows how many of Ressam's chums had their new documentation.

Every day, these people are probing, testing, finding the weak spots in the system. The government has to stop all of them each and every time. They just have to get through once. Richard Reid was within a few seconds of blowing up a transatlantic jet before his fellow passengers jumped on him. Maybe the next Richard Reid will find himself seated next to a Todd Beamer type. Or maybe he'll get lucky and the adjoining seat will be filled by an Ivy League professor immersed in a long article in *Harper's* about how crass and misguided America's war on terrorism is because we're not concentrating on the "root causes" and he won't notice the smoking loafer until it's too late. The enemy has a simple war aim: kill Americans – and if, along the way, you happen to kill a few Aussies, Japanese, Pakistanis or the nationals of some 70 other countries who died on September 11th, well, that's no big deal. Mission accomplished.

None of us wants to think about this or live like this. When the FBI urges us to be extra vigilant, we pay no attention. When it emerges that a "shadow government" has been set up, we make jokes about it. But every American should know that there've been plenty of plans for a second September 11th and be grateful that they were all foiled, or fell apart, or got stalled because some bureaucrat at a DMV in Orlando or a passport office in Toronto or a check-in counter at Amsterdam was being a little more careful than he would have been six months ago.

The probability is that al-Qaeda and their network of allies have the capability of detonating a "dirty nuke". America can hunker down, shut the borders, close the ATMs, and demand you get to the airport five hours early for a 40-minute puddle-jump. Or it can take the war to Islamofascism's center of operations and destroy it there. In other words, it can besiege the American people, or it can besiege the enemy.

Not a tough choice, you'd think. But the six-month suspension of normal politics is taking its toll on Democrats. "We seem to be good at developing entrance strategies," Senator Robert C Byrd, West Virginia's porkmeister par excellence, whined the other day, "and not so good at developing exit strategies."

Well spotted, Senator. Here's something else that will shock you: Churchill didn't have an "exit strategy" for World War Two. Exit strategies are for optional foreign adventures, when you go into the People's Republic of Basketcazia because you think General Ruthlez Bastardo would be a mild improvement on President Sy Kotik but otherwise you've no vital interest at stake. You don't have exit strategies when your national territory's been attacked; you have a responsibility to see the war through to the end.

It's a shame Senator Byrd can't seem to understand that. Maybe if we applied the traditional courtesies of West Virginia politics and agreed to rename Afghanistan Robert C Byrdistan, he could see his way to being supportive for a couple more months. Honestly, I don't like to complain but, given that the Senate has a talent pool of 200 million to draw on, the 100 members of "the world's greatest deliberative body" have performed abysmally since September 11th. The headline on Jules Witcover's column in *The Baltimore Sun* read "Democrats Ask Tough Questions On War". In fact, tough questions would be welcome. But Byrd's and Tom Daschle's criticisms are pathetic: they're about spin, posturing, about how it'll play on TV. In war, grown-ups don't have time for silly games in the Congressional schoolyard.

Six months on, it's clear that, in the ops room, the grown-ups are in charge: Bush, Rummy, Condi. The downside, alas, is that on the non-war fronts the Bush Presidency has died. But most Presidents get to pick their priorities. Bush has no choice in his. If Senator Byrd wants to know the "end game", here's a few signs of how things will look when it's over:

~ Regime changes in Iraq and Iran.

~ The liquidation of Saudi Arabia, with the territory partitioned between Jordan and the less unenlightened Gulf Emirs.

~ The dissolution of Nato: America needs to stop over-guaranteeing European security.

~ The embrace by the Middle East of the same reforms Turkey embarked on 80 years ago.

In other words, these are early days, and there are plenty of horrors to come. It's war, there's more, get used to it.

MR ATTA GETS HIS PAPERS

March 14th 2002
The National Post

THIS WEEK, Tom Ridge, Director of Homeland Security, unveiled his new system of colour-coded alerts. Henceforth, the situation will be graded on a scale from red (severe risk) to green (low risk). Today is a yellow day: elevated risk.

What does America on Yellow Alert look like? Well, on Monday, six months to the day after terrorists killed 3,000 people, Rudi Dekkers received a letter from the US Immigration and Naturalization Service. Mr Dekkers runs a flight school in Venice, Florida, and the INS were writing to inform him that two of his pupils, Mohammed Atta and Marwan al-Shehhi, had been approved for student visas.

Unfortunately, Messrs Atta and al-Shehhi will be unable to use their visas. Mr Atta died on September 11th at the controls of the plane which hit World Trade Center Tower One. Mr al-Shehhi died a few minutes later at the controls of the plane which hit Tower Two.

Presumably, that's why we're merely on Yellow Alert: it's okay, folks, the Federal Government is issuing visas to terrorists, but only dead ones. If the Federal Government were issuing visas to live terrorists, you can bet that we'd be on Red Alert.

Then again, maybe not.

A few days after September 11th, I called for the resignation of Federal Aviation Administration honcho Jane Garvey and other top officials on the grounds that "what happened on Tuesday was not the odd guy slipping through a few 'cracks in the system', but a completely cracked system, whose failure was total." I didn't expect the President to pay any heed to me, but I assumed hundreds of more illustrious opinion-formers in Washington and New York would also be affronted.

Not a bit of it. Six months on, the only prominent resignation has been that of my old comment-page confrere and Bush speechwriter David Frum, and, as far as I know, David didn't quit because they'd found out he'd issued a green card to Mullah Omar. If he had, they'd make him Director of the CIA.

For some reason, the Administration, Congressional Democrats and the pundits reached an unspoken agreement to wipe the slate clean, and allow every Federal deadbeat and time-server to start afresh. Since then, anyone who's used a US airport has gotten used to having their nail clippers confiscated, their gifts for Junior torn open and broken, and their jewellery stolen. Passengers have put up with this harassment because of a not entirely logical assumption that the more the government pisses on you the more likely it is it's pissing all over the bad guys.

We now know that's not the case – that "big government" is carrying on just as before. How much faith should Americans have that the INS can spot living, potential terrorists when they can't even spot world-famous dead terrorists? What conclusions should we draw from Mr Dekkers' puzzling letter from the Government of the United States? It's goofy in every respect – right down to its alleged date of mailing: though sent last week, the envelope, according to NBC, bears the postmark July 5th 2002. Is this a missive from some strange comic-book alternate universe where a bizarro Uncle Sam celebrates a perversion of Independence Day by bureaucratically regulating America's enemies back to life?

Well, it makes as much sense as the official explanations. Asked why the INS is issuing visas to dead terrorists, spokesman Russ Bergeron was positively breezy: it's all perfectly routine, the terrorists had received verbal notification a few months back, most likely when they were still alive, but the paperwork got tied up at the processing centre in London, Kentucky. "Because of a backlog of data entry, materials are just now arriving at the school," said Mr Bergeron, so it's nothing to make a fuss about, it's just "back-up notification". Almost right. It's the sort of notification that should get every American's back up.

Former INS District Director Tom Fischer said it's "a case of the right hand not knowing what the left hand was doing". But neither hand of the INS should be issuing visas to terrorists: this is a case of the left cheek not telling the right cheek which side of their butt they're meant to be talking through.

Though they took another five months to be delivered, the visas were actually issued by an INS clerk on October 1st 2001 – three weeks after the attacks, when Mohammed Atta's face was being flashed up on TV screens every hour of the day and Mr Dekkers' flight school was getting a lot of publicity. But, even if Mr Atta's name and Mr Dekkers' school failed to ring any bells with this INS clerk, you'd sort of hope that, in a more general sense, they'd be keeping an eye on flight-training applications by young men from the Middle East. At the very least, you'd think some pedantic pen-pusher would say, "Hey, this form has an invalid place of residence. It says Venice, Florida even though he's now at Big Hole In The Ground, Lower Manhattan. He needs to apply for a ZB47 Amendment Of Address (Foreign National, Non-Breathing) Permit. I *knew* something smelled phoney on this."

But no, he didn't even do that. It's nothing to do with money or computers, only dopey employees in a Federal bureaucracy so secure in its complacency that not even mass murder can rouse it. What other visas did this particular clerk issue that day? Is there a record? Does anyone know? Or is the US Government too busy at La Guardia confiscating the miniature plastic screwdriver from Little Johnny's Bob The Builder kit?

Mr Bergeron is quite right, of course. There is nothing "unusual" about this incident. The only justification for any application taking two years would be if the INS were doing what it's supposed to do – looking into applicants' backgrounds. But that's not what happens: In July 2000, the application arrives and is placed on Pile A. One year later, it's dusted off and moved from Pile A to Pile B. Three months after that, it's moved to Pile C. Five months after that, it's moved to Pile D, the one next to the envelopes. It takes two years to shuffle the paper, not to verify the application. If they were to attempt the latter, you'd be talking, oh, 12, 15 years, and they only do that if you want to get a foreign nanny for your kids before they reach early middle-age. So go on, try it yourself. Fill in an RU1-2 green card application in the name of Mohammed Atta, list infidel-killing as your profession, Osama as your reference, and those 72 virgins as your dependents. What are the odds you'd slip through? Better than even?

What's clear since September 11th is that Bush's foreign and defence heavyweights are in a different league from his domestic team. This is not good news for the American people: at best, Underperformin' Norman Mineta, the Transportation Secretary, will merely inconvenience folks; at worst, he'll kill them. Meanwhile, the big-government left and the authoritarian right have a new wheeze: Americans will be more secure with a National Identity Card! And who will issue the new card? Why, the INS! Just as soon as they finish up the paperwork on this temporary agricultural-worker permit for a Mr O. B. Laden. The post-9/11 amnesty needs to end: if Bush can't use Mohammed Atta's visa as a cue to clean out these Federal agencies, then it's the Administration that needs to get some student visas and go back to school, because they're obviously the world's slowest learners.

~

MY, HOW YOU'VE SHRUNK

March 10th 2002
The Sunday Telegraph

ABOUT A MONTH ago in these pages, I had cause to complain about the headline appended to my review of George W Bush's first year: "My, How You've Grown." I pointed out that, as I've always regarded the President as a colossus who bestrides the planet, he could hardly grow any more in my eyes. Well, if the Executive Editor (Headlines) is short of inspiration this weekend, feel free to use my suggestion: My, How You've Shrunk.

Last Tuesday was the absolute low point of the Bush Presidency. Even in the wobblier moments of September 11th and 12th, he never said or did anything flat-out stinking-to-high-heaven wrong. But last week he slapped tariffs of 30% on imported steel. Canada and Mexico are exempt, because of Nafta, and so are selected developing countries, beneficiaries of the new Bush Doctrine of "compassionate protectionism". But among those stiffed by the President are pretty much everybody with troops on the ground fighting alongside the 10th Mountain Division in Afghanistan –

fellows like Australia, whose Prime Minister, John Howard, summed up his country's support for the US better than anyone else in the days after September 11th: "This is no time to be an 80% ally."

No, indeed. Bush to Howard: You're now a 30% ally.

Presumably, the Administration figures it can afford to slough off the Aussies. But this decision also flips the finger at the only two allies who really matter, Britain and Russia. Steel is important to Moscow, and it may yet prove significant in whether or not Tony Blair can bring his reluctant party with him on toppling Saddam. Britain is still one of the largest steel producers in the world, though not a lot of it goes to the US. Nevertheless, it does, as they say, "send conflicting messages" to slap a hypocritical penalty on your ally's goods in the same week you ask him for a 25,000-man troop commitment in Iraq.

Whoever George W Bush is "protecting", it isn't the American people: according to the columnist George Will, for every steel-producing job these tariffs save, they'll cost ten jobs in the steel-consuming sector. So, if it's any consolation to beleaguered Bush supporters in Britain, Australia and Russia, he's not doing anything for Americans with this decision either.

I wouldn't mind what's effectively the introduction of a covert sales tax: there's a war on and we must all make sacrifices. The problem is that this particular sales tax undermines the war effort – or, at any rate, the moral basis for it. In the autumn, with America fretting over the economic consequences of September 11th, the President declared that the attack on New York was an attack on "free trade". "We will keep our country open," he insisted, "and our markets open for business."

But that was then. A couple of years back, I found myself in conversation with, ahem, a senior member of the Royal Family who opined that it was just awful that Rolls-Royce had been swallowed by Volkswagen. I like being an oleaginous Royal suck-up as much as the next guy, but this was too much. I replied that one of the refreshing aspects of US capitalism was its open-mindedness: when Daimler takes over Chrysler – manufacturers of the Jeep – Americans don't go around whining about the loss of this powerful national symbol and why doesn't the government intervene. If Sony grabs Columbia Pictures, big deal. If you can make it, ship it and sell it, the American market is yours for the taking. As the Treasury Secretary, Paul O'Neill, said barely a week ago: "Freer trade can help stimulate growth: It fuels competition, and innovation."

I heard the President say words to that effect at the Summit of the Americas in Quebec City last year, and, being foolish enough to take him at face value, repeated it to the anti-globalisation mobs outside the perimeter fence, whenever they stopped lobbing bits of concrete at your humble correspondent long enough for me to get a word in. Giving the rest of the planet access to G7 markets is the best way not only to improve the living standards of the world's poor, but also to bring them within the purview of civilised (or anyway non-deranged) nations.

Lest anyone doubt the relevance of this, consider that 50 years ago Egypt and South Korea had more or less identical per capita incomes. Today, Egypt's is less than 20 per cent of South Korea's. This isn't the leftie's lamebrain poverty-breeds-resentment argument: the fact that Egypt is a fetid backwater is nobody's fault but the Egyptians'. South Korea, on the other hand, has transformed itself, and is, among other things, a significant exporter of cheap steel to grateful American manufacturers. So Bush has chosen to penalise the Koreans – to blame the chronic sickness of the US steel industry on the foreign steel industry.

Scapegoating breeds resentment, and so it should. Free trade is the mitigating circumstance of America's unprecedented global hegemony: it says, "Yes, we're a behemoth never before seen in the history of the world, but you can grab a piece of that. We're loaded, sell us something." Take that away and what you're left with is perilously close to the global bully *The Guardian* and the Euroweenies drone on about. If you're a deadbeat Saudi loser who'd rather hole up in Tora Bora than put in a decent day's work, we'll drop a daisycutter on you. But, if you're a wiry little Korean slogging away in the factory all week, we'll still screw you over.

So put another nail in the coffin of Bush's domestic Presidency. Last Tuesday he pulled off the remarkable feat of making Bill Clinton look principled. With hindsight, Clinton had two bedrock convictions: he believed oral sex didn't qualify as adultery and he believed in free trade. Bush, by contrast, thinks a little bit of union featherbedding doesn't count as political adultery, and will swing enough votes among the Red Robboes of the Appalachians to make the difference. Don't bet on it. Protectionism breeds ingrates. By November, some pandering West Virginia Democrat will be agitating for 40% tariffs. In 2004, Bush will win or lose for reasons entirely unconnected with an irrelevant, dying industry.

But, in the meantime, some of us conservatives are wondering: if he weren't killing Islamofascist nutters in the Hindu Kush, why exactly would we support this guy? The sooner the invasion of Iraq starts, the better.

MARCH

Tensions

March 4th 2002
The National Post

JOANNE JACOBS, formerly a columnist with *The San Jose Mercury News*, spotted a dandy headline in her old paper last week. A Muslim mob, you'll recall, had attacked a train full of Hindus, an unfortunate development which the *Mercury News* reported to its readers thus: "Religious Tensions Kill 57 In India".

Ah, those religions tensions'll kill you every time. Is there an Ex-Lax you can take for religious tension? Or an extra-strength Tylenol, in case you feel a sudden attack coming on? I haven't looked out the *Mercury News* for September 12th but I'm assuming the front page read "Religious Tensions Kill 3,000 In New York", a particularly bad outbreak.

If I were an Islamic fundamentalist, I'd be wondering what I had to do to get a bad press. *The New York Times* had a picture the other day of a party of Palestinian suicide bombers looking like Klansmen, all dressed up and ready to blow. They were captioned "Hamas activists". Take my advice and try not to be standing anywhere near an activist when he activates himself.

You gotta hand it to the Islamofascists: while the usual doom-mongers are now querying whether America's up to fighting a war on two fronts (Afghanistan and Iraq), the Islamabaddies blithely open up new fronts every couple of weeks. At the World Trade Center, Muslim terrorists killed mainly Christians. In Israel, they're killing mainly Jews. In India, they're killing mainly Hindus. Let's not get into the Sudan or the Philippines. Now, okay, there are two sides to every dispute, but these days one side can pretty well be predicted: Muslims vs Jews, Muslims vs Christians, Muslims vs Hindus, Muslims vs [Your Religion Here]. If war were tennis, they'd be Grand Slam champions: they'll play on anything – lawn, clay, rubble. And yet the more they kill, the more frantically the press cranks out the "Islam is a religion of peace" editorials.

Now it would be absurd to claim that all Muslims are terrorists. But the idea that the forces at play in New York, Palestine, Tora Bora and Kashmir are some sort of tiny unrepresentative extremist aberration of Islam is equally ludicrous. The other day *The Boston Globe* reported from the Saudi town of Abha on the subtleties of the Kingdom's education system: "At a public high school in this provincial town in the southwest part of the country, 10th grade classes are forced to memorize from a Ministry of Education textbook entitled 'Monotheism' that is replete with anti-Christian and anti-Jewish bigotry and violent interpretations of Islamic scripture. A passage on page 64 under the title 'Judgment Day' says: 'The Hour will not come until Muslims will fight the Jews, and Muslims will kill all the Jews.'"

That's pretty straightforward, isn't it? In fact, pretty much everything about Saudi Arabia, except for the urbane evasions of their Washington Ambassador, Prince Bandar, is admirably straightforward. Saudi citizens were, for the most part, responsible for September 11th. The Saudi Government funds the madrassahs in Pakistan which are doing their best to breed a South Asian branch office of Saudi Wahhabism. Admittedly, the Saudis are less directly responsible for the Israeli/Palestinian conflict, except insofar as they have a vested interest in it as a distraction from other matters and they financially reward the families of Palestinian suicide bombers. Still, if we don't want to be beastly about Muslims in general, we could at least be beastly about the House of Saud in particular.

Instead, the Saudi question has become the *ne plus ultra* of the Islamo-euphemist approach, and a beloved staple of comment pages and cable news shows. By now, the familiar "The Saudis Are Our Friends" op-ed piece may even have its own category in the Pulitzers. Usually it turns up after the Saudis have done something not terribly friendly – refused to let Washington use the US bases in Saudi Arabia, or to comply with post-9/11 security requests. Then the vast phalanx of former US Ambassadors to Saudi Arabia fans out across *The New York Times*, CNN, ABC's "Nightline", etc, to insist that, *au contraire*, the Saudis have been "enormously helpful". At what? Recommending a decent restaurant in Mayfair?

Charles Freeman, a former Ambassador to the Kingdom and now President of something called the Middle East Policy Council, offered a fine example of the genre the other day when he revealed that Crown Prince Abdullah, the head honcho since King Fahd had his stroke, was "personally anguished" by developments in the Middle East and that that was why he had proposed his "peace plan". If, indeed, he has proposed it - to anyone other than Thomas Friedman of *The New York Times*, that is. And, come to think of it, it was Friedman who proposed it to the Prince – Israel withdraws to the June 4th 1967 lines, Palestinian state, full normalized relations with the Arab League, etc. "After I laid out this idea," wrote Friedman, "the Crown Prince looked at me with mock astonishment and said, 'Have you broken into my desk?'

"'No,' I said, wondering what he was talking about.

"'The reason I ask is that this is exactly the idea I had in mind...'"

What a coincidence! Apparently, the Prince had "drafted a speech along those lines" and "it is in my desk". It's just that he hadn't got around to delivering the speech. Still hasn't, in fact. Seems an awful waste of a good speech. Unless – perish the thought – it's just something he keeps in his desk to flatter visiting American correspondents. In any case, it's the same peace plan the Saudis dust off every ten years – they proposed it in 1991, and before that in 1981. It's just a couple of months late this time round. But book a meeting around October 2011 with King Abdullah (as he plans on being by then) and he'll gladly propose it to you one mo' time. Prince Abdullah has no interest in Palestinians: it's easier for a Palestinian to emigrate to Toronto and become a subject of the Queen than to emigrate to Riyadh and become a subject of King Fahd. But the Prince's peace plan usefully changes the subject from more embarrassing matters – such as the Kingdom's role in the events of September 11th.

There are only two convincing positions on the House of Saud and what happened that grim day: a) They're indirectly responsible for it; b) They're directly responsible for it. There's a lot of evidence for the former – the Saudi funding of the madrassahs, etc – and a certain amount of not yet totally compelling evidence for the latter – a Saudi "humanitarian aid" office in the Balkans set up by a member of the Royal Family which appears to be a front for terrorism. Reasonable people can disagree whether it's (a) or (b) but for Americans to argue that the Saudis are our allies in the war on terrorism is like Fred Goldman joining OJ in his search for the real killers. The advantage of this thesis to fellows like Charles Freeman is that it places a premium on their nuance-interpretation skills. Because everything the Kingdom does seems to be self-evidently inimical to the west, any old four-year old can point out that the King is in the altogether hostile mode. It takes an old Saudi hand like Mr Freeman to draw attention to the subtler shades of meaning, to explain the ancient ways of Araby, by which, say, an adamant refusal to arrest associates of the September 11th hijackers is, in fact, a clear sign of the Saudis' remarkable support for Washington. If the Saudis nuked Delaware, the massed ranks of former Ambassadors would be telling Larry King that, obviously, even the best allies have their difficulties from time to time, but this is essentially a little hiccup that can be smoothed over by closer consultation.

Do they know what they're talking about? You'll remember the old-school Kremlinologists, who'd watch the Red Army parades and tip as the coming man the 87-year old corpse with the luxuriant monobrow and the waxy complexion propped up against the 93-year old Commissar of the Sverdlovsk gas works and people's hall of culture. The Kremlinologists got everything wrong, of course, and they only had a couple of dozen guys to divine the intentions of. Saudi Arabia has 7,000 princes – at the time of writing; it may be up to 7,600 if you're reading this after lunch. Many of us have never met a Saudi who isn't a prince. Chances are you can find princes to represent any view you want. But the awkward fact is that the dominant faction in the House of Saud right now is anti-American.

Instead of presenting Prince Abdullah with Israeli/Palestinian peace proposals, Americans ought to be handing him US/Saudi peace proposals: clean up your own education system and stop destabilizing Asian Muslim culture, for starters. Washington (and London, too) needs to figure out what it wants from Saudi Arabia and whether it's likely to get it from King Fahd and his bloated clan. We know already one thing we're not going to get: the Taliban had two major allies before September 11th, Pakistan and Saudi Arabia, and it's clear the Royal house has no inclination to do a Musharraf. If the west has a medium-term aim in the Middle East, it ought to be the evolution of Arabic Islam into something closer to the more moderate Muslim temperament of Turkey or Bangladesh. I know, I know, all these things are relative, but even that modest goal is unattainable under the House of Saud.

The Royal Family derives such legitimacy as it has from its role as the guardian and promoter of Wahhabism. It is, therefore, the ideological font of militant Islamism in the way that Saddam and Boy Assad and Mubarak and the other Arab thugs aren't. Saddam is as Islamic as the wind is blowing: say what you like about the old mass murderer, but his malign activities are not, in that sense, defined by his religion. One cannot say the same for the House of Saud, or Prince Abdullah, who for all his "personal anguish" is at best not pro-western and, by some accounts, quite fiercely anti-American. And, if the issue is "religious tensions", who's fomenting them, from Pakistan to the Balkans to America itself? Saudi Arabia should be a "root cause" we can all agree on.

But sadly not. John O'Sullivan, editor-in-chief of UPI, wrote recently that "reforming the House of Saud will be a formidable and subtle task. But it offers a great deal more hope for everyone than blithely burning it down." I disagree. Reforming the House of Saud is all but impossible. Lavish economic engagement with the west has only entrenched it more firmly in its barbarism. "Stability" means letting layabout princes use western oil revenues to seduce their people into anti-western nihilism. On the other hand, blithely burning it down offers quite a bit of hope, given that no likely replacement would provide the ideological succour to the Islamakazis that Saud-endorsed Wahhabism does. My own view – maps available on request – is that the Muslim Holy Sites and most of the interior should go to the Hashemites of Jordan, and what's left should be divided between the less wacky Gulf Emirs. That should be the policy goal, even if for the moment it's pursued covertly rather than by daisycutters.

Borders are not sacrosanct. The House of Saud are not Royal, merely nomads who found a sugar daddy. There's no good reason why every time a soccer mom fills her Chevy Suburban she should be helping fund some toxic madrassah. In this instance, destabilization is our friend.

~

LETTER TO THE EDITOR
Forgive the Islamabaddies

March 23rd 2002
The Spectator

From His Excellency Ghazi Algosaibi
Sir: Ever since Mark Steyn, maps at the ready, threatened to dismantle Saudi Arabia, our population has been living in a state of high anxiety and fear. Our children are having nightmares and our old men and women are quaking in terror. We are desperately trying to save ourselves.

We promise to be good boys and carry out Mr Steyn's demands to the letter. We shall stop all foreign aid, desist from all charitable activities, drink our own oil, love the Generalissimo, Ariel (Baby Face) Sharon, teach nothing in our schools except pornography and devil worship, and refer to all Muslims, ourselves included, as either "Islamofascists" or "Islamabaddies".

I do hope that Mr Steyn will find it in his warm, loving and tolerant heart to forgive us our trespasses and give us a second chance.

Ghazi Algosaibi
Ambassador
Royal Embassy of Saudi Arabia
London W1

TOYS BIN US

March 9th 2002
The Daily Telegraph

I WASN'T SURPRISED to hear the Iranian government has gone into the doll business. A subsidiary of the Ministry of Education has introduced "Sara", dressed in traditional Islamic garb, and her brother "Dara" to counter the influence of dolls from the Great Satan. "Dara and Sara are strategic products to preserve our national identity," toy seller Mehdi Hedayet told the BBC. "It is an answer to Barbie and Ken." Barbie, with her prominent bust and wanton clothing, has caused some concern among Iranian parents, and, as for Ken, there've been persistent rumours that he's a bit light on his loafers. "I think every Barbie doll is more harmful than an American missile," said Mehdi's fellow retailer, Masoumeh Rahimi.

Well, it wasn't news to me. A few days earlier, I'd swung by the new store Toys bin Us, only to find my old friend, style guru Armand Croissant, behind the counter. "Culturally appropriate dolls are where it's at," he said. "Just ask UN Barbie." He delved in his box and produced Human Rights Commissioner Mary Barbieson. "She comes with ten pairs of sensible shoes but only one speech. What's that, Mary?" He bent down and held her close to his ear. "She says we need to do more to reach out to Middle Eastern countries."

"And how do we do that?" I asked.

"Easy," said Armand, and pulled out a familiar bearded figure with a green camo jacket over his robes. "Meet Osama ken Laden. One of our biggest sellers. He's completely lifelike. In every respect."

I peeked under his tunic. "But he's got no private parts."

"Hold him up to the light," said Armand.

I peered closely. "Oh, yeah. Now I see." I put him back on the counter. "But his beard's too dark. It should be greyer."

"Well, that's Osama when he was younger," explained Armand. "It's like Barbie. We've got him in several different models."

I said I wouldn't mind seeing the latest and Armand passed over the box. "There's nothing in here," I said.

"It's DNA Osama," he sighed wearily. "You have to look carefully. He comes with his own cave and you can have endless hours of fun sprinkling him in different corners."

"To be honest, I was looking for something I could dress up," I said. "Mix'n'match outfits."

Armand disappeared below the counter and emerged with a trim little doll and a huge box of multicoloured clothes. "Meet Hamid Barbai, the interim leader of Barbistan. He comes with 270 chapans and 632 different lambskin karakuls in assorted colours. But, while he's changing in and out of his many outfits, Warlord Ken is

217

consolidating his grip on the remote northern province." He held up a ferocious looking Tajik doll.

"Phew," I grimaced. "He's a bit ripe."

"Well, he only has one tunic and he's been wearing it all winter. He comes complete with his fair-weather friend Talibarbie. Whoops, is that the Northern Alliance coming?" He pressed a button in Talibarbie's back and the full beard fell away and dropped to the floor. "Voila! Uzbek Ken. He's never liked Mullah Omar."

But by now I was in the mood for something a little different. Armand showed me Saudi Ken with the detachable head in case he turns out to be gay, and Suicide Ken, complete with plastic explosives to strap to his chest and 72 Virgin Barbies to pleasure him in paradise, and the new culturally authentic Nigerian doll, Female Circumcised Barbie. But he could see I felt faint and moved swiftly on.

"We've got the exclusive contract from the Zimbabwean Government for this one. Southern Africa's hottest seller, here he is – Robert Mubarbie." He turned the key in the back and the Zimbabwean leader loped along the counter in his familiar camp gait.

"Is he easy to wind up?"

"I'll say." Armand whipped out a Ken doll. "Hey, Bob. Didn't I see you in Heaven last night?"

The Mubarbie doll spun around and his little jaw moved up and down. "You filthy British homosexual!" he yelled at Ken in a tinny voice. "You are lower than pigs!"

"I'm impressed," I admitted. "Does he have any friends?"

"More than you'd think," said Armand, and handed me Kommonwealth Konference Ken.

I pulled the string in his back, but nothing happened. "He's useless," I complained. "He doesn't do a thing."

"Nonsense," said Armand. "Look at him. He's expressing 'deep concern'."

Well, I decided I was looking for something a little more robust. So Armand unveiled his latest doll, Tony Blarbie, who didn't seem to care much for either Robert Mubarbie or Kommonwealth Konference Ken. "Tony has three statements of moral indignation, and he repeats them over and over regardless of whether you pull his string or not."

"And then what does he do?"

"Oh, he doesn't do anything. He talks and talks and then just seizes up. We may have to send him back to the factory."

"Presumably," I said, "like Ken and Barbie, Tony is a wholly owned franchise of Mattel?"

"That's right," said Armand. "Lakshmi Mattel. But he'd rather you didn't mention that."

~

WE WERE SOLDIERS

March 9th 2002
The Spectator

THE BEST THING about *We Were Soldiers* is how bad it is. I don't mean "bad" just in the sense that it's written and directed by Randall Wallace, screenwriter of *Braveheart* (which won Oscars for pretty much everything except its screenplay, which was not overlooked without reason) and *Pearl Harbor* (whose plonking dialogue has been dwelt on previously in these pages). Mr Wallace is as reliably awful as you can get. And yet it serves him well here. *Pearl Harbor* was terrible, but it was professionally terrible, its lame dialogue and cookie-cutter characters and butt-numbingly obvious emotional manipulation skillfully woven together into state-of-the-art Hollywood product. By contrast, in its best moments, *We Were Soldiers* feels very unHollywoody, as if it's a film not just about soldiers, but made by soldiers. It's the very opposite of Steven Spielberg's fluid ballet of carnage in *Saving Private Ryan*, and yet, in its stiffness and squareness, it manages to be sad and moving in the way real military men are.

This is all the more remarkable considering that it's about the first big engagement of the Vietnam War, in the Ia Drang valley for three days and nights of November 1965, back when Vietnam had barely registered with the American public and the US involvement still came under the vague heading of "advisors". In essence, the 1st Battalion of the 7th Cavalry walked – or helicoptered – into an ambush and, despite being outnumbered five to one by the Viet Cong, managed to extricate themselves. Colonel Hal Moore, the commanding officer of the AirCav hotshots, and Joe Galloway, a UPI reporter who was in the thick of the battle for two days, later wrote a book – a terrific read – from which this movie is drawn, with Mel Gibson as Moore and Barry Pepper as Galloway.

We Were Soldiers opens with a brisk, unsparing prelude – a massacre of French forces in the same valley, 11 years earlier. Then we're off to Fort Benning, Georgia a decade later, where Colonel Moore and his grizzled old Sergeant Major, Basil Plumley (Sam Elliott), are training youngsters for a new kind of cavalry. "We will ride into battle and this will be our horse," announces Moore, as a chopper flies past on cue. Basil Plumley, incidentally, is not in the least bit plummy or basil-esque. He's the hard-case to Moore's Harvard man, a social inversion of the "Dad's Army" command, with lower middle-class Arthur Lowe and his posh deputy John LeMesurier.

I'm not sure why I started thinking of "Dad's Army" 20 minutes into the movie, but maybe it's because Wallace has made the textbook error of turning a great book into a bad text, taking a vivid real-life story and shaving all the edges off to fit the usual clichés. The Fort Benning scenes become incredibly irritating in their bland gee-whizzery. There's always some kid around to prompt Moore to wax philosophical, as when his five-year old cute-as-a-button daughter asks him, "Daddy, what's a war?" Meanwhile, Mrs Moore (Madeleine Stowe) serves as den mother to the army wives, clustered around the living room like a convention of 1960s sitcom spouses. One of them is puzzled because she's just been into town and discovered that the local laundromat won't let her wash her coloureds: there's a sign in the window saying "Whites Only". As in *Pearl Harbor*, the clothes and hairdos look just right, but the characters and emotional moment feel phoney.

Once Moore and co hit 'Nam, though, *We Were Soldiers* lives up to its title, as if happy to have its studio-mandated soppy-girly scenes behind it. It's been fascinating to watch the hasty and not entirely voluntary evolution of the Hollywood war movie post-September 11th. You'll recall the moment in *Saving Private Ryan* when Tom Hanks says, in all seriousness, that maybe saving Private Ryan will be the one good thing to come out of this lousy war. Hollywood still can't bring itself to be patriotic, to fight for a cause, so in the modern war movie military values – honour, courage, comradeship – exist in a vacuum, the soldier's professionalism its own *raison d'être*.

That's a problem dramatically, but it's an amazing transformation nevertheless. A Vietnam movie like this would have been unthinkable 10 or 20 years ago, or at any time since John Wayne made *The Green Berets*. This is a film where soldiers lie burned and bleeding and say "I'm glad I could die for my country" without a trace of Altmanesque irony or Oliver Stoned mockery.

Perhaps the scene that sums up what's changed is the moment when Joe Galloway's fellow members of the press corps are choppered in after the battle. He's been transformed by what he's experienced. Meanwhile, they cluster around Colonel Moore asking the usual idiot how-do-you-feel questions: "How do you feel about the loss of your men, sir? Have you notified their families?" In this film, soldiers are intense, heroic, highly skilled, and the media are a bunch of droning boneheads in safari suits. Who'd have thought it? Considering that for 30 years the media have congratulated themselves for being the real heroes of Vietnam – getting the truth back to the American people – this scene seems almost heresy.

Mel? Oh, he's fine, if you make allowances for the wandering southern accent. The real problem is the characterisations of his men, whom Wallace completely fails to distinguish from one another. That's a pity. One of the reasons Colonel Moore wrote his book was to memorialise as individuals, as personalities, the men under his command. It's worth reading.

~

THE ROBERT C BYRD INSTITUTE OF TIME-SERVERS

March 23rd 2002
The Spectator

UPDATE: LAST week, I wrote about the US Immigration and Naturalisation Service, which marked the semi-anniversary of September 11th by issuing visas to two of the terrorists who'd died on that day. Since then, under pressure from the President to show the agency would not tolerate such a fiasco, INS Commissioner James Ziglar has acted decisively by moving four INS officers "sideways". For example, Janis Sposato has been transferred to the post of "assistant deputy executive associate commissioner for immigration services". I'm not sure what post Ms Sposato was transferred sideways from – possibly that of associate executive deputy assistant commissioner. At any rate, this is a serious blow for Ms Sposato. It may well be that her dreams of rising to deputy executive associate assistant commissioner, and perhaps one day even assistant associate deputy executive commissioner, have gone up in smoke. I shouldn't be surprised if none of the other assistant deputy executive associates want to associate with her.

The agency contends its problems are due not to its swollen bureaucracy but to a "lack of resources". The visa-processing system is apparently "paper-based": every mom'n'pop hardware store has its inventory on computer, but, when it comes to which terrorist is eligible for which visa, it's all down to ledger files and carbon copies. Perhaps they don't have a computer system because they're spending all their money on custom-built extra-large business cards to fit Ms Sposato's title on. Unfortunately, Commissioner Ziglar needs to have a lot of vague, generalised titles at his disposal because he lacks the power to fire anyone. All he can do is move them sideways, and you can only do that if your bureaucracy has a fairly sizeable chunk of meaningless positions for the sideways types to be moved into. The Justice Department has now asked Congress to give it the power to dismiss INS employees. Will they get it? Who knows? The Administration doesn't seem to be getting a lot of what it wants these days.

No-one looking at Washington right now could seriously argue that this is a government culture on a war footing. It would not have been possible for Messrs Atta and al-Shehhi to kill thousands of Americans without the unwitting cooperation of the INS, FBI, CIA, the Federal Aviation Administration and sundry other agencies. Yet, while supposedly "the world changed" on September 11th, the relevant Federal bodies are carrying on just as before. Six months on, not a head has rolled. The Transportation Secretary, Underperformin' Norman Mineta, is continuing his harassment of octogenarian nuns at airport check-ins. The newly federalised security scanners fall asleep on the job as often as the minimum-wage illegal-immigrant no-spikka-da-English felony-warrants-in-three-neighbouring-states old-school security scanners. Anyone who's spent ten minutes at the departure gate soon spots that half these security guys operate not "random checks" but a plonkingly obvious rota system, singling out every nth person for a special pat-down and feel-up, so as long as you graciously wave the nun ahead of you and go through as the nth plus one, you'll slip through.

In fairness, if the line's slow moving, it's not always the government's fault. Last Saturday, at Des Moines, an America West flight from Phoenix landed with a dead man on board. The cabin crew described him as "kind of stiff" during the flight - in two and a half hours, he hadn't moved and had periodically dripped saliva. But, although some witnesses have suggested he was dead at the gate back in Phoenix, America West is insistent that there was no breach of security and that he fully qualified under FAA regulations as a living human being when he boarded the 737, wheeled on by his son and daughter-in-law. The FAA forbids dead people from boarding, presumably in order to prevent al-Qa'eda corpses from picking up their green cards. Meanwhile, the airline pilots want to be armed with guns, the public wants them to have them, but Underperformin' Norman has nixed the idea.

Worried about bioterror? Don't worry, the Centers for Disease Control is busy researching tobacco advertising and state variations in intimate-partner homicide. Congress? They've done nothing useful since the day of the attacks, when they appeared on the steps of the Capitol and spontaneously sang "God Bless America". Then they resumed normal service: God help America. Mr Bush did appoint a "Director of Homeland Security", Tom Ridge, but no-one has a clue what he does all day. Supposedly, he "coordinates" 80 different agencies. So, when the FBI puts Mullah Omar on their "Most Wanted" list, Director Ridge passes it on to the INS, who tell him they gave Mr Omar a visa in February and he's now working as a pool boy in Palm Beach. Mr Ridge, formerly Governor of Pennsylvania, is a "moderate Republican" whom the press spent much of 2000 urging on Mr Bush as the ideal Vice-Presidential running-mate. Being "pro-choice", etc, Governor Ridge would allegedly appeal to all kinds of key demographics Bush could never reach. All I can say is thank God for Dick Cheney. Since becoming Director of Homeland Security, Governor Ridge isn't appealing to anybody, except maybe to some higher force to put him out of his misery. Within ten minutes of taking the job, word was out that he didn't have the President's ear and the agency heads thought he was a loser. He spent his first weeks coming up with proposals to merge various competing acronyms like the INS into one streamlined super-acronym agency, but the President didn't seem interested. So now he's mostly the guy who goes on TV and looks like someone's twisting a pineapple up his bottom as he introduces new fodder for the late-night comics. Last week, it fell to Mr Ridge to unveil America's new system of daily colour-coded security alerts – from blue (low risk) to red (severe risk) via green, yellow and orange. As I write, it's officially a yellow day: elevated risk. But it all depends where you're looking from. President Bush is seeing red but acting yeller, Tom Ridge is too green, I'm feeling blue, and my orange was confiscated for security reasons.

The New York Post's John Podhoretz has observed that, when you meet Republicans, they talk about the war, whereas, when you meet Democrats, they talk about campaign finance reform, Enron, environmental issues, etc. This is very true. The current political scene resembles a recent misprint in *The Independent*, in which, in the course of a good Eurosneer at the expense of the President, their leader writer commented that Mr Bush had choked on a pretzel "while watching the Green Bay Packers take on the San Francisco Giants". This seems unlikely, given that the Packers are a football team, the Giants a baseball team. But, in a way, that's what Washington feels like. In contrast to the British media, where even the *Speccie* is riven by disputes about civilian deaths in Afghanistan, in the mainstream US press, those of us on the warmongering side have the field to ourselves: say anything you want about toppling Saddam, overthrowing the Ayatollahs, nuking the Channel Islands, and nary a voice is raised in protest. The leftie pundits, for the most part, don't want to touch the subject, preferring to drone on about "soft money", racist judges, the North-East Dairy Compact and other pressing matters. And, as the right does on the war, the left has a pretty free run on these subjects. One team's playing football, the other's playing baseball. Occasionally Tom Daschle, Washington's most powerful Democrat, will put a finger in the wind and venture some criticism of the war effort – where's Osama? We wanna see some results here - but he gets slapped down pretty quickly and the Dems have sensibly concluded that things work pretty well if they let Bush concentrate on Iraq and Afghanistan while they get on with what's important to them.

I gather this is what it was like in the previous Crusades, with Dubya the Lionheart off in foreign parts slaying the foe leaving the treacherous Prince Tom of Daschle to run amok at home. One day, some of us hope fondly, the war will be over and Dubya will return to do to the teachers' unions and the eco-crazies what he did to the Taleban. Dream on, says Dick Morris, the toe-sucker turned thumb-sucker. His theory is that Bush is Churchill – i.e., he's a loser. The public will stick with him as long as the war's on, but the minute it's over he's toast and they'll turn to Clem Attlee in the shape of Daschle, Dick Gephardt, Al Gore, whoever. According to Morris, if the war's still raging in 2004, Bush gets re-elected; if not, he's a one-termer like his dad. The total collapse of the non-war aspects of the Bush Presidency suggests there may be something to the Morris thesis.

Well, so be it. If you only have one priority, saving the civilised world is as good as any. But, in this post-Taleban pre-Saddam lull, even the war Presidency isn't looking so good. The Dems, sniffing blood, have figured that, while you're on a hiding to nothing taking on Rummy, the home front is wide-open. Senator Daschle has threatened to subpoena Ridge to force him to appear before Congress. Subpoena! Like he's some Enron exec. Ridge is on the Presidential staff rather than a Cabinet Secretary confirmed in office by the Senate, so he says he's not obliged to appear formally before the old windbags. He told Robert C Byrd, the Senate's most illustrious sanctimonious old coot, that he'd be happy to brief him in private, but the Senator's demanding public hearings so that he can hector the hapless Ridge in front of the TV cameras. Byrd sees himself as "the conscience of the Senate" – a revered constitutionalist, a sort of Lord Blake of West Virginia. But, more to the point, he's the Duke of Pork, and over the years he's steered many worthy public-works projects to his state. West Virginia is now home to the Robert C Byrd Rural Health Center, the Robert C Byrd Academic and Technology Center, the Robert C Byrd Life Long Learning Center, the Robert C Byrd Locks and Dam, the Robert C Byrd Green Bank Telescope; the Robert C. Byrd Institute for Advanced Flexible Manufacturing, the Robert C Byrd Hilltop Office Complex, etc, etc. Senator Byrd wants the war to be less about bombing foreigners and more about homeland security. Specifically, he would like a new anti-terrorist command centre to be set up at West Virginia's state-of-the-art Robert C Byrd Regional Training Institute.

I would prefer to set up the Robert C Byrd Business As Usual Center, a West Virginia retirement home for the many Senators, Congressmen, cabinet secretaries and Federal officials who don't seem to realise that there's a war on, that thousands of Americans were killed, and that, just for once, it's not about pork and time-serving and turf disputes. But Bush needs to act, too, to reclaim the home front from the present bunch of deadbeats. The wilier Dems dismiss those approval ratings, betting that the President is in about as healthy a state as that passenger to Des Moines: flying high but already expired.

REALITY CHECK

March 16th 2002
The Daily Telegraph

"The BBC faces a torrent of criticism over a 'real-life documentary' series which pits volunteers against the conditions endured by the millions who died in the trenches of northern France in World War I." – The Daily Mail

Your guide to this week's new BBC reality shows:

THE TRENCH
Set in a Rwandan latrine, this historically accurate series recreates the conditions of an African refugee camp. Twelve attractive young people from Penge (the Hutus) and twelve from Stockton-on-Tees (the Tutsis) compete to see who can produce the most distended bellies in just two weeks! As on "Big Brother", there'll be lots of opportunities to see the participants with their kit off writhing around – but this time in agony, as they wait for that UN food convoy to arrive! You'll see hot horny Brits too doubled up with the dysentery to bonk!

And as if the cholera wasn't bad enough several forgotten pop and soap stars from the Eighties will be swinging by to film their all-star charity fundraising hit. How many retakes of Wet Wet Wet's

Marti Pellow singing "And it's hard to find snow in Africa at Christmas" can our boys and girls take?

Each episode comes complete with authentic doom-laden period voiceover by Michael Buerk. (Obviously, it would be inhumane to subject the series' participants to the full gruelling horrors of the situation, so the part of Marti Pellow will be played by Shakin' Stevens.)

THE WENCH

Set in an 18th century bawdy house, this historically accurate series shows what happens when ten healthy young men from Stoke-on-Trent are confined for two weeks with a buxom, apple-cheeked, pox-ridden barmaid. And remember, every boil or pustule raises £50 for the BBC's Children In Need Appeal!

THE FRENCH

Set in an authentic recreation of the Elysée Palace in the car park at BBC Clwyd, this scrupulously accurate series gives members of the Bush Administration the chance to experience life as a snotty French politician.

See Pentagon hawk Don Rumsfeld as sophisticated French Foreign Minister Hubert Védrine scoffing at "ze simplisme" of Bush's State of the Union Address. Watch American warwolf Dick Cheney as worldly Prime Minister Lionel Jospin sneering at the absurd Texas cowboy's obsession with fighting terrorism. Marvel at National Security dominatrix Condi Rice's performance as exquisitely cultured former Defence Minister Jean-Pierre Chevènement complaining that the Americans are dedicated to "ze organised cretinisation of our people". Thrill to cowboy Bush himself as he takes on the role of effortlessly subtle EU External Affairs Commissioner Chris Patten, chuckling merrily at his droll play on words as he observes that "smart bombs are not as important as smart development assistance". (One of these people is not French, but who can tell?)

Bush's old Texas Rangers baseball team appear as the French diplomatic corps, and the *Telegraph*'s very own leading extremist Zionist Jewess, Barbara Amiel, will be dropping in to award bonus points for anti-Semitism. Although the blundering Americans will be immersed in Gallic cynicism round the clock, they will be allowed one 15-minute bathroom break every eight hours in order to use words like "good" and "evil" non-ironically.

THE BENCH
In this disturbingly lifeless series, a trio of judges from Britain, Jamaica and South Korea are confined to a small room in Holland listening to Slobodan Milosevic pretend to cross-examine a witness for two or three weeks.

THE DENCH
Set on a brilliantly lifelike recreation of a movie set, a troupe of British actors attempt to stick it out on a dreary British movie shoot in hopes of an Oscar nomination only to find that yet again it's gone to Judi bloody Dench. Tom Courtenay plays the young Alan Bates. Alan Bates plays the young Tom Courtenay. Eileen Atkins and Anna Massey play bridge. Kate Winslet wonders why all the good parts go to Cate Blanchett. Cate Blanchett wishes that *Charlotte Gray* had gone to Kate Winslet. Blanche Winslett plays Kristin Scott Thomas.

THE MENSCH
Filmed on location, this historically accurate series gives Islamic fundamentalists the chance to experience life as a group of Jewish comics at a 1950s Catskills hotel as they argue over who should get the plaque for Humanitarian of the Year. See top Saudi imam Marwan bin Hamada al-Nihar as Brooklyn's Bernie Kaplan: "You know why Jewish mothers make great parole officers? They never let anyone finish a sentence. (Rim shot.) So the big-time Hollywood producer calls me and he says, 'We got this great role for you. You play the Jewish husband.' And I say, 'Forget it. I want a speaking part.' (Rim shot.) You know those Arabs? Every time they pray, they gotta face Mecca? Big deal. My wife, every time she prays, she faces Bloomingdale's. Oy..."

Will the imam survive his two-week engagement? How will Mullah Omar cope with all that kibitzing? Can he make it all the way through "Bei Mir Bist Du Schon" with the special lyrics about the Borscht Of The Day Special?

THE STENCH
Filmed in Bulawayo, this disturbingly accurate series recreates the experience of voting in last weekend's election. Hundreds of citizens wait patiently in a sweltering polling station for their chance to cast their ballots, only to find that lackeys of Zimbabwean strongman Robert Mugabe are turning away the white, middle class

and well-educated. Happily, this saves the producers a lot of time, as lackeys of BBC strongman Gavyn Davies had given them exactly the same directive.

~

AMONG THE EQUIVALISTS

March 25th 2002
The National Post

THERE WERE no other passengers in my car on the Eurostar except for an American couple and their precocious little girl. Bored by the Kent countryside, she announced that she was going to tell her parents all the facts she had amassed about France. Though they were many and varied in number, as we emerged from the Channel Tunnel and onto the soil of the Fifth Republic itself, she began to falter. "I don't know a whole lot about World War Two. I know we were the good people. So the French would be, like, the bad people?"

"No, sweetie," said Daddy, patiently. "The French were the good people, too."

Hmm. I'd have given a more nuanced answer myself, but let it go. The moppet wanted to keep things straightforward. "So who were the bad people?" she asked.

"Well, there aren't really bad people, sweetie. Not whole countries of them."

I gave an involuntary snort behind my copy of *Le Monde*. Daddy and Mommy glanced over in my direction, but I hastily exuded a passing imitation of Gallic charm. Though Daddy's characterization of the Second World War – no bad people were involved in the making of this global conflict – is not yet received opinion, the same disinclination to take sides colours our view of almost all contemporary disputes. Countries A and B may be at war, but there is no good side and no bad side, just two parties "trapped" in a "mindless" "cycle of violence" that "threatens the peace process". The "peace process" tends to be no peace and lotsa process, in which western panjandrums have invested considerable amounts of their prestige. That's why in Paris this weekend most of my dining companions were outraged not by the deaths of Palestinians or Israelis but by the shelling of Palestinian Authority buildings. "These buildings," one indignant Frenchman told me, "were built with money direct from the Union!" – i.e., the European Union. "We have given billions, and now it is rubble."

"Oh, your money's perfectly safe," I said. "It's sitting in the Hamas bigshots' numbered bank accounts in Zurich."

Fortunately, the World Trade Center was not an EU aid project, so the French are far less mad at Osama. "The great question facing us all today," declared one old acquaintance of mine gravely, "is how to halt and reverse American power before it destroys the world."

"No doubt many agreeable dinners will be devoted to exploring this question," I said, ordering another cognac. Everyone professed to "understand" how America felt about September 11th, but more importantly they also understood how everybody else felt, too.

"Your Mister Bush," said his wife, a chic lawyer, "he sees always the B-movie western: America is the good guy so her enemies must be the bad guys."

"Well, in the case of al-Qaeda, he's not actually wrong, is he?"

Pitying looks from around the table. "Bush is crippled," said someone else, "by his Rambo view of the world."

"I very much doubt Bush reads Rimbaud," I said.

And on and on, round the clock. The following point was made to me twice within the space of 24 hours, so I assume it's the current sophistry doing the rounds. "Ah, Mark," said the first, with a wry self-congratulatory twinkle, "the British and Americans, they go on all the time about democracy. But you do realize there are six billion people in this world and that, if you gave them the opportunity to vote for Mr Bush or Mr bin Laden, why, one billion would vote for Bush and five billion for bin Laden." Pause for stunned reaction from boneheaded North American, and then, with a sardonic courtly nod: "I myself would, of course, vote for Bush."

The second time I heard this observation the speaker gave a slightly different tag: "I myself would, of course, *probably* vote for Bush." Take Two sounds about right.

Leaving aside the precision of the math, this droll jest neatly encapsulates the French world view: naïve Washington thinks all will be well if you liberate the will of the people, the European elite knows that civilization depends on restraining it. At heart, they believe the opposite of the American tourist on the train: there are no good peoples, just different groups of bad peoples whose baser urges have to be adroitly managed – as Western Europe failed to do between the wars but which it has done with some success since. That's why the EU likes the Emirs and the Ayatollahs, old Arafat and Boy Assad. They feel those fellows are engaged in the same project as theirs: holding the excesses of the people in check.

This worldly cynicism would have more to commend it if it weren't for the overwhelming evidence that the opposite is, in fact, the case – that these regimes preserve themselves by actively encouraging their people's worst instincts. Take my old friends the Saudis. In London, His Excellency the Saudi Ambassador to the Court of St James, Sheikh Ghazi Algosaibi, has been amusing himself with my plans for his kingdom, as recently outlined in these pages. "Ever since Mark Steyn, maps at the ready, threatened to dismantle Saudi Arabia," says His Excellency, "our children are having nightmares and our old men and women are quaking in terror. We are desperately trying to save ourselves." Ah, that famous Saudi sense of humour.

I don't know whether the Saudi people are quaking in terror, and nor, I suspect, does Ambassador Algosaibi. If their children are having nightmares, it may be because they fret over finding themselves, as recently happened to some young girls in Mecca, fleeing from a blazing schoolhouse and being beaten by the mutaween (the religious police) and forced back inside the building to perish in the flames. Why would officials of the Commission for the Promotion of Virtue and Prevention of Vice do such a thing? Because the girls, in their haste to escape the inferno, had neglected to put on their head scarves. Fifteen of them died. They were, to quote Ambassador Algosaibi, desperately trying to save themselves, but in Saudi Arabia that's not allowed, not for girls. The Saudis, in an attempt at damage control with the western media, have suggested that the beaters were not bona fide members of the mutaween but impostors. I'll bet it's those Jews again.

The other day, the Saudi government daily *Al-Riyadh* ran a column headlined "The Jewish Holiday Of Purim": "For this holiday the Jewish people must obtain human blood so that their clerics can prepare the holiday pastries," wrote Dr Umayma Ahmad Al-Jalahma of King Faysal University. "The victim must be a mature adolescent who is, of course, a non-Jew." Wow. That's some recipe, I thought. But, of course, the average Arab reader just yawns and sighs, "Big deal. So the Jews use gentile blood in their cookies. Is the Pope catholic? What else is new?"

John Derbyshire, in *National Review*, argues that we shouldn't be sending peace negotiators to the Middle East, but teams of psychiatrists. The majority of its 300 million inhabitants are, he says, "nuts". And he has a point. It's possible to believe in "the plight of the Palestinians". It's just about possible to believe that Israel wishes to kill all the Palestinians and that therefore the Jews should be driven into the sea. It's even possible to believe that Mossad are so ingenious that they pulled off the September 11th attacks and framed a bunch of innocent Arabs. But no rational person can seriously believe that your average Jew cookery show begins "First, take your Gentile victim and drain his blood".

Yet such an assertion passes without comment in the Saudi press. Do the majority of Saudis go along with this stuff? We don't know. But we do know that their government's mouthpiece thinks it useful to propagate the old blood libels. Whether or not you can make rational human beings of the Middle Eastern peoples is unclear, but there's no question that you're never going to do it as long as the present gang's in charge.

Forget the "cycle of violence" and the "peace process". History teaches us that the most lasting peace is achieved when one side – preferably the worst side – is decisively defeated and the regime's diseased organs are comprehensively cleansed. That's why National Socialism, Fascism and Japanese militarism have not troubled us of late. One can imagine how World War Two would have played out had, say, Mary Robinson, the UN Human Rights poseur, been sitting in Downing Street instead of Winston Churchill. Her crowd should not be running World War Four.

~

THE NEW SERIOUSNESS

March 28th 2002
The National Post

PERSONALLY, I thought this year's Academy Awards just zipped by in no time. But that's because I'm on the road in Europe. Because of the time difference, the rest of the world gets the big show a day late, edited down to a little over an hour in some countries and barely longer than a Billy Crystal opening number in others.

The non-starry awards – Best Documentary Short, Best Original Score – are the first to get chopped. That cuts it down to three hours forty-five. What else can we lose? How about some of those lifetime achievement and humanitarian things? Arthur Hiller and his hairdo of the night wound up on the cutting-room floor. But so did Robert Redford's woozy ramblings, Barbra Streisand warm-up and all.

That leaves 'em with three hours. What else can go? Well, here's what the BBC, among others, decided to do: every single reference to September 11th got deleted. The moment of silence. Kevin Spacey's sonorous platitudes about the need to celebrate life in the face of death. Whoopi Goldberg spinning round and revealing the New York Fire and Police Department acronyms emblazoned on the back of her frock. The lame jokes about how "America suffered through a great national tragedy, but we have recovered. Mariah Carey has already made another movie." All scrupulously excised by the publicly funded broadcasters of America's allies, leaving nary a trace except for the occasional weird jump in mid-speech.

Given that the message of the evening was supposed to be the "new seriousness" of post-9/11 Hollywood, the removal of any mention of the dread date meant what was left was flat and subdued but with no particular reason why. It was like watching a celeb show played by lookalikes recruited from a funeral home. The dress code no longer made sense. Actor after actor appeared not in "black tie" – ie, bow tie and tux – but in long, droopy, black necktie, sober shirt, dark suit, as if they'd just dropped in to present a Best Screenplay award on the way back from Auntie Mabel's interment. Otherwise, all that survived of the show's big theme was the sub-text to Tom Hanks' assertion, before the nominations for Best Picture, that "when we're at the movies, we're not alone".

This is a traditional theme: movies make us a community, they're therapeutic, they bind us together to heal the wounds of the world by showing how art transcends the petty divisions of our troubled times, etc. Well, I'm in Europe and every multiplex you pass in London, Paris and Berlin is showing five Hollywood films plus one token local product. In London, the biggest poster on the concourse of Waterloo Station advertises "The West Wing". In Paris, the oldies station plays American records you never hear in America anymore ("Honey" by Bobby Goldsboro, good grief). In Berlin, I switch on the TV and Sarah Michelle Gellar is speaking German. Around the world, everyone's watching American movies – and they all hate America.

Sometimes they actively hate it, sometimes they just quietly despise it. But, if decades of exposure to the healing balm of Tom Hanks and his fellow "artists" have really united the world, it would appear to be mostly in the cause of anti-Americanism. Somewhere right now, in a council flat in the English Midlands, in Frankfurt or in Rotterdam, an Islamic terrorist is sitting in a Yankees cap, Disney T-shirt and Nike sneakers plotting to blow up the White House.

One of the lessons of September 11th is that every day millions of people wear baseball caps, listen to Britney, watch "Friends", eat at Dunkin' Donuts, and go see *Ali* – and they don't have a clue about America. In London, the broadsheet newspapers that devote most space to American cultural trends – *The Guardian, The Independent* – are the most vehemently anti-American. You can easily like American pop culture without liking America. On the other hand, if you dislike American pop culture, it'll make you dislike America even more. Thus Jean-Pierre Chevènement, French Presidential candidate, and his famous statement that the United States is dedicated to "the organized cretinization of our people". There was a whiff of this yesterday when another Presidential candidate, Alain Madelin, described this week's massacre in a French town hall as an "American-style by-product". One Frenchman – a left-wing eco-nut - kills eight other Frenchmen, but somehow it's evidence of America's malign cultural influence.

You can sort of see what he's getting at. Wherever you live around the world, the landscape of the imagination is America: in the movie in your mind, the car chase takes place on the Golden Gate Bridge, the love scene in Central Park, the massive explosion at the

World Trade Center. The world watches Hollywood's America in a kind of post-neutron-bombed way: you get the sex and the shoot-outs, but the spirit of the country remains as foreign as ever.

In Britain, they played up the "black Oscars" angle because, being a racially relaxed society, they find American breast-beating and self-flagellation on the subject hugely enjoyable. On the Continent, where real racism of all kinds is pervasive, they took Hollywood's bizarre determination to muscle in on the civil rights struggle 40 years too late as confirmation things must be far worse over there. I'd gladly award a lifetime achievement Oscar to each of Halle Berry's breasts, which reportedly received half-a-million apiece for their exposed role in *Swordfish* – that's $19 million less than John Travolta got, and they gave a much better performance. I'm certainly happy that Los Angeles' limousine liberals have finally caught up with those right-wing racist Republicans who long ago handed out starring roles to Condi Rice and Colin Powell. But to suggest that giving one beautiful, talented actress a statuette is some kind of civil-rights breakthrough is ridiculously self-regarding even by Hollywood's standards. It was compounded by the "tribute" to Sidney Poitier, which solicited testimonials only from black actors and thereby ghettoized his achievement, making "black acting" seem a specialization award, like Best Foreign Language Film.

When Hollywood has such difficulty liking America, it's no wonder its foreign audiences find it so hard. Deprived by their networks of the 9/11 content, the Europeans weren't missing anything: it was victim stuff, strangely outdated, like a movie that's been in development too long. The stars expressed sympathy for New York, but not the Pentagon. They saluted the firemen, but not the heroic passengers of Flight 93, never mind the brave men of the 10th Mountain Division – or, if we're being multicultural, the Princess Patricias and the Australian SAS. The montage of vox pops that opened the show included Laura Bush plus Willie Brown, Mayor of San Francisco; Jerry Brown, Mayor of Oakland; Lani Guinier, onetime Clinton Administration nominee; and Al Sharpton, New York's pre-eminent race-baiter. That's not just a four-to-one Democratic advantage, that's four far-left ideological Dems to one non-political Republican spouse: a very Hollywood idea of balance. No wonder that when Robert Redford started peddling his boilerplate about how it's more important than ever to cherish "freedom of expression", Mr and Mrs America switched off in record numbers.

Hollywood has had a problem since September 11th. It knows the plot has changed but it can't quite find the tone. It wants to be in tune with the masses, but can't quite bring itself. On Sunday the only unashamedly patriotic sentiment was voiced by Julian Fellowes. Picking up the Best Screenplay Award for *Gosford Park*, he kept the lists of lawyers' and agents' names to a minimum, thanked the US for being so welcoming to foreigners and ended with the words "God bless America". And so at the post-9/11 Oscars, the one participant who expressed any love of America was a Briton, a Tory and an occasional Conservative Party speechwriter. How did he get past security?

APRIL

Never again. Again.

April 4th/14th 2002
The National Post/The Sunday Telegraph

A LL CIVILIZED people can agree that killing Jews is wrong. Well, killing six million of them 60 years ago is wrong. Killing a couple of dozen every 48 hours or so, that's a different matter. For example, the official position of Canada's Foreign Affairs Minister, Bill Graham, speaking from his beach in Barbados, is that Israel's response to the Passover massacre is "disproportionate".

Mr Graham did not specify what would be proportionate. But presumably, if he were Prime Minister of Israel, he'd respond by fishing some girl out of her Home Ec. class at Tel Aviv High, loading her blouse with Semtex, and pointing her in the direction of the nearest Ramallah pizzeria to blow the legs off Palestinian grannies. Alas, I fear even this proportionate, measured, reasonable response would be unlikely to win Israel any sympathy in the chancelleries of the west.

"The Zionist entity" is now more isolated diplomatically than at any time in its history. "The whole world is demanding that Israel withdraws," said Kofi Annan in Madrid, standing alongside various panjandrums from the EU, UN, US and Russia. "I don't think the whole world, including the friends of the Israeli people and government, can be wrong."

Oh, I don't know. The "whole world" has a pretty good track record of being wrong, especially where Jews are concerned. Fifty million Frenchmen *can* be wrong, and never more so than when they're teamed with the EU (which has called on Israel to "lower the violence"), the European Parliament (which has demanded sanctions against Israel), the German Government (which has announced an arms embargo against Israel), the brand-new International Criminal Court (which - in its very first 24 hours! - started mulling the question of "Israeli war crimes"), the Norwegian Parliament (which had a visitor thrown out the building for wearing a provocative Star of David on his lapel), never mind the members of Calgary's "Palestinian community" who marched through the streets carrying placards emblazoned "Death To The Jews", a timeless slogan but not hitherto a burning issue on the prairies. The French President is "appalled" by what the Dutch Foreign Ministry calls Israel's "military repression". Meanwhile, the Pope "rejects unjust conditions and humiliations imposed on the Palestinian people as well as the reprisals and revenge attacks which do nothing but feed the sense of frustration."

Oh, that ol' "frustration", it's so easy to feed. In Marseilles, where within four days one synagogue was burned to the ground and another less conclusively torched, the Grand Mufti, Soheib Bencheikh, told UPI that so long as "the violence in the Middle East" persisted "Arab youths in France would likely continue their campaign of attacks". They're not Palestinians, they're mostly French citizens of North African extraction. But "frustration" at what Israel is doing on the West Bank of the Jordan justifies French Muslims burning French Jews' houses of worship.

It was a lively Passover weekend *sur le Continent*. In Brussels, a synagogue was firebombed. In Berlin, two Orthodox Jews were attacked on a busy street and a Jewish memorial was defaced with a swastika. In France, three synagogues were burned. A kosher butcher's shop was shot up in Toulouse. In Villeurbanne, near Lyons, a young Jewish couple, the woman pregnant, were badly beaten.

"Ah, those Jews," sighed an attractive, intelligent, sophisticated Parisienne at dinner the other night. "They cause problems everywhere they are."

I spluttered and sprayed soup down my shirt front.

"You must be more sensitive in front of our friend," chuckled our host, musing on Barbara Amiel's recent observations about French anti-Semitism. "In the English world, they think Europe is planning the Second Holocaust."

Well, no. There won't be a Second Holocaust in Europe, if only because they did such a thorough job first time round. France's excitable Arab youth are perforce engaged in no more than a belated mopping up operation. Its significance is as a portent of what the Continent can expect once Mr Bush's war on terror moves on to Iraq. The only question is whether Western Europe's millions of young, unassimilated Muslim men succeed merely in paralysing their governments or destabilizing them. Even in Britain, Downing Street is bracing for massive Muslim riots.

But, even if there are no longer enough European Jews for big-time genocide, one is struck by the similarities between then and now. In 1960, when the Israelis seized Adolf Eichmann, the government-controlled Saudi newspaper ran the story under the headline, "Arrest Of Eichmann, Who Had The Honour Of Killing Six Million Jews". Today, Israel's population is about six million, a fifth of them Arabs but that still leaves a nice round number of five million Jews and, then as now, great honour attaches to killing them: your face on posters all over town, a revered place in society for your family, 25,000 bucks from Saddam Hussein. Then as now, the old libels – the Protocols of the Elders of Zion, Jews drink human blood – are peddled daily in government-approved publications – then in Germany, now in Egypt, Syria, Saudi Arabia. Then as now, the world's diplomats are determined to see no evil, hear no evil. In 1933, this chap Hitler was a bit rough and ready, but he's better than most of the alternatives, and there's no need to pay any attention to all this stuff about the Jews, just a lot of talk, and besides he's got a point with this "lebensraum" business, legitimate grievance and all that. In 2002, Saudi Arabia is our "friend", Egypt is "moderate", and Chairman Arafat, according to the Swiss Foreign Ministry spokeswoman Muriel Berset-Kohen, is "our legitimate interlocutor because he has been democratically elected".

Not exactly, Muriel. He was elected once, in a deeply flawed and corrupted poll, shortly after the establishment of the "Palestinian Authority". His term expired in 1999 but, rather than submit to the tiresome disruption of a re-election campaign, he simply extended his "Presidency" indefinitely, thus following in the long tradition of dictators installed by a cynical west: one man, one vote, one time.

The big difference is that, whereas in the Thirties the Jews were David, now they're Goliath – the massive military sledgehammer crushing an oppressed and captive people. That's how Peter Preston in *The Guardian* sees it, arguing that, as the Palestinians have no tanks, they have to improvise with what they can get their hands on – plastic explosives and willing schoolgirls. In fact, the West Bank Arabs had plenty of tanks: the only reason they're living under "Israeli occupation" is because in 1967 their then government, Jordan, sent its heavy machinery into action against Israel. To claim that this is a dispute between Israel and the "Palestinians" is to ignore that the latter are supplied with money and arms by Iraq, Iran, Syria and Saudi Arabia. Objectively, they're the Goliath.

As George Jonas pointed out the other day, the Arabs resent Europe for solving its Jewish problem by moving it offshore, by dumping it in their lap, making it the Arabs' problem. I have some sympathy for this view: with hindsight, it might have been better to give the Zionists France or Austria. The problem now for the Arabs is that they cannot rid themselves of the Jews by conventional military means: they have tanks, missiles, aircraft, but every time they use them against Israel, they lose. So their chosen weapon is the Palestinians: Iraq and the other patrons of terror have figured out that the only block of the supposedly explosive "Arab street" that's rousable is in the West Bank, and they're pouring their resources in accordingly. Effectively, they've designated "Palestine" as one big suicide bomb to take out the Jews, and it's going so swimmingly the last thing they want is to have to go back to primitive weaponry like tanks. Either it'll wear them down by attrition – there are already signs that young Israelis are drifting into a "post-Zionist" fatalism – or it will hold them until the finishing touches are put to that eagerly awaited Muslim nuke that Hashemi Rafsanjani, one of those famous Iranian moderates, has sworn will settle the Jewish question forever. It's not tiny Palestine versus big Israel, anymore than it was tiny Sudetenland versus big Czechoslovakia in the Thirties. It's six million Israelis versus a solid hostile Muslim bloc of 300 million.

Meanwhile, what have we learned from this last extraordinary month? Not much about the Middle East, but quite a lot about Europe. What happens when Palestinian civilians strap on plastic explosives and head for Israeli pizza parlours? Europe says Israeli checkpoints for Palestinians are "humiliating". Palestinian Red Crescent ambulances permit themselves to be used as transportation for bombs and explosives - and Europe attacks Israel for refusing them free movement. Documents are found signed by Arafat authorizing funding for a suicide bombing on a young girl's bat mitzvah, and members of the Nobel committee publicly call for taking back the 1994 Peace Prize - from Shimon Peres. Synagogues are firebombed in France, Belgium and Finland, and the EU deplores the wanton destruction of property - in Ramallah.

What the Europeans call "Muslim-Jewish tensions" on the Continent do not involve Jewish gangs attacking Mosques or beating up women in hejabs, only Muslim gangs attacking synagogues and stoning a bus of Jewish schoolchildren. In France, Jew-bashing incidents are currently running at the rate of 12 per day, though the authorities seem positively insouciant about investigating them. In fairness, the Prime Minister did bestir himself last week. "No matter what is happening in the Middle East," said Lionel Jospin, "anti-Semitic acts are totally unacceptable" – a formulation which, even as it disapproves of the assaults, somehow manages to validate their motivation. For, as Messieurs Jospin, Chirac and Védrine have assured us, "what is happening in the Middle East" is the fault of the famously "shitty little country". France's leaders and their excitable Arab youth are, to that extent, on the same song sheet.

This is not virulently anti-Jew, just the familiar European urge to appease. France has seven million Muslims. If, from one million Palestinians, Hamas and co can recruit enough to blow up a couple of dozen Israelis every 48 hours, how many recruits could they find in France from an unassimilated population five times the size? The Europeans are scared of their Muslim populations, scared of what perceived slight might turn them from shooting up kosher butchers to shooting up targets of more, shall we say, concern to the general population.

When the war with Iraq starts, we'll find out. No wonder Paris and Brussels are as keen to postpone it as Baghdad and Riyadh. The "whole world" is agreed that if anybody has to be blown up it might as well be the Israelis. Ah, those Jew troublemakers: why won't they just lie there and take it?

I hate writing about this stuff. I've never been a "Zionist", never written a column on the subject pre 9/11. I'm sick of getting e-mails sneering, "What was your name ...originally?" (Just for the record, originally my name was "Anthony Wilson-Smith", but you can't get anywhere in modern multiculti Canada with some WASP throwback moniker like that.) To those who always complain that I weep for Jewish children but not Muslim ones, let me say I weep for Ayat Mohammed al-Akhras, the straight-A high-school student who blew herself up in a supermarket last week. She spent eight years in a contaminated education system run by Yasser Arafat, she grew up in a culture that glorifies human sacrifice promoted by Yasser Arafat, she was recruited by subordinates of Yasser Arafat, supplied with explosives paid for by Yasser Arafat, and dispatched as a human bomb with the blessing of Yasser Arafat. I weep for every Arab child so perverted by a contemptible cowardly old man.

There are two sides in this struggle: one is prepared to offer land, the other is prepared to offer "the right to exist". That argument should have been settled six decades ago. As it says on the wall at Dachau, "Never Again".

But, as the old song says, "I'll Never Say 'Never Again' Again."

~

THE ROAD TO PEACE LEADS THROUGH THE ROAD TO WAR

April 8th 2002
The National Post

ANOTHER WEEK, another high-level mission to the Middle East. This time, Colin Powell is flying to the region to bring peace; last time round, Dick Cheney was flying to the region to whip up war fever. It seems a lifetime ago now, but it's just the other day that the Vice-President was released from his "secure location" and dispatched to Araby to shore up support for toppling Saddam from our "friends" in the region.

As it happens, the axis of evil – Iraq, Iran – is causing far less trouble at the moment than the axis of pals – Saudi Arabia, Egypt – but such are the mysterious ways of the Orient and, indeed, of Washington that it was deemed a priority to kiss up to the "good" guys and attempt to bring them on side. Saddam had nothing to do with September 11th, the House of Saud had everything to do with it. But for some reason the Administration thought it would appeal to that famous Saudi sense of humour (see Ambassador Algosaibi's droll letter) if the old Butcher of Baghdad got stiffed for their mess. In order to establish his bona fides with these "moderate" regimes, President Bush slapped Israel around a little and declared military action against Palestinian terrorists "not helpful", while the Vice-President talked up Saudi Crown Prince Abdullah's "peace plan" for the region and made sympathetic murmurings about the "desperation" of the suicide bombers.

And what happened? The "moderates" told Cheney to get lost, and went off to the Arab League summit to shower the Iraqi delegation in more kisses than Halle Berry got on Oscar night. Prince Abdullah himself planted a smackeroo on the lips of the Iraqi Vice-President, the first tongue sarnie between the two parties since the Gulf War. Speaking of which, Baghdad promised not to invade Kuwait for the foreseeable future. And the League as a whole signed on to some Natoesque collective security deal, declaring that an attack on Iraq would be regarded as an attack on them all.

Meanwhile, Ariel Sharon did as he was told, exercised "restraint" and put away his stick, and the carrot of a meeting with Cheney was dangled in front of Chairman Arafat, Israel's eternal "partner for peace". The upshot was an explosion of multiple suicide bombings culminating in the Passover massacre at a ballroom in Netanya. If this is interventionist diplomacy, the sooner they take Cheney back to his "secure location" and throw away the key the better.

Aside from the grim body count, these missions are a deranged exercise in unrealpolitik, with all parties negotiating fictions. The Vice-President wanted Saudi Arabia to pretend to be his friend, the Arab League to pretend the peace plan is for real, Ariel Sharon to pretend that Yasser Arafat is cracking down on terrorism, and Arafat to pretend that he wants to crack down on terrorism. Fortunately, none of this matters. The cynic's view of the Cheney-Powell missions is that they were necessitated by a scheduling conflict over scheduling conflicts: Washington had booked the Middle East for a war with Iraq only to discover the joint being used for some other guys' war. The US would like peace in the Middle East in order to launch a massive conflagration there. The opposite is more to the point: you need a war against Iraq in order to bring peace to the Middle East. And on that, if little else, Bush shows no signs of going "wobbly". Indeed, interviewing the President on Britain's ITV network a week ago, Trevor McDonald seemed to have difficulty taking yes for an answer. "Have you made up your mind that Iraq must be attacked?" he asked.

"I made up my mind that Saddam needs to go," said the President.

"And, of course, if the logic of the war on terror means anything," continued Sir Trevor, "then Saddam must go?"

"That's what I just said," confirmed the President. "The policy of my government is that he goes."

"So you're going to go after him?"

"As I told you, the policy of my government is that Saddam Hussein not be in power."

Among Britain's snooty elite, the President was much mocked for lapsing mid-interview into one of his famous Bushisms: "The invisible part of everything that you thought you could see, you can't see." But the problem with the Middle East is that so many world leaders persist in seeing things that aren't there, notably Yasser Arafat's commitment to peace. The only consolation is that Saddam's rapprochements with his neighbours are also illusory. The Arab armies make Belgium look butch: when the Marines go into Iraq, they won't be running into any Egyptian or Syrian units.

Nor is it worth fretting over Saddam's call to use the oil supply as a weapon: right now, those guys need to sell the stuff more than the west needs to buy it. On the other hand, if the old monster's wheeze was to postpone the US invasion by whipping up the West Bank into full-scale war, everything's going to plan. The Iraqis and Saudis need to keep this war going in order to postpone the next one – hence, their generous subvention of the extensive infrastructure required to keep Palestinian schoolgirls loaded up with explosives.

The only useful contribution in recent days has been made by Brigadier Sultan Abul-Aynayn, Arafat's head man in Lebanon, who's now threatening to extend his differences with the Zionists to the Great Satan itself. "If one hair on the head of Arafat is harmed, the US had better protect its interests around the world. I mean what I am saying," he said. "We are not like Osama bin Laden, but we have our own style of response."

No doubt. The Brigadier reminds us that, if you've declared war on terrorism, you can't pick and choose. A suicide bomber detonating himself in a restaurant and a suicide pilot detonating his plane in a skyscraper are differences merely of degree. Bush can't claim the right to root out the perpetrators of anti-American terrorism in a lawless Taliban state like Afghanistan and deny others the right to root out the perpetrators of anti-Israeli terrorism in a lawless Arafat statelet.

NEVER AGAIN. AGAIN.

Just to emphasize the point, here's some of the things the Israelis found in Arafat's compound since the tanks rolled in last Friday:

> 40 pistols,
> 19 sniper rifles,
> 200 MK 47 Kalashnikovs...

Well, so far, nothing unusual. If I cleared out my basement, I could probably muster a similar tally. But that's not all they turned up:

> 43 RPG missiles,
> 4 pipe bombs,
> an unspecified number of empty suicide bomber belts,
> hundreds of thousands of counterfeit Israeli bills in denominations of 50, 100 and 200 shekels,
> printing plates for counterfeiting millions more,
> $100,000 in counterfeit US bills...

Hmm. Under the terms of that Oslo "peace process" that the EU's so keen on, the "Palestinian Authority" is meant to be not the West Bank mob concession but an internally autonomous embryo state. The Chairman is supposed to be busy with health, education, employment, international trade, public works... oh, and tourism, if you're interested in a weekend break in Ramallah. But Mr Arafat has no interest in governing. Barely had the ink dried on those Oslo "peace accords" than the ink was drying on the first of those 50-shekel bills.

The "plight of the Palestinian people" is that, after a quarter-century living under Israeli occupation, they were transferred to living under Arafat occupation, and he wasn't up to the job. So, after almost a decade under his administration, the big career opportunities in the Palestinian Authority lie in strapping on one of those Yasser souvenir belts, filling it with explosives, wandering into a shopping mall and blowing up Jews. That's the way to set your family up for life, especially now that Saddam has upped the martyr jackpot to 25,000 bucks per successful self-detonation and Saudi TV has just had a hugely successful charity telethon raising $56 million for the families of Palestinian "martyrs". King Fahd and Crown Prince Abdullah both chipped in. One Saudi Princess donated both her Rolls and her ox, a double jackpot sure to inspire any West Bank suicide bomber hoping to transform his relicts into a two-car family. Maybe they'll make it a weekly show: "Who Wants To Be A Million Air Particles?"

It's very difficult to negotiate a "two-state solution" when one side sees the two-state solution as an intermediate stage to a one-state solution: ending the "Israeli occupation" of the West Bank is a tactical prelude to ending the Israeli occupation of Israel. The divide among the Palestinians isn't between those who want to make peace with Israel and those who want to destroy her, but between those who want to destroy Israel one suicide bomb at a time and those who want to destroy her through artful "peace processes". Ayat Mohammed al-Akhras, the straight-A high-school student who blew herself up in a supermarket last week, devoted her farewell video to castigating the Arab League bigshots for pussying around with peace plans and leaving the real work to Palestinian schoolgirl bombers. Her view would appear, from the polls, to be the opinion of the overwhelming majority.

That's why America needs to be equally focused. The stability junkies in the EU, UN and elsewhere have, as usual, missed the point. The Middle East is too stable. In Africa and Latin America and Eastern Europe, rare is the dictator who dies in harness. But, in the Arab world, they get to pass their fetid crowns on to their designated heirs: old Assad bequeathed Syria to his son, Saddam hopes to do the same with Iraq. There has been "stability" for three decades, longer than anywhere else in the non-democratic world. But, when a dysfunctional regime stays in power, that's not stability, but a cesspit. Yasser Arafat and his PLO were anointed the "sole legitimate representative of the Palestinian people" in 1974, and after 28 years he's anything but legit: he's printing up foreign currency in the basement.

So if you were Washington and you wanted to destabilize the Middle East, where would you start? In the Gulf a week ago, I listened as a British diplomat bemoaned the coming war with Iraq: lot of nonsense; until the Yanks buggered everything up Saddam was a sound fellow, indifferent to Islam, pro-western, a bit rough on the Kurds but our man through and through. "Good heavens, he wears a trilby!" said my British chum, as if the fact that he likes dressing up as the Queen Mum's bookie decisively settled the matter. London invented the country and gave it its name – Iraq, "the well-rooted land" - and, as this quintessential British Arabist noted with pride, the Iraqi people are secular, tolerant, literate, the antithesis of those wacky fundamentalists in Egypt and Saudi Arabia. Their Deputy Prime Minister is Christian – admittedly a Kurd-gassing, Scud-lobbing, terror-funding Saddamite Christian, but nevertheless this is what passes for pluralism in the Middle East.

I agreed entirely with the Brit guy's analysis, disagreeing only with his conclusion. As far as he was concerned, these were all reasons for not invading Iraq; to me, they're all reasons for pressing ahead. If you had to pick only one regime to topple, this is the one. Once you've got rid of the ruling gang, it's the west's best shot at incubating a reasonably non-insane polity. In Iraq and Iran, there's a sporting chance regime change would bring about improvement. In Egypt, Syria and Saudi Arabia, it's far more problematic. The best way to destabilize the Islamist regimes is by destabilizing the non-Islamist one first. Sorry, Saddam. Them's the breaks.

In the end, the Middle East has to be fixed. As for the Palestinians, they're a wrecked people. It's tragic, and, if you want to argue about who's to blame, we can bat dates around back to the Great War. But it doesn't matter. It doesn't even matter whether you regard, as the Europeans appear to, the Palestinians' descent into depravity as confirmation of their victim status: as PA spokesman Hasan Abdul Rahman said on CNN after a new pile of Jew corpses, it's the fault of Israel for "turning our children into suicide bombers". Even if it were true, it makes no difference. They can't be allowed to succeed, because otherwise the next generation of suicide bombers will be in Bloomingdale's and Macy's.

That's why Arafat will never be President of a Palestinian state, and has begun his countdown to oblivion. And that's why the unravelling of the Middle East has to start not in the West Bank but in Baghdad. At the moment, all that prevents Islamofascism being a truly global threat is its practitioners' stupidity and inefficiency. Say what you like about Saddam but, by Middle Eastern standards, he's a very shrewd genocidal maniac. All the more reason to be rid of him sooner rather than later. Yes, it's a stylish trilby, but it's time to say here's your hat and what's your hurry.

~

MARK STEYN

REFUGEE CAMP GOLDEN JUBILEE

April 20th 2002
The Daily Telegraph

DON'T GET ME wrong. I like the British papers, if only when compared with the unreadable US broadsheets. But it has to be said that, since September 11th, Fleet Street hasn't done its reputation any favours, stampeding herd-like toward one mirage after another – "the mighty Pashtun warrior, humbler of empires"; "the fast-approaching brutal Afghan winter", due to arrive any day now; the "living hell of Guantanamo", where the medical staff outnumber the detainees, etc.

All very entertaining. But sooner or later I think readers have the right to expect their newspapers to get something right. Aside from "Sven And Ulrika's 3am Tryst", I mean.

Instead, we have the alleged Israeli massacre of civilians at Jenin. In yesterday's *Telegraph*, Terje Roed-Larsen, the "UN Special Coordinator for the Middle East Peace Process", described the devastation at the refugee camp as "horrific beyond belief". It may yet prove the worst human-rights atrocity since, oh, the Dutch took charge at Srebrenica, but so far one can't help noticing a curious sameness about this week's fevered dispatches. All rely on the same couple of eyewitnesses – "Kamal Anis, a labourer" (*The Times*), "Kamal Anis, 28" (the *Telegraph*), "A quiet, sad-looking young man called Kamal Anis" (*The Independent*) – and the same handful of victims – "A man named only as Bashar" (the *Telegraph*), "the burned remains of a man, Bashar" (*The Evening Standard*), "Bashir died in agony" (*The Times*). You'd think with so many thousands massacred there'd be a bigger selection of victims and distraught loved ones, wouldn't you? But apparently not. I do hope my friends in the British press aren't being led up the humanitarian garden path one mo' time.

For a more balanced view, one turns to the Egyptian papers. *Al-Ahram* this week contains a fascinating interview with "Omar", a top bomb-maker who managed to escape from Jenin on Wednesday. "Of all the fighters in the West Bank we were the best prepared," he says. "We started working on our plan: to trap the invading soldiers and blow them up." So Omar and his pals booby-trapped more than

248

50 houses in the camp. "We cut off lengths of mains water pipes and packed them with explosives and nails. Then we placed them about four metres apart throughout the houses – in cupboards, under sinks, in sofas."

That was just the interior décor. Outside, they placed more powerful bombs in garbage cans and cars. But don't worry about all those "innocent" civilians. As *Al-Ahram* reported, "According to Omar, everyone in the camp, including the children, knew where the explosives were located so there was no danger of civilians being injured." Thank goodness for that.

Omar's account is confirmed by the state of the corpses ("What appeared to be pipe bombs were partially hidden under a coat"). So you can understand why the UN's head man, Mr Roed-Larsen, would rather talk about "unacceptable" Israeli conduct than why his "refugee" camp (funded by British taxpayers) is, in fact, a bomb factory with on-site demonstration facilities. Mr Roed-Larsen's operation is a large part of the problem in the region. It's possible he himself hasn't a clue what's going on: that appeared to be the case 18 months ago, when Hezbollah guerillas crossed over from Lebanon in UN-marked cars, abducted three IDF soldiers and murdered them, and Mr Roed-Larsen's subordinates embarked on a nine-month cover-up of relevant video evidence. The intemperate grandee might once again merely be out of the loop. But it beggars belief that officials on the ground in the UN-managed camp weren't aware of the scale of terrorist activities: there are only so many blind eyes you can turn. That's what's "horrific beyond belief": that the UN is complicit in terrorism.

Which raises the one question that matters: why is the Jenin refugee camp still there? The Palestinians are the only people on earth with their own permanent UN agency – the Union Nations Relief and Works Agency for Palestine Refugees, established shortly after the Arabs lost their first dumb war against Israel in 1948. It was assumed UNRWA would be a temporary effort, as they usually are, and that the Arab nations would soon take over responsibility. But the Arabs shrewdly calculated that the Palestinians were more use to them in UN hands. So here we are in Jenin, a "refugee camp" about to celebrate its golden jubilee. Founded in 1953, it's been a refugee camp under Jordan, under Israel, under the Palestinian Authority. It's a refugee camp older than most African, Caribbean or Pacific states. But the

UNRWA still launches its "emergency" appeals, for an emergency from 54 years ago, when the IDF halted the Iraqis at Jenin.

Go back to the other great refugee tides of that time: Imagine if the millions of displaced persons in Europe at the end of the war or in the Indian sub-continent after partition were today maintained in camps, along with their children, and grandchildren, and great-grandchildren - three generations none of whom had ever lived in the places they're supposed to be refugees from. In whose interest would that be?

In Jenin, it's the UN that breeds "hopelessness" and "frustration", and enables and shelters terrorism. There was no massacre, just the natural consequence of the UN's putrid administration: if you let your charges build a bomb factory, don't be surprised if it blows up in your face.

AN INSULT TO FRANCE!

April 25th 2002
The National Post

ON SUNDAY, Jean-Marie Le Pen, the alleged extreme right-wing madman, managed to place second in the first round of the French Presidential election. Since then, many Europhile commentators in the English-speaking world have been attempting to reassure us that the significance of this event has been much overplayed – Le Pen only got a little more than he usually gets, pure fluke he came second, nothing to make a fuss about, all perfectly routine. The best response to this line of thinking was by the shrewd Internet commentatrix Megan McArdle: "They're completely missing the point, which is that it's *hilarious*."

Absolutely. You'd have to have a heart of stone not to be weeping with laughter at the scenes of France's snot-nosed political elite huffily denouncing Sunday's result as an insult to the honour of the Republic. I was in Paris a couple of weeks ago and I well remember the retired French diplomat who assured me that "a man like George

W Bush is simply not possible in our politics. For a creature of such crude, simplistic and extreme views to be one of the two principal candidates in a Presidential election would be inconceivable here. Inconceivable!"

Please, no giggling. Somehow events have so arranged themselves that French electors now face a choice, as the papers see it, between "*la droite*" et "*l'extrême droite*". The French people have taken to the streets in angry protests against ...the French people! Which must be a relief to the operators of McDonald's franchises, British lorry drivers and other more traditional targets of their ire, but is still a little weird. Meanwhile, the only thing that stands between M Le Pen and the Elysée Palace, President Chirac, has declared himself the representative of "the soul of the Republic". In the sense that he's a shifty old crook up to his neck in kickbacks and with no political principles, he may be on to something.

While M Chirac has cast himself as the defender of France, M Le Pen is apparently the defender of the Jews. While I was over there, he was the only candidate who was seriously affronted by the epidemic of anti-Jew assaults by French Muslims. The Eurosnots told me this was "cynical", given that M Le Pen is notoriously anti-Jew and not above doing oven jokes in public. But that doesn't necessarily make him cynical. Maybe he just loathes Arabs even more than Jews (which, for linguistic pedants, would make him technically a perfect anti-Semite). Maybe he just resents the Muslims muscling in on his turf: "We strongly object to the Arab attacks on the Jews. That's our job." But, given that Chirac and Jospin brushed off the Jew-bashing epidemic like a speck of dust on their elegant suits, Le Pen's ability to co-opt it into his general tough-on-crime/tough-on-immigrants approach showed at the least a certain political savvy.

Still, despite the racism and bigotry, I resent the characterization of M Le Pen as "extreme right". I'm an extreme right-wing madman myself, and it takes one to know one. M Le Pen is an economic protectionist in favour of the minimum wage, lavish subsidies for France's incompetent industries and inefficient agriculture; he's anti-American and fiercely opposed to globalization. In other words, he's got far more in common with Naomi Klein than with me. He would fit right in as a guest host on the CBC's "CounterSpin". Even the antipathy toward Jews is more of a left-wing thing these days – see the EU, UN, Svend and Mary Robinson, etc.

Insofar as anyone speaks up for Jews in the west, it's only a few right-wing columnists, Newt Gingrich, Christian conservatives and Mrs Thatcher – or, as a reader e-mailed the other day, "all you Hebraic assholes on the right". M Le Pen is a nationalist and a socialist – or, if you prefer, a nationalist socialist. Hmm. A bit long but, if you lost a syllable, you might be in business.

But terms like "left" and "right" are irrelevant in French politics. In an advanced technocratic state, where almost any issue worth talking about has been ruled beyond the scope of partisan politics, you might as well throw away the compass. The Presidential election was meant to be a contest between the supposedly conservative Chirac and his supposedly socialist Prime Minister, Lionel Jospin. In practice, this boils down to a candidate who's left of right of left of centre, and a candidate who's right of left of right of left of centre. Chirac and Jospin ran on identical platforms – they're both in favour of high taxes, high unemployment and high crime. So, with no significant policy differences between them, the two candidates were relying on their personal appeal, which, given that one's a fraud and the other's a dullard, was asking rather too much of French voters. Faced with a choice between Eurodee and Eurodum, you can't blame electors for choosing to make it a real race by voting for the one guy running on an openly stated, clearly defined manifesto.

M Le Pen wants to restrict immigration; Chirac and Jospin think this subject is beneath discussion. Le Pen believes the euro is a "currency of occupation"; Chospin and Jirac think this subject is beneath discussion. Le Pen wants to pull out of the EU; Chipin and Josrac think this subject is beneath discussion. Le Pen wants to get tough on crime; Chispac and Jorin think this, too, is beneath discussion, and that may have been their mistake. European union and even immigration are lofty, philosophical issues. But crime is personal. The French are undergoing a terrible wave of criminality, in which thousands of cars are routinely torched for fun and more and more immigrant suburbs are no-go areas for the police. Chirac and Jospin's unwillingness even to address this issue only confirmed their image as the arrogant co-regents of a remote, insulated elite.

Europe's ruling class has effortlessly refined Voltaire: I disapprove of what you say, but I will defend to the death my right not to have to listen to you say it. You might disapprove of what Le Pen says on immigration, but to declare that the subject cannot even be raised is profoundly unhealthy for a democracy. The problem with the old one-party states of Africa and Latin America was that they criminalized dissent: you could no longer criticize the President, you could only kill him. In the two-party one-party states of Europe, a similar process is under way: if the political culture forbids respectable politicians from raising certain topics, then the electorate will turn to unrespectable politicians – as they're doing in France, Austria, Belgium, the Netherlands, Denmark and elsewhere. Le Pen is not an aberration but the logical consequence.

The Eurosnots, of course, learn nothing. President Chirac has announced that he will not deign to debate his opponent during the remaining two weeks of the campaign. M Le Pen beat M Chirac in nine of France's 22 districts. Unlovely he may be, but he is the legitimate standard bearer for democratic opposition to Chirac. By refusing to engage, the President is doing a grave disservice to French democracy. Similarly, Gerhard Schröder, facing difficult electoral prospects this fall, is now warning German conservatives that he will decline to participate in a "campaign of fear" – i.e., on touchy issues. But the way you defeat poisonous ideas is to expose them to the bracing air of open debate. In Marseilles, they're burning synagogues. In Berlin, the police advise Jews not to leave their homes in skullcaps or other identifying marks of their faith. But Europe's political establishments insist that, on immigration and crime, there's nothing to talk about.

A century and a half ago, Tsar Nicholas I described Turkey as "the sick man of Europe". Today, the sick man of Europe is the European – the urbane Continental princelings like Chirac, gliding from capital to capital building their Eutopia, oblivious to the popular will except on those rare occasions, such as Sunday, when the people do something so impertinent they finally catch the eye of their haughty maitre d'. I've said before that September 11th will prove to be like the Archduke's assassination in Sarajevo – one of those events that shatters the known world. To the list of polities destined to slip down the Eurinal of history, we must add the European Union and France's Fifth Republic. The only question is how messy their disintegration will be.

⁓

A FOREIGN FIELD

April 29th 2002
The National Post

THERE HAVE been two news stories about the Princess Pats this last week. If you're the sort of Canadian who gets his news from the CBC, *Globe And Mail*, etc, you'll only know about one of them: the deaths of four of our solders in Afghanistan. The other, less reported story – the Pentagon's wish to honour five of our snipers – is at least as revealing of our country's vexed relationship with its military.

I felt a little out of it during the media's attempts to whip up a Dianysian grief jamboree. The practice of returning fallen soldiers to their homeland is an American one. In our soldiering tradition – that's to say, the British and Commonwealth tradition – the dead are buried where they fall. In Rupert Brooke's famous lines,

> *If I should die, think only this of me:*
> *That there's some corner of a foreign field*
> *That is for ever England. There shall be*
> *In that rich earth a richer dust concealed...*

In western Europe, you don't have to go far to find foreign fields that are forever Canadian. Old soldiers, in my experience, like that idea: they hold the terrain they fought for in perpetuity, as their comrades press on.

By contrast, the desire to pull the dead out and ship them home has the whiff of a posthumous retreat about it – or at least a portent of retreat. And so, in last week's moving funerals, the anti-war faction found the most potent symbolism yet to bolster their call to chuck it in. "The terms of engagement were not clear enough," said renowned military analyst Alexa McDonough, saying she felt a "sense of rage" that Canadians were being "taken for granted". "If Canadian troops cannot be certain that they're not going to be fired on by Americans, we have no business being there," huffed Svend Robinson, the suicide bombers' favourite gay infidel. In Saturday's *Toronto Star*, readers were uniformly critical of our participation in an American war: "Canada should question its role in the war on terror...", "I think the

Prime Minister should advise the Governor-General to pull our troops out…"

Some of these guys are just the usual reflexive anti-Yank types. But the more artful ones managed to whip up a most unbecoming hysteria about Bush's insufficient prostration before his touchy neighbour to the north. Bush should have said sorry quicker and more feelingly! He should pay compensation! He should have personally called the families of the four soldiers!

Of course, if he had made calls to the widows and parents, these same critics would have been the first to cry that this was an outrageous assault on our sovereignty, that Bush was treating our boys as his - as if he were their commander-in-chief and they mere colonial conscripts to the Yank army. Australia, the first ally to lose a man in Afghanistan, didn't carry on like this, nor did the British, who in the Gulf War lost far more men (including an old friend of mine) to US friendly fire. But even the more sober commentators managed to produce a convoluted argument that, precisely because Canada's military contribution is so small and thus fatalities are so rare and so few, Bush should have been aware that he needed to make a bigger deal about it.

Leaving aside the predictable opportunism in these effusions, a reasonable person would conclude that ours is a culture no longer at ease with soldiering. This was confirmed by the other story involving the Pentagon and the Pats: America's wish to honour five PPCLI snipers with the Bronze Star for being so good at …killing the enemy. As *The National Post* and nobody else reported, the Canadian Government put this request on hold on the curious grounds that the Americans hadn't observed the correct protocol. Apparently, what's meant to happen is that the Deputy Under Assistant Secretary of State notifies the Assistant Under Counsellor for Paperwork at the Canadian Embassy who shuffles it to the Deputy Chief of Carbon Copies at the Department of Obfuscation in Ottawa who runs it by the Prime Minister on the 14th hole at Royal Montreal who forwards it to the Conrad Black Memorial Committee for Honours Incompatible With Canadian Citizenship at its headquarters on an ice floe in Queen Maud Gulf, where the matter can be expedited at their next biennial meeting.

After the *Post* drew attention to this strange delay, the government lifted the Conradian freeze and announced that they had no objections to the Bronze Stars. Indeed, Art Eggleton, the Defensive Minister, declared that this was the first he'd heard of it.

This seems to be Canada's newest military tradition. Whenever our soldiers are discovered to have done anything heroic, such as capturing or killing al-Qaeda terrorists, Mr Eggleton steps into the limelight and bravely deflects attention on to himself. If successful Canadian military operations have to be mentioned in public at all, it should be in the context of unsuccessful Parliamentary enquiries into the vortex of the Defensive Minister's reverse-Nixonian persona: What did Mr Eggleton not know and when did he not know it? The "fog of war" has nothing on the fog of Grits.

You'll recall how the Patricias wound up in Kandahar. Ottawa assumed, after the fall of Kabul, that they'd be a shoo-in for a little light peacekeeping in the stabilization force. Instead, the British gave us the brush and Mr Chretien was faced with being a non-participant in the "war on terror": at G8 meetings, when the talk turned to the war, he'd be the eunuch in the harem – observer status only. So Ottawa pleaded and begged and eventually Washington said okay, you can string along in Kandahar. Because this was a combat mission, Ottawa got to swan around telling folks that, sure, the Brits had their little peacekeeping operation going but frankly we Canadians have been there, done that and this time we were looking for something a little more macho. They were so busy spinning they forgot that for once what they were saying was actually true: our boys were going to be over there killing Johnny Foreigner.

So now they have done, and very impressively so. Washington wants to reward their bravery, Ottawa isn't even sure this is something you discuss in polite company. Everywhere from the government primer for putative citizens to the Molson ads to the new $10 bill, we're told that Canadian soldiers don't wage war, they make peace. So, when the Pentagon says, "Hey, guys, don't be so hard on yourselves", it's understandable that the Defensive Minister doesn't quite know what line to take.

Pace Svend and co, the Princess Patricias died in the service of Queen and country, not of Uncle Sam and his global hegemony. They are not in Kandahar to "help out" in America's war. This is our war, too – as much a threat to us in the long run as to America. So it is in our interest for the Pats to kill as many al-Qaeda fighters as possible.

This sits uncomfortably in a culture that, on the evidence of the last weeks, prefers to see its soldiers as victims rather than warriors.

The anti-Americans know what they're doing: the four soldiers buried last week are far more use to them dead than they ever were alive. If you're opposed to this war, then obviously the only good soldier is a dead soldier, and preferably dead at the Americans' hands. But an amazing 69% of Canadians resisted the media barrage and told the pollsters they don't believe our troops should be pulled out. They're the ones the government and the miserable Eggleton should be speaking to. Instead of telling us what he doesn't know, why doesn't he tell us something he should know? That our guys are doing a great job there, that some of them have done an extraordinary job, and that we're proud their heroism is being recognized by our allies. I think that's what their four comrades would have wanted — that the Pats stay and see it through.

I am grateful for the service of Sergeant Léger, Corporal Dyer, Private Green and Private Smith. But I am also grateful for that of the five snipers, and a government that was truly committed to this war wouldn't need a protocol row to force them to acknowledge their existence. A Canadian serviceman shouldn't have to die to get in the papers.

MAY

Who's ugly now?

May 4th 2002
The Spectator

O N SEPTEMBER 12th 2001, *The New Yorker*'s theatre critic John Lahr, musing on the events of the day before, wrote: "I do smell destabilising violence in the wings. In fear, the nation, to my mind, has always proved mean-spirited and violent."

Mr Lahr is American but lives in London. And, among both his European neighbours and members of America's Lahrfable tendency back home, this view was widely held. Though Rana Kabbani, writing from Paris for *The Guardian*, piously offered the hope that "the painful lesson that Americans have had to learn is not drowned out by cowboy ravings about 'getting the bastards'", it was more or less assumed by her chums that the Yanks' crude, xenophobic, redneck instincts would quickly reveal themselves. Members of the Muslim American community, if they weren't all rounded up, would be forced into hiding. Some feminist groups began organising a network of safe houses for Muslim women, on the assumption that "women of cover" (as President Bush calls them) would soon have to go into deep cover.

Well, sure enough, the crude, xenophobic rednecks did assert themselves. But not in America. In Europe. Muslims kill thousands of Americans in America, and there's a big anti-Muslim backlash …in France! Oh, and also Denmark, the Netherlands, Portugal and those other provinces of the land of sophistication where explicitly Islamophobic parties are now a significant part of the political calculus. What d'you reckon Le Pen'll get this weekend? Just his 17% base? Maybe 20? And how many voters will stay home? France's domestic intelligence agency has apparently advised the government that Le Pen will pull at least 30%. That seems rather high for a chap BBC announcers, demonstrating their famous impartiality, describe as "virulent". There can't, surely, be that many French electors willing to vote for a virulent hatemonger, can there? I mean, this isn't Mississippi, is it?

For the Europhiles in the US media, the events of recent weeks are bewildering. It's barely two months since they were reporting approvingly every snooty crack by Chris Patten and Hubert Védrine and regretting that Washington was so out of step with Europe. But then the synagogue attacks became too frequent to ignore, and M Le Pen whupped poor old Jospin, and frankly, if you can pick only one place to be out of step with, Europe's an excellent choice. Like the man almost said, I do smell destabilising violence in the wings. In fear, the Continent, to my mind, has always proved mean-spirited and violent. M Le Pen is certainly "mean-spirited"; the synagogue burners and kosher-butcher shooter-uppers and Jewish schoolbus stoners are certainly violent. And somehow, when Messrs Patten and Védrine were deploring American "simplisme", it never occurred to us their idea of sophistication was a culture in which the most interesting political question is which strain of literal anti-Semitism – anti-Jew or anti-Arab or anti-both - is more potent.

The rise of the anti-immigrant parties in France, Belgium et al is supposedly due to crime. It's true there seems to be a lot of it over there. You're six times more likely to be mugged in London than New York. The Royal Borough of Kensington and Chelsea has a worse crime rate than Harlem. In *The Los Angeles Times*, Sebastian Rotella was perplexed: "As crime has dropped in the United States in recent years, it has worsened in much of Europe, despite generous welfare states designed to prevent US-style inequality and social conflict."

"Despite"? Try "because". In December in this space I lent my support to Mickey Kaus, the thinking conservative's thinking liberal, who advanced the theory that welfare causes terrorism. Among the examples I cited was Zacarias Moussaoui, the so-called "20th hijacker", who became an Islamofascist nutter while living on welfare in London. What else is there to do all day? Go down the pub? Lie on the floor listening to your neighbour's car being stolen? If you're putting in a ten-hour grease-monkey shift at Fat Dave's Auto Body, you're too wiped out to wipe America out. But in the public housing of Paris, Frankfurt and Rotterdam the government will pay you to sit around the flat all day plotting world domination.

It's a scheme worthy of a Bond villain: flood high-unemployment Europe with unassimilated low-skilled young men, whom the state is obliged to put on welfare just to keep them from rioting, and hey presto, your enemies will be funding their own downfall – *On Her Majesty's Social Service*. Say what you like about that so-called "American Taleban" but at least his loopy Marin County parents put him through terrorist training school on their own nickel and not at the taxpayers' expense. At the moment, alongside the ranks of Europe's terrorist welfare queens, Jihad Johnny has the distinction of being the west's only private-sector Islamabaddy.

It should by now be dawning on US Europhiles that the Continent's done everything American progressives have wanted for years and it doesn't seem to be working out. Thanks to the recent body counts at Erfurt and Nanterre, Europe's currently outpacing the Yanks at high-scoring gun massacres. At the last attempted US massacre, at the Appalachian School of Law in West Virginia, there were a couple of gun-totin' students on hand to pin down the would-be mass murderer until the cops arrived. But in Europe – "a gun-control utopia", as *The Los Angeles Times* sees it – there's no one to stop the corpses piling up.

Americans have gun massacres because Americans have guns - masses of them, on every bedside table, in every glove pocket. Americans have guns because, philosophically, they believe that deterring crime is the citizen's responsibility. If you've a yen to steal, say, Stephen Glover's TV set in London, you'll probably get away with it. If you try to steal mine in New Hampshire, I'll blow your head off. So what in London is a 50-quid robbery would be a gun death over here. I say "would be" because, while Stephen's highly likely to get his TV stolen, my end of the deal will remain strictly hypothetical: the chances of an occupied property being broken into in my part of northern New England are statistically insignificant. That's the trade-off: a slightly increased risk of gun death in exchange for a dramatically reduced rate in everything else – hot burglaries, street crime, sexual assault, fatal stabbings. It takes some considerable skill to wind up, as Europe has, with every indicator going haywire: total gun control plus rapidly increasing gun violence plus stratospheric property crime.

Whose fault is all this? Hey, that's easy! According to Charles Pasqua, a former French Interior Minister, "There is a general climate of violence that has developed over the years and an American-style evolution of French society." According to Vicente Verdu, writing in *El Pais* last Saturday, it's the McDonaldsisation of crime. The Big Mac was invented in America, but now it's everywhere. Likewise, the Big Massacre. This is a familiar argument. When I was TV critic at *The Evening Standard*, I sat through innumerable gabfests at which media grandees and Labour arts spokesmen would explain that, without the BBC license fee, we'd wind up with nothing to watch but "lowest common denominator" "American-style quiz shows and soap operas". At that time, there were no soaps or game shows on US network primetime but there were a ton of them on UK telly. Almost every "American" nightmare the elites warn against is, in fact, an already well-established European reality: downmarket TV, xenophobic electorates, Wild West lawlessness.

Of course, the BBC license fee does fund upmarket fare such as …Tom Paulin, obscure poet but prominent telly personality, a towering intellectual of a kind America can barely dream of. Though his lively interview with Egypt's *Al-Ahram* was characterised as anti-Jew, it also managed to be anti-American. While he evidently has little regard for Israelis in general, he reserves especial vehemence for those "Brooklyn-born" settlers on the West Bank, who "should be shot dead… They are Nazis… I feel nothing but hatred for them." Mr Paulin will be delighted to hear that *Al-Ahram*'s Palestinian readers have risen to his challenge. Last Saturday, Palestinian "activists" murdered four settlers, among them five-year old Danielle Shefi, who was shot in her bed in an attack that left her mother and two brothers wounded. I don't believe Danielle was "Brooklyn-born", but maybe her parents were and that's close enough. What matters is that the little Nazi moppet was "shot dead", just as Mr Paulin wants, and, in another blow to vulgar American culture, her Mickey Mouse sheets were left soaked in blood. Hamas and the Popular Front for the Liberation of Palestine both claimed responsibility for this glorious victory, so presumably one of them's lying, perhaps just to impress Mr Paulin. Only four gone, Tom, but it's a start. Maybe time to give another interview?

Are there any BBC viewers so offended by Tom Paulin's incitement to murder that they're willing to withhold that portion of the license fee that goes to pay him? Are there any co-panellists who'll refuse to sit there kibitzing with him? Or will he get away with it?

Here's another suggestion, this time for any Berlin readers. In the days immediately after September 11th, when American Muslim women were supposedly afraid to leave the house, their neighbours took to wearing headscarves in solidarity and standing guard outside mosques. The few anti-Islamic incidents never became a widespread epidemic because the common decency of Americans quickly asserted itself. The Berlin police recently advised Jews not to go out in public wearing skull caps or other identifying marks of their faith. Given that their predecessors were keener to mandate identifying marks – yellow stars, arm tattoos, etc – perhaps we should look on the Berlin constabulary's recommendations as progress. But are there any Germans minded to mimic those American women who took up the hejab in solidarity with their Muslim sisters? Perhaps you'd like to wear skull caps in solidarity with their Jewish brothers? Don't all raise your hands at once.

For Goran Persson, the Prime Minister of Sweden, the point of the EU is that it can be a counter-balance, a "moderating" influence on those wacky Americans. But, for a moderating influence, it's remarkably immoderate. If you look at that first round of French Presidential voting, between Le Pen, the guy who broke away from Le Pen, the Trot, the other Trot and the rest of the cranks, the zany fringe candidates drew about 45% of the vote. Olivier Duhamel, a French Socialist Member of the European Parliament, regrets that "we've gone back to a degenerate democracy of the kind you find in the United States." *Bien-sûr!* Austria's Joerg Haider got 29%, Le Pen 17%, the anti-Muslim Danish People's Party's 12%. You know what "strident" "extreme" Pat Buchanan got in the 2000 Presidential election? 0.42%.

About a year ago, I wrote a column about the Euro-elite for *The Wall Street Journal* hailing the age of the "ugly European". Back then, the ugliness was strictly rhetorical – the smugness of the Pattens and the Perssons. But in the course of 12 months the ugliness has gotten a lot uglier. Muslims killed thousands of Americans, but America doesn't have anti-Muslim political parties, just a goofy President who hosts a month of Ramadan knees-ups at the White House. America has millions of Muslims, but they don't firebomb synagogues and beat up Jews and, if they did, the police wouldn't turn a blind eye. Meanwhile, France has a Presidential candidate who makes oven jokes, a Foreign Minister who believes in the international Jewish conspiracy, and a Number One bestseller which claims the plane that crashed into the Pentagon never existed. Heigh-ho, look on the bright side: Europe may be "mean-spirited and violent", but at least it's not American.

THE BRUTAL AFGHAN WINTER HITS JENIN

May 4th 2002
The Daily Telegraph

I USUALLY save the I-told-you-so gloat for the year-in-review column, but I can't resist noting that Yasser Arafat's Fatah organisation has now come round to my way of thinking on the Jenin refugee camp. "There was no massacre," I wrote here two weeks ago, when Robert Fisk and Fleet Street's other sob-sisters were running around weepin' and a-wailin' about mass graves and war crimes.

The Israeli government's latest figures for Jenin put the death toll of Palestinians at 52. The Palestinians themselves put the death toll at – wait for it – 56.

That's right. 56. There are no missing zeroes on the end. The only missing zeroes are those gullible British hacks who swallowed that line about hundreds of dead civilians but have fallen mysteriously silent as the figures have been revised downward. The total of 56 dead was announced by Kadoura Moussa, the Fatah director for the northern West Bank, after four Palestinian Authority investigators reported their findings to him at his office in the camp. Unlike all those leathery flak-jacketed foreign correspondents, I'm no expert, but, just as a matter of interest, is a discrepancy of four enough to qualify as a "massacre"? 23 Israeli soldiers died at Jenin, so the comparative death tolls sound less like a "massacre" and more like a – what's the word? - "battle".

So the Israelis and Palestinians are more or less agreed. The only guys who don't agree are excitable chaps like Gerald Kaufman, who's demanding sanctions against Israel, and my colleague Armando Iannucci, whose droll killer-Jews-on-the-rampage column appeared on this page yesterday. Considering that the Telegraph Group is routinely dismissed by Richard Ingrams and co as a Zionist lackey, I do think we could do a little more to live up to the name.

Anxious to lend the west's agitated humanitarians a helping hand, a group of Palestinians in Jenin held a funeral a week ago for one of their massacred compatriots and invited a cameraman along. The deceased, covered in a shroud, was being borne on a stretcher to his final resting place, when, alas, his bearers stumbled and he fell to the ground. The "corpse" picked himself up, dusted himself off and climbed back on the stretcher to start all over again. Unfortunately, the clumsy pallbearers managed to drop him a second time. At this point, the crowd, who apparently weren't in on the scheme, fled in terror. The stiff, meanwhile, had had enough of his bungling bearers, and flounced off in a huff.

Oh, dear. Jenin, tragically, seems to be the first massacre with a shortage of corpses. Would it have been too much for the Hamas PR guys to get one of their eager schoolgirl volunteers to detonate herself in the backyard?

Even Europe's most anti-Israel papers are beginning to wise up. The other day *The Independent's* Phil Reeves criticised "the Palestinian leadership, who instantly, and without proof, declared that a massacre had occurred in which as many as 500 died. Palestinian human-rights groups made matters worse by churning out wild, and clearly untrue, stories." They obviously weren't quite so clearly untrue a week and a half earlier, when a presumably entirely different Phil Reeves wrote about Israeli "atrocities committed in the Jenin refugee camp, where its army has killed and injured hundreds of Palestinians."

So, 52-56. Hmm. Where have I heard those numbers before? Why, in another famous media illusion – "the brutal Afghan winter", under whose gruelling conditions Kabul this January had to cope with average daytime temperatures of …52-56! It would, however, be unfair to suggest that in every ludicrous Fleet Street fiction the correct figure will eventually prove to be 52-56. For example, when the Yanks were torturing al-Qa'eda suspects in "the searing heat of Guantanamo", the overnight low was 66 and breezy, or about the same as a late January day in Kandahar in the brutal Afghan winter, when the warlords and their catamites stroll arm in arm down the sun-dappled streets.

Nonetheless, in recognition of my colleagues' spectacularly inept record since September 11th, I am proud to announce the inauguration of the British Press Award For Total Fantasy. Journalists can enter as many of their reports as they wish. Can't decide whether that story based on a Hamas press release is more risible than that dispatch based on the Radio Taleban lunchtime news? Hey, send us both! Winners will receive a grand prize of FIVE THOUSAND POUNDS!!!! However, in keeping with traditional Fleet Street standards of numerical accuracy, when the cheque eventually shows up a month later it'll be for £8.47. The lucky winners will also get a year's subscription to *The Independent,* which will expire after six weeks.

We'll announce the results in mid-September – the first anniversary of early sightings of "the fast-approaching brutal Afghan winter". Who knows? It may even have shown up by then.

But that's not the only columnar innovation this week. I gather Mr Kaufman is upset that Kofi Annan has called off his UN investigation into Jenin. The reason, according to taste, is either that the Israelis are being uncooperative or that there wasn't much point in the commission schlepping all that way just to discover that it wasn't 52-56, but 58, or 61, or 47. One of the three members was Cornelio Sommaruga, the former President of the International Red Cross who once compared the Star of David to the swastika. Anyone interested in pondering this comparison further can find the two emblems conveniently displayed in close proximity at an increasing number of European synagogues.

Anyway, as Kofi's commission isn't going ahead, I'm pleased to announce my own fact-finding investigation into – drumroll, please - the UN. Ex-ambassadors, European Foreign Ministers and former presidents of humanitarian organisations are welcome to apply to join my commission, but, if they're too busy, we'll make do with jes' regular folks. Among the issues we'll be examining:

- UN participation in the sex-slave trade in Bosnia;

- the UN refugee extortion racket in Kenya;

- UN involvement in massive embezzlement in Kosovo;

- the UN's cover-up of the sex-for-food scandal in West Africa involving aid workers demanding sexual favours from children as young as four;

- the UN-fuelled explosion of drugs, Aids and prostitution in Cambodia;

- the UN's complicity in massacres in pre-liberated Afghanistan.

Oh, and, if we've any time left, we may even investigate the Jenin refugee camp. Not what the Israelis have been doing there for the last month, but what the UN's been doing there for the last half-century. There's a good prima facie case to be made for their collusion in terrorism. I'd say that's worth investigating, wouldn't you? Our final report will, of course, make a detailed list of proposals, starting with this one: given the amount of money the UN spends on Jenin, they could at least hire better actors for fake funerals.

WALKING THE TALK

May 9th 2002
The National Post

"JAW-JAW IS better than war-war," said Churchill, and on the whole he's right. It's better to talk to people than to kill them. That's why the Europeans are so thrilled to see Yasser Arafat sprung from his compound in Ramallah. Now he can get a shower and a shave – well, okay, maybe not a shave – and a change of bandolier, and get the "peace process" "back on track".

The Bush Administration was also pleased to see Israel's "partner for peace" freed up and his fax line reconnected. And, waddayaknow, at the very moment the President was discussing this latest hopeful development with Ariel Sharon at the White House, the "peace process" did indeed get back on its customary track with the detonation of a brand new suicide bomber in a pool hall in Rishon Lezion. 16 dead Israelis, and much joy from the heroic martyr's proud parents: "Yasser, that's my baby! Do we get a cheque from Saddam? Or the Saudis? Or both?"

And, of course, there's nothing like the cheery sound of Palestine's baby ka-boomers to intensify the need for a new round of talks. All we need now is some guy to lend his name to a new plan which would open the way to get us back to "Tenet", which would get us back to "Mitchell", which would get us back to "Wye River", which would get us back to "Oslo", which would get us back to Kansas. Have I forgotten someone? Zinni? Did he have a plan? Or was his plan not to have a plan?

On Tuesday, one suicide bomber killed almost as many civilians as the entire Israeli army did during the notorious Jenin "massacre". Where are the condemnations from the EU? Where's the UN inquiry? Oh, wait, I forgot. When Palestinians kill Israelis, that just means Israel needs to do more to redouble its efforts to get the "peace process" back on that long and winding track.

It's instructive to contrast the eternal forbearance the EU demands of Israel with their own behaviour. On Sunday, the French Presidential election ended with a result that the Republic's establishment claimed had strengthened their democracy. Can't quite see it myself. For a start, President Chirac refused point blank to "jaw-jaw" with his opponent, the dreaded M Le Pen: why, to debate him would only dignify him! No-one else wanted to "jaw-jaw", either: instead, there were large demonstrations by the left urging people to vote for "the crook, not the fascist". To make the street-theatre look a little better on TV, schools gave their pupils the day off to go and make up the numbers in a demonstration against a fellow most of them had barely heard of. To some of us, there's always something a little totalitarian about the state conscripting children in its propaganda efforts, but Chirac, though undoubtedly the crook, seemed appreciative of these fascistic touches.

The media rallied overwhelmingly to his soiled banner. Under France's onerous electoral laws, neither candidate is allowed to campaign on the day before the election, so instead, in an unprecedented display of cheerleading, the press urged voters to turn out for Monsewer Sleaze. Four out of five people voted for "the crook", but that still left a fifth of French electors to support a "fascist" who in any healthy political culture would have been a joke candidate: putting aside his views, he's 74 and he's never held government office. If an election with only one viable candidate, no debate, a biased media, a blind eye to corruption, and public demonstrations with bussed-in schoolchildren "strengthens" your democracy, then I'm moving to Zimbabwe.

The day after the French election attention turned to the Netherlands. Like President Chirac, the Prime Minister Wim Kok had declared that his principal opponent, Pim Fortuyn, was someone who was beneath debate. So on Monday someone shot him dead. A militant vegan, if reports are to be believed. From across the North Sea, Tony Blair issued a heartfelt tribute to the first victim of political assassination in Holland in 350 years: "No matter what feelings political figures arouse, the ballot box is the place to express them."

In Rotterdam, voters had done just that: 35% of electors in the Netherlands' second largest city had cast their ballots for Pim Fortuyn. Yet that wasn't enough to get him a debate with Wim Kok, and even in death he remained, at least to the grudging Mr Blair, beyond the pale (to coin a phrase). Fortuyn and Le Pen had virtually nothing in common: Le Pen's a Vichy nostalgist; Fortuyn was a beneficiary of Dutch liberalism who boasted about the ethnic diversity of his many lovers. Le Pen's a left-wing protectionist; Fortuyn was a Thatcherite on economic issues. But in the shorthand of European politics both were dismissed as "extreme", "hateful" and, naturally, "right-wing".

A recent poll in Canada revealed that 75% of people have no idea what the terms "left" and "right" mean, and who can blame them? But here's a layman's guide: "left" has been withdrawn from circulation, you never hear it any more; and "right" just means the side you're meant to dislike.

Apart from their mutual antipathy to Muslim immigration, Fortuyn and Le Pen would have loathed each other. But they cocked their individual snooks at the pieties of contemporary Eurofantasy and so they were beyond debate: *Mais non*, said Chirac and Blair and Kok, we cannot talk with these men, no matter how many people vote for them. To engage them would only legitimize them.

What did either Fortuyn or Le Pen do to deserve having their voters ignored by the political establishment? Did they kill anyone? Did they issue orders for murders and bombings? Did they fund terrorism? Did they supply terrorists with weapons and training? Yasser Arafat has done – is doing – all these things, and yet the Europeans insist he is their "friend", a legitimate leader, a constructive "partner for peace", and someone whom the Israelis must keep talking to, no matter how huge the mountain of corpses grows. Oh, and as we all know, it's Ariel Sharon who is "extreme" and "right-wing": the side you're meant to dislike.

European humbug has reached almost deafening levels in the last few weeks. There's the Pope's emissary high-fiving with the Chairman as he's liberated from his compound, while back home, legitimate political leaders who submit themselves to the ballot box are disdained and then assassinated. Yasser, of course, has postponed indefinitely his "re-election" campaign, but that doesn't stop the generous European Union subsidies which indirectly fund Palestinian suicide bombers. Smug, intolerant and decadent, Continental politics are in an advanced state of disease. When the establishment is too arrogant to "jaw-jaw", "war-war" – or at least massive civil unrest - isn't too far behind.

~

THE NEW RIGHT

May 11th 2002
The Daily Telegraph

"**G**OOD EVENING," I said, reading the autocue at rehearsal. "Europe was stunned today by the resurgence of the extreme right-wi... Hang on, isn't this last week's script?"

"That was France," explained Ron, my producer. "This is Holland."

"Gotcha," I said. "So this guy, Pim, is another charismatic, hateful right-winger like Le Pen, who believes in..." I reached under the desk and pulled out the BBC's handy "How To Spot A Right-Wing Madman" chart. "So, like Le Pen, he believes in right-wing policies like economic protectionism, minimum wage, massive subsidies to inefficient agriculture and incompetent industries. He's opposed to globalisation, fiercely anti-American, admires Saddam..."

"No, no," said Ron. "Pim doesn't believe any of that conventional right-wing stuff. He's the other kind of right-winger."

"What other kind?"

"The kind that's a sociology professor who believes in promiscuous gay sex and recreational drugs. We've got a call in to Norman Tebbit and Baroness Young asking if they'd like to pay tribute to him from one of their favourite gay bathhouses."

"Fabulous," I said. "Great pictures. But how many kinds of right-wingers are there?"

"Well, we're adding new categories every week. But, for the purposes of headline updates, just stick with this easy précis." The floor manager slid the BBC *At-A-Glance Guide To Who's Right* on to the desk: "'Far right' equals old-time right-winger; 'extreme right' equals bald right-winger; 'hard right' equals bald gay right-winger; and 'incendiary right' equals divisive right-wing corpse who unduly provoked vegan peace activists."

It's tough keeping on top of this stuff. "So," I asked Ron, "the guy who killed Pim was a fruitarian?"

"No," he said. "Pim's the fruit Aryan."

"Got it," I said. "So I'll start with a little scene-setting colour stuff – not since the Thirties have we witnessed the disturbing spectre of so many gay sociology professors on the march across Europe in their screamingly camp jackboots, blah blah, and then we'll go to Jean-Marie for a quick comment on how he and his fellow Zionist homosexuals are taking the news…"

"Right," said Ron. "Then he wallops you in the solar plexus and we cut to a still of Joerg Haider as the BBC Radio Orchestra plays 'The Man That Got Away'. Then, after you've been patched up, we bring on Tony…"

With his usual professionalism, the Prime Minister's Presidential motorcade roared into the studio, demolishing the set and scattering terrified make-up girls. "Good to see you, Mark. But I must make it clear that I won't debate directly with hateful extremists like M Le Pen. President Chirac was absolutely right to insist that we cannot enter into dialogue with these people. To do so would only legitimise them and we need to send a clear signal that these hard-right bigots have no place in our democracy."

"You mean by shooting them?"

"Er, well, no, not that. No matter what feelings political figures arouse, the ballot box is the place to express them."

"You mean by electing a bloke in a monkey suit like they did up north?"

"Er, well, no, obviously, that calls into question the whole business of direct elections. We may be better returning to a system whereby we simply…"

"Appoint Chris Patten to the post?"

"Exactly," said Tony, clearly relieved. "Chris can't get elected to anything, but it seems to have worked out pretty well for him. And the advantage of appointing a reasonable moderate European democrat like Chris is that…"

"It's easier to take away the people's passports and hand them over to Red China!" I slapped Tony on the back. "Hey, you're on fire tonight, Prime Minister! The argument's brilliant, but keep it light, keep it breezy. Okay, Ron, I'll say, 'Later on the programme,

Tony Blair explains why the best response to right-wing fascism is to have fewer elections and give more power to Chris Patten...' Then we'll go down the line to Queen Beatrix in our Amsterdam studio."

"Right," said Ron. "If Pim's successor, Joao Varela, becomes Prime Minister, she's planning to refuse to take tea with him because his party are right-wing racists."

"Good for Her Majesty!" I said. "It's great to see someone who won't have any truck with white bigots who hate immigrants."

"Well, actually, this Varela feller's a black guy from Cape Verde. But for Holland to elect the first black immigrant Prime Minister in Europe would send a frightening message that virulent racist nationalism is once again on the rise."

"Makes sense," I said, chugging down a half-dozen Aspirin. "Okay, then we go to one of these reactionary right-wingers campaigning for casual gay sex. And presumably there's a liberal progressive party that wants to restrict casual sex?"

"You mean Blok Wim Kok," said Ron.

"It's all Dutch to me," I said. "Then we'll cross to Denmark to talk to the new hardline conservatives..."

"Whoa, hold on," Ron interrupted. "Check your BBC *Who's Right* guide this minute! 'Hardline conservatives' is a designation we apply only to unreconstructed Marxists on the North Korean politburo plus Don Rumsfeld."

"Sorry," I said, "It's a lot to take in without bigger cue cards. 'Racist right' equals black immigrant right-wingers. 'Conservatives' equal Communists. Hey, here's one for you. How about 'moderate conservatives'?"

Ron guffawed. "'Moderate conservatives'? There's no such thing, not in this news department. "Oh, wait a minute..." He flipped through the BBC guide. "You're right. Page 47. 'Moderate conservative', a term strictly reserved for reformist Ayatollahs."

~

LOOMING DEADLINE

May 23rd 2002
The National Post

IT FEELS LIKE August, said Rich Lowry, the editor of *National Review*, the other week. August 2001, he meant.

In Britain, Tony Blair has assured his Cabinet there'll be no war on Iraq without UN approval. In Canada, the Government has confirmed the Princess Patricias are heading home from Afghanistan and won't be replaced. We stood "shoulder to shoulder", as the Prime Minister said we would, but it's been six months now and our shoulder's getting kinda stiff. Besides, we went in because we didn't want to be left out. Now we don't want to be left in. On the road to war, France, Germany and the rest of America's Nato "allies" are parked shoulder to shoulder on the shoulder.

And even in the US the "sleeping giant" has resumed his slumbers. Poor Chandra leads the news once more, as she did last August, and the "war on terror" is now merely this month's Enron, the latest thin straw with which the Democrats hope finally to break the Republican elephant's back. Consider this item from the CBS News website last weekend:

"*The Washington Post* said Saturday that a top-secret briefing memo presented to President Bush in 1998 focused on efforts by Osama bin Laden to strike at targets in the US."

President Who in 1998? As I recall, it was the 42nd guy, Clinton, William J, and in 1998 he was too busy declaring his pants a Federal Disaster Area to do much about terrorist masterminds. This shock report raises the critical question: What doesn't CBS know and why don't they know it? In the course of the afternoon, after Dan Rather's hair stylist was dispatched to Barnes & Noble to buy *The Bumper Picture Book Of American Presidents*, America's hard news leader wised up to the error and "corrected" it:

"*The Washington Post* reported Saturday that a 1998 top-secret briefing memo to the President…"

"The President"? One can forgive the mistake – the natural exuberance of CBS reporters to stick it to Bush – but it's the cheap evasion of the correction that's revealing: the network's happy to name names when Bush is in the line of fire, but they turn all generalized and protective when it comes to the other fellow.

I'm all for accountability: I called for resignations and firings in this space on September 17th, and, let me tell you, it was a lonely job back then. The obvious failures at the FAA, INS, CIA, FBI were of no apparent concern to America's political and media establishment. They were happy to bide their time, let the dust settle, wait for Bush to become a viable target. What that little correction at CBS tells you is that for Dan and his playmates this isn't a war anymore, but just (oh, happy phrase) "politics as usual" – it's not about the defence of the nation, or the deaths of thousands of civilians, but just another campaign finance reform, arsenic in the water, caribou breeding grounds in ANWR.

Sure, the country's at Code Yellow, and boring bureaucrats keep warning that something may be happening somewhere sometime, but at the moment nothing is happening nowhere, except for the odd discovery of an arms cache in Tora Bora, and even then it's some non-telegenic Brit Royal Marines who stumble on it. After all the tedious, suffocating sobriety of the last eight months, it's now safe for funereal Tom Daschle, would-be undertaker to the Presidency, to announce that he's "gravely concerned" in his usual concernedly grave way. He's so gravely concerned that he's willing to imply, with a nudge and wink, that the President knew thousands of American civilians were going to be slaughtered – and let it happen anyway! In the immortal word of Marv Albert: *Yessss!!* The spin shall set you free! As John and Yoko so sagely observed, Happy Xmas (War is over)!

If the war is just politics now, then let's consider the Bush position. The Republican Party base is feeling sorely put upon: the White House caved to *The New York Times* on campaign finance reform, to the unions on steel tariffs, to Ted Kennedy on education. But, even on the war, Bush's heavyweights have concentrated on the overseas stuff and left the pipsqueaks in charge of the home front. This week, Norman Mineta, the Transport Secretary whose resignation I called for in September, confirmed that he'd nixed the idea of allowing pilots to carry guns. Underperformin' Norman is so September 10th, in thrall to all the old shibboleths – gun control good; profiling bad. You can't blame the public for concluding that a war effort which targets 86-year old nuns with tweezers is all effort and no war.

So the domestic agenda's dead, the home front's a joke, and anything overseas is fast receding beyond the far horizon. You can go to the people and sell the nation on a war presidency if the B52s are walloping Saddam, but not if there's nothing happening except a exciting new irrigation project in Jalalabad. If Bush hasn't been planning war with Iraq these last few weeks, he might as well have been golfing. Recent polls show, to no one's surprise, that the American people once again tick "education" as the most pressing issue facing the nation.

The distinguished conservative commentator John Derbyshire has now declared that war with Iraq ain't gonna happen. Meanwhile, the same crowd making a big song'n'dance about the President "ignoring" "warnings" about September 11th are saying that there's no justification for doing anything about Saddam, as he hasn't yet done anything to us. But, unless Bush II is as languid and purposeless as his dad, war with Iraq has to happen, and soon. Ignore Colin Powell's recent assurances that the Administration has "no plans" to attack. That's the way he was talking in early October last year: every time Bush made a speech deploring the "evildoers", Powell went on TV and said the Administration was interested in reaching out and working with moderate evildoers. Then the bombing started and that was the end of the outreach.

It has to be the same now. Bush, in his "axis of evil" speech, claimed that "time is running out". What's he going to say on September 11th this year? Time's still running out, but we feel it's important not to rush into things? It's not plausible. So sometime between the G8 summit at Kananaskis in June and the first anniversary of 9/11 war will start – out of the blue, with a huge bang of colossal overwhelming force, and preferably on a Sunday so that Dan Rather and Peter Jennings have to rush back from the Hamptons. Personally, I'd like it to start during Kananaskis, just to put Chrétien, Chirac and Schröder on the spot. But that's not the Bush style. So summer or early fall it is. There are compelling international security reasons for removing Saddam, but, as CBS News reminds us, there are also persuasive domestic political ones. If war isn't underway by the beginning of autumn, George W Bush might as well nickname himself President Juan Term.

THE GRAND TOUR

May 25th 2002
The Daily Telegraph

*"Bush Visit Highlights Rift With Europe: President's Tour Appears
Unlikely To Lift Relations From Historic Low"* – The Guardian

From: **potus@whitehouse.gov**
To: **george41@aol.com**

...so it's goin' pretty well, dad. Lot of Germans in the street with signs sayin' somethin' about "COWBOY" and "TOD". Don't know this Cowboy Tod, but he sounds a good man. Afterwards Jacques and Gerhard and the Belgian foreign minister guy say, c'mon, let's grab a little lunch at the EU cafeteria, and I'm at the table lookin' at the menu and this big ol' French waiter dude says, *"Oui, monsieur?"* An' I'm thinkin', well, now's my chance to be all multilateral, so I say, *"Qu'est-ce que c'est la soupe du jour?"*

And the Belgian foreign minister guy goes, "It means 'soup of the day', idiot."

Which I thought was pretty funny for a Belgian, and I was about to say "Hey, they should get you for *Austin Powers III*", but instead Jacques yells, *"Mer de Crete, tiens!"*, which Condi's interpreter helpfully translates for me: "Sea of Crete, hey!"

An' I'm thinkin', what's the deal with that? Flippin' through the ol' mental Rolodex an' comin' up blank, pop.

But I tell Jacques, "Yeah, Crete. Could get messy there, Landslide. Got Colin keepin' an eye on things...

From: **lagloiredelarepublique@elysee.fr**
To: **lagrandehorizontale@hotmail.com**

...and the Belgian clod says, "It means 'soup of the day', idiot." So I explode, *"Merde! Crétin!"*, and I kick the buffoon Michel under the table and am about to remind him in Flemish that we are dealing with a monstrously arrogant simpleton who would add us to his moronic axis of evil at the drop of his 37.8451-litre hat. But the cowboy does not seem to notice! Instead, the halfwit slaps me on the back and calls me "Landslide" again, which I regard as an insult to the honour of the Republic, and I also do not care for him always touching the suit, as it cost 45,703 euros according to my official government expenses claim.

On the subject of which, now that I have driven a stake through the black heart of Fascism for another six weeks or so, you might remind your husband that the regular transfers can safely be resumed through the usual account.

Anyway, just when I think things cannot get any worse, up comes Christopher Patten, the Englishman who tries so laughably hard to fit in. You would think these MI6 plants would be a little less obvious…

From: **chris@emissionselectroniquesofficielsducommissioneuropean.eu**
To: **jiang@politburo.cn**

…so Jacques goes, "*Vous connaissez Chris Patten, naturellement.*" And Bush drawls in that absurdly provincial way of his, "Sure. The guy who handed over all those fellers to the Commies in Beijing, right?" And he cracks up and giggles, "Look, ma, no briefing papers!"

Honestly, Jiang. Then he slaps his knee and says, "Pull up a chair, Marshal Pétain. Any pal of Landslide's is a pal of mine, amigo!" So I patiently explain to him that it's "*ami*" not "amigo" and that Jacques doesn't like being thwacked round the shoulder. "He would prefer, Mr President, if you just gave him the traditional double-kiss on both cheeks."

"Whoa, buddy!" says Bush. "I thought that was what they call in these parts *le vice anglais*." And Gerhard and Jacques and Louis are all weeping with laughter at that one. And I'm just about to bring up the question of human rights – in Texas, Jiang, relax – when Romano shows up and says, "Ah, *Signor* Booosh. How appropriate that we meet again, President to President, at this epic juncture in the rhythm of history, as the American moment ends and the European era begins."

And Bush says, "*Que sera, sera*, man." And just as I'm explaining to him that that's Spanish and President Prodi is Italian, Romano totally humiliates me. "Strictly speaking, Chris, he could have been saying '*Che sera, sera*'. We have no way of knowing until we get the transcript."

"Or more likely," says Jacques, "he was speaking French out of consideration *pour moi*."

"But it's obvious he's referring to the famous song by Doris Da – " I catch myself, but too late. Michel's already sniggering…

From: **louis.michel@celebritybelgo.be**
To: **strongman@congo.com**

…and then the fool Englishman babbling about moronic American pop culture decides to share with us his preliminary findings on what binds us together in a common European identity. Europeans are defined by:

1) Our opposition to American steel tariffs.
2) Our opposition to the American team at the Ryder Cup.

"Excellent," says Chirac. "Furthermore, Europeans are united in feeling that McDonald's has a deplorable wine list."

"Also," I point out, "the topless girls on the beach at St Tropez are a good 70 kilos lighter than at Atlantic City, even if you factor in the heavier-set Eastern European women we're being forced to take."

"Well," says the nincompoop cowboy. "I'm jes' here to thank you all for your vital contributions to the war on terror: The British Royal Marines, the French ship that's only six weeks away from being somewhere in the general area, the Greeks' spare filing cabinet and the Belgians' very generous gift of a fully operational paperweight of Manekin Pis…"

"Sure to brighten up any barracks," Chirac sneers.

He is even more insufferable than usual, but fortunately the waiter arrives with my steak frites. "Take it back," I hiss. "It is more charred than the Israeli Embassy in Paris…"

JUNE

Flying while Arab

June 1st 2002
The Spectator

WHEN POLITICAL correctness got going in the Eighties, the laconic wing of the conservative movement was inclined to be relaxed about it. To be sure, the tendency of previously pithy identity labels to become ever more polysyllabically ornate ("person of colour", "Native American") was time consuming, but otherwise PC was surely harmless. Some distinguished persons of non-colour, among them Sir Peregrine Worsthorne, even argued that conservatives should support political correctness as merely the contemporary version of old-fashioned courtliness and good manners.

Alas, after September 11th, this position seems no longer tenable. Instead, we have to ask a more basic question: Does political correctness kill?

Consider the extraordinary memo sent three weeks ago by FBI agent Coleen Rowley to the agency's director Robert Mueller, and now all over *Time* magazine. Ms Rowley works out of the Minneapolis field office, whose agents, last August 16th, took action to jail a French citizen of Middle Eastern origin. Zacarias Moussaoui had shown up at a Minnesota flight school and shelled out 8,000 bucks in cash in order to learn how to fly 747s, except for the landing and take-off bit, which he said he'd rather skip. On investigation, he proved to have overstayed his visa and so was held on an immigration violation. Otherwise, he would have been the 20th hijacker, and, so far as one can tell, on board United Flight 93, the fourth plane, the one which crashed in a Pennsylvania field en route, as we now know, to the White House. In Mr Moussaoui's more skilled hands – Flight 93 wound up with the runt of Osama's litter - it might well have reached its target.

Ms Rowley and her colleagues established that Moussaoui was on a French intelligence watch list, had ties to radical Islamist groups, was known to have recruited young Muslims to fight in Chechnya, and had been in Afghanistan and Pakistan immediately before arriving in the US. They wanted to search his computer, but to do that they needed the okay from HQ. Washington was not only uncooperative, but set about, in the words of Ms Rowley's memo, "thwarting the Minneapolis FBI agents' efforts", responding to field-office requests with ever lamer brush-offs: How could she be sure it was the same guy? There could be any number of Frenchmen called "Zacarias Moussaoui". She checked the Paris phone book, which listed only one. After September 11th, when the Minneapolis agents belatedly got access to Moussaoui's computer, they found among other things the phone number of Mohammed Atta's roommate.

What was the problem at HQ? According to *The New York Times'* William Safire, "Intimidated by the brouhaha about supposed ethnic profiling of Wen Ho Lee, lawyers at John Ashcroft's Justice Department wanted no part of going after this Arab." Wen Ho Lee was a Taiwan-born scientist at Los Alamos accused in 1999 of leaking nuclear secrets to the Chinese. His lawyers mobilised the Asian-American lobby, his daughter embarked on a coast-to-coast speaking tour, and pretty soon the case had effectively collapsed leaving the Feds with headlines like "Investigator Denies Lee Was Victim Of Racial Bias" (*The San Francisco Chronicle*).

This was during an election campaign in which Al Gore was promising that his first act as President would be to sign an executive order forbidding police from pulling over African-Americans for "driving while black". Dr Lee had been arrested, wrote the columnist Lars-Erik Nelson, for "working in a nuclear weapons laboratory while Chinese". In August 2001, invited to connect the dots on the Moussaoui file, Washington bureaucrats foresaw only scolding editorials about "flying while Arab".

Example Number Two: another memo from last summer, this time the so-called "Phoenix memo" sent by Kenneth Williams. This is Kenneth Williams the crack FBI Arizona agent, not Kenneth Williams of *Carry On Up The Khyber* fame, though in the end it might just as well have been. Agent Williams filed a report on an alarming trend he'd spotted and, just to make sure you didn't have to plough through a lot of stuff to get to the meat, the Executive Summary at the top read: "Usama bin Laden and Al-Muhjiroun supporters attending civil aviation universities/colleges in Arizona."

Three weeks ago, FBI Director Mueller was asked why the Bureau had declined to act on the memo. He said: "There are more than 2,000 aviation academies in the United States. The latest figure I think I heard is something like 20,000 students attending them. And it was perceived that this would be a monumental undertaking without any specificity as to particular persons."

A "monumental undertaking"? Okay, there are 20,000 students. Eliminate all the women, discount Irv Goldbloom of Queens and Gord MacDonald of Winnipeg and Stiffy Farquahar-ffarquahar of Little Blandford-on-the-Smack and just concentrate on fellows with names like ...oh, I dunno, Mohammed, and Waleed, and Ahmed. How many would that be? 150? 200? Say it's 500. Is Mueller really saying that the FBI with all its resources cannot divert ten people to go through 2,000 names apiece and pull out the ones worth running through the computer?

Well, yes, officially, he is. But what he really means is not that the Bureau lacked "any specificity as to particular persons", but that the specificity itself was the problem. In August 2001, no FBI bureaucrat was prepared to fire off a potentially career-detonating memo saying "Check out the Arabs."

On September 15th Director Mueller said: "The fact that there were a number of individuals that happened to have received training at flight schools here is news, quite obviously. If we had understood that to be the case, we would have - perhaps one could have averted this." Indeed. There weren't a lot of dots to connect. Last summer, within a few weeks of each other, the Phoenix flight-school memo and Moussaoui warrant request landed on the desk of Dave Frasca, head of the FBI's radical-fundamentalist unit. He buried the first, and refused the second.

Example Three: On August 1st, James Woods, the motion picture actor, was flying from Boston to Los Angeles. With him in the first class cabin were half-a-dozen guys, four of whom were young Middle Eastern men. Woods, like all really good actors, is a keen observer of people, and what he observed as they flew west persuaded him they were hijackers. The FBI has requested that he not reveal all the details, but he says he asked the flight attendant if he could speak to the pilot. After landing at LAX, the crew reported the incident to the Federal Aviation Administration. The FAA did ...nothing. Two of the four were on board the September 11th planes. Woods turned out to be sitting in on a rehearsal for the big day.

After 9/11, the standard line was that Osama bin Laden had pulled off an ingenious plan. But he didn't have to be ingenious, just lucky. And he was luckiest of all in that the obviousness of what was happening paradoxically made investigating it all the more problematic. His agents aren't that smart – not in the sense of IRA smart, or Carlos the Jackal smart. The details Woods is permitted to discuss are in themselves very revealing: The four men boarded with no hand luggage. Not a thing. That's what he noticed first. Everyone going on a long flight across a continent takes something: a briefcase, a laptop, a shopping bag with a couple of airport novels, a *Wall Street Journal* or a *Boston Herald*.

But these boys had zip. They didn't use their personal headsets, they declined all food and drink, they did nothing but stare ahead to the cockpit and engage in low murmurs in Arabic. They behaved like conspirators. And Woods was struck by the way they treated the stewardess: "They literally ignored her like she didn't exist, which is sort of a kind of Taleban, you know, idea of womanhood, as you know, not even a human being."

So they weren't masters of disguise, adept at blending into any situation. They weren't like the Nazi spies in war movies, urbane and charming in their unaccented English. It apparently never occurred to them to act natural, read *Newsweek*, watch the movie, eat a salad, listen to Lite Rock Favourites Of The Seventies, treat the infidel-whore stewardess like a human being. Everything they did stuck out. But it didn't matter. Because the more they stuck out, the more everyone who mattered was trained not to notice them. The sort of fellows willing to fly airplanes into buildings turn out, not surprisingly, to be fairly stupid. But they benefited from an even more profound institutional stupidity. In August 2001, no-one at the FBI or FAA or anywhere else wanted to be seen to be noticing funny behaviour by Arabs. In mid-September, I wrote that what happened was a total systemic failure. But, as the memos leak out, one reason for that failure looms ever larger. Thousands of Americans died because of ethnic squeamishness by Federal agencies.

But that was before September 11th. Now we all know better … don't we?

Well, here's an easy experiment any *Spectator* reader can perform while waiting to board at Newark or LaGuardia. 15 of the 19 hijackers were young Saudi males, Osama himself is (was) a youngish Saudi male, and some 80 per cent of all those folks captured in Afghanistan and carted off to Guantanamo turn out to be young Saudi males (though, out of the usual deference to our Saudi friends, the Administration is keeping studiously quiet on the last point). So you're at Newark standing in line behind a young Saudi male and an 87-year old arthritic nun from Des Moines. Who'll be asked to remove his or her shoes? Six out of ten times, it'll be the nun. Three out of ten times, you. One out of ten, Abdumb al-Dumber. Even if this is just for show, what it's showing is profound official faintheartedness.

Norm Mineta, the Transportation Secretary, is insistent that fairness demands the burden of inconvenience be spread among all ethnic and age groups. "Any specificity as to particular persons" is strictly forbidden. Meanwhile, his colleagues have spent the last three weeks assuring us that another catastrophe is now inevitable. "There will be another terrorist attack," Robert Mueller told the National Association of District Attorneys the other day. "We will not be able to stop it."

We must, I suppose, take him and Cheney and Rummy and all the rest at their word. They wouldn't scare us if they hadn't done all they believe they can do. So, naturally, the mind turns to all the things they haven't done: as I write, young Saudi males are still arriving at US airports on routinely issued student visas. If it lessened the "inevitability" just ever so slightly of that second attack, wouldn't it be worth declaring a temporary moratorium on Saudi visitors, or at least making their sojourns in the US extremely rare and highly discretionary? Oh, no. Can't be done.

Ask why the Saudis are allowed to kill thousands of Americans and still get the kid-glove treatment, and you're told the magic word: oil. Here's my answer: blow it out your Medicine Hat. The largest source of imported energy for the United States is the Province of Alberta. Indeed, whenever I'm asked how America can lessen its dependence on foreign oil, I say it's simple: annex Alberta. The Albertans would be up for it, and to be honest they're the only assimilable Canadian province, at least from a Republican standpoint. In 1972, the world's total proven oil reserves added up to 550 billion barrels; today, a single deposit of Alberta's tar shales contains more than that. Yet no Albertan government minister or trade representative gets the access in Washington the Saudis do. No Premier of Alberta gets invited to Bush's Crawford ranch. No Albertan bigshot, if you'll forgive the oxymoron, gets Colin Powell kissing up to him like "Crown" "Prince" Abdullah and "Prince" Bandar do. In Washington, an Albertan can't get ...well, I was going to say an Albertan can't get arrested, but funnily enough that's the one thing they can get. While Bush was Governor of Texas, he even managed to execute an Albertan, which seems to be more than the Administration is likely to do with any Saudis.

So it's not oil, but rather that even targeting so obvious an enemy as the Saudis is simply not politically possible. Cries of "Islamophobia" and "racism" would rend the air. The Saudis discriminate against Americans all the time: American Jews are not allowed to enter the "Kingdom", nor are American Episcopalians who happen to have an Israeli stamp in their passports. But America cannot be seen to take any similar measures, though it has far more compelling reasons to.

James Woods puts it very well: "19 of 19 killers on September 11th were Arab Muslims - not a Swede among them." Nevertheless, in a world where the EU officially chides the BBC for describing Osama as an "Islamic fundamentalist", we must pretend that al-Qa'eda contains potentially vast numbers of Swedish agents, many female and elderly. Even after September 11th, we can't revoke the central fiction of multiculturalism – that all cultures are equally nice and so we must be equally nice to them, even if they slaughter large numbers of us and announce repeatedly their intention to slaughter more. *National Review*'s John Derbyshire calls this "the reductio ad absurdum of racial sensitivity: Better dead than rude."

Last October, urging Congress to get tough on the obvious suspects, the leggy blonde commentatrix Ann Coulter declared: "Americans aren't going to die for political correctness."

They already have.

~

THE LOAN ARRANGER

June 10th 2002

The National Post

WHEN LAST in this space, ten days ago, I was writing about whether political correctness kills: "Everything they did stuck out. But it didn't matter. Because the more they stuck out, the more everyone who mattered was trained to look the other way."

I didn't know the half of it. The other day, Johnelle Bryant, an official with the US Department of Agriculture, gave an interview to ABC News in which she revealed that Mohammed Atta and three other September 11th terrorists had visited her Florida office seeking government loans. America, it seems, came *this* close to having the World Trade Center incinerated at the taxpayers' expense.

Mr Atta swung by in May 2000, and Ms Bryant remembers quite a bit about it. "At first," she says, "he refused to speak with me," on the grounds that she was, in his words, "but a female". After he'd reiterated the point, she pulled rank: "I told him that if he was interested in getting a farm-service agency loan in my servicing area, then he would need to deal with me." Throughout the hour-long interview, he continued to dismiss her as "but a female".

Ms Bryant says the applicant was asking for $650,000 to start a crop-dusting business. His plan was to buy a six-seater twin-prop and then remove the seats. "He wanted to build a chemical tank that would fit inside the aircraft and take up every available square inch of the aircraft except for where the pilot would be sitting."

Hmm.

When she explained that his application would have to be processed, Mr Atta became "very agitated". He'd apparently been expecting to leave the office with cash in hand. "He asked me," recalls Ms Bryant, "what would prevent him from going behind my desk and cutting my throat and making off with the millions of dollars in that safe." Try this with your Royal Bank loan officer – I find it works every time. But Ms Bryant replied politely that there was no money in the safe because loans are never given in cash, and also that she was trained in karate.

His fiendish plan stymied at every turn, Mr Atta then spotted an aerial view of Washington hanging on the wall behind her. He told her he particularly liked the way it got all the famous landmarks of the city in one convenient picture, pointing specifically to the Pentagon and the White House. "He pulled out a wad of cash," says Ms Bryant, "and started throwing money on my desk. He wanted that picture really bad."

She told him it wasn't for sale, but he only tossed more dough at her. "His look on his face became very bitter at that point," Ms Bryant remembers. "He said, 'How would America like it if another country destroyed that city and some of the monuments in it,' like the cities in his country had been destroyed?"

Hmm.

Mr Atta then moved on to other prominent landmarks in other American cities, and enquired about security at the World Trade Center. Ms Bryant had a Dallas Cowboys souvenir on her desk, and he asked her about their spectacular stadium and, specifically, the "hole in the roof".

At that point, the chit-chat turned to Mr Atta's own country, which he claimed was Afghanistan. "He mentioned Osama bin Laden," she says. "He could have been a character on *Star Wars* for all I knew." Obi bin Kenobe. So Mr Atta helpfully explained that this bin Laden guy "would someday be known as the world's greatest leader."

Sadly, the interview ended badly from the terrorists' point of view when Ms Bryant informed her visitor that the loan program is for farm-based projects and a crop-dusting business did not qualify.

A few weeks later, another September 11th killer showed up, Marwan al-Shehhi, seeking half-a-million bucks supposedly to buy a sugar-cane farm. Accompanying him was Mr Atta, but he was cunningly disguised with a pair of glasses and claiming to be someone else entirely – to whit, Mr al-Shehhi's "accountant". Sportingly, Ms Bryant went along with the jape. The safe-breaking, the throat-slitting, the fake specs… why, Mr Atta was just being charmingly multicultural! "I felt that he was trying to make the cultural leap from the country that he came from," she says. "I was attempting, in every manner I could, to help him make his relocation into our country as easy for him as I could."

Unfortunately, his imaginative business plan for a crop-duster capable of crop-dusting Texas was frustrated by the unduly onerous restrictions and bureaucratic torpor of the USDA program. By late summer, Mr Atta and his chums had concluded the government was never going to buy them their own twin-props and they'd have to make do with the aircraft that were already up there. So they switched their flight training courses from small planes to large jet simulators, and told their instructors to skip all that take-off and landing stuff.

Ms Bryant has come forward now because she thinks "it's very vital that the Americans realize that when these people come to the United States, they don't have a big 'T' on their forehead."

No, indeed. In some cases, they have a big "T-E-R-R-O-R-I-S-T" flashing in neon off the end of their nose. Ten days ago, I pointed out that these fellows made virtually no effort to blend in. They weren't in "deep cover", they were barely covered at all. Atta was the brains of the operation, and he did a marginally better job of it than Leslie Nielsen would have. His one great insight into western culture was his assumption that he could get a government grant to take out the Pentagon. Yet no matter how dumb he was, officialdom was always dumber.

"If they watch this interview and they see the type of questions that Atta asked me," Ms Bryant told ABC News, "then perhaps they will recognize a terrorist, and make the call that I didn't make." Meanwhile, here are some signs to look for:

1) He threatens to cut your throat.
2) He talks about the destruction of prominent landmarks.
3) He enquires about security at said landmarks.
4) He hails Osama bin Laden as a great leader.

There'll be more of these stories, tales of men virtually screaming their intentions but up against a culture sensitivity-trained into a coma. A stump-toothed Appalachian mountain man would get slung out on his ear if he was that misogynist and abusive in a government office. In a Hollywood movie, the guy refusing to deal with the little lady and demanding to see the real boss would be a sexist Republican Congressman. In the new motion-picture blockbuster *The Sum Of All Fears*, the Islamic terrorists of Tom Clancy's novel have been replaced with neo-Nazis – a safe villain that won't offend our delicate multicultural sensibilities.

The good news is we're up against idiots. The bad news is we're also up against the suppler idiocies of current western orthodoxy. Thus, the US Government's new plans to photograph and fingerprint visitors from countries "believed to harbour terrorists" have already been attacked by Mary Robinson, the UN Human Rights junketeer who's never met an Arab dictator she didn't like. Islamists want to kill us in the name of Islam. Regrettable, but there it is. If we pretend otherwise, the Council on American-Islamic Relations, the Canadian Islamic Congress and the Islamic Society of Britain might be nice to us. But, speaking personally, I can't say I care. If Islamic lobby groups throughout the western world really want to hitch their star to a bunch of psychopathic morons, good luck to them. It's a free country. Hey, we'll even give you a government grant to tell us how racist we are.

~

HYPERPOWER

June 22nd 2002
The Daily Telegraph

AND SO THE dream dies. The boys gave it their best, they played well, but it wasn't to be. They're out of the World Cup, to the bitter disappointment of their supporters.

I refer, of course, to the US team – the first team in World Cup history with more players than fans. Across America yesterday, all nine of them gathered in bars to watch the big match only to find that the other patrons preferred to see the "Golden Girls" re-run dubbed into Spanish on Channel 173 or the last half of "Bud Answers Your Plastering Queries" on the Sheetrock Channel. Twiddling my own dial in New Hampshire, I couldn't find the game on anywhere except a French-language station from Quebec.

Is there any other sport where you can only follow the US team by watching foreign channels? No-one was singing "'Ere we go, 'ere we go, 'ere we go!" – even though it's by *an American composer!* But, cursed to be born in the US, that poor schmuck Sousa couldn't even make a living in the soccer business, forced to stick to his day job as a

conductor. In fact, all the great football songs are by Americans –
Rodgers and Hammerstein ("You'll Never Walk Alone") and
Livingston and Evans, whose "Que Sera, Sera" has a British lyric of
endearing directness:

Mi-illwall, Millwall
Millwa-all, Millwall, Millwall
Millwa-all, Millwall, Millwall
Mi-illwall, Millwall.
(Repeat until knife fight)

But, aside from the music, the American contribution to soccer
has been minimal, and American interest in it even minimaller. Every
four years, the same bien-pensants who urge the Administration to be
more "multilateral" and to work through the UN also commend the
virtues of the World Cup: the game is supposedly more poetic than
American sports, as subtle and nuanced as French foreign policy. But
Americans like their international competitions to be international in
the sense of the current "international coalition against terror" at
Kandahar air base – that's to say, overwhelmingly American but with a
few token Canadians. The World Series extends to the Toronto Blue
Jays, but that's it.

But for the last couple of weeks the World Cup has been going
very oddly. I didn't spot it at first because, like 99.9999% of the US
population, I had no idea the World Cup was even on. But once the
back-issues of the *Telegraph* started arriving, I couldn't help noticing
the Cup's strange approximation of the world beyond footie. No
sooner had the Saudi Ambassador to London, Sheikh Algosaibi, hailed
the heroism of "martyrdom operations" than his national team
heroically martyred themselves eight-nil. Either that or the entire squad
are Mossad Jew infiltrators.

Even more unnerving was the success of the American team.
What more damning evidence could you have of the global reach of
the hyperpower than for the World Cup to go to the one country that
has absolutely zero interest in soccer? And, if the sleeping giant can
sleepwalk its way to Number One football nation, who's to say it
couldn't also sew up a Test Series or two?

Would winning have changed anything? I like to think not. In
defeat, magnanimity. In victory, complete and utter indifference. One

fondly imagines the news bulletins: "At the White House, aides were alarmed when the President slumped to the floor and passed out during the early minutes of the match. Surgeons operated immediately to remove the pretzel only to find there wasn't one. 'I guess I just find it hard to stay awake during soccer,' Mr Bush later reassured the American people. 'I was fine once we switched over to the "Antiques Roadshow".' However, the President added that he wanted 'to take this opportunity to congratulate our team on their incredible victory over the ...er, evildoers.'

"At CNN, reporters fanned out across the country to ask Americans if they had World Cup fever. 'Well, I heard you got it from sharing drinking receptacles in sub-Saharan Africa,' said Sindy Vimmerstedt, 54, of Cleveland, 'so it's just as well we're going to Florida.'

"Many famous football faces from Britain have found themselves in demand on US television. 'It's a game of two halves, Larry,' Bobby Charlton said on 'Larry King Live'. 'Is it really?' said Larry. 'Well, you'd know better than I would. And are the helmets expensive?' Few Americans seemed familiar with even the most basic technical terms. At a Hollywood victory party, a BBC reporter asked Richard Gere if he was planning to get rat-arsed, but the colour drained from his cheeks and he had to be helped to a chair."

What an interesting philosophical question America's total disinterest in its national team raises: if a goal is scored in the forest and there's no-one around to cheer it, is it still a GO-O-O-O-O-O-O-O-O-O-O-OALLLLLLL? One can't but feel that, like those unmanned "drones" dropping bombs in Afghanistan, the unfanned team is an eerie glimpse of the future. My prediction is that by 2006 France, Argentina, the Saudis and maybe even England will be attempting to mimic America's winning indifference streak. You'll Never Walk Alone – unless you're an American footballer at a homecoming ceremony.

~

LETTER TO THE EDITOR
Football fix

June 25th 2002
The Daily Telegraph

From His Excellency Ghazi Algosaibi
Sir: I am grateful for Mark Steyn's generosity in trying to explain away the humiliating defeat of the Saudi football team at the hands of the Germans by offering an interesting theory: "The entire [Saudi] team are Mossad Jew infiltrators" (Comment, June 22). This is very comforting but, alas, untrue. The defeat was well earned. However, I am surprised that Mr Steyn neglected to mention a well-known fact. It was a Wahabi Islamo-fascist masquerading as a German player who used his terrorist head to score the goal against the American team.

Ghazi Algosaibi
Ambassador
Royal Embassy of Saudi Arabia
London W1

~

EIGHT'S A CROWD

June 27th 2002
The Daily Telegraph/The National Post

Kananaskis, Alberta

THERE ARE supposedly seven grizzlies prowling the perimeter fence here, one for almost every G8 leader, leaving Jean Chrétien to be pecked to death by a harlequin duck or smothered by a swarm of long-toed salamanders.

But I expect it will be a quieter summit than that. George W Bush would rather be anywhere else than in Kananaskis this week, and not because of the topic under discussion: an "action package" on Africa. If one were to poll the American media on the subject least likely to command column inches, an initiative on Africa would rank pretty high, an initiative on Canada would come higher, but a Canadian initiative on Africa would be unbeatable. Nonetheless, for his brief moment in the international spotlight, the Canadian Prime Minister has decided to turn the lights off. When some reporter asks whether Bush will attempt to use the G8 summit to discuss the war on terror rather than aid to Africa, M Chrétien replies that, as he's the chairman, he'll see to it that, no matter what the President wants, the conference will not be "hijacked by terrorists". Tasteful. He's da guy in da cockpit and he'll be sticking to da course no matter how dat crazy Bush sit in the back fuming and attempting to light his shoe.

In fact, the G8 focus on Africa suits Bush. It may not do anything to solve Africa's problems but at least it won't add to his. This is, in effect, the first summit of the post-summit era. The behaviour of the elite clubs – Nato, the EU – since September 11th has confirmed Bush's skepticism about multilateralism: the few useful contributions to the war on terror have come about through focused bilateralism – Australia's SAS boys aren't in Afghanistan because the Aussies and the Yanks belong to the same international talking shops; likewise, Mr Blair's helpfulness isn't because of the EU but, if anything, in spite of it. Geopolitically speaking, two's company, eight's a crowd. Meaningful international agreements signed by the United States will henceforth be as rare as the long-toed salamander in the Kananaskis woods, in whose interests the Mounties warn you not to urinate in the same place twice. There's another metaphor for global summitry.

So the Bush plan on the Middle East and the G8 plan on Africa are not just differences in priorities but in fundamental approach. NEPAD (The New Economic Partnership for Africa's Development) is in the grand tradition of multilateral plans; the Palestine plan is a plan for those who are sceptical of plans. M Chrétien really thinks he can save Africa; Mr Bush is under no illusions that he can bring peace to the Middle East and his plan is to have no plans on the subject until those involved get serious. He's not "imposing" "onerous" "conditions" on the Palestinians. His message to them is a simple one: No shirt, no shoes, no service. They're not conditions, only a statement of the obvious: it may be "up to the Palestinians" (as President Chirac, Prime Minister Chrétien et al insist) to choose their leaders but if they choose corrupt and duplicitous terrorism-facilitators like "Chairman" Arafat there's no reason on earth why the United States should help them to statehood.

If M Chrétien had decided to devote this summit to Palestine, he would have had a big plan brokered with the EU, he'd have flown in Arafat and Assad and Saudi "Crown" "Prince" Abdullah and a bunch of Arab League bigwigs – and nothing would have come of it, because it would have been predicated on a fiction. The acronym for M Chrétien's African plan – NEPAD, pronounced "kneepad" – could just as easily be applied to the Euro-Canadian approach to Mr Arafat: if you spend enough time on your kneepads, the guy'll come round. He won't. Mr Bush has seen the Arafat memo authorising a payment of US $20,000 to the family of that last suicide bomber – the one the Chairman supposedly "condemned". The President has declared that you can't plan on a fellow like that. Mr Bush's plan is, in fact, a superb explanation of why he doesn't have a plan.

No wonder his G8 colleagues and the rest of the all-plans-all-the-time set are furious with Bush. If the no-plan plan were to catch on with the international community, it'd be the end of summits like Kananaskis. In declaring that the present diseased Palestinian institutions are worthless negotiators, Mr Bush has usefully clarified the situation in ways that a thousand "Oslos" and "Wye Rivers" and "Mitchells" and "Tenets" never can. Had he kept it to himself and quietly offered it to his pals around the table at Kananaskis, Chirac would have pronounced it unacceptable, Chrétien would have ummed and awed, Blair would have sought to find some middle ground, and the result would have been a compromise statement of utter worthlessness – like the Commonwealth on Zimbabwe, or the EU on anything. Much better to pre-announce the plan, and give the other guys a few days to catch up. If they don't want to, what's the difference?

Mr Bush has called, so to speak, the bluff of summits.

DUST BIN

June 29th 2002
The Spectator

HE'S BACK! Or he will be. Any day now. Just you wait. "I want to assure Muslims," said bigshot Islamofascist Suleiman Abu Ghaith the other day, "that Sheikh Osama bin Laden… is in good and prosperous health and all what is being rumoured about his illness and injury in Tora Bora has no truth." He's tanned, rested, and ready to rumble. "America," warned Suleiman, "must prepare itself and fasten its seat belt."

Wow. These guys don't just slash the throats of stewardesses, they memorise their lines. And it seems they've made sure that Osama, like your tray table, is stowed and, like your seat-back, is in an upright position. Or so our friend Suleiman claims. If it is Suleiman. His words were on an audio tape delivered to al-Jazeera, and al-Jazeera claims to have identified the voice as that of Suleiman, the baby-faced al-Qa'eda sidekick who briefly became a familiar figure on the news bulletins last September and early October and has apparently survived the rumours of his own demise in December. I think I'd want a something a little more date-specific if a new Osama video turned up. You can't expect him to hold up that morning's paper as it would give a little too much away – *The Peshawar Bugle, The Baghdad Sycophant, The Teheran Fundamentalist* – but at the very least I'd expect him to cite not just his usual ancient grievances but some more recent ones - say, the Saudi World Cup team's eight-nil humiliation.

I said in *The Sunday Telegraph* a couple of weeks ago that Osama was "deceased" and in *The Daily Telegraph* back in March that he was a few specks of DNA somewhere in the Hindu Kush. Everyone else seems to think he's alive and well. Recently, several hundred of the Princess Patricia's Canadian Light Infantry exhumed every corpse in an al-Qa'eda cemetery near Kandahar and, failing to find a body with a very long beard and a very short penis, concluded that Osama had gotten away. (He had at one point ten lookalikes to confuse the Americans, but, of course, even the most convincing doppelganger would be unlikely to match Osama's unusual deficiencies in the trouser department.)

Where did he go? The alleged experts seem inclined to favour either the Greater Kandahar area or the Pakistani tribal lands. Supposedly, he's trimmed his beard, and is receiving dialysis from machines supplied by rogue elements of the ISI, Pakistan's intelligence services, while waiting for a doctor to be flown in to perform a kidney transplant. I doubt it. On the Afghan side of the border, while the Taleban's top execs have melted back into a not unsympathetic general population, the foreign occupiers – Osama and his Arabs and other miscellaneous hirings – remain very unpopular. In the Pakistani badlands, meanwhile, he could perhaps rely on the fact that the $25 million bounty on his head is too large to have any meaning to your average Baluchistani villager, unschooled in such matters as exchange rates. But those duplicitous ISI guys are another matter, and I wouldn't trust any doctor they ushered into the room.

Oh, well. Hamid Karzai says he's in Pakistan. General Musharraf says he's in Afghanistan. From this we can deduce the general rule that, whatever country you happen to be in charge of, you'd rather Osama were in someone else's. The obvious question for those who say the weirdbeard's getting dialysis treatment in Iraq or Iran is: why would Saddam and the Ayatollahs feel differently from Karzai and Musharraf? Are they that fond of the old terrorist mastermind? The evidence suggests that both regimes are currently trying to avoid attracting Washington's attention in the hope that this whole unfortunate axis-of-evil business will just fade away. Booking him into the Saddam Hussein Saviour Of The People And Humiliator Of The Great Satan Ear, Nose, Cutthroat And General Hospital's Renal Ward would be like pasting a big ol' target on your forehead. The Iranians, in particular, would be aware of a potential historical symmetry: it was Jimmy Carter's decision to allow the exiled Shah into the US for medical treatment that provoked the American Embassy siege.

Conceivably, the Saudis are cocky enough to figure they could get away with it. They've funnelled money to Osama, they've supplied most of his manpower, and their man in London – *Spectator* letters-page mainstay Ambassador Algosaibi – says he'd like to be a suicide bomber if only he weren't so old and out of shape. And yet "Crown" "Prince" Abdullah still gets invited to Crawford to pal around on the President's ranch. The House of Saud could be forgiven for concluding that they can do anything they like and the White House will still hail them as a "staunch ally". If Osama is alive, Saudi Arabia's his most likely location. That would explain why the Americans haven't found him in any of the places they've looked for him: they're choosing not to look in Saudi.

In any case, Washington is in no hurry to pronounce him dead. In a celebrity culture, it's useful to be able to put a face to what would otherwise be a shadowy menace. The Chinese get away with a ton of stuff just because they eschew the Colonel Gaddafi pillbox hat and the Saddamite turtleneck and run their tyranny with a bunch of boring interchangeable guys in specs and cheap lounge suits. Osama's generated websites and bumper stickers and T-shirts and song parodies, and announcing that you'd found his DNA in the rubble of a daisy-cuttered cave would only prompt even more Americans to tune out the war.

Likewise, it's the open-endedness of the Bush crusade (whoops) that rattles the Europeans: if Osama were dead, the Eurosophists would be saying, "C'mon, you got your man, you had your revenge, now declare victory and go home." With the guy directly responsible out of the way, the European inclination to render terrorism as an impersonal abstraction born of "desperation" and "hopelessness" would be unstoppable. Thus, for Bush, at home and abroad, it is politically necessary for Osama to remain alive until the invasion of Iraq is under way. If I were choreographing this war, some conclusively distinguishing characteristics would turn up around September 11th.

Nonetheless, he's already stiff, he's six feet under, he's bin Laiden to rest, he's in paradise being pleasured by those 72 virgins and wondering if they're tittering about his shortcomings. The alleged Suleiman insists that Osama, his Number Two Ayman al-Zawahiri, Mullah Omar and "98% of the leadership of al-Qa'eda are safe and are running their affairs perfectly." But, in that case, where are they? Holed up in the hills far from a video camera? Unlikely. Your average run-of-the-mill schoolgirl suicide bomber can make a farewell video. Ah, say the clever-clogs, but suppose he's been injured and can't appear on camera. Come off it. The killers of *Wall Street Journal* reporter Daniel Pearl filmed his decapitation and then had his final moments plus the severed swinging head augmented with news footage and music and captions, and widely circulated via the Internet. It is a vile and disgusting video, but it is technically accomplished. No matter how badly injured Osama's arms or legs are, they could have filmed his head up tight like Pearl's, and broken up the film with other material. They could have slapped on some pancake and dunked his beard in a vat of industrial-strength Grecian. If Daniel Pearl's murderers can get access to a professional studio and editing facilities, surely "98%" of al-Qa'eda's leadership can. If they could have, they would have – if not Osama, then al-Zawahiri or Mullah Omar or any of the other hotshots who've been silent these last six months. They can't all be recuperating from kidney transplants.

Here's what we know about al-Qa'eda: the Number One and Two guys haven't been heard from since December; Number Three, Mohammed Atef, is dead; Number Four, Abu Zubaydah, is in US custody; so are hundreds of others, 80% of them Saudis captured in Afghanistan. Not all Osama's lieutenants are dead or in detention, but intelligence reports have spotted surviving individual members of his elite personal bodyguard in various spots around the globe, which would appear to suggest that they've been reassigned: there's no point being a bodyguard when the body's no longer in a state worth guarding.

Al-Qa'eda has always been a decentralised organisation, but under a snooty all-Arab officer class. It shouldn't surprise us that they find it hard to recruit top-quality psychopaths willing to kill themselves to protest the fall of Andalusia in 1492 or whatever other ancient grievance is itching Osama's yak-wool undies. As the number of incompetent Palestinian suicide bombers suggests, in this field it's hard, by definition, to get people with experience. But, even so, it's clear the misfit conscripts have been promoted way beyond their natural ability: the network's dependent on incompetent street punks like Jose Padilla, the "dirty bomb" guy captured in Chicago, and Richard Reid, the damp squib of a shoebomber, purely because they travel on respectable passports issued by Her Britannic Majesty or the United States. If Reid had invested a handful of euros in a lighter instead of relying on a damp, bent book of matches from the airport EconoLodge, he'd have detonated the plane over the Atlantic. Instead, he's destined to be the most pitiful footnote in terrorist history: a man who couldn't even blow his legs off when his loafers were packed with explosives.

So the alleged Suleiman Abu Gaith had nothing to boast of in his audio statement except the attack on a synagogue in Tunisia that killed 14 German tourists. "This operation was carried out by al-

Qa'eda network," he said proudly. "A youth could not see his brothers in Palestine butchered and murdered... while he saw Jews cavorting in Djerba." But that's pretty pathetic, isn't it? Some "network": it can kill barely any more people than a novice schoolgirl suicide-bomber acting out of Cherie Blairite desperation.

Go back to that video of Tiny bin Laden and the big-time sheikh yakking on about what a great day September 11th was and rolling around with laughter because some of the boys didn't know it was a suicide mission until they boarded the plane. It's clear the so-called evil genius never expected the twin towers to collapse. He just got lucky. His pa may know about construction, but Junior's just a peculiarly advanced model of the useless idiot son – a criticism routinely made of Bush but actually far more applicable to Osama, who took his dad's fortune and literally threw it down a hole in the ground. The anthrax attacks, which the FBI persists in attributing to domestic sources, seem to me to be almost certainly al-Qa'eda, both because they ceased around the time Osama and co disappeared from view and because of their ineffectiveness. It was *National Review*'s Jonah Goldberg who suggested that al-Qa'eda's operatives in Florida had been instructed to send anthrax to the American media and were boneheadedly literal enough simply to look up "American Media" in the phone book, it being the name of the publishers of *The National Enquirer*. Similarly, instructed to attack American airlines, they attacked "American Airlines".

Now I could be wrong and Suleiman could be right. Maybe Osama's fit as a fiddle and he's ready to take out DisneyWorld or Rockefeller Center. Americans are worried about terrorist attacks on Fourth of July parades. Gays are worried that he'll target Gay Pride parades, which have traditionally been very lightly policed. Perhaps al-Qa'eda have plans to fly crop-dusters into the infidel sodomites. Perhaps it'll be a flop, like the shoe-bombing and the anthrax and the dirty nuke. Or perhaps the idiots will get lucky again. An idiot with a nuke or chemical weapons could get very lucky.

But the real story here is not September 11th, or the attack on the USS Kohl, or the embassy bombings in Africa, or even Oklahoma City, which seems more and more likely to have had a radical Islamic component. These events are separated by months, years, but in between the splashy headline-grabbers the real work goes on day after day in the Saudi-funded madrassahs radicalising Muslims in South

Asia, Pakistan, the Balkans, Western Europe and America. The President's speech on Monday was, among other things, a colossal rebuff to "Crown" "Prince" Abdullah's fictional Saudi peace plan and may or may not signal a full-scale re-evaluation of America's long-turned blind eye to Saudi misdeeds. Is Osama dead? Yes. Is American cosseting of the House of Saud dead? That's harder to say. But it's time to move on to the real Mister Bigs.

~

LETTER TO THE EDITOR
Secret weapon

July 6th 2002
The Spectator

From His Excellency Ghazi Algosaibi
Sir: In his most recent hilarious-as-usual masterpiece, Mark Steyn ('Dust bin', 29 June) refers, directly and indirectly, three times to Osama bin Laden's 'trouser department'.

Your readers should not misunderestimate his obsession. Mr Steyn is looking for a dirty bomb, and he is looking in the right place.

Ghazi Algosaibi
Ambassador
Royal Embassy of Saudi Arabia
London W1

JULY

Independence

July 7th 2002
The Sunday Telegraph

ON THURSDAY, to celebrate America's Independence Day, I celebrated America's independence – not just from George III but from the rest of what passes for the civilised world. You only have to listen to a couple of minutes of any BBC current affairs show or glance at the front pages of any Continental newspaper (or even, on particularly bad days, read selected *Telegraph* columnists) to realise that America is the western world's odd man out, and has been increasingly since September 11th.

Personally, I couldn't be happier about it. I'm delighted the United States is "out of step" with, say, Belgium. Not because I'm Belgophobic. If the Belgians want to support the International Criminal Court, keep Saddam in office until his nuke arsenal is ready to fly, and continue subsidising Yasser Arafat's pay-offs to the relicts of suicide bombers, that's fine, go ahead, you're an independent nation.

Unfortunately, on the European side, it's the very concept of independence that's at issue. The Rest Of The West disputes not America's positions so much as their right to have positions. To do so is "unilateralist" – which is, when you think about it, just another word for "independent". When your positions are as independent of the global consensus as those of Mr Bush then you must be – all together now – "arrogant". Or so we are assured by such famously modest types as John Simpson, the liberator of Kabul, and his anonymous interviewee in these pages last week, the "leading British civil servant" who complained about the President's "arrogance" while describing him as "a bear of very little brain".

One sympathises with Sir Hugh Sless-Auld-ffarquahar, GCMG or whoever it was. Obviously, the Presidency of the United States has never attracted the same calibre of talent as the Deputy Permanent Under-Secretaryship of the Ministry of Car Parks. But I wonder if this

299

is quite the way to ensure Britain's voice is heard in Washington. In their haste to line up at the Eurinals and spray their contempt over Bush, the Smug-ffarquahars of the world have settled on the line that Mr Bush is presuming to "announce to the Palestinians who should and shouldn't be their leader." Actually, that's not what the President said and, in fact, it's the Euro-elite who tell people who they can vote for. In February, Louis Michel, the Belgian Foreign Minister, speaking on behalf of the EU, threatened sanctions against Italy if they voted for Umberto Bossi's Northern League. Nothing "arrogant" about that, apparently.

In other words, the Michels and Pattens and Smug-Pratts are indulging in what the psychologists call displacement. Mr Bush is a polite, modest fellow. He speaks softly because he carries the world's biggest stick. Conversely, the Europeans speak ever more shrilly because their twig is even tinier than Osama bin Laden's notoriously small penis. If they wanted to, they could make the twig bigger, by spending more on defence. But they've made a conscious decision not to: the EU has embarked on a unique scheme for world domination dependent on hectoring the rest of the planet into submission. If Mr Bush is allowed to go his own way, the European strategy of noisy impotence – all mouth and no trousers – will be exposed as a sham.

But America is also an historical anomaly: the first non-imperial superpower. It has no colonies and no desire for any. For almost 60 years, it's paid for the defence of the west virtually single-handed while creating and supporting structures – the UN, Nato, G8 – that exist only to allow its "allies" to pretend they're on an equal footing. For "allies", read dependencies: it's because the US provides generous charity defence guarantees that the European governments have been free to fritter away their revenues on socialised health care and lavish welfare and all the other entitlements the Euro-progressives berate America for not providing for its own citizens. The non-arrogance of Washington is unparalleled in human history: it's American muscle that tames Bosnia but it's the risibly pompous Paddy Ashdown who gets to swank about the joint playing EU viceroy.

In Washington, meanwhile, cooler assessments are being made. America knows now what multilateralism boils down to: There's no point pooling resources with people who have no resources to pool. There's no point getting together and forming a whole that's less than the sum of your individual part.

If that sounds "arrogant" to Europe, well, do something about it. You don't want Bush to topple Saddam? Fine. Sign a mutual defence pact with Baghdad. You like Yasser that much? Send your mythical Rapid Reaction Force to guard Ramallah. That's what real powers do. But sneering civil servants being patronising about colonials isn't going to cut it. That argument was settled in 1776.

~

FANCY THAT!

July 8th 2002
The National Post

I'M A DEAD WHITE male, as you can tell from the picture accompanying this column. Suppose on Martin Luther King Day I went to the offices of the National Association for the Advancement of Colored People and shot the receptionists. How many nano-seconds do you think it would take before the attack was being characterized as racially motivated? Your top Olympic hotshot could ingest every steroid on the planet and he couldn't beat that time.

Suppose it was Judy Garland's birthday and I went to my local gay bathhouse and opened fire on the fetching young men handing out the towels. How many minutes would tick by before the word "homophobia" was heard?

Or suppose it was the anniversary of Roe v Wade, and me and my semi-automatic swung by the abortion clinic...

Well, you get the idea. On the Fourth of July (hint) a guy went to the airport in Los Angeles, sauntered up to the ticket counter of El Al (hint) and fatally shot two people and wounded three. How many folks hearing the news on a quickie radio update honestly expected it to be anyone other than a Muslim male of Middle Eastern origin? Obviously, Underperformin' Norman Mineta, the scrupulously sensitivity-trained US Transportation Secretary, would have been wary of jumping to conclusions. Were he running the LAPD, he'd have pulled in a couple of elderly spinsters from the Baptist Missionary Society and Kelli-Sue, a trainee hairdresser from Cleveland.

But, fortunately for the final death toll, El Al has its own security and so the suspect, after firing ten rounds, was himself killed. And whaddaya know? He wasn't an elderly spinster but a 41-year old Egyptian male! His name wasn't Kellie-Sue, it was Hesham Mohamed Hadayet!

Mohamed! What are the odds on that?

This stunning development seems to have completely disoriented the FBI. I quote from the *New York Times* headline: "Officials Puzzled About Motive Of Airport Gunman."

Hmm. Egyptian Muslim kills Jews on American national holiday. Best not to jump to conclusions. Denial really is a river in Egypt. "It appears he went there with the intention of killing people," said Richard Garcia, the Bureau's agent in charge. "Why he did that we are still trying to determine."

CNN and the Associated Press all but stampeded to report a "witness" who described the shooter as a fat white guy in a ponytail who kept yelling "Artie took my job." But, alas, this promising account proved to be a prank. Saudi Arabia's popular *Arab News* suggested that Mr Hadayet had made the mistake of doing business with El Al and that "the Israeli airline had been late in paying for two limousine rentals from the Egyptian immigrant's company". If a couple of late cheques were a motive for murder, Izzy's and Conrad's heads would now be stuffed and mounted in my trophy room. But, sadly, this cautionary tale about the Jew bloodsucker's commercial wiles proved also to be false.

That left the police with no leads. Nothing to go on. The trail's stone cold. All the FBI has is an Egyptian male, who'd complained to his apartment managers after his neighbours post-9/11 began displaying the American flag; who'd posted a banner saying "READ KORAN" on his own front door; who told his employees that he hated Israel, that the two biggest drug dealers in New York were Israelis, and that Israel was trying to wipe out the Egyptian population by flooding the country with Aids-infected Jewess prostitutes.

Could even the most expert psychological profiler make sense of such confusing and contradictory signs? Beats me, Sherlock. But, as Agent Garcia says, there's no indication of "anti-Israel views or any other type of racial views." Orange County's Muslim Public Affairs Council has praised Agent Garcia for his exceptionally advanced levels of sensitivity. Any moment now, they'll be demanding to know why Governor Davis has failed to visit a mosque to reassure Muslims.

Meanwhile, a London newspaper says that Mr Hadayet may have met with Osama bin Laden's deputy on at least two occasions in Cairo. If last Thursday's shooting is the spectacular Fourth of July massacre al-Qaeda have been promising for months, then they're to be congratulated for a bloody slaughter on an epic scale never before seen in America except from incompetent grade-school psychos who steal Uncle Bud's hunting rifle but forget to take any extra ammo.

Oh, speaking of the late Mr bin Laden, whatever happened to that new video we were promised any day now? Well, apparently, that's been pushed back to the new fall season, too, and should be premiering the same week as the new romantic comedy in which I star as the world's most eligible bachelor unable to choose between Julia Roberts and Cameron Diaz and so forced to make love to both repeatedly. I offered Osama a small part, but he said, "I've got one already."

Credit where it's due. Between September 11th and July 4th, there were no terrorist attacks on American soil. That's a longer period of peace than the British ever managed in the 30 years it took them to surrender to the IRA. Much of this ten-month calm is due to increased vigilance but some of it is also due to al-Qaeda's preference for hiring morons. If their glorious Fourth was really the follow-up to 9/11, then I'd say that's the worst-grossing sequel since Dudley Moore made *Arthur II*.

But let's take the Feds at their word when they insist there's "no connection" between the LAX killer and any terrorist organizations. In its way, that's even more disturbing. Mr Hadayet doesn't fit the poverty-breeds-desperation-breeds-resentment routine: he lived in prosperous suburbia and ran his own business. America had been good to him, at least when compared with the economic basket-case he emigrated from. On July 4th, he had plenty of reasons to get out the bunting and firecrackers. Instead, he went Jew-killing.

Osama and al-Qaeda are a small problem, which since September 11th has been managed about as well as can be expected. But the broader culture of "intolerance" in certain unassimilated communities is a potentially much bigger problem. You win wars not just by bombing but by argument, too: Churchill understood this; he characterized the enemy as evil, because they were and because it was important for the British people to understand this if they were to muster the will to see the war through. In Vietnam, the US lost the rhetorical ground to Jane Fonda and co, and wound up losing the war, too. It's critical that the same thing does not happen here. The organizations which purport to represent Muslims in North America and Europe have their own excuses for soft-pedaling the torrent of hate from respectable sources within the Muslim world – mosques, media, government. There's no reason why the FBI and other US agencies should sign on to their fictions.

In the meantime, spare a thought for Thursday's victims, Victoria Hen, 25, and Yaakov Aminov, 46. Mr Hadayet successfully orphaned eight children – and a ninth on the way. Congratulations to another heroic Islamist martyr!

But, in the midst of so much regrettably predictable behaviour, this column is pleased to inaugurate the David Atkin Muslim Balls Award. As readers may recall, the other week, David Atkin of Windsor wrote to say that I "don't have the balls to write anything positive about Muslims". So let me salute those Muslim Pakistani police currently searching for three men wanted for carrying out the gang-rape to which an 18-year old girl was sentenced by a Punjabi tribal council. Let me also salute the many Muslim Pakistanis said to be "outraged" by the girl's treatment: she was punished by the council because her brother had been seen unchaperoned with a woman from a higher social class; her father was made to witness the multiple rape. Let me salute, too, Muslim strongman General Musharraf who is ordering compensation of US$8,000 to be paid. It's not a lot – indeed, it would be insulting in a western court – but at least he recognizes something's wrong. That's a start. Returning his country to English Common Law would be even better.

BOG STANDARDS

July 6th 2002
The Daily Telegraph

Pop star George Michael's controversial music video, which portrays Tony Blair as a poodle to Mr Bush, was being premiered today. – The South Wales Echo

SO I WAS IN the gents at Regents Park, when I suddenly noticed a foot had slid under the wall of the cubicle on my right and was twirling daintily at me.

"Psst!" hissed a familiar voice. "It's me. George Michael."

"Are you insane, man?" I gasped. "You want to go through this again? You're already notorious the world over for your criminal record."

"That's unfair," he snapped. "It got to No 78 in Norway and was given a rave review from the rock critic of *The Bournemouth Echo*."

"Look, I'm in a hurry," I said. "I'm not narrow-minded or anything but I'm a respectable citizen and, like the majority of the British people, I find the very thought of certain activities utterly disgusting. So I don't mind performing a lewd act with you, but please, please don't make me listen to your new CD."

"You're just like all the rest," said George sulkily, withdrawing his foot and giving a petulant kick at the door. "I do a savage indictment of the war on terror and Blair's relationship with Bush, and no-one's interested. They just want the old stuff."

"Whoa, hold up there, buddy. The old stuff *is* a savage indictment of Tone's relationship with me."

I looked up and there was President Bush poking his head over the wall of the left-hand cubicle.

"Yeah, I didn't get it at first. I said to Colin, 'These Brits keep goin' on about a "special relationship". What's the deal with that?' An' Colin goes, 'Just think Wham!' An' he explains that I'm George W Michael and Tone's the other guy, Wossname."

"Give me a minute," said George Michael. "It'll come to me."

"Well, anyway," said the President, "Colin says 'Sure, you and Tony are officially a duo, but everyone knows who's doing all the work, right? So you got to be careful not to make him look even

305

more dorky and useless.' This was back in late September and I knew Tone was worried that we was jes' gonna launch the Afghan thing in the middle of the night and he'd have to read about it in the papers, like all the other allies. 'Exactly,' says Colin. 'What Tony's trying to tell you is "Wake Me Up Before You Go-Go/Don't leave me hanging on like a yo-yo/Wake Me Up Before You Go-Go/I don't wanna miss it when you hit that high."'

"Then Colin says, 'And what you have to tell him is: 'I'm not planning on going solo.'

"I say, 'But I *am* planning on going solo. I'm a globally reviled unilateralist.' And he says, 'Yeah, but we don't need to tell Tony that just yet. It's called the Michael Doctrine.' I say, 'Wow, this guy Michael seems to be right on top of geopolitical affairs. Do I need to get all his records?' But Colin says, 'No, just the early, big-selling ones.'"

"That's all wrong," said a voice from the cubicle down the end, and there hanging halfway up the wall clinging to the cistern was the Prime Minister himself. "As I see it, there have been few more eloquent summaries of Anglo-American relations in the George Michael oeuvre than..." And here Mr Blair began to sing in a high, plaintive voice: " 'Last Christmas/I gave you my heart/But the very next day/You gave it away...' I mean, if you take out 'my heart' and replace it with 'my Royal Marines' and instead of 'gave it away' sing 'introduced steel tariffs and massive farm subsidies that damage his few remaining allies'."

"Gotcha," said George M. "How about...?" And instantly all the tedious unlistenable tracks of his serious-artist period were forgotten and he was once again the swarthy young heartthrob bellowing out his Xmas classic:

> Last Christmas
> I gave you my troops
> But the very next day
> You subsidised hay...

"Brilliant!" cried Tony, losing his balance and clutching desperately at the chain as the cistern pipe came away from the wall and he crashed to the floor in a torrent of water and frothing Toilet Duck.

Scarcely had he landed then the door of my cubicle was kicked open and there was an angry Chris Patten with his fly

306

undone. "I've been standing at the Eurinal listening to this rubbish," he snorted. "Yes, the President's right. He is George W Michael in the sense that he's a manufactured bubblegum product of the big multinationals who's under the absurd illusion that he's a towering genius. But he doesn't realise that this war will only succeed if we approach it like 'Do They Know It's Christmas?' Okay, George got a couple of solo lines, but there were a lot of other singers on that single. And, frankly, this coalition won't work unless we hear from Jacques Chirac as Simon LeBon, Gerhard Schröder as Bono, and the Benelux guys as Bananarama."

But George seemed to have lost interest and had once again slid his toes under the partition and was playing footsie with me. Suddenly a voice cut through the hubbub with the most famous of all Michael lyrics: "Guilty feet have got no rhythm."

"Hmm," said George, thoughtfully. "You mean America is hampered by an awareness of its own culpability?"

"No," said the chap, knocking down George's cubicle door. "I mean I'm PC Hotchkiss and you're nicked."

~

BEARS OF VERY LITTLE BRAIN

July 13th 2002
The Spectator

I SEE MY COLLEAGUE Matthew Parris is fighting vainly the old ennui. He is, in a word, Bushed. He can no longer be bothered being pro-American or anti-American, he just wants to tend to his garden.

As it happens, despite being a ferocious pro-Bush warmonger, I feel exactly the same. It's not so much that Britain and America are in disagreement as that they seem to lack the minimal shared assumptions necessary to conduct any kind of rational argument. Alan Watkins in *The Independent On Sunday*, for example, proposes that Americans should not be invited to Glyndebourne or Covent Garden. I do not think this will unduly discombobulate many members of the Bush Administration. The President himself likes to be in bed by nine, so good luck finding a 25-minute opera. I think Matthew was nearer the mark a few months back when he complained that the problem with America was that it was falling into the hands of people who don't throw dinner parties. (I paraphrase.) In Whitehall, meanwhile, "senior civil servants" brief John Simpson that Bush is "a bear of very little brain" and his Middle East speech was "puerile", "absurdly ignorant" and "ludicrous", and Mr Simpson for some reason thinks this is worth passing on to his *Sunday Telegraph* readers as evidence of a sea-change in Anglo-American relations.

It doesn't really matter what Bush does anymore. He's appallingly isolationist except when he's being dangerously interventionist. He's an arrogant, swaggering cowboy except when he's being a shrinking violet. I saw him play the latter role in Alberta a couple of weeks back at the G8 summit. He jetted in, kept a low profile, stood in the back row for most of the group photos, and flew out quietly without giving a press conference. It was *The Magnificent Seven* plus one non-speaking cowboy extra bringing up the rear. And you've never heard such bitching and moaning from the other guys. "He's stealing our man's thunder," complained a Canadian.

"But you'd hardly know he's here," I said.

"That's my point. Everybody's focusing on how low-key he is. He's stealing our thunder by going to such extreme lengths to be seen not stealing it."

Now it's true that Bush did everything but turn up in a false beard and check in as Mr Smith. But that's because, aside from shooting a little bilateral breeze with Vlad and Tone, he knew the whole thing was going to be a waste of time. Anyone wondering why the Bush Administration pays no attention to its allies should go back to those "senior civil servants" of Mr Simpson's. I'll bet Sir Humphrey had been polishing that "bear of little brain" crack before John showed up: you can almost hear the guy preening as he delivers it. But, frankly, the Bush moron gags have all been done. Sir Humphrey cracking Dubya dummy jokes is like your gram'pa putting on a Travolta suit and doing *Saturday Night Fever*: even if he could pull it off, it's still squaresville.

But that's Europe's problem all over, isn't it? There's a terrible reluctance to change the script: the old jokes are the best, and so are the old policies. Obviously, a "senior civil servant" would find Bush's Middle East speech "puerile", "absurdly ignorant" and "ludicrous".

The President gets up and announces that the present Palestinian leadership is worthless and he'd like to see a new constitution, separation of powers, an autonomous legislature, and independent municipal institutions. Independent municipal institutions? In the Middle East? No wonder *The Guardian*'s Jonathan Freedland described it as a "fantastic speech. That's to say, literally fantastic." How "absurdly ignorant". Why, all Bush's "ludicrous" speech will do is ensure that the Palestinians vote Arafat in by an even huger majority than he would already get.

For the benefit of any senior civil servants who read *The Spectator*, a short recap may be helpful:

December 9th 2001: In *The Chicago Sun-Times*, puerile columnist Mark Steyn writes that "Arafatism is a crisis for the Palestinians: if their cause remains mortgaged to the Chairman, their prospects of any kind of viable future are precisely zero," and concludes: "I see *The New York Times* is warning the Israelis not to try getting rid of Arafat. They have a point. It's time the Palestinians got rid of him."

April 6th: In a *Spectator* story headlined "Say Goodbye, Yasser Arafat", absurdly ignorant columnist Mark Steyn says that "Arafat will never be president of a Palestinian state and has begun his countdown to oblivion."

June 24th: In a speech in Washington, President Bush says much the same thing.

June 30th: Arafat offers to meet Bush "anytime, anywhere", but Colin Powell says he's not interested, no time, nowhere, no how. The London-based newspaper *Al-Hayat* reports: "It appeared yesterday that US efforts to replace President Arafat are gaining momentum. Some well-informed Palestinian sources revealed to Al-Hayat that some US parties 'offered' several Palestinian personalities the post of 'prime minister' during the last few days."

July 1st: Arafat flunkey Saeb Erekat criticizes Arabs for "their strange silence on Bush's speech". President Mubarak, asked whether Egypt is working with Washington on replacing Arafat, says only that he has not "discussed that with US officials". Four thousand demonstrators storm Arafat's Gaza headquarters chanting, "We want jobs! We want food!"

July 3rd: Two officials fired by Arafat refuse to accept their dismissals.

July 4th: Oman's pro-government *Al-Watan* newspaper runs a story headlined "Is Arafat The Weakest Link?"

July 6th: In the latest Arafat order to be ignored by his subordinates, Palestinian security officers tell the Chairman that the man he's appointed as their new leader is unacceptable.

July 7th: A source within the Israeli General Staff says it's concluded that "Arafat's stature is dropping so precipitously that there is no need for Israel to push him out of the territories". He will, they say, "be displaced within six months".

July 8th: the Jordanian magazine *Al-Majd* reports that Yasser Arafat is "expected to step down in the coming weeks".

July 10th: Egyptian, Jordanian and Saudi figures are said to be urging the Chairman to settle for a "ceremonial role", as the alternative position might well involve lying down in a plywood box.

Arafat isn't just toast, he's buttered, covered in Marmite and being dipped in the soft-boiled egg of history. Israel knows it, the Egyptians, Saudis, Jordanians and Syrians know it, Hamas knows it, Arafat's cronies know it, and ol' man Yasser knows it. The only folks who haven't figured it out are senior British civil servants, European foreign ministers and, alas, readers of *The Spectator*, who, responding to an online poll asking "Is President Bush right to call for the removal of Yasser Arafat?", voted six to one against. Oh, and the Danish Prime Minister, who speaking in his capacity as the EU's new Queen-for-a-day has requested an urgent meeting with the US to get "the peace process" "back on track".

By "peace process", our Danish friend means "Oslo". Sorry, pal. That show's been cancelled. For the last two-and-a-half weeks we've been in the post-Oslo era, but the EU's still standing around wearing footer bags in cricket season. The only thing that's "puerile" is those snot-nosed Brit civil servants who can manage no more insightful reaction to an extraordinary moment in Middle Eastern affairs than to make lame-o Winnie-the-Pooh cracks. The ground is shifting under your feet: if you want to wind up in the heffalump pit while the world passes you by, carry on. Europe's in danger of being the only guys in Yasser's Rolodex who still return his calls.

At the G8 meeting it was fascinating to see the other delegations react to Washington's eve-of-summit spanner-in-the-works. Mr Bush didn't bother giving anyone a head's-up on the speech, it being much more fun just to deliver it and then watch the rest of the gang scramble to re-position themselves. A few hours after the Bush speech, Canada's Jean Chrétien was asked what he thought of it and said that he could not reply because he had not yet been briefed; by the following morning, the Chrétien position on Arafat had subtly evolved: he now had no view on the fellow one way or the other. Tony Blair managed to come up with a form of words that left him looking less like an incompetent boob – obviously, it's for the Palestian people to decide, blah blah, but no-one knows better than Tone how perennially disappointing Arafat is. But Mr Blair was essentially following the same trajectory as his Canadian colleague: moving toward the new American position while trying to give the impression he's always been there. The Continentals, on the other hand, seem to be the last people on the planet who believe that Yasser really is Chairman-for-Life.

Best case scenario: Arafat runs in 2003 and is elected to a Palestinian Presidency stripped of all power – like President Vossname of Germany or President O'Itllcometome of Ireland. Worst case scenario: carried out by the handles. To Bush, either solution will do. Some rare Palestinian "moderates" (the term is relative: I mean progressive types who think suicide-bomber classes shouldn't start till junior high) might yet emerge. On the other hand, some repellent Arafat lieutenant or Hamas honcho might carry the day. Doesn't matter: an unashamed terrorist would be easier to deal with than a frontman for terrorists.

To the realpolitik set, the Arafat equation was very simple: a strongman state was a better bet than a weak democracy doomed to collapse into chaos. But, in launching the intifada, Yasser blew up his own raison d'être. You can't warn *"Après moi le déluge"* when the deluge is already in full flood. There will be disreputable fellows at the heart of the Palestinian question for some years to come, but never again will the Palestinian people's future be mortgaged to one man for decade after decade after decade.

As to the Europeans' assumption that Bush, merely by advising them not to, will provoke the Palestinians into voting for the grizzled old loser, that assumes the West Bank and Gaza electors are as unsophisticated as those of Greater London, who voted for Red Ken just to spite Mr Blair and are now paying the price (£1,260 per annum). But in any case the hypothesis is a false one: when the election comes, Chairman Arafat will not be a candidate.

For Bush, it's a win-win situation. If the Palestinians elect the Hamas crowd, he can say, "Fine, I respect your choice. Call me back when you decide to put self-government before self-detonation." If they opt for plausible state and municipal legislators, Bush will have re-established an important principle: that when the Americans sign on to nation-building they do so only to bring into being functioning democratic, civilised states – as they did, against the odds, with post-war Germany and Japan. Who's to say it couldn't work in Palestine? Not being a colonial power, the Americans don't have that win-a-few-lose-a-few attitude – here a Canada, there a Zimbabwe – that the British have. So the Bush plan is perfect: heads we win, tails you lose. That's also how some of these other international questions are being framed: heads, the International Criminal Court will be modified to our satisfaction; tails, we won't have to do any more lousy UN peacekeeping.

The question Matthew Parris might to like to ask as he weeds his borders is why could no European leader make a speech like that. How did it come about that the entire EU reflexively stuck with an aging terrorist who cancelled the last scheduled elections? Which bear is really the one with the little brain? The one who in under three weeks has changed the dynamic of the Palestinian question? Or the one whose gags are as stale as his world view?

Europeans expend an awful lot of energy explaining why nothing can change: it's "absurdly ignorant" even to suggest getting rid of Arafat; it's preposterous to pursue "crackpot" (John Simpson) plans for missile defence because it would "humiliate" the Russians. But Bush went ahead, and the Russians are fine about it, and Yasser's packing, and, behind the scenes, the Aussies and Canucks and not a few others are relieved the unilateralist cowboy has killed Kyoto. Bush tosses a pebble in the water and the ripples spread across the lake; the EU drops a huge rock of conventional wisdom and it sinks without trace. I've said before that, if America's Coke, the world could use a Pepsi. If the EU doesn't have the will to fulfill that role militarily, it could at least try to do it intellectually, with a bit of fresh creative thinking about some of these issues. But instead it clings to 1970s environmental doom-mongering, 1970s missile treaties and 1970s terrorists. Poor old Europe: never mind walking the walk, it can't even talk the talk.

OSAMA AND BIRT

July 13th 2002
The Daily Telegraph

"LOOK AT THIS," said Sulayman abu Ghaith, tossing last Sunday's *Observer* down on the table. The headline read "Bin Laden Plans Fresh Terror For September" and the opening sentence was chilling: "Terrorists are planning a series of spectacular attacks on American, British and Israeli targets to coincide with the anniversary of the destruction of the World Trade Centre on 11 September last year." "You can't buy publicity like that!" crowed Sulayman. "We will rain down death upon the Great Satan!"

But I wasn't the only non-executive director of al-Qa'eda to be unimpressed. "That's what you said before Fourth of July," sighed Walid. "And Easter, and Christmas, and Halloween. What are you going to tell them on September 12th after another big nothing?"

"Fear not, my brothers," said Sulayman. "We have huge plans for October 5th, the birthday of revered 21st President Chester Arthur."

"This is just what you were like at the East Midlands Gas Board in the Seventies," said Hafiz, who goes back with Sulayman a long way. "You said you'd be there Tuesday, I'd take the day off, no sign of anyone, so I'd call up the 24-hour helpline when it re-opened at 11am on Wednesday and you'd promise it would definitely be Friday, and then on Monday morning I'd ring again and you'd say a week on Thursday."

"That's not fair," protested Sulayman. "I was the most feared gasman in Nuneaton."

"You were pulling this stuff all the time when you were George Michael's agent," pointed out Ibrahim, who used to be at DreamWorks. "I lost count how often you'd promise, 'No, no, this next album is really the big comeback, honestly.'"

"Hmm," said Abdel. "What's Osama make of this plan? And why isn't he here? He hasn't made a board meeting in months. And whatever happened to that big new video you said would be out by now?"

"Well, er, we pushed that back to the fall season," said Sulayman. "We didn't want to get into some silly box-office thing with *Men In Black II*. And Sheikh Osama wanted to re-shoot a couple of…"

"Jews?" I said hopefully.

"…scenes," he said. "But you can ask him yourself. He's waiting in there."

"The broom cupboard?"

"For security," said Sulayman. "I'll just get him." He disappeared into the cupboard and a minute later Osama came out. I found it hard to contain my shock at how he'd aged: his snowy-white beard looked like that of the infidel Santa on my last shopping trip to Macy's.

"Sulayman's staying in the broom cupboard," he said in a muffled voice, "to, er, count the brooms. Inventory. But let's get down to business, praise be to Allah."

Walid leaned over and yanked Sheikh Osama's beard. To my astonishment, it came off, and there was Sulayman!

"What kind of idiots do you take us for? US immigration?" Hafiz sneered. "Face it, Sully, second quarter results are plummeting faster than Mohammed Atta in an overloaded crop-duster. We've decided to bring in someone new, someone even more ruthless than Osama." He pressed the intercom. "You can send him in now, Miss Jones, you infidel whore."

A strange figure in spectacles and an effete suit of disgusting hue entered the room. "May I present our new leader, Lord Birt – or, to give him his Muslim name, Armani bin Fitted," said Hafiz. "Lord Birt comes to us direct from the United Kingdom, where he is famed for his ability to turn around poorly managed industries. The Bush poodle Blair put him in charge of crime, and the crime figures have gone way up! He is the man who made the trains run on time! Nothing could demonstrate more clearly our determination to implement much-needed reforms than the presence of this renowned management expert."

Lord Birt said, "First, we need to establish a corporate framework within which business units can develop a cost-benefit matrix to prioritise greater flexibility within the parameters of core guidelines, Allah be praised," he added.

I looked at Ibrahim nervously. "What page of the Koran is that on?"

"Secondly, implementing the internal market will require focusing on inter-departmental targets..."

"You mean we have to kill each other, O Imam Birt?" I said, puzzled.

He gave me a pitying look. "Under our new strategy of 'bomber choice', martyrdom consultants will work with suicide bombers to set budget priorities. Say, you're a shoe-bomber on a Miami flight. Does it make more sense to outsource the footwear or contract it from an in-house facility? Every suicide bomber – or 'business outreach unit' – will have to fill in a post-operation performance assessment of his strategic choices."

"But I'll be in Paradise being pleasured by 72 virgins," I objected. "I'm not going to want to fill in a lot of paperwork."

"We've cut it back to two virgins and 112 virgin-assessment consultants," he said. "Oh, and you'll be needing one of these."

"Ah," I said, recognising every jihadi's favourite fashion accessory. "The good old suicide-bomber belt."

"Yes, but now it's a memo belt," beamed Mullah Birt. And indeed, instead of explosives, every pocket was jammed with requisition and evaluation forms. "The infidels will flee in terror!"

I began to feel a vague nagging doubt about the way the jihad was going...

AUGUST

Leak du jour

August 1st 2002
The National Post

WELCOME TO August, or as we in the newspaper business call it "the silly season", because nothing important ever happens in August, unless you count the outbreak of the First World War (August 1914), the greatest financial crisis in the history of the British Empire (August 1931), the Molotov-Ribbentrop pact heralding the Second World War (August 1939), the nuking of Hiroshima and Nagasaki (August 1945), the Soviet invasion of Czechoslovakia (August 1968), the only Presidential resignation in American history (August 1974), etc, etc.

What sort of August are we in for this year? Another desultory month like August 2001? Or something more explosive? Stop me if you've heard this one before, but on Monday the London newspaper *Ash-Sharq al-Awsat* reported that al-Qaeda were planning a spectacular series of attacks for August, after which terrorist mastermind Osama bin Laden would appear in a new video.

This doesn't entirely square with the other reported development of the week – that al-Qaeda is now being run by Osama's 20-year old son, Scott bin Laden. No, hang on a minute, Scott's the name of Dr Evil's son. If you've seen *Goldmember*, you'll know that Scott does indeed wind up taking over his dad's evil operation. It couldn't be that al-Qaeda have been reduced to taking inspiration from *Austin Powers*, could it?

Anyway, just for the record, Osama bin Evil's son is called Saad, and I'd be saad too if I found I'd inherited a business whose principal asset is the executive latrine at Sub-Basement Level 14 in Tora Bora. But, as readers will recall, I said a couple of months back that the old has-bin was pushing up daisycutter bits in the Hindu Kush and I don't figure we'll be seeing him on video again unless he's dancing with Fred Astaire in a new Dirt Devil commercial.

316

Meanwhile, what of Washington's own spectacular series of attacks? I had war with Iraq tentatively scheduled for sometime between the G8 summit and the anniversary of September 11th. *The New York Times* and *The Washington Post* have spent the last few weeks running their hugely entertaining Leak Of The Day features, each with a brand-new top-secret plan revealing how the Pentagon intends to invade Iraq from bases in Jordan/Qatar/Diego Garcia/Sarnia with a two-pronged strike/three-pronged strike/three-strikes-you're-pronged strike/radical no-prong strike using a rather stylish spatula/post-prong approach with plans for post-war reconstruction (the prong is ended but the military lingers on). Who knew there were so many ways to flatten Iraq? How does August 11th work for you? Say, 3pm Eastern?

Don Rumsfeld wrote a tough internal memo demanding the leaks cease, only to have the memo leaked to *The Los Angeles Times*. Poor old Saddam, who'd wanted to spend this summer on his fourth romantic novel (when he's not gassing Kurds, he's the Barbara Cartland of Baghdad), is instead having to wrap his head round dozens of tedious *New York Times* analyses of in-depth war plans while trying to bring his ebola factory on-stream before the end of the week.

The end of the big Baghdaddy would also put the skids under many of the surrounding regimes. The Saudis have figured that out, which is why they want the old Saddamite to stay in power indefinitely. Hence, the hilarious story in yesterday's *National Post*:

> *Islamic extremists are threatening to take control of Saudi Arabia's corrupt and autocratic regime, fuelling fears in Washington that the United States might lose its most powerful Muslim ally in the war against Islamic terrorism.*
>
> *Despite brutal suppression of any public dissent, anti-government demonstrations have swept the kingdom in recent months to protest the pro-American stance of Crown Prince Abdullah, Saudi Arabia's de facto ruler.*

The way to find out what this story really means is to hold it up to the mirror and read it backwards. First, and most obviously, Saudi Arabia is not America's "most powerful Muslim ally in the war against Islamic terrorism", but the principal underwriter and fomenter of Islamic terrorism. Second, Crown Prince Abdullah is not "pro-

American", but, compared to the ailing King Fahd, noticeably anti-pathetic and uncooperative. Third, anti-government demonstrations "sweeping" the kingdom? A little evidence might help. Dates and places?

Now there are certainly unstable regimes in that part of the world - the Ayatollahs in Iran are loading up the steamer trunks – and life expectation among the Saudi Royal Family has taken a sudden turn for the worse. Three princes have died within a week: on July 22nd, Prince Ahmed bin Salman bin Abdul Aziz (owner of the champion racehorse War Emblem) had a fatal heart attack at the age of 43; on July 23rd, Prince Sultan bin Faisal bin Turki al-Saud, 41, died in a car accident on the way to the funeral; on July 29th, Prince Fahd bin Turki bin Saud al-Kabir, 25, was found dead in the desert from "thirst". I'd put money on War Emblem, but what are the odds on that trifecta?

I'm certainly willing to believe there's a struggle going on in the House of Saud between those who are actively pro-al-Qaeda and those who'd rather buy 'em off – there are no "pro-American" elements in any meaningful sense – but, much as I'd like it, the Saudi powder keg is not about to blow. The *Post*'s account drew heavily on a story in Britain's *Observer* on Sunday, which was looking pretty ropey by Monday. "The condition of the King, in hospital in Switzerland, is 'unstable'," reported *The Observer*. In fact, he was there for a cataract operation, which seems to have gone swimmingly.

The Observer's source was most likely Arabists in the British Foreign Office who rarely miss an opportunity to give the House of Saud the full Monica. And I wouldn't mind waging the Lawrence of Arabia fetishists got it direct from the horse owner's mouth – Prince Abdullah. Abdullah needs a diversion to stall the Iraqi invasion. His hilarious Palestinian "peace plan" did a dandy job this spring, his "Saudi collapse imminent" scare is designed to take care of the summer and fall. But it's not true: the House of Saud will collapse *after* the fall of Saddam, not before.

So here's the likely schedule: pencil in Iraq this August, the Saudi revolution next August. How bad will the Iraqi war get? I see Bill Clinton told an audience in Toronto this week that, if Saddam's boys ever crossed the Israeli border, "I would personally get in a ditch, grab a rifle, and fight and die." The Toronto crowd applauded wildly, in acknowledgment of a true knee-slapper. "In Surprise Move, Clinton Enlists": now *that's* a silly-season story.

~

BREAST ALERT

August 10th 2002
The Daily Telegraph

I WASN'T SURPRISED to hear that airport security at Los Angeles had seized from a British granny the 2" toy rifle of a GI Joe she'd bought for her grandson. Nor by the news that security at Reno Airport inspected a woman's breasts to check it was only underwiring she had in her brassiere. Nor by the news that a Long Island mom boarding at JFK had been made to drink bottles of her own breast milk in front of other passengers to prove it wasn't a dangerous liquid. Here at the US Transportation Security Administration, we regard these as important victories in the war against terrorism.

Whether these three suspects are, indeed, the world's most wanted evil masterminds – where's my secretary's Post-It note? Ah, yes, here we are... Whether these three suspects are indeed the notorious Osama bin Lactate, Mullah Ol' Bra and Saddam Hippain it's too early to say, but we do know that it would have been all too easy to insert a toy miniature rifle in the top of the rubber nipple of a baby bottle, give it a surreptitious squeeze and send the plastic projectile flying into the aisle to give the stewardess a nasty nick in her pantyhose. The day that happens you'll know we're not doing our job.

The breast feel? That came from the top, my boss, Transportation Secretary Norman Mineta. "Think about it," he said. "If Osama's still alive, he's not wandering around looking like some crazy bearded Islamist terrorist. He'll have had the best plastic surgery money can buy – Pamela Anderson's collagen lips, Anna Nicole Smith's hooters. Take it from me, Osama bin Stacked, baby! We need to keep a lookout for any breasts over 38D. Oh, what the hell, 36B."

"Now that's what I call profiling!" I said.

The Secretary had swung by because I'd mentioned to him that we needed a bigger holding facility. "I got wall-to-wall terrorist suspects in there," I told him. "Unless you'd rather I didn't detain quite so many."

"Remember what I told you that first day?" said Norm. " 'You know the rules. Go by the book.' "

"I went and bought the book," I said. "*The Rules* by Ellen Fein and Sherrie Schneider. They had it at the airport newsstand and, boy, thanks for the tip. It's got a lot of great dating advice and, for those of us at the metal detector, it sure helps while away the mid-afternoon lull when they're boarding the flight to Riyadh."

But we were at the detention centre and I could tell the Secretary was impressed by the number of suspected terrorists we'd managed to cram in. He peered at their cold terrorist faces as they pressed up against the wire mesh of the cage. "Hang on," said Norm. "You've filled up the joint with a lot of nancy boys."

"That's just their brilliant cover," I explained. "They showed up at the US Air counter claiming to be the touring company of a famous Broadway production. Yet, when I asked them to name the show, they shouted, 'Annie, get your gun!' Fortunately, we wrestled them to the ground before they could yell any further instructions to their accomplice. We shut down the terminal for four hours but so far we haven't managed to find this 'Annie'.

"But I'm confident we can get more out of this one," I said, indicating Ronnie Twinkle, his chilling Islamist fanaticism all too obvious even in his cunning disguise of leotard and tap-shoes. "I asked him, 'What do you know about bombs?', and he said, 'Well, I did Sondheim in Des Moines.'"

"Bitch!" hissed Ronnie.

"Good work, Mark!" said Norm. But suddenly he spotted a whimpering figure at the back of the pen, her terrorist nerve utterly broken, though we'd given her a copy of the Koran and her own prayer mat. "Isn't that Anna Wintour, the celebrated longtime editor of *Vogue*? What on earth did you arrest her for?"

"You told me to be alert for alarming bangs," I replied.

"Excellent!" said Norm. "But who's that fellow over there?"

"That's the critically acclaimed poet Thom Gunn. I asked to see some picture ID and he produced his California driver's license. It was a very good likeness, so I arrested him for attempting to board a plane while carrying a replica of a Gunn."

"You'll go far in this department," said Norman. "Hey, what's that awful smell?"

"Striped bass," I said. "It's a couple of days old now, but we're still waiting for the lab results to come back. I went to grab a bite and I found this terrorist had managed to infiltrate the terminal restaurant and was slipping firearms to his terrorist pals under the guise of being a waiter. The buddy, posing as a customer, says, 'So what are your specials?' and then this terrorist guy, Walter, says, 'Well, today, for $12.95 we have a striped bass in a saffron sauce on a Ruger.'"

Walter exploded and lunged at the cage wire. "For the thousandth time, you jerk! It's striped bass in a saffron sauce on arugula."

I grabbed the striped bass and slapped him hard on the cheek with it. "The mullahs can't help you now, punk!" As I tossed aside the fish, I whispered to the boss, "Seems this 'arugula' is Italian for 'rocket'. Could be we intercepted something real big here."

"You've done a terrific job," said Norman, as we strolled back down the concourse past a man with dark black eyes and a long grey beard who seemed vaguely familiar. "Nabbing that British granny was a stroke of genius. Hey, what's that on the security camera? More suspicious old ladies?"

"No, that's the 'Golden Girls' rerun," I said. "The guys on the conveyor belt scanner like to switch over once in a while. Like to join me?"

Yet, even as we settled down to watch, I felt vaguely uneasy, as if we were missing something. "Surely, Mr Secretary, if Osama's the fiendish mastermind he's supposed to be, he'll know you're on the look-out for a gal with colossal knockers and he'll have had a reduction job like Pammy did. He could be wandering around with small but exquisitely pert breasts."

"Good thinking, Mark," Norm said. "Okay, from now on we check out all the racks."

I glanced around. "Wow!! Get a load of the bazookas on that bombshell!!!"

"What are you on about?" said Norm, scanning the gate. "There's not a hot-looking gal with stand-out mammaries anywhere in sight."

"I was referring to that young swarthy male coming out the men's room with an old bomb shell he's fitted a couple of bazookas on to."

"Try and stay focused on the job," said Norm sternly. "Here come the Dallas Cowgirls. I get to frisk first."

~

FIRST WE TAKE BAGHDAD

August 10th 2002
The Spectator

WAR WITH IRAQ looms and not everyone is happy about it. "I think the principle of 'first things first' does apply," says Al Gore, "and has to be followed if we are to have any chance of success." By this he means that, instead of Saddam's removal, Afghanistan's stability "needs to be assured first" – just as in the Second World War we wisely concentrated on nation-building in the Solomon Islands for two or three years instead of rushing on to liberate a lot of other places. I'd say it's Al Gore's stability that needs to be assured first.

In Britain, those two old pantomime dames, Ted Heath and Denis Healey, are pursing their lips and hoisting their bosoms, not for the first time. Wisely, Lord Healey is not being quite as specific in his predictions of doom as he was in 1991, when he confidently asserted that war with Saddam would "push up the price of oil to $65 a barrel for about a year, produce a collapse in the American banking system …and produce a world recession". Meanwhile, the Continentals are all hot for Unmovic. I assumed Unmovic was the new and even more obstinate Serb strongman, but apparently it's the latest inspections regime – the UN Monitoring, Verification and Inspection Commission – that Saddam's suddenly all eager to invite in. Now why do you think that might be?

Of course, his vice-president, Taha Yassin Ramadan, wants an assurance from the UN that its inspections won't be "intrusive", and no doubt they'd be happy to go along. Give Saddam a quick glide with the electronic wand, no need for a full cavity search, it's all just for show anyway. That the old butcher is developing weapons of mass destruction is not in doubt. The only question is whether or not he'll use them – or, more to the point, use them on anybody we give a toss about. The Eurosophists reckon he won't. Washington would rather make sure he can't.

Beyond that, the President isn't really interested in making a case. Those who want to do so on his behalf draw attention to a pre-September 11th meeting in Prague between Saddam's man and Mohammed Atta. Others say that, if the new Bush Doctrine of "pre-emption" means anything, Saddam's the obvious place to start. But I prefer to look at it this way: What's the real long-term war aim of the United States?

I'd say it's this – to bring the Middle East within the civilised world. How do you do that? Tricky, but this we can say for certain: you'll never be able to manage it with the present crowd – Saddam, the Ayatollahs, the House of Saud, Boy Assad, Mubarak, Yasser. When Amr Moussa, Secretary-General of the Arab League, warns the BBC that a US invasion of Iraq would "threaten the whole stability of the Middle East", he's missing the point: *that's* the reason it's such a great idea. Suppose we buy in to Moussa's pitch and place stability above all other considerations. We get another 25 years of the Ayatollahs, another 35 years of the PLO and Hamas, another 40 years of the Baathists in Syria and Iraq, another 80 years of Saudi Wahhabism. What kind of Middle East are we likely to have at the end of all that? The region's in the state it's in because it's *too* stable.

And no-one sums it up better than the butcher of Baghdad. What dictator wouldn't be tickled by being "monitored"? Saddam's eternal participation in an ongoing field study of dictatorship is the reductio ad absurdum of "stability" fetishisation, ever since the stability junkies prevailed on Bush Sr to leave the Saddamites in power 11 years ago. Just about every ten minutes somewhere on your radio or TV dial these days you can hear bigshot Democrat Senator Joe Biden retailing for the umpteenth time a pompous little anecdote in which he explains how he's warned Bush Jr against taking out Saddam. "Mr President," he claims to have said, "there is a reason your father stopped and did not go to Baghdad. The reason he stopped is he didn't want to stay for five years."

And your point is…? By my arithmetic, that means we'd have been out in spring 1996. Sounds a good deal to me. Instead, it's late summer 2002 and Britain and America are still ineffectually bombing Iraq every week while somehow managing to get blamed for systematically starving to death a million Iraqi kids - or two million or whatever it's up to by now – through UN sanctions, though funnily enough UN sanctions don't seem to have so tightened Saddam's purse strings that he can't find 25,000 bucks to give to the family of each Palestinian suicide bomber. More than that, he's still here. And, simply by being still here, he's what passes for a success story in the Arab world. He's living proof to the boneheads on the "Arab street" that you can be violently anti-American, anti-Israel, anti-everything, and get away with it. Today, French flights are once again landing at Saddam Hussein International Airport in Baghdad. With every week he survives, the will to take him out diminishes. With every month, the will even to constrain him does, too. And, with every year, his legend throughout the region increases.

So Saddam has to go. He will fall quickly, as quickly as the "mighty Afghan warrior, humbler of empires" fell. What happens then is harder to predict. I doubt whether any coherent post-Saddam administration can come from the disaffected freaks, creeps and losers assembled by the realpolitik set in London the other week and launched as the "Iraqi National Movement". But, as Al Gore would say, first things first: it's not strictly necessary for a new regime in Iraq to be better than its predecessor, only different. That sends the important message that whose fingernails you rip out in the dungeon of the Presidential palace is your affair but start monkeying with us and you've written your last romantic novel, moustache boy. That's the immediate and critical US aim.

Nonetheless, whoever succeeds Saddam will almost certainly be an improvement. That's to say, he will, at worst, be a post-September 11th General Musharraf –a non-deranged dictator who'll stick the anthrax program on the back burner, attend to more pressing economic matters and thereby set in motion a chain of events, state by state. Just to run through a few:

SAUDI ARABIA

One reason why the House of Saud wants Saddam to stick around is because the first thing a new Iraqi regime will do, liberated from UN constraints on oil exports, is start pumping an extra couple million gallons a day. It's a small point but one worth noting that, by keeping Saddam in power but restricting his ability to sell oil, the west to a certain extent punishes itself. A new regime in Baghdad, whether democratic or not, means more oil, which means cheaper prices at the pump, which means more pressure on the House of Saud, whose underpants get tightened a notch with every per barrel dollar drop. Thus, Saddam's removal could be seriously crushing. There are no good guys in Saudi Arabia - the choice is between those who are openly pro-al-Qa'eda and those who are quietly buying them off – but even without total internal collapse, the less money they're getting from oil the less they have to fund Islamist recruitment in Europe, South Asia and North America, and the more internal dissension there is in the kingdom, the more likely their excitable young men are to wage the jihad at home rather than abroad. Leaving Saddam as the regional muscle man means allowing the Saudis to continue providing the ideological heft to Islamist terrorism.

JORDAN

There are rumours doing the rounds in London and Washington that King Abdullah has been more or less bought by Saddam, and pretty cheaply, too. This is in the grand tradition of King Hussein's decision to stick with his Iraqi "brother" during the last Gulf War, when even the Syrians signed up with the Americans. It's obvious that the longer Saddam stays in power the more Jordan will be corrupted, and eventually we'll wind up with one more Arab sewer state. The Hashemite Kingdom is already an important route for Iraqi sanctions-busting, and Saddam would quite like to use it as a military highway, too. Of all the hardline anti-Jew rejectionist regimes in the Middle East, the Saddamites are the only ones anxious to send their troops into combat against Israel. All that's restraining them is the Arab countries they'd have to pass through en route. Every year Saddam stays in power increases the chance he'll turn Jordan into a de facto colony and thruway to the battlefield.

I'm not a Hashemite romantic: when you actually sit down and try and work out why Jordan gets such a good press, it seems to boil down mainly to the Royal Family's taste in hot-looking westernised babes. But, if their good points remain kinda mysterious, it's nevertheless the case that they've got fewer bad points than any of their neighbours. Getting Saddam off the Hashemite windpipe will be the first step in letting the most reformable Arab regime start reforming. Leaving Saddam in power means losing Jordan.

IRAN

As I write this, the original Islamist nutters are firing on their hapless citizens in Teheran, Esfahan, Ghazvin and other Iranian cities. The popular demonstrations are to mark the 96th anniversary of the constitutional monarchy and, so far as one can tell from the patchy reports, it sounds more like Hungary 1956 than Czechoslovakia 1989. But there are some interesting details. Protesters report that the regime's riot police are speaking Arabic. That confirms rumours that the mullahs have hired Saudis, Iraqis and others to do the heavy work of shooting civilians. The likelihood that a young pro-western population will be cowed by Arab outsiders decreases significantly after Saddam's gone: they'll no longer be the crack troops of the regional superpower but only the despised remnants of a loser regime. The liberation of Iraq will hasten the revolution in Iran.

THE PALESTINIAN AUTHORITY

The Palestinian people are perhaps the best testament to the defects of stability. They've been kept in an artificially stable environment for half a century: the faux "refugee camps" of Jenin and the like, which are effectively UN-supervised terrorist training facilities now populated by three generations of "refugees" who've never lived in the places they're supposed to be refugees from. All-out war to the death would have been preferable, regardless of who won. Either the Arabs would have got their way and pushed the Jews into the sea or the Arabs would have been decisively beaten once and for all. But neither scenario would have led to the remorseless descent into depravity that the Palestinians have accomplished in their UN-mandated limbo. The death-cult psychosis doesn't exist in isolation: it's armed by Iran, bankrolled by Iraq, and philosophically sustained by Saudi Islamism. It will not survive the liquidation of its state patrons. This is good news for any Palestinians interested in actual life.

None of the above will happen without a massive humiliating military defeat of the Arab world's Number One loonitoon. Shortly thereafter, the Ayatollahs and ol' man Yasser will be gone, and the House of Saud, Junior Assad and Mubarak will follow. Think I'm crazy? Look at the map the last time we went to war with Saddam. In 1991, Afghanistan was still Communist, as were the Central Asian republics, and Pakistan was under the corrupt Sharif regime. Eleven years later, General Musharraf is trying his hardest to be Washington's new best friend, and American forces are in Afghanistan, Kyrgyzstan, Uzbekistan and even Georgia. The Middle East's eastern and northern borders have quietly become an American sphere of influence. The regimes on the ground are of varying degrees of unattractiveness, but none of 'em is causing the west any trouble. That's the way Araby will look in a couple of years. It starts in Baghdad, and soon.

THE FABRICATIONS OF WAR

August 17th 2002
The Daily Telegraph

TO BE HONEST, I didn't pay much attention to the story in Thursday's *Telegraph* – "World Faces Polyester Crisis" – in which our Science Correspondent revealed that we could be reeling under massive polyester shortages by 2008. But I bumped into famed war correspondent John Pilger at the bar that evening and he was waving the paper triumphantly.

"See?" he said. "Now do you get it? Now do you understand what your so-called 'War on Terror' is really about?"

"What do you mean 'so-called' War on Terror?" I huffed indignantly.

"Because it's an abbreviation," crowed John. "Just another chilling Pentagon euphemism to hide what's really going on. 'War on Terror'. Short for 'War on Terylene'. " He unrolled a map. "Look at this. 85% of the world's known polyester resources are found in this arc from the Republic of Crimplenistan in Central Asia through the vast desert waists of al-Asticated down to the Gulf of Aqrilaq.

Washington's been looking for an excuse to seize them ever since things flared up in the Seventies and they were at the mercy of OPEC."

"OPEC? You mean...?"

"Optional Permanent Easi-Crease. Look at Rumsfeld's trousers. Thing is, if the Yanks run their huge fibre-optic cables down to their bases at the Gusset of Slaq, they'll control the world's entire polyester supply. After all, what's the most vital element of the American economy?"

"Er, oil?" I suggested.

"Oh, come on," scoffed John. "Go to any mall in Jersey and count the stretch pants. Take away the polyester and the bottom will drop out of the US economy. Literally."

"I dunno," I said sceptically. "The Middle East isn't somewhere I associate with casual clothing."

"Really?" chuckled John. "You've never heard of the Grand Mufti of Jerusalem?"

I had to concede he had a point.

~

THE UNREALITY OF REALISTS

August 25th 2002
The Sunday Telegraph

YOU CAN HARDLY open an American newspaper these days without finding another "senior Republican" "breaking ranks" with President Bush over toppling Saddam: House Majority Leader Dick Armey, Senator Chuck Hagel, former Secretary of State Henry Kissinger, former National Security Advisor Brent Scowcroft, former Secretary of State Larry Eagleburger, former this, former that... To hear *The New York Times* tell it, the entire Bush Sr Administration except for Dad is out in the street chanting "Hell, no, we won't go!", and it's only a matter of time before Pop himself joins in ("Bush Says He Cannot Support Bush").

In Baghdad, the wily Saddam is no doubt wondering why the massed ranks of Nixon/Ford/Reagan/Bush grandees are so eager to kick a sitting Republican President in the teeth over the his sole surviving policy on the eve of tight midterm elections in which control of both the House and Senate are at stake. Presumably, he's written it off as a laughably crude psy-ops disinformation campaign by the Great Satan designed to sucker him into easing up on the anthrax production and getting back to work on his latest romantic novel.

But in America, alas, the naysayers are being taken seriously, even Dick Armey and Chuck Hagel. A couple of months ago, Congressman Armey's latest wheeze was that the entire Palestinian population should be removed from the West Bank, a policy initiative *The New York Times* thought it kindest not even to mention. But there's nothing like disagreeing with your own President to transform a Republican from a laughingstock into a respected geopolitical thinker.

It even works with Senator Hagel, who recently explained his opposition to Bush's "axis of evil" concept thus: "I think the reaction the President has gotten from our allies and almost every nation around the world is that words have meaning, meanings mean commitments, and commitments lead to expectations. And sometimes those expectations turn into unintended consequences." It is, in every sense, hard to argue with that. Words have meaning, but not always when strung together by Chuck Hagel. It seems to me the most likely explanation is that he's giving a coded signal to Iraqi dissidents in Basra to take out the power lines on Thursday at 0430 GMT.

That leaves the wise old foreign policy owls. When it comes to unsavoury foreigners, Eagleburger, Scowcroft and Kissinger are all famously "realist", though there's a fine line between realism and lethargy. A decade ago, Brent Scowcroft advised Bush Sr to stick with Gorbachev and the preservation of the Soviet Union over Yeltsin and a democratic Russia. Last autumn, he argued in favour of leaving the Taleban in power. Inevitably Scowcroft now supports letting Saddam be because, if we start a war, "we could have an explosion in the Middle East. It could turn the whole region into a cauldron."

I agree. The only difference is that I think an explosion is long overdue and turning the whole region into a cauldron is a necessary step toward taming and then reforming it. But you can't expect Scowcroft, a notorious stability junkie, to accept such a premise. Just over a year ago, I sat next to him at dinner and it wasn't so much that he disagreed with this or that Administration initiative as that he was congenitally suspicious about the very concept of initiatives. He believes everything – the Soviets, the Taleban, Saddam – can be "managed". And so it was that Scowcroft advised the first President Bush that it was better not to defeat Iraq but to manage it, to eschew victory in favour of "inspections regimes". The "management" tendency always sounds more moderate and reassuring, if you don't mind little details like huge numbers of corpses: a decade ago, Scowcroft's Cold War attachment to the old Titoist bulwark of Yugoslavia persisted long after the federation had in any meaningful sense ceased to exist and the Serbs were already butchering thousands in Croatia and Bosnia. (In fairness to Scowcroft, it's his fellow muddle-management types in the EU who deserve the principal credit for the worst bloodshed in Europe in half a century.)

That's why Henry Kissinger's contribution is the most important. Despite the best efforts of *The New York Times*, the good doctor is not opposed to war with Iraq. He states explicitly that there's an "imperative for pre-emptive action" and sooner rather than later. Not only does Kissinger not break ranks with Bush, but, more remarkably, he breaks ranks with himself, acknowledging that Kissingerian "realism" is no longer sufficient in an age of enemies unsusceptible to concepts like "deterrence". If his support for war seems hedged with qualifications, that's more to do with the philosophical argument he's having with himself over the magnitude of what Bush is proposing. To Kissinger, the President's "pre-emption" doctrine is a repudiation of international relations as understood since the 1648 Treaty of Westphalia. But in a world where enemies with no negotiable demands can strike without warning, the Treaty of Westphalia no longer seems inviolable. Kissinger wants a "comprehensive strategy" drawn up for this new world, but at least he recognises he's in one. Scowcroft's stuck in September 10th.

That's the nub of it. Bush and Cheney themselves came to office with a realist, managerial view of affairs, and it's only as the true horrors of the Middle East have revealed themselves after September 11th – from the House of Saud's bankrolling of al-Qa'eda to the EU's indirect subsidy of the intifada – that "realism" has been revealed to be totally divorced from reality. Unlike his dad, Bush Jr has acquired a "vision thing" without going looking for one: it just sort of snuck up on him as the awesomeness of the task post-9/11 became clear. It's a huge vision - to remove the real "root cause" of terrorism by remaking the Middle East – and for the moment it's too huge to be fully spelled out in the face of opposition by Colin Powell and a vast swathe of the Federal bureaucracy.

The State Department, through proxies like Scowcroft and Eagleburger, is waging a war for control of the Bush foreign-policy agenda. Sometimes they win a battle or two: Secretary Powell will be especially please that Saudi Prince Bandar, a senior member of the biggest terror-funding family on the planet, will be out at the ranch this Tuesday so that the President can hail him as a "staunch friend standing alongside America in the fight against terror". But eventually reality will dawn even on the "realists", and with luck before another 3,000 are murdered. One thing's for sure, if a fellow ever needed a sign he was on the right track, the criticisms of "senior Republicans" this past fortnight are surely it.

HOLD THE TEDDY BEARS

September 1st 2002
The Chicago Sun-Times

WE ARE IN THE season of anniversaries – Elvis, Diana, the World Trade Center. August 16th 1977, August 31st 1997, September 11th 2001.

If the comparison is trivial and demeaning, don't blame me. Five years ago, my mistake was to compare Diana to Elvis. I thought her luster had the staying power of the other big-time celebrity demises. I was wrong.

But grant me at least a sense of proportion: the throngs howling on the streets of London insisted we were on the brink of something far bigger, that the Princess of Wales' death had, to coin a phrase, "changed the world" – or at any rate that section of it under the rule of the House of Windsor. Britain was in the grip of a psychosis that week, a weird hybrid of American victim culture and English yob culture, with mobs outside Buckingham Palace – the "Ice Palace" – demanding that the Queen come out and feel their pain or they'd come in and give her some pain of her own to feel.

Her Majesty rode out the storm, as she has ridden out others. Five years on, Diana is a faded presence. "The people's princess" has been shrugged off by the people; her incandescent celebrity has guttered and died. But what's endured is a kind of ongoing karaoke Diana cult, with new and ever more transient personages briefly shunted into the limelight for the usual routine of teary candlelight vigils and mountains of teddy bears. In England this month, two girls were abducted. Eventually, their bodies were found. It is an appalling, grotesque, despicable murder and their parents' grief must be truly inconsolable. But, for the rest of a transfixed nation, "this vile crime," as the doctor and columnist Theodore Dalrymple wrote, "has been turned into something of an entertainment". The length and breadth of the realm there are public displays of Diana-like "mourning", though, as Dalrymple says, there must be something "tinny or ersatz in the outpouring of grief". How can there not be? Regret and quiet sorrow is one thing. But, when people surrender to Dianysian emotional feasting on the bier of someone unknown to them, they debase the very meaning of feeling.

These English spasms of masturbatory mawkishness are useful, because, in their crudely menacing way, they make explicit the coercive element in mass sentimentality. On this side of the Atlantic, the media have been looking for a Di phenomenon for some time, and did their best to fake one when John F Kennedy Jr died: if Diana was "the people's princess", then John-John was the people's socialite, the people's obscure magazine publisher, whatever. In fairness to those baying Brit morons, they did at least bother showing up. By contrast, the so-called floral tributes outside JFK's apartment were only ever shown in close-up, because the truth is that not only did they not begin to match the fields of tributes in Kensington Gardens, there was barely any more of a memorial than the roadside crosses and bouquets you see on the edge of a state highway when some anonymous kid gets hit by a drunk.

Which brings us to September 11th. As I wrote a year ago, in those first moments, no-one quite knew what was happening, and so the events themselves set the tone:

One plane hit, then another, then the Pentagon was smoking, the White House was evacuated, the towers crumbled, a plane crashed in Pennsylvania, there were other flights missing, there were bomb scares... For a few hours that Tuesday it felt like the Third World War, and so commentators fell into war mode. And by the time the networks had shuttled Diane Sawyer, Barbara Walters and the other empathetic glamour gals to the scene it was too late to revert to the banality of "healing" and "closure" and all the other guff of a soft-focus grief wallow.

It's very, very rare for the media to be caught so off-guard by an event that they lose control of their ability to determine its meaning. Within minutes of JFK Jr's plane going down, for example, you know Dan Rather was dusting off his *Camelot* lyrics and the producers were ordering up their "America's Son" and "America's Prince" graphics.

But a year has gone by. And there seems to be an effort to do on the anniversary what they were unable to accomplish on the day: to make September 11th 2002 an occasion for "coping". The National Education Association sees the day as an opportunity for therapy, complete with "healing tools, routines and rituals" and a "circle of feelings" designed to help students "feel better" and "comfort each other" by having their "feelings" about September 11th "validated" in a "non-judgmental" way.

If you think America's largest teachers' union is just some minor fringe group of no consequence, then what are we to make of the ceremonies at Ground Zero itself? New York's woeful mediocrity of a mayor, Mike Bloomberg, has decreed there are to be no speeches: instead, Governor Pataki will recite the Gettysburg Address, just as the third-graders do on small-town New England commons on Memorial Day. The Gettysburg Address is a fine address, but it's nothing to do with September 11th. It's as if at Gettysburg Lincoln had been told, "Well, this speech looks a little controversial. Couldn't you just stand up and recite the Declaration of Independence?" The nullity of Bloomberg's planned commemoration is an acknowledgment, even in the most sorely wounded city in America, that one year on there is no agreement on what September 11th means. To some, it calls forth righteous anger and bestselling kick-ass country songs. To others, far more influential in the culture, it demands "healing circles".

Look, I'm sorry if some schoolkids aren't feeling chipper. Tough. But 3,000 people died on September 11th, leaving a gaping hole in the lives of their children, parents, siblings and friends. Those of us who don't fall into those categories are not bereaved and, by pretending to be, we diminish the real pain of those who really feel it. That's not to say that, like many, I wasn't struck by this or that name that drifted up out of the great roll-call of the dead. *Newsweek*'s Anna Quindlen "fastened on", as she put it, one family on the flight manifest:

> *Peter Hanson, Massachusetts*
> *Susan Hanson, Massachusetts*
> *Christine Hanson, 2, Massachusetts*

As Miss Quindlen described them, "the father, the mother, the two-year old girl off on an adventure, sitting safe between them, taking wing." Christine Hanson will never be three, and I feel sad about that. But I did not know her, love her, cherish her; I do not feel her loss, her absence in my life. I have no reason to hold hands in a "healing circle" for her. All I can do for Christine Hanson is insist that the terrorist movement which killed her is hunted down and prevented from targeting any more two-year olds. We honor Christine Hanson's memory by righting the great wrong done to her, not by ersatz grief-mongering.

Elvis, Diana, September 11th. I was wrong to compare Diana with Elvis. Don't let them Dianafy September 11th.

SEPTEMBER 11th 2002

Winning and losing

September 7th/11th 2002
The Spectator/The Daily Telegraph/The National Post

WE ARE BACK to September 10th 2001, at least if the National Education Association is anything to go by. Their attractive series of classroom lessons and projects for September 11th, sponsored by Johnson & Johnson, begins with a little light non-judgmentalism: the NEA advises teachers not to "suggest any group is responsible" for the, ah, "tragic events". Just because Osama bin Laden and al-Qa'eda boasted they did it is no reason to jump to conclusions:

> *Blaming is especially difficult in terrorist situations because someone is at fault. In this country, we still believe that all people are innocent until solid, reliable evidence from our legal authorities proves otherwise*

- which presumably means we should wait till the trial and, given that what's left of Osama is currently doing a good impression of a few specks of Johnson's Baby Powder, that's likely to be a long time coming.

Furthermore:

> *We have no reason to believe that the attacks were part of an organised plan of any other country. The terrorists acted independently, without the sanction of any nation.*

Er, well, okay, if you overlook the meetings between Mohammed Atta and the bigshot Iraqi in Prague, and the millions of dollars al-Qa'eda got from the House of Saud, and the fact that Osama and Mullah Omar were married to each other's daughters.

But instead the NEA thinks children should:

*Explore the problems inherent in assigning blame to populations
or nations of people by looking at contemporary examples of
ethnic conflict, discrimination, and stereotyping at home and
abroad."*

And by that you mean...?

*Internment of Japanese Americans after Pearl Harbor and the
backlash against Arab Americans during the Gulf War are
obvious examples.*

Not that obvious: for one thing, the "backlash against Arab
Americans during the Gulf War" is entirely mythical. But you get the
gist. Don't blame anyone. But, if you have to, blame America.

This is more or less where we came in. Last September 11th,
my friend's daughter Rachel went to school and was told by her teacher
that, as terrible as the unfolding events were, the allies had killed far
more people in Dresden. Lehigh University in Pennsylvania banned
the American flag from its campus "so non-American students would
not feel uncomfortable". At the University of North Carolina, students
dressed in Muslim garb to express solidarity. The interim pastor at my
local Baptist Church warned us not to attack Muslims, even though
finding any Muslims to attack would have involved a good three-hour
drive.

And so this September 11th, across the continent, millions of
pupils, from kindergarten to high school, will be studying such central
questions as whether the stereotyped images on 1942 War Bonds
posters made German-Americans feel uncomfortable. Evidently, they
made German-American Dwight D Eisenhower so uncomfortable that
he went off and liberated Europe. But I don't suppose that's what the
NEA had in mind.

I don't think the teachers' union are "Hate America" types.
Very few Americans are. But, rather, they're in thrall to something far
craftier than straightforward anti-Americanism, a kind of enervating
cult of tolerance in which you demonstrate your sensitivity to other
cultures by being almost totally insensitive to your own. The NEA
study suggestions have a bit of everything in them: your teacher might
pluck out Roosevelt's "Four Freedoms", on the other hand, she might
wind up at the discussion topic about whether it was irresponsible for

the media to show video footage of Palestinians celebrating September 11th as this allegedly led to increased hostility toward Arabs. Real live Arab intolerance is not a problem except insofar as it risks inflaming yet more mythical American intolerance.

This stuff went away for a while last October, and some of us were foolish enough to think it might go away for good. That it didn't has a lot to do with George W Bush and the strategy that brought him to power. You'll recall that he campaigned in 2000 as a "compassionate conservative". On his first trip to New Hampshire, he declared, "I'm proud to be a compassionate conservative. And on this ground I will make my stand!" Those of us who ventured on to the ground to stand alongside him found it pretty mushy and squelchy, but figured the bog of clichés was merely a cunning ruse, a means of co-opting all the Democrats' touchy-feely words and thereby neutralising their linguistic advantage. My distinguished colleague Barbara Amiel felt differently. As she put it two years ago:

> *Those of us who give a tinker's farthing about ideas knew we were in* merde *up to the waist. Conservatism is by definition "compassionate". It has a full understanding and tender spot for the human condition and the ways of our world. A need to qualify conservatism by rebranding it as a product now found in a sweet-smelling pink "compassionate" version is hideous and a concession to your enemies right at the beginning.*

I was wrong and Barbara was right. It didn't seem important at the time, but it is now. I thought the clumsy multicultural pandering of the Bush campaign was a superb joke, but with hindsight it foreshadowed the rhetorical faintheartedness of the last year. Bush, we right-wing types were assured in 2000, would do the right thing, even if he talked a lot of hooey. Many of us stuck to this line after September 11th: okay, the Muslim photo-ops and the non-stop White House Ramadan-a-ding-dong got a bit tedious, but for all the Islamic outreach you could at least rely on the guy to take out the Taleban, and, when the moment comes, Saddam as well.

But words matter, too. As noted previously, Churchill wasn't just down in the ops room sticking pins in maps but all over the airwaves explaining why the Nazis were evil and why they needed to be wiped from the earth. Lose the rhetorical ground at home and you lose the war overseas – Vietnam being the most obvious example. This time round, the very name of the conflict was the first evasion. It's not a "war on terror", it's a war on radical Islamism, a worldwide scourge operating on five continents. But the President is too much of a compassionate warmonger to say so.

And so the evasions continue. Here's Thomas Friedman in *The New York Times*:

> *The ruckus being raised by conservative Christians over the University of North Carolina's decision to ask incoming students to read a book about the Koran - to stimulate a campus debate - surely has to be one of the most embarrassing moments for America since Sept. 11.*
>
> *Why? Because it exhibits such profound lack of understanding of what America is about, and it exhibits such a chilling mimicry of what the most repressive Arab Muslim states are about. Ask yourself this question: What would Osama bin Laden do if he found out that the University of Riyadh had asked incoming freshmen to read the New and Old Testaments?*

Blow it up, I guess. But Friedman's being supremely disingenuous. What most of us object to at UNC is the decision to promote not the reading of the Koran, a very worthwhile activity, but the reading of a highly selective book about the Koran, which makes a point of ignoring all the troublesome passages. The university is not "stimulating a debate" – something increasingly few American educational institutions are interested in – but promoting a particular view in line with all the usual delusions. I'm all in favour of studying Islam, so long as we're honest about it.

After all, our enemies are perfectly honest, and remarkably straightforward. Just tune in any Arab TV station for Friday prayers with the A-list imams:

> *O God, destroy the Jews and their supporters. O God, destroy the Christians and their supporters and followers, shake the ground under them, instil fear in their hearts, and freeze the blood in their veins.*

That's Sheikh Akram Abd-al-Razzaq al-Ruqayhi, some hotshot imam live from the Grand Mosque in Sanaa on August 9th on Yemeni state TV. It's the local equivalent of "Thought For The Day", and even more predictable. Here's the same dude a week earlier:

> *O God, deal with Jews and their supporters and Christians and their supporters and lackeys. O God, count them one by one, kill them all, and don't leave anyone.*

This isn't some fringe crank sentiment, but what appears to be a standard formulation from the Middle Eastern equivalent of the Book of Common Prayer. Another state TV channel, another mosque, another imam, same script:

"O God, deal with the occupier Jews for they are within your power," said Sheikh Anwar al-Badawi on August 2nd live from the Umar Bin-Al-Khattab Mosque in Doha on Qatar Television. "O God, count them one by one, kill them, and don't leave any one of them."

Same Sheikh a week later: "O God, destroy the usurper Jews and the vile Christians."

Hmm. Perhaps we need to call in Bletchley Park. Must be some sort of code.

As a matter of fact, you don't even need to go to the Middle East to catch the death-to-Jews-and-Christians routine. I stayed in the heart of Paris a couple of months back, at the Plaza Athenée, and the eight Arab TV channels available in my room had more than enough foaming imams to go round.

The old-time Commies at least used to go to a bit of effort to tell the western leftie intellectuals what they wanted to hear. The Islamists, by contrast, cheerfully piss all over every cherished western progressive shibboleth. Women? The Taleban didn't just "marginalise" women, they buried them under sackcloth. Gays? As *The New Republic* reported a week ago, the Palestinian Authority tortures homosexuals, makes them stand in sewage up to their necks with faeces-filled sacks on their heads. Yet Canadian MP Svend Robinson, Yasser's favourite gay infidel, still makes his pilgrimages to Ramallah to pledge solidarity with the people's "struggle". Animals? CNN's showing videos all this week of al-Qa'eda members testing various hideous poison gases on dogs.

Radical Islamists aren't tolerant of anybody: they kill Jews, Hindus, Christians, babies, schoolgirls, airline stewardesses, bond traders, journalists, dogs. They use snuff videos for recruitment: go on the Internet and a couple of clicks will get you to the decapitation of Daniel Pearl. You can't negotiate with them because they have no demands – or at least no rational ones. They've nothing they want to talk about. It takes up valuable time they'd rather spend killing us.

President Bush has won the first battle (Afghanistan) but he's in danger of losing the war. The war isn't with al-Qa'eda, or Saddam, or the House of Saud. They're all a bunch of losers. True, insignificant loser states can cause their share of trouble when they're proxies for the great powers. But, in a unipolar world, it's clear that the most powerful enemy in this war is ourselves, and our determination to sleepwalk to cultural suicide in order to demonstrate our sensitivity. By "our", I don't mean the American people or the Canadian people or even the French people. I don't even mean the Democrats: American politics is more responsive and populist than Europe's, and when war with Iraq starts, Hillary will be cheerleading along with the rest of them. But against that are all the people who shape our culture, who teach our children, who run our colleges and churches, who make the TV shows we watch – and they haven't got a clue. Bruce Springsteen's blurry equivalist mope of a 9/11 album, *The Rising*, is a classic example of how even a supposed "blue-collar" icon can't bring himself to want America to win. On my car radio, John McCain pops up on behalf of the Office of Civil Rights every ten minutes sternly reminding Americans not to beat up Muslims.

And, of course, let us not forget Britain's great comic figure Baroness Kennedy of the Shaws, QC, who thinks that it's too easy to go on about "Islamic fundamentalists". "What I think happens very readily," she said, "is that we as western liberals too often are fundamentalist ourselves. We don't look at our own fundamentalisms." And what exactly does Lady Kennedy mean by western liberal fundamentalism? "One of the things that we are too ready to insist upon is that we are the tolerant people and that the intolerance is something that belongs to other countries like Islam. And I'm not sure that's true."

If I follow correctly, Lady Kennedy is suggesting that our tolerance of our own tolerance is making us intolerant of other people's intolerance. To complain about Islamic fundamentalism is to ignore how offensive others must find our own western fundamentalisms – votes, drivers' licenses for women, no incentives to mass murder from the pulpit of Westminster Cathedral.

****

AMERICA'S had a year to wise up, but instead it's retreating to its illusions. George W Bush had a rare opportunity after September 11th. He could have attempted to reverse the most poisonous tide in the western world: the gloopy multiculturalism that insists all cultures are equally valid, even as they're trying to kill us. He could have argued that western self-loathing is a psychosis we can no longer afford. He could have told the teachers' unions that there was more to the Second World War than the internment of Japanese-Americans and it's time they started teaching it to our children.

But he chose not to. Anyone who followed George W Bush during the 2000 Presidential campaign will recognise the pattern:

He stacked up more money and a bigger poll lead than anyone had ever seen in a competitive race – and then he didn't bother campaigning in New Hampshire. So he lost the primary.

But he clawed his way back and won the nomination – and then he pretty much disappeared from sight to spend the summer working on his new ranch house back in Texas. So by Labour Day Al Gore was ahead in the polls.

But he stirred himself and eked out a small lead in the run-up to November – and then, in the wake of a damaging last-minute leak about an old drunk-driving conviction, he flew back home and took the final weekend of the campaign off.

But he just about squeaked through on election day, even though his disinclination to rebut the drunk story almost certainly cost him the popular vote and a couple of close states.

This is the way George W Bush does things and his rendezvous with history on September 11th – the day that "changed the world" – did not, in the end, change the Bush modus operandi. A few weeks after the attacks, he had the highest approval ratings of any President in history. But he didn't do anything with them. And, in political terms, he might as well have spent this summer playing video golf and watching the director's cut of *Austin Powers*. On election day in November, without Saddam's scalp on his bedpost, Bush will be right back where he was on September 10th 2001: the 50% President, his approval ratings in the fifties, his "negatives" high, the half of the country that didn't vote for him feeling no warmer toward him than if the day that "changed the world" had never happened.

If this sounds familiar, that's because it is. Last autumn, Bush aides were at pains to emphasise that the son would not make his father's mistake: unlike George Bush Sr, the new President understood that political capital can't be banked; you have to spend it when you have it because it won't be there in six months' time. The 90% poll numbers were always going to come down. It was just a question of where they stabilised, and what Bush would manage to accomplish while they were up in the stratosphere. By that measure, he squandered his opportunity.

In devoting his energies to the war, the President let his domestic agenda die. Even as the USAF were strafing Tora Bora, Senator Pat Leahy, a wily Vermont Democrat, continued to stall the President's judicial nominations; Ted Kennedy gutted the Bush education bill; and their fellow Democrats obstructed plans for oil-drilling in the Arctic National Wildlife Refuge. At that moment, with his poll numbers in the eighties, it would have been so easy for Bush to do to Leahy what Clinton did to Gingrich. The President could have said that, with so many suspected terrorists and their accomplices in custody, we can't afford vacancies and backlogs in our courthouses and my good frien' Pat needs to stop playin' politics with the Federal judiciary. September 11th is not just an event, hermetically sealed from everything before and after, but a context. Everything that's wrong with the environmental movement, with the teachers' unions, with the big-government bureaucracies can be seen through the prism of their responses to that day.

But the President's greatest mistake was his failure to take on the debilitating Oprahfied therapeutic culture that, in the weeks after September 11th, looked momentarily vulnerable. There were two kinds of responses to that awful day. You could go with "C'mon, guys, let's roll!", the words of Todd Beamer as he and the brave passengers of Flight 93 took on their Islamist hijackers, and, at the cost of their own lives, prevented a fourth plane from slamming through the White House. Or you could go with "healing" and "closure" and the rest of the awful lifeless language of emotional narcissism. Had Mr Bush taken it upon himself to talk up the virtues of courage and self-reliance demonstrated on Flight 93 he would have done a service not just to his nation but to his party, for a touchy-feely culture inevitably trends Democratic.

But he ducked the rhetorical challenge. Bush has allowed the culture to lapse back into its default mode of psychobabbling self-absorption.

Increasingly dispirited as the summer wore on, Republican foot-soldiers pondered a basic question: when your leader puts his domestic agenda on hold to switch to a war Presidency and then puts the war Presidency on hold, what's left? In the end, even Mr Bush's magnificent moral clarity faded away into a Colin Powellite blur. Long after it became clear that 3,000 Americans were killed by Saudi citizens with Saudi money direct from members of the Saudi Royal Family, Mr Bush was still inviting Saudi princes to the Crawford ranch and insisting that the Kingdom was a "staunch friend" in the war against terror. This is not just ridiculous but offensive. Even if it's merely "rope-a-dope" and behind the scenes all kinds of plans are being made, the public dissimulation diminishes the President's authority. Symbolism matters: the White House is for business, the privilege of kicking loose at the ranch ought to be reserved for real friends; Yet Australia's John Howard, whose boys fought alongside the US in Afghanistan, didn't get an invite to Crawford and the fellows who bankrolled al-Qa'eda did. Words matter, too: Bush's remarks about the Saudis come perilously close to lying to the American people about who murdered their friends and family.

In January, naming Iraq as part of the "axis of evil", Bush declared that "time is running out". Eight months later, time had run back in again. "I'm a patient man," said the President. You can't blame the American people - the "sleeping giant" – for dozing off again.

****

MONA CHAREN summed it up in a column on the increasing pressure to pretend that September 11th 2001 was not what it was – an act of war – but instead some sort of unfortunate "tragedy". It is, she says, "a kind of moral disarmament of the nation. Before there can be an army, navy and air force capable of protecting us, there must be a citizenry that believes we are worth defending."

If it sounds extreme to put it in those terms, consider how far many in the west are prepared to go *not* to defend themselves. In August, in Sydney, the pack leader of a group of Lebanese Muslim gang-rapists was sentenced to 55 years in gaol. I suppose I ought to say "Lebanese-Australian" Muslim gang-rapists, since the accused were Australian citizens. But, identity-wise, the rambunctious young lads considered themselves heavy on the Lebanese, light on the Australian. During their gang rapes, the lucky lady would be told she was about to be "fucked Leb style" and that she deserved it because she was an "Australian pig".

But, inevitably, it's the heavy sentence that's "controversial". After September 11th, Americans were advised to ask themselves, "Why do they hate us?" Now Australians need to ask themselves, "Why do they rape us?" As Monroe Reimers put it on the letters page of *The Sydney Morning Herald*:

> *As terrible as the crime was, we must not confuse justice with revenge. We need answers. Where has this hatred come from? How have we contributed to it? Perhaps it's time to take a good hard look at the racism by exclusion practised with such a vengeance by our community and cultural institutions.*

Indeed. Many's the time, labouring under the burden of some or other ghastly government policy, I've thought of pinning some gal down and sodomising her while 14 of my pals look on and await their turn. But I fear in my case the Monroe Reimers of the world would be rather less eager to search for "root causes". Gang rape as a legitimate expression of the campaign for social justice is a privilege reserved only unto a few.

Mr Reimers, though, will be happy to know his view is echoed across the hemispheres. Five days before 9/11, the Norwegian newspaper *Dagbladet* reported that 65% of the country's rapes were committed by "non-western" immigrants – a category which, in Norway, is almost wholly Muslim. A professor at the University of Oslo explained that one reason for the disproportionate Muslim share of the rape market was that in their native lands "rape is scarcely punished" because it is generally believed that "it is women who are responsible for rape".

So Muslim immigrants to Norway should be made aware that things are a little different in Scandinavia? Not at all! Rather, the professor insisted, "Norwegian women must take their share of responsibility for these rapes" because their manner of dress would be regarded by Muslim men as inappropriate. "Norwegian women must realize that we live in a multicultural society and adapt themselves to it." Or to modify Queen Victoria's wedding-night advice to her daughter: lie back and think of Yemen.

France? Well, I can't bring you any ethnic rape statistics from the Fifth Republic because the authorities go to great lengths not to keep any. But, even though the phenomenon of immigrant gang rape does not officially exist, there's already a word for it: the "*tournante*" – or "take your turn". Last year, 11 Muslim men were arrested for enjoying a grand old *tournante* with a 14-year old girl in a cellar. It's now a widely accepted communal "rite of passage" in the North African *quartiers* of French cities.

Whether or not certain cultures are more prone to rape is a delicate question we shall explore another day. But what's interesting is how easily even this most extreme manifestation of multiculturalism is subsumed within the usual pieties. Norwegian women must learn to be, in a very real sense, less "exclusionary". Lebanese male immigrants, finding refuge in a land of peace, freedom and opportunity, are somehow transformed into gang rapists by Australian racism.

After September 11th, a friend in London said to me she couldn't stand all the America-needs-to-ask-itself stuff because she used to work at a rape crisis centre and she'd heard this blame-the-victim routine a thousand times before. America was asking for it: like those Norwegian women, it was being "provocative". Even so, it comes as a surprise to realize the multiculti apologists do exactly the same to actual rape victims. After the OJ verdict, it was noted by some feminists that "race trumped gender". What we've seen since September 11th is that multiculturalism trumps everything. Its grip on the imagination of the western elites is unshakeable. Thus, President Bush, in the month after September 11th, went around declaring "Islam is peace" while surrounded by representatives of organisations whose literature claims Jews are apes.

On this "Islam is peace" business, Bassam Tibi, a Muslim professor at Goettingen University in Germany, gave a helpful speech a few months back: "Both sides should acknowledge candidly that although they might use identical terms these mean different things to each of them," he said. "The word 'peace', for example, implies to a Muslim the extension of the Dar al-Islam - or 'House of Islam' - to the entire world. This is completely different from the Enlightenment concept of eternal peace that dominates Western thought." Only when the entire world is a Dar al-Islam will it be a Dar a-Salam, or "House of Peace".

On the face of it, that sounds ridiculous. The "Muslim world" – the arc stretching from North Africa through South Asia – is economically and militarily moribund. But, looked at through the lens of Norwegian rape or French crime, the idea of a Dar al-Islam doesn't sound so ridiculous. The "code of silence" that surrounds rape in tightly knit Muslim families is, so to speak, amplified by the broader "code of silence" surrounding multicultural issues in the west. If all cultures are of equal value, how do you point out any defects?

As I understand it, the benefits of multiculturalism are that the sterile white-bread cultures of Australia, Canada and Britain get some great ethnic restaurants and a Commonwealth Games opening ceremony that goes on till two in the morning. But, in the case of those Muslim ghettoes in Sydney, in Oslo, in Paris, in Copenhagen and in Manchester, multiculturalism means that the worst attributes of Muslim culture – the subjugation of women – combine with the worst attributes of western culture – license and self-gratification. Tattooed, pierced Pakistani skinhead gangs swaggering down the streets of Northern England are as much a product of multiculturalism as the turban-wearing Sikh Mountie in the vice-regal escort at Rideau Hall. Yet even in the face of the crudest assaults on its most cherished causes – women's rights, gay rights – the political class turns squeamishly away.

Once upon a time we knew what to do. A British district officer, coming upon a scene of suttee, was told by the locals that in Hindu culture it was the custom to cremate a widow on her husband's funeral pyre. He replied that in British culture it was the custom to hang chaps who did that sort of thing. There are many great things about India – curry, pyjamas, sitars, software engineers – but suttee was not one of them. What a pity we're no longer capable of being "judgmental" and "discriminating". We're told the old-school imperialists were racists, that they thought of the wogs as inferior. But, if so, they at least considered them capable of improvement. The multiculturalists are just as racist. The only difference is that they think the wogs can never reform: good heavens, you can't expect a Muslim in Norway not to go about raping the womenfolk! Much better just to get used to it.

As one is always obliged to explain when tiptoeing around this territory, I'm not a racist, only a culturalist. I believe western culture – rule of law, universal suffrage, etc – is preferable to Arab culture: that's why there are millions of Muslims in Scandinavia, and four Scandinavians in Syria. Follow the traffic. I support immigration, but with assimilation. Without it, like a Hindu widow, the west is slowly climbing on the funeral pyre of its lost empires. You see it in European foreign policy already: they're scared of their mysterious, swelling, unstoppable Muslim populations.

Islam For All approvingly reported the other day that, at present demographic rates, in 20 years' time the majority of Holland's children (the population under 18) will be Muslim. It will be the first Islamic country in western Europe since the loss of Spain. Europe is the colony now.

Or as Charles Johnson of the *Little Green Footballs* website drolly suggested: "Maybe we should start a betting pool: which European country will be the first to institute shari'a?"

****

A couple of days after September 11th, I wrote:

> *Those western nations who spent last week in Durban finessing and nuancing evil should understand now that what is at stake is whether the world's future will belong to liberal democracy and the rule of law, or to darker forces.*

But a year later, after a brief hiccup, the western elites have resumed finessing and nuancing evil all the more enthusiastically, and America's "compassionate conservative" shows no stomach for a fight at least as important as any on the battlefield.

The great imponderable of this war is how widespread among Muslims is support for radical Islamism. The evidence is conflicting: On the one hand, the supposedly incendiary "Arab street" is relatively calm. On the other, few imams in North America or Europe are prepared to stand up and give an unqualified denunciation of Osama bin Laden and al-Qa'eda. It's clear there's a struggle going on in the Muslim world along a continuum with Turkish and South Asian Islam at one end and the psychotic death cult of the jihadi at the other. Victory over the latter requires wholesale reconstruction of the Middle East, and the free world long ago lost faith in its moral authority to embark on such projects. This isn't a "clash of civilisations" so much as two clashes within civilisations – in the west, between those who believe in the values of liberal democracy and those too numbed by multiculturalist bromides to recognise even the most direct assault on them; and in the Islamic world, between what's left of the moderate Muslim temperament and the Saudi-radicalised death-cult Islamists.

The Islamists are militarily weak but ideologically secure. A year on, the west is just the opposite. There's more than one way to lose a war.

****

SEPTEMBER 11th was the day everything changed. Everyone said so, and some still do. But nations don't change in a day, much less the world. The change that occurred on September 11th was a simple one. When Osama bin Laden blew up the World Trade Center, he also blew up the polite fictions of the pre-war world. At Ground Zero, they've been working frantically to clear away the rubble. Likewise, at the UN, EU and all the rest, they've also been working frantically not so much to clear away the mess but to stick it back together and reconstruct the great fantasy world as it existed on September 10th, that bizarro make-believe land where Nato is a "mutual defence alliance" and Egypt and Saudi Arabia are "our staunch friends". Even in America, some people are still living in that world. You can switch on the TV and hear apparently sane "experts" using phrases like "Bush risks losing the support of the Arab League".

The easiest way to understand how little has changed is to consider the two UN Conferences in South Africa which bookend the year. The weekend before 9/11, at the UN Conference Against Racism, Colonialism, Whitey, Hymie and Capitalism, Robert Mugabe's government was cheered to the rafters for calling on Britain and America to "apologise unreservedly for their crimes against humanity". Last week, when the world's jetset luddites convened at the Church of the Sustainable Conception for the so-called Earth Summit, who got the biggest roar this time? Why, ol' Starver Bob, for a trenchant assault on the wickedness of Tony Blair.

A few weeks earlier, Libya was elected to chair the UN Human Rights Commission. Washington doesn't expect much from the UN, but why did it have to be Libya? Okay, it's never going to be America or Britain, but how about Belize or Western Samoa? Why did it have to be something so utterly contemptible of reality as the elevation of Colonel Gaddafi's flunkey? If the multilateral world is irrelevant, it's because its organs – the UN, EU, Nato – are diseased and it has shown no willingness in the last year to address the fact.

Does that mean Bush is a unilateralist? Not at all. Bilateralism is booming. Since September 11th, US-Russian, US-Chinese, US-Indian and US-Turkish relations have all improved, all of which are arguably more important than whether Washington sees eye to eye with Chris Patten. Only a very blinkered self-absorbed Eurocentric would assume that because Mr Bush (as quoted in *The Spectator*) says he doesn't "give a shit about the Europeans", he doesn't give a shit about anyone else: within a year, for example, the US has built productive relations with the Central Asian republics.

So, whether or not the world changed, America's relationship with it did. A year on, there's still no agreement as to the meaning of September 11th. To some of us, it was an act of war. To *Guardian* columnists, it was the world's biggest "but": yes, it was regrettable, BUT it was also a logical consequence of America's "cowboy arrogance" blah blah. To the Muslims who celebrated openly in Ramallah and in Denmark and at Concordia University in Montreal, it was the most spectacular blow yet against the Great Satan. To other Muslims, it was obviously the work of Mossad. To John Lahr, theatre critic of *The New Yorker*, it was possibly the work of George W Bush trying to distract attention from Democrat criticism of his missile-defence plans.

When an opinion-former's caught unawares, he retreats to his tropes, however lame, as Lahr did, and Pilger, Chomsky et al. But the clearest way to understand the meaning of the day is to look at those who were called upon to act rather than theorise. We now know that the fourth plane, United Flight 93, the one that shattered across a field in Pennsylvania, was heading for the White House. Had they made it, it would have been the strike of the day. It might have killed the Vice-

President and who knows who else, but, even if it hadn't, think of the symbolism: the shattered façade, smoke billowing from a pile of rubble on Pennsylvania Avenue, just like the money shot in *Independence Day*. Those delirious Palestinians and Danes and Montrealers would have danced all night.

But they were denied their jubilation. Unlike those on the first three flights, the hostages on 93 knew what their fate would be. They understood there would be no happy ending. So they gave us the next best thing, a hopeful ending. The plane crashed, not into the White House, but in some pasture outside Pittsburgh

The most significant development of September 11th is that it marks the day America began to fight back: thanks to the heroes of Flight 93, 9/11 is not just Pearl Harbor but also the Doolittle Raid, all wrapped up in 90 minutes. Those passengers were the only victims who knew what the hijackers had in store for them, and so they acted. The improvisations of Flight 93 foreshadowed the innovations of the Afghan campaign, when men in traditional Uzbek garb sat on horses and used laser technology to guide USAF bombers to their targets. The B2s dropped their load and flew back to base – Diego Garcia or Mississippi.

The Flight 93 hijackers might have got lucky. They might have found themselves on a plane with John Lahr ("You guys are working for Bush, right?") or Robert Daubenspeck of White River Junction, Vermont, who the day after September 11th wrote to my local newspaper advising against retaliation: "Someone, someday, must have the courage not to hit back but to look them in the eye and say, 'I love you.'" But, granted these exceptions, chances are any flight full of reasonably typical Americans would have found a group of people to do the right thing, to act as those on Flight 93 did. When you face these psychotic death-cultists, when you "look them in the eye", you see there's nothing to negotiate.

On Flight 93, Todd Beamer, Jeremy Glick, Thomas Burnett, Mark Bingham and others did not have the luxury of amused *Guardian*esque detachment. So they effectively inaugurated the new Bush Doctrine: when you know your enemies have got something big up their sleeves, you take 'em out before they can do it.

Everything that mattered after September 11th – Bush's moral clarity, the Afghan innovations, and the crystal-clear understanding that this is an enemy beyond compromise – was present in the final moments of Flight 93. They're the bedrock American values, the ones you don't always see because everyone's yakking about Anna Nicole Smith or the new "reality-based" "Beverly Hillbillies". But we know that when you need them in a hurry they're always there.

Bush will need them in the years ahead because he has chosen to embark on the most ambitious change of all, a reversal of half-a-century of US policy in the Middle East. The polite fictions – Prince Abdullah is "moderate", Yasser Arafat is our "partner in peace", the Syrian Foreign Minister is as respectable as New Zealand's – will no longer do. They led to slaughter.

Europe, for one, hasn't caught up to September 11th: when it comes to Saddam, the Continentals are like the passengers on those first three planes; they're thinking he's a rational guy, just play it cool and he won't pull anything crazy.

But America learned the hard way: it's the world of September 10th that's really crazy.

MARK STEYN RETURNS…

…in this Sunday's Chicago Sun-Times;

…in Monday's New York Sun;

…in Thursday's National Post;

…in Friday's Spectator;

…in this weekend's Daily Telegraph *and* Sunday Telegraph;

…in this month's New Criterion;

…and at SteynOnline.com